Human Rights in the Indian Armed Forces

An Analysis of Article 33

Human Rights
in the Indian Armed Forces

An Analysis of Article 33

by

Wg Cdr (Dr) U C Jha

&

Dr Sanghamitra Choudhury

Vij Books India Pvt Ltd

New Delhi (India)

First Published in 2019

Published by

Vij Books India Pvt Ltd
(Publishers, Distributors & Importers)
2/19, Ansari Road
Delhi – 110 002
Phones: 91-11-43596460, 91-11-47340674
Fax: 91-11-47340674
e-mail: vijbooks@rediffmail.com
web : www.vijbooks.com

Contents

Preface

The Indian Constitution guarantees the essential human rights in the form of the Fundamental Rights (Part III) and the Directive Principles of State Policy (Part IV), which are the cornerstone of governance of the country. The important rights and freedoms granted under the Constitution are equal protection under the law, freedom of speech and expression, freedom of worship and religion, freedom of assembly and association, freedom of person, freedom against double jeopardy and against *ex post facto* laws. Article 13 of the Constitution states that the State shall not make any law which takes away or abridges the rights conferred by Part III and that any law made in contravention of this provision shall be void. The term 'law' includes any ordinance, order, by-law, rule, regulation, notification, custom or usage having the force of law within the territory of India.

A notable feature of the Constitution is that it accords a dignified and crucial position to the judiciary. Article 13 confers a power and imposes a duty and an obligation on the courts to declare a law void if it is inconsistent with a Fundamental Right. Article 32 gives the judiciary the power to protect the people's fundamental rights from any undue encroachment by any organ of the State. The jurisdiction so conferred on the Supreme Court and high courts is a part of the inviolable fabric of the Constitution.

The Fundamental Rights have been liberally construed by the Supreme Court in the last five decades, keeping in view the International Covenants to which India is a party.[1] For instance, the right to protection of life and personal liberty, which is confined to 18 words in Article 21, has received the widest possible interpretation.[2] The Constitution Bench of the Supreme Court has held that access to justice is a Fundamental Right

---

1 *People's Union for Civil Liberty v. Union of India*, (2005) 2 SCC 436.

2 Article 21 of the Constitution lays down, "No person shall be deprived of his life or personal liberty except according to procedure established by law."

guaranteed to citizens by Article 14 and Article 21 of the Constitution. The Bench observed that if "life" implies not only life in the physical sense but a bundle of rights that makes life worth living, there is no juristic or other basis for holding that denial of "access to justice" will not affect the quality of human life so as to take access to justice out of the purview of the right to life guaranteed under Article 21.[3]

Article 33 of the Constitution, however, constitutes an exception to the Fundamental Rights. It empowers the Parliament to restrict or abrogate the fundamental rights of certain categories of government servants so as to ensure the proper discharge of their duties and the maintenance of duties amongst them. Besides the three wings of the armed forces, these rights have been abrogated in respect of members of the forces charged with the maintenance of public order, persons employed in any bureau or organization established for the purposes of intelligence or counter-intelligence, and those employed in communication systems set up for the purposes of any force, bureau or organization.

Article 33 does not by itself abrogate any right; its applicability depends upon parliamentary legislation. Parliament, in exercise of powers conferred by Article 33, can restrict or abrogate the Fundamental Rights in their application to the members of the armed forces. For example, it has abrogated certain powers of persons subject to the Navy Act, 1957, under Section 12 of the Act. In other cases, Parliament has empowered the Central Government to make rules to restrict certain Fundamental Rights of the members of the forces. For instance, the Central Government, exercising its rule-making power under the Army Act, 1950 and the Air Force Act, 1950 has abrogated certain Fundamental Rights of the members of the Indian Army and the Air Force. These rights relate to the freedom of speech and expression, the freedom of assembly, and the freedom to form associations and unions and are part of Article 19 of the Constitution.

The Indian Armed Forces are governed by the respective service Acts which owe their origin to British laws drafted in the post-Mutiny era to govern native soldiers, who were considered uneducated, uncultured and undisciplined. Unfortunately, no honest attempt has been made since Independence to modernize the military legal system, keeping in mind the expanding horizon of international human rights laws and the changes made by other democratic countries. Let us take an example. In 1982, the Supreme Court of India in *PPS Bedi's* case, made a critical assessment

---

3 *Anita Kushwaha v. Pushap Sudan*, Transfer Petition (C) No. 1343 of 2008, with other petitions, decided on 19 July 2016.

of the Indian military legal system for the first time. It commented that the winds of change blowing over the world necessitated a second look to bring the provisions of military law in conformity with the liberty-oriented Constitution and the rule of law which formed the uniting and integrating force in our political society. The Supreme Court urged the Parliament to reform military law in view of the changed value system, and commented that fair play and justice could not always be sacrificed at the altar of military discipline. The government did nothing except making a few minor amendments to the legal system. Some of these amendments were made after the judiciary made scathing remarks on the antiquity of the military legal system, while others were made after the corresponding provisions of the civil criminal justice system was amended.

The Parliamentary Standing Committee on Defence (2005-06) in its Tenth Report said, "… it is high time that these (service) Acts be reviewed in totality in the light of the judgments delivered by the courts to make their provisions more democratic." The Committee recommended that "An expert committee be constituted to thoroughly review the Acts and make recommendations to bring them in tune with the norms being followed in other democratic countries." The Committee also desired that a common disciplinary code be created so as to bring uniformity in the dispensation of justice to the armed forces personnel.

The reaction of the government to these criticisms and recommendations has been indifferent and slow. Twenty-five long years after the Supreme Court's comments in the *PPS Bedi* case, Parliament finally woke up and the Armed Forces Tribunal Act was passed to pave the way for the establishment of the Armed Forces Tribunal. The Tribunal has been functioning with congenital defects. It has no power of civil contempt and therefore its decisions cannot be enforced. It does not have jurisdiction in issues relating to leave, postings, summary trial, and summary court martial where punishment is less than three months of detention. In case of any dispute relating to these issues, the final authority remains with the military hierarchy or the central government. In other words, arbitrariness or unreasonableness on the part of the authorities in these matters cannot be questioned in any court of law.

The higher judiciary often chooses the path of least resistance by supporting the military organization in any controversial case. The few cases in which the courts have intervened have had little impact on military governance. The courts are generally of the opinion that any adverse comment on military higher-ups may erode discipline in the armed forces.

The judiciary believes in good faith that by supporting the organization, they are affording an opportunity to the military hierarchy as well as the government to rectify the defects in governance and the justice delivery system.

In a hierarchical system, it is natural for the judiciary to assign greater weightage to the higher authority than the junior. Therefore, the benefit of the doubt always goes to the organization. Senior commanders are gratefully viewed by civilians as well as the judiciary as custodians of national security. Thus, in cases of alleged bias, or denial of rights, or injustice at the hands of a commander, the courts are tempted to rule out the possibility of culpability or malice on the part of the superior. Recently, while referring a case back to the Defence Minister, the Supreme Court said, "We repose full faith in the Raksha Mantri and are confident that she would consider the entire matter in a totally dispassionate manner, with utmost objectivity and depicting total fairness. ... and are hopeful that the decision shall be taken within a week."[4]

Outside the armed forces not many are aware that military personnel are at the mercy of an antiquated and outmoded legal system that has hardly been altered since the Mutiny Acts. Discontent with the system has driven an increasing number of military personnel to approach the armed forces tribunal and the Supreme Court for the resolution of their grievances. Cases of fratricide and suicide are on the rise in all three services, especially the army. There have also been a few disturbing incidents in which soldiers have used physical force against their officers or refused to carry out orders. In a couple of incidents they have refused to work in the undignified role of "batman" or "orderly" for their officer.[5] The social media was exploited by some to air their opinions and grievances against their superiors and the organization. This trend is disturbing. In an attempt to find an answer, this book examines the following issues:

> ➤ Can the rights contained in international human rights treaties to which India is a party, be denied to the members of the armed forces, even if they do not have any impact on their discipline or performance of duty?

> ➤ Are the members of the armed forces entitled to enjoy the

---

4 *Union of India v. Maj Gen Manomoy Ganguly*, Civil Appeal No. 5800 of 2018, decided on 1 August 2018.

5 Wilkinson Steven I., 2015, *Army and Nation: The Military and Indian Democracy since Independence*, Ranikhet: Permanent Black.

Fundamental Rights subject to the limitations imposed by Article 33?

➢ Can they be denied every right contained in Part III/IV of the Constitution for the sake of maintenance of discipline and proper performance of duty?

➢ Can they be subjected to forced labour and inhuman and degrading treatment at the hands of their superiors in the name of discipline?

➢ Can they be forced to work under inhumane conditions and denied wages for extra work?

➢ Do they have the right to suitable service accommodation, and respect for their private and family life?

➢ Can the government force them to undertake peacetime functions endangering their life?

➢ What remedy do they have when the privilege of grievance redressal granted by an Act of Parliament is made so coercive and marred by the regulation that it loses its effectiveness?

➢ Can they be denied the right to a fair and just trial that is available to civilians under the criminal justice system?

➢ Should they be subjected to the unfair, unjust and arbitrary system of summary courts martial when no other modern military in the world follows such a systems of trial?

➢ Are the provisions of the three services Acts immune from challenges of unconstitutionality?

➢ Does the higher judiciary have any positive duty in interpreting the Fundamental Rights of the members of the armed forces?

➢ Is there a need to redefine the rights and duties of military personnel in India?

This book is divided into six chapters. The introductory chapter examines the position of the armed forces under the Constitution, the restrictions on the fundamental rights of the members of the armed forces under Article 33, and its relation to the Army Act, 1950 and other subordinate legislations made under the Act. Chapter II contains a discussion of the conditions of military service which have a direct bearing on the fundamental rights of armed forces personnel. This chapter raises a pertinent question: should the members of the armed forces be exposed to situations where their lives would be put at risk without a clear and legitimate military purpose or where the threat to life has been disregarded? Article 14 of the International Covenant on Civil and Political Rights provides that everyone shall be entitled to a fair and public hearing by a competent, independent and impartial tribunal established by law. Chapter III highlights how the right to a fair trial is violated under the military legal system in India. Chapter IV discusses the role played by the Supreme Court in analysing cases related to Article 33. Chapter V provides a brief analysis of the constitutions of a few States as regards the restrictions placed on the fundamental rights of the members of their armed forces. Chapter VI makes recommendations on safeguarding the rights of the members of the armed forces.

This book has two appendices. Appendix I contains the Constituent Assembly debate of 9 December 1948 relating to Article 33 of the Constitution, and the text of the Lok Sabha debate of 22 and 23 August 1984 on the Constitution (Fifty-Second Amendment) Bill. Appendix II provides the texts of the Supreme Court cases and a few high court cases relating to Article 33.

In this book, the terms 'military' and the 'Army Act' have been used in the generic sense and include the three services and laws relating to the air force and navy, unless specifically stated.

This book is dedicated to soldiers, sailors and airmen.

We thank Vij Books India Pvt Ltd, New Delhi for their cooperation in bringing out this book.

Wg Cdr (Dr) U C Jha

01 November 2018   Dr. Sanghamitra Choudhury

Chapter – I

Introduction

The concept of the modern State has undergone numerous changes since its formal conception at the Peace of Westphalia in 1648. In international law, a State is defined as an independent political society, occupying a defined territory, the members of which are united together for the purpose of resisting external forces and preservation of internal order.[1] In a State, there is a need to have a predictable body of norms and rules from which various governmental organs can draw their powers and functions. A State in modern time does not confine to merely a 'police' and 'law and order' functions, it also tends to become a social welfare state. To meet this requirement, the constitution of a State establishes apex organs of government and administration, describe their structure, composition, powers and principal functions, and define their inter-relationship with

---

1   Phillips O. Hood, 1987, *Constitutional and Administrative Law*, Seventh Edition, London, Sweet & Maxwell, ELBS, p. 5. The most accepted definition of the term "State" is contained in Article 1 of the 1933 Montevideo Convention on the Rights and Duties of States, which sets the traditional criteria for statehood: the entity must possess a permanent population, a defined territory, an effective government, and capacity to enter into relations with other states. Crawford is of the view that States possess certain exclusive and general legal characteristics, which he has divided into five principles that constitute in legal terms the hard core of the concept of statehood. These are: (1) States have full competence to perform acts in the international sphere, such as entering into treaties. (2) States are exclusively competent with regard to their internal affairs. (3) States cannot be compelled to take part in international processes, settlements, or jurisdiction unless they consent to such exercise. (4) States are considered "equal" in international law. (5) Finally, it is only possible to derogate from these principles if it has been clearly established. Crawford J., The Criteria for Statehood in International Law, *British Yearbook of International Law*, Vol. 48, 1977, p. 93-182.

1

one another.[2] In its narrower meaning, a constitution means a document having a special legal status which sets out the framework and principal functions of the organs of government and declares the principles or rules by which those organs must operate.[3] Traditionally, the structure of a country's government is divided into three institutional components in the constitution: (i) legislative to make laws; (ii) executive to implement and execute laws; and (iii) judiciary to interpret the laws and administer justice.[4] The constitution may also create other organs which it may regard as significant; for instance, the Indian Constitution provides for the Election Commission to ensure free and fair elections in the country. An important aspect of the relationship between the government and the people is guaranteeing of certain Fundamental Rights to the people.

The Armed Forces and Constitution

The notion of State is somewhat akin to the concept of armed forces. Number-wise, the armed forces remain the most important organ of the State; their principal object is to fight and win wars. According to Finer (2006), the armed forces have three political advantages over civilian organizations: (i) a marked superiority in organization, (ii) a highly emotionalized symbolic status and (iii) a monopoly of arms.[5] The highly peculiar features of the armed forces are: centralized command, hierarchy, discipline, intercommunication, and *esprit de corps* and self-sufficiency. The armed forces are unlike any other state organization because they are allowed to do things that no other organization is permitted to do (such as using lethal force), and their personnel are required to do things that no other employees are required to do (such as submit to military discipline or ultimately give up their lives in the line of duty).[6] These special rights and obligations make the armed forces a very powerful organ of a State.

The armed forces world over are undergoing a profound shift in

---

2   Wade E.C.S. and Phillips George Godfrey, 1985, *Constitutional and Administrative Law*, Longman.

3   Bradley, A.W., Ewing, K.D. and Knight, C.J.S., 2015, *Constitutional and Administrative Law*, UK: Pearson Education Limited, p. 4.

4   Jain M.P., 2005, *Indian Constitutional Law*, Nagpur: Wadhwa & Company, p. 2.

5   Finer Samuel E., 2002, *The Man on Horseback: The Role of Military in Politics*, USA: Transaction Publishers, p. 6.

6   The Armed Forces, Roles and responsibilities in good security sector governance, SSR backgrounder, Geneva Centre for the Democratic Control of Armed Forces, Geneva: DCAF, 2015.

their core function. The emergence of new security challenges in the form of terrorism and insurgency, coupled with the increasing role in internal security situation have refocused military role in a modern state.[7] Governments and societies have been contemplating the appropriateness of newly defined purposes for their armed forces, which extend beyond their core role of providing security against external threats.[8] It is necessary that this power is used effectively and efficiently with respect for human rights and the principles of good governance.

The position of the armed forces in the Indian constitution is as follows. List 1, Entry 1 (Seventh Schedule), provides for the defence of India while Entry 2 provides for the naval, military and air forces of the Union. The President is the supreme commander of the defence forces of the Union and the exercise of this command is to be regulated by law.[9] It is the duty of the Union to protect every state against external aggression and internal disturbance.[10] In a federal state where internal security becomes the responsibility of the police, the function of protection against external aggression is performed by the Centre through its armed forces.

Fundamental Rights

The Indian Constitution is a unique document. It contains not only the fundamental principles of governance but also many administrative details such as the provisions regarding citizenship, official language, government services, electoral machinery, etc. The Constitution of India being written constitutes the fundamental law of the land. It is under this fundamental law that all laws are made and executed, all government authorities act and the validity of their functioning adjudged. No act of legislative, executive, judicial or quasi-judicial, or any administrative agency would be lawful if it is contrary to the Constitution.[11] The Indian Constitution guarantees essential human rights under Part III and directive principles

---

7   Timothy Edmunds, What Are Armed Forces For? The Changing Nature of Military Roles in Europe, *International Affairs*, Vol. 82, No. 6, November 2006, pp. 1059-1075.

8   Schnabel Albrecht and Marc Krupanski, Evolving Internal Roles of the Armed Forces, *Prism*, Vol. 4, No. 4, pp. 119-137.

9   Article 53 (2) of the Constitution of India states: Without prejudices to the generality of the foregoing provision, the supreme command of the Defence Forces of the Union shall be vested in the President and the exercise thereof shall be regulated by law. Article 74 (1), Constitution of India provides that the President has to act on the advice of the Council of Ministers.

10 The Constitution of India, Article 355.

11 Jain, M. P., 2018, *Indian Constitutional Law*, Gurgaon: LexisNexis, p. 21.

of State policy in Part IV of the Constitution which are fundamental to the governance of the country. The Fundamental Rights cannot be taken away by any legislation; a legislation can only impose reasonable restriction on the exercise of the right.[12] Part III of the Indian Constitution guarantees that every person (limited to non-citizen in some cases) shall be entitled to certain Fundamental Rights irrespective of race, caste, creed, sex or place of birth. These rights are judicially enforceable which encompass all the civil and political rights and are contained in Articles 12 to 35.[13] Unlike Constitutions of some developed States, no fundamental right in India is absolute in nature. Reasonable restrictions can be imposed on such Fundamental Rights. A reasonable restriction on the exercise of the right is always permissible in the interest of the security of the State.[14] The Supreme Court of India has interpreted the Constitution's Fundamental Rights guarantees expansively. The Court has held that in interpreting the Fundamental Rights, its approach "should be dynamic rather than static, pragmatic and not pedantic, and elastic rather than rigid."[15]

Article 13 of the Constitution is a key provision as it gives teeth to the Fundamental Rights and makes them justifiable. Article 13 not only declares pre-constitution laws as void to the extent to which they are inconsistent with the Fundamental Rights, it also prohibits the State from making a law which either takes away totally or abrogates in part a fundamental right.[16] The effect of Article 13(2) is that no Fundamental Right can be infringed by the State either by legislative or administrative action. Article 13 makes the Supreme Court, as the guardian, protector and the interpreter of the

---

12 *Dharam Dutt v. Union of India* (2004) 1 SCC 712.

13 The Part III of the Constitution consists of 26 Articles which are arranged under the following subheadings : (i) Articles 12 and 13, (ii) Right to Equality (Articles 14 to 18), (iii) Right to Freedom (Articles 19 to 22), (iv) Right against Exploitation (Article 23 & 24), (v) Right to Freedom of Religion (Articles 25 to 28), (vi) Cultural and Educational Rights (Articles 29 and 30), (vii) Right to Property (Articles 30A, 31 A, 31B and 31C), (viii) Right to Constitutional Remedies (Articles 32 to 35).

14 Basu Durga Das, 2012, *Shorter Constitution of India*, Vol. I, Gurgaon: LexisNexis Butterworths Wadhwa, p. 43.

15 *Pathumma v. State of Kerala*, AIR 1978 SC 771. The Supreme Court in *Maneka Gandhi v. Union of India* (1978) 1 SCC 248 held that the framing and structure of part III of the Constitution by the founding fathers calls for the guarantees embodied in it to be interpreted in a liberal way, so as to subserve the purpose for which the constitution-makers intended them, and not in any pedantic or narrow sense.

16 *State of West Bengal v. Committee for Protection of Democratic Rights, West Bengal*, AIR 2010 SC 1476.

Fundamental Rights.[17] A statue is declared unconstitutional and void if it comes in conflict with a Fundamental Right.

The Constitution guarantees the right to equality through Article 14-18. The underlying object of Article 14 is to secure all persons, citizens and non-citizens, the equality of status and opportunity referred in the Preamble to the Constitution. The rights protected by the Constitution include "equality before the law" and "equal protection of the laws", which embody a broad guarantee against arbitrary or irrational state action. In course of time Article 14 has evolved into a very meaningful guarantee against any action of the administration which may be arbitrary, discriminatory or unequal.[18] This manifests itself in the following propositions: (A) A law conferring unguided and unrestricted power on an authority is bad, as its use could be discriminatory; (B) Article 14 illegalizes discrimination in the actual exercise of any discriminatory power; and (C) Article 14 strikes at arbitrariness in administrative action and ensures fairness and equality of treatment.[19]

Article 19 confers to the citizen of India six freedoms: of 'speech and expression', 'peaceable assembly', 'association', 'free movement', 'residence' and 'practicing any profession and carrying on any business'; although Parliament may legislate "reasonable restrictions" on some of these rights in the interests of the "sovereignty and integrity of India," "security of the state," or "public order." These Fundamental Rights are basic rights and must be harmoniously construed so that they are properly promoted with a minimum of such implicit and necessary restrictions.[20]

The term "reasonable" does not have a precise definition and each case is to be adjudged on its own merits, and no abstract or general pattern of reasonableness is applicable uniformly in all aces. The court evaluating the reasonableness on the restrictions imposed on a Fundamental Right guaranteed by Article 19 enjoys a vast discretion. The Supreme Court is of the view that the following principles and guidelines should be kept in mind while considering the constitutionality of a statutory provision upon a challenge on the alleged vice of unreasonableness of the restriction imposed by it:

---

17 *Brij Mohan Lal v. Union of India* (2012) 6 SCC 5602.

18 *YSrinivas Rao v. J Veeraiah* AIR 1993 SC 929.

19 Jain, M. P., 2018, *Indian Constitutional Law*, Gurgaon: LexisNexis, p. 943.

20 *Dharam Dutt v. Union of India* (2004) 1 SCC 712; *M H Devendrappa v. Karnataka State Small Industries Development Corporation*, (1998) 3 SCC 732.

(a) The restriction sought to be imposed on the Fundamental Rights guaranteed by Article 19 of the Constitution must not be arbitrary or of an excessive nature so as to go beyond the requirement of felt need of the society and object sought to be achieved.

(b) There must be a direct and proximate nexus or a reasonable connection between the restriction imposed and the object sought to be achieved.

(c) No abstract or fixed principle can be laid down which may have universal application in all cases. Such consideration on the question of quality of reasonableness, therefore, is expected to vary from case to case.

(d) In interpreting constitutional provisions, courts should be alive to the felt need of the society and complex issues facing the people which the Legislature intends to solve through effective legislation.

(e) In appreciating such problems and felt need of the society the judicial approach must necessarily be dynamic, pragmatic and elastic

(f) It is imperative that for consideration of reasonableness of restriction imposed by a statute, the Court should examine whether the social control as envisaged in Article 19 is being effectuated by the restriction imposed on the Fundamental Rights.[21]

Article 20 of the Constitution prohibits *ex-post facto* laws, double jeopardy, and compelled self-incrimination. An *ex-post facto* law is a law which imposes penalties retrospectively, that is, upon acts already done, or which increases the penalty for the past acts. Article 20(2) which run as, "No person shall be prosecuted and punished for the same offence more than once", contains the rule against double jeopardy.[22]

Article 21, the core of all the Fundamental Rights provisions in the Constitution, states: "No person shall be deprived of his life or personal

---

21 *Papnasam Labour Union v. Madura Coats Ltd* 1995 AIR 2200, 1995 SCC (1) 501.

22 The provisions of double jeopardy though not found under the Navy Act, 1957 and deleted in 1992 under the Army Act, 1950, still exist in the Air Force Act, 1950. Section 126 of the Act dealing with successive trials by a criminal court and a court martial, provides, "A person convicted or acquitted by a court-martial may, with the previous sanction of the Central Government, be tried again by a criminal court for the same offence, or on the same facts." This is a gross violation of Article 20(2) of the Constitution.

liberty except according to procedure established by law." The Supreme Court has interpreted the term "life" to include the right to possession of each organ of one's body and a prohibition of torture or inhuman or degrading treatment by Police. In *Francis Coralie Mullin v. The Administrator, Union Territory of Delhi*,[23] the Supreme Court held that "life" couldn't be restricted to mere animal existence, or physical survival. The right to life means the right to live with dignity and all that goes with it - the basic necessities of life such as adequate nutrition, clothing, shelter and facilities for reading, writing and expressing oneself."

The judiciary has interpreted 'the right to life and personal liberty' to encompass all basic conditions for a life with dignity and liberty. The expression 'personal liberty' was given an expansive interpretation by the Supreme Court in *Maneka Gandhi v. Union of India*.[24] The Court reiterated the proposition that Article 14, 19 and 21 are not mutually exclusive. This means that a law prescribing a procedure for depriving a person of 'personal liberty' has to meet the requirement of Article 19. In addition, the procedure established by law in Article 21 must answer the requirement of Article 14. Such an approach allows it to come down heavily on the system of administration of criminal justice and law enforcement. It also brings into the fold of Article 21 all those directive principles of state policy that are essential for a "life with dignity".[25] While some people have a very simplistic notion of human dignity, that it's just some sort of aura or something of property that hangs around people and can be violated. In fact, human dignity is a relation between people and one is respected by others as a human. Others respect one's right, which doesn't mean they can never violate them, but there have to be reasons and justifications that are sound in order to override one's rights.

The Supreme Court has held that the Constitution guarantees the right to privacy [26] and freedom from torture or cruel, inhuman, or degrading treatment.[27] It has also recognized a constitutional right to a fair criminal trial, including among other elements the presumption of innocence; independence, impartiality, and competence of the judge; knowledge by the accused of the accusations; trial of the accused and taking of

---

23 AIR 1981 SC 746.

24 *Maneka Gandhi v Union of India* (1978) 1 SCC 248.

25 *Olga Telllis v. Bombay Corporation*, AIR 1986 SC 180.

26 *Kharak Singh v. State of UP*, AIR 1963 SC 898.

27 *Francis Coralie Mullin v. Union Territory of Delhi*, AIR 1981 SC 746.

evidence in his presence; cross-examination of prosecution witnesses; and presentation of evidence in defence.[28] The Court has held that speedy trial is a fundamental right implicit in the broad sweep and content of Article 21 of the Constitution; and the law must ensure "reasonable, just and fair" procedure.[29]

The rights of a person, arrested and detained by the State authorities, are provided in Article 22 of the Constitution. These include the right to be informed of the grounds of arrest, the right to legal advice and the right to be produced before a magistrate within 24 hours of arrest (except where one is arrested under a preventive detention law). Individuals arrested and taken into custody must be provided with the basis for arrest "as soon as may be" and produced before a magistrate within 24 hours. The Supreme Court in its landmark case of *D.K. Basu v. State of West Bengal*, extended the Constitution's procedural guarantees further by requiring the police to follow detailed guidelines for arrest and interrogation.[30] The Constitution also guarantees the right to counsel of the defendant's choice; and the Supreme Court has held that legal assistance must be provided to indigent defendants at government expense.[31] The insufficiency of legal aid to the accused during a court-martial is a serious defect of the present system; the most significant is the absence of the services of an experienced legal counsel for the accused.[32] Article 23 of the Constitution prohibits forced

---

28 *State of Punjab v. Baldev Singh*, AIR 1999 SC 2378.

29 *Moti Lal Saraf v. State of J&K*, (2006) 10 SCC 560.

30 *D.K. Basu v. State of West Bengal*, (1977) 1 SCC 416.

31 Article 22(1) of the Constitution gives a guarantee to a person arrested and detained to be defended by a legal practitioner of his choice. However, the law governing the armed forces does not provide the right to engage a counsel, when is accused marched in front of the commanding officer for determination of charges against him. It is only when the charges against an accused have been finalized, summary of evidence against him has been completed and the convening authority has issued an order for assembly of court martial; he is asked, whether he would like to be defended by a counsel, which he will have to arrange for himself, or a military office to be detailed to defend him at trial.

32 The Army Rules permit an accused to engage a civilian lawyer at his own expense or to be defended by a military officer known as the defending officer. In reality, very few of the accused can engage a civilian lawyer at their own expense and service officers normally detailed for the duty are inexperienced and unwilling to undertake this commitment. The infrastructure required to meet this obligation of legal aid has not been developed in the armed forces. Consequently, cases before the court martial are not adequately defended, which is in violation of the provisions of Article 22(1) of the Constitution.

labour not only against the State but also against private citizens.[33] The Supreme Court in the *People's Union for Democratic Rights v. Union of India* has given an expansive significance to the term 'forced labour'.[34]

The Fundamental Rights are enforceable in a court of law. In fact, the remedial right of obtaining the enforcement of these is also a guaranteed constitutional right. These Fundamental Rights are rooted in the recognition of the dignity of the individual as well as the rights of groups and the rights of the society. The executive, legislature and judiciary have been entrusted with the job of balancing the rights of the individual and the interest of the society. However, if Fundamental Rights are to be restricted or abrogated, keeping in mind the good of the society as a whole, it has to be done by the Constitution itself. Article 33 is an exception to the general provisions contained in Part III of the Constitution. It gives Parliament the power to modify the rights conferred by Part III in their application to armed forces personnel.

Article 33

The makers of the Constitution specified, with great precision, the circumstances under which the Fundamental Rights may be curtailed or abrogated by the State in the interest of the nation or of social progress. One of the points that came up for consideration before the provisions related to the Fundamental Rights were given their final shape, was the extent to which these rights would apply to members of the armed forces. Their position made it necessary for them to be subjected to a code of conduct not entirely consistent with the exercise of the Fundamental Rights as they would apply to the ordinary citizen. This was recognized during the preliminary stages of the discussions of the sub-committee. It was provided in the draft that the Union Legislature would be entitled to determine the extent to which the Fundamental Rights should be restricted or abrogated in respect of the members of the armed forces or other forces

---

33 The old British term "orderly" continued into the post-independence Indian Army. It has now, however, been replaced with the Hindi word *sahayak*, which translates as "assistant" or "helper". There have been suggestions to do away with the practice, as the Indian Navy and Indian Air Force already have. In the Pakistan Army, civilian personal are employed in this role and are designated as NCB (Non-Combatant Bearer); they work only as a personal servant to each officer. In the US, the Department of Defence policy provides, "No officer may use an enlisted member as a servant for duties that contribute only to the officer's personal benefit and that have no reasonable connection with the officer's official responsibilities." In the French Army the batmen were officially abolished after the World War II.

34 AIR 1982 SC 1473.

charged with the maintenance of public order to ensure the fulfilment of their duties and the maintenance of discipline.[35] The sub-committee on Fundamental Rights accepted this reservation at its meeting of March 30, 1947; there was no controversy and no discussion.[36] The clause figured as Clause 31 in its report to the Advisory Committee. It was duly adopted by the committee and incorporated as Clause 23 of its interim report. The Constituent Assembly also adopted this provision without any discussion on 2 May 1947. The provision was later adopted by the drafting committee without any material change and figured as Article 26 of the draft Constitution of February 1948:

> The Union Legislature may by law determine to what extent any of the rights guaranteed in this part shall in their application to the members of the armed forces or forces charged with maintenance of public order be restricted or abrogated so as to ensure the proper discharge of duties and the maintenance of discipline among them.

The article was non-controversial. No amendment of substance was moved and it was adopted by the Assembly on 9 December 1948, with a minor change suggested by Dr. Ambedkar substituting the words "conferred by" for "guaranteed in". At the revision stage, the Drafting Committee numbered it as Article 33.[37]

> **Power of Parliament to modify the rights conferred by this part in their application to Forces**:- Parliament may by law determine to what extent any of the rights conferred by this Part shall, in their application to the members of the Armed Forces or the Forces charged with the maintenance of public order, be restricted or abrogated so as to ensure the proper discharge of their duties and the maintenance of discipline among them.

The provision under Article 33 is an exception to the universal applicabil-

---

35 Sen Mr Justice D. M., Former Judge Advocate General (Army) and Judge of Guwahati High Court, as spoke in the seminar organized by The United Services Institution of India, New Delhi on "*The Relationship of Military law and Discipline with the Judicial System of the Country*", held at Vigyan Bhawan on February 26, 1982: "When the first Draft of the Constitution was circulated amongst the Service HQ, Articles 33, 136, 227 and 310 were not there. These were submitted by the services HQ and subsequently were redrafted by Dr. Ambedakar."

36 Minutes of the Meeting of the Sub-Committee on Fundamental Rights, 27 February -31 March 1947; The Framing of Indian Constitution: Select documents, Vol. II, Bombay: N.M. Tripathi Pvt. Ltd, pp. 114-143.

37 Constituent Assembly Debates of 9 December 1948, see p. 159 of the book.

ity of Fundamental Rights. The scope of Article 33 was enlarged in 1984. Clause 2 of the Constitution (Fifty-Second Amendment) Bill, 1984 states that for Article 33 of the Constitution, the following article shall be substituted, namely:-

"33. **Power of Parliament to modify the rights conferred by this Part in their application to Forces, etc**.- Parliament may, by law, determine to what extent any of the rights conferred by this Part shall, in their application to-

(a) the members of the Armed Forces; or

(b) the members of the Forces charged with the maintenance of public order; or

(c) the members of the Forces charged with the protection of property belonging to, or in the charge of or possession of the state; or

(d) persons employed in any bureau or other organisation established by the State for purposes of intelligence or counter intelligence; or

(e) persons employed in, or in connection with, the telecommunication systems set up for the purposes of any Force, bureau or organisation referred to in clauses (a) to (d)

be restricted or abrogated so as to ensure the proper discharge of their duties and the maintenance of discipline among them."

Upon an amendment moved by the Minister of Home Affairs, sub-clause (c) was deleted and consequential changes were made in sub-clause (d) and (e).[38] Section 2 of the Constitution (Fiftieth Amendment) Act, 1984 was adopted as follows:

For Article 33 of the Constitution, the following article shall be substituted, namely:-

"33. **Power of Parliament to modify the rights conferred by this Part in their application to Forces, etc**.- Parliament may, by law, determine to what extent any of the rights conferred by this Part shall, in their application to,-

---

38 For Lok Sabha debates on the Constitution (Fifty-Second Amendment) Bill, 1984, see page 160 of the book.

(a) the members of the Armed Forces; or

(b) the members of the Forces charged with the maintenance of public order; or

(c) persons employed in any bureau or other organisation established by the State for purposes of intelligence or counter intelligence; or

(d) persons employed in, or in connection with, the telecommunication systems set up for the purposes of any Force, bureau or organisation referred to in clauses (a) to (c) be restricted or abrogated so as to ensure the proper discharge of their duties and the maintenance of discipline among them."

The 1984 amendment to the Article 33 enlarging the scope of the Article has been held valid and not destructive of the basic features of the Constitution.[39]

Scope of Article 33

A reading of Article 33 suggests that Parliament can make a law abrogating or restricting the Fundamental Rights of members of the armed forces or the forces charged with the maintenance of public order only for two reasons. First, 'for ensuring the proper discharge of their duties' and, second, 'for the maintenance of discipline among them'. However, Article 13 cl. (2) runs: "The state shall not make any law which takes away or abridges the rights conferred by this part (Part III of the Constitution) and any law made in contravention of this clause shall, to the extent of the contravention, be void."

Article 33 is thus an exception to the provisions of Article 13 (2) of the Constitution. While recognizing the immutability of the Fundamental Rights, the Constitution has, under Article 33, provided for the suspension or the modification of Fundamental Rights under specific circumstances. The article applies not only to the armed forces but also to other forces such as the police and intelligence bureau. However, it does not apply to other classes of government servants not covered by the provision. Nor does it apply to those who have left armed forces. The article has given the power

---

39 The 1984 amendment to the Article 33 enlarging the scope of the Article 33 has been held valid and not destructive of the basic features of the Constitution. *Intelligence Bureau Employees' Association v. Union of India* (1997) 11 SCC 348, decided on 24 April 1996 [Two Judge Bench].

to abridge or abrogate the rights of the personnel covered by its provision only to the Parliament and not to the state legislature or the executive. The President exercising the power of the state legislature under Article 356 is not competent to make a law as contemplated by Article 33.[40]

The Army Act, 1950

In pursuance of the provisions under Article 33 of the Constitution, Section 21 of the Army Act, 1950 states:

21. **Power to Modify certain Fundamental Rights in their application to persons subject to this Act:** Subject to the provisions of any law for the time being in force relating to the regular army or to any branch thereof, the central government may, by notification, make rules restricting to such extent and in such manner as may be necessary the right of any person subject to this Act:-

    (a) to be a member of, or to be associated in any way with, any trade union, or any society, institution or association or any class of societies, institutions or associations;

    (b) to attend or address any meeting or to take part in any demonstration organized by anybody or a person for any political or other purposes;

    (c) to communicate with the press or to publish or cause to be published any book, letter or document.[41]

Section 21 of the Army Act, 1950, empowers the Central Government to make rules restricting 'to such extent and in such manner as may be

---

40 *Dalbir Singh v. State of Punjab* AIR 1962 SC 1106.

41 Similar provisions are contained in Section 21 of the Air Force Act, 1950. The Navy Act, 1957, Section 4, dealing with Fundamental Rights provides, "The rights conferred by Part III of the Constitution in their application to persons subject to naval law shall be restricted or abrogated to the extent provided in this Act." See Manual of Military Law, Vol. II, 2011: A note below Army Act, section 21, states that the right to be defended by legal practitioner of his choice provided by Article 22(1) of the Constitution has been restricted by Army Rules 96 and 129. This is an incorrect statement. Section 21 of the Army Act gives power to the central government to make rules restricting Fundamental Rights only for three specified purposes, i.e., to be member of a trade union, to attend public meeting for political purpose, and to communicate with the press. Thus, if the rules made by the central government restrict Fundamental Rights for any other purposes not linked to discipline and performance of duty (as envisaged under Article 33), those rules would be in violation of power given by the Parliament under section 21 of the Army Act.

necessary' three categories of rights of any person subject to the Act. Briefly, these are: (i) to be member of a trade union, (ii) to attend or address political meetings, and (iii) to communicate with the press or publish any document. These rights are part of the Fundamental Rights under Article 19(1) cls (a), (b) and (c) and under the constitutional scheme they cannot be restricted by executive action unsupported by law. But the section 21 of the Army Act is saved by Article 33 which carves out an exception in so far as the applicability of Fundamental Rights to members of the armed forces and the forces charged with the maintenance of public order is concerned.

The Central Government exercising rules making powers under section 191 of the Army Act has made the Army Rules, 1954. The restrictions imposed by the Parliament under section 21 of the Army Act are found in Rules 19, 20 and 21 of the Army Rules, 1954. These are as follows:

Rule 19

Unauthorised organization

No person subject to the Act shall, without the express sanction of the Central Government:

(i) Take official cognisance of, or assist or take any active part in any society, institution or organisation, not recognised as part of the Armed Forces of the Union; unless it be of a recreational or religious nature in which case prior sanction of the superior officer shall be obtained;

(ii) Be a member of, or be associated in any way with, any trade union or labour union, or any class of trade or labour unions.

Rule 20

Political and non-military activities

(1) No person subject to the Act shall attend, address, or take part in, any meeting or demonstration held for a party or any political purposes, or belong to or join or subscribe in the aid of, any political association or movement.

(2) No person subject to the Act shall issue an address to electors or in any other manner publicly announce himself or allow himself to be publicly announced as a candidate or as a prospective candidate for election to Parliament, the

legislature of a State or a local authority, or any public body or act as a member of a candidate's election committee, or in any way actively promote or prosecute a candidate's interests.

Rule 21

Communications to the Press, Lectures, etc

No person subject to the Act shall:-

(i) Publish in any form whatever or communicate directly or indirectly to the Press any matter in relation to a political question or on a service subject or containing any service information, or publish or cause to be published any book or letter or article or other document on such question or matter or containing such information without the prior sanction of the Central Government, or any officer specified by the Central Government in this behalf; or

(ii) Deliver a lecture or wireless address, on a matter relating to a political question or on a service subject or containing any information or views on any service subject without the prior sanction of the Central Government or any officer specified by the Central Government in this behalf.

Explanation; For the purposes of this rule, the expression "service information" and "service subject" include information or subject, as the case may be, concerning the forces, the defence or the external relation of the Union.[42]

---

42 Similar provisions are contained the Air Force Rules, 1950 and placed at Rule 19-21. In the case of Indian Navy, there are no regulations, thus, Section 19 of the Navy Act, 1957, dealing with restriction respecting right to form associations, freedom of speech, etc, provides:

(1) No person subject to naval law shall, without the express sanction of the Central Government: (a) be a member of, or be associated in any way with, any trade union, labour union, political association or with any class of trade unions, labour unions or political associations, or (b) be a member of, or be associated in any way with, any other society, institution, association or organisation that is not recognised as part of the Armed Forces of the Union or is not of a purely social, recreational or religious nature. Explanation: If any question arises as to whether any society, institution, association or organisation is of a purely social, recreational or religious nature, the decision of the Central Government thereon shall be final.

(2) No person subject to naval law shall attend or address any meeting or take any part in any demonstration organised by any body of persons for any political purposes or for such other purposes as may be specified in this behalf by the Central Government.

However, the restriction to communicate with the press or delivering lectures is not absolute, but is controlled by the Central Government.[43]

The Rights of the Members of the Armed Forces

Nearly 1.4 million Indians serving in the armed forces, as well as retired members of the three service and their families have stake in the social and legal issues affecting the armed forces. No one would disagree with the fact that the armed forces, entrusted with the defence of a country, need to be highly disciplined and efficient. The government has to make every effort to ensure that its armed forces are capable of guarding the frontiers of the country. However, the large number of cases which have come up before the superior civil courts and the recently established benches of the Armed Forces Tribunal show that the governance and the justice delivery system of the armed forces has not been able to satisfy the aspirations of men in uniform. There has been an unusual increase in the filing of petitions by serving as well as retired military personnel. This trend shows a gradual erosion of faith in the system of governance as well as violation of human rights in the armed forces. The recent judgments of the Supreme Court and Armed Forces Tribunal have found the existing system of governance and military justice unjust and antiquated and out of step with the liberal spirit of the Indian Constitution.[44] India is also a signatory to a number

---

(3)   No person subject to naval law shall communicate with the press or publish or cause to be published any book, letter or other document having bearing on any naval, army or air force subject or containing any fact or opinion calculated to embarrass the relations between the Government and the people or any section thereof or between the Government and any foreign country, except with the previous sanction of the Central Government.

(4)   No person subject to naval law shall whilst he is so subject practise any profession or carry on any occupation, trade or business without the previous sanction of the Chief of the Naval Staff.

43   **The Regulations for the Army, Volume I (1987), paragraph 322, dealing with communication to the press, lectures, provides:** "Applications for obtaining permission of the Central Government to publish a book or letter or an article or deliver a lecture or wireless address as mentioned in Army Rule 21 will be submitted to the Vice Chief of the Army Staff (MI-11) through staff channels together with two copies of the book, letter, article, lecture or address and of any enclosure, sketch or photograph relating thereto, and will be accompanied by a statement from the authority under whom the applicant is immediately serving that such authority has no objection to the application. This, however, does not apply to the publication of articles in regimental of service journals, which do not refer to political or controversial issues, and lectures on professional subjects in service associations which are not reported to the press.

44   *Lt. Col. P. P. S. Bedi v. Union of India* (1982) 3 SCC 140; *R.S. Bhagat v. Union of India*

of international human rights instruments.[45] The domain of these human rights instruments have tended to globalize the perspective of constitutional jurisprudence and extend the scope of fundamental human rights in India. In the recent past the governance and military justice system in most of the democracies has undergone a sea change. A few states see the members of the armed forces as citizen-in-uniform and have bestowed them with every constitutional right. There is thus a need to strike a fair balance between the pressures of a democratic society and the requirements of military discipline in India. The next two chapters consider certain rights of the members of the armed forces which may not have any impact on their discipline or performance of duty.

AIR 1982 DELHI 191; *Ranjit Thakur v. Union of India* (1987) 4 SCC 611, *Bhuneswar Singh v. Union of India* (1993) 4 SCC 327; *Union of India v. Charanjit Singh Gill* AIR 2000 SC 3425.

45 Post-Constitution India has signed a number of international treaties and conventions. These include International Covenant on Civil and Political Rights, 1966 (ICCPR), Convention on the Elimination of All Forms of Discrimination Against Women, 1981 and Convention Against Torture and Other Cruel, Inhuman or Degrading Treatment or Punishment, 1984. The United Nations has, in the last 25 years also passed a number of resolutions relating to the administration of justice. This includes, 'guidelines on the role of prosecutor', 'basic principles on the role of lawyers', 'principles on the independence of judiciary' and 'body of principles for the protection of all persons under any form of detention or imprisonment. Signature/ ratification of these treaties make it binding upon the State to follow human rights treaty obligations relating to administration of justice to its citizens.

Chapter – II

Conditions of Service and Fundamental Rights

Introduction

The members of the armed forces are citizens of India and are entitled to the Fundamental Rights contained in the Constitution of India. However, some of their rights have been restricted or abrogated by the Constitution itself to ensure discipline and the proper discharge of duties by them.[1] These rights relate to membership of any trade union, addressing political meetings and taking part in demonstrations for political purposes and communication with the press or publication of any document.[2]

---

1   Article 33 of the Constitution provides: Parliament may, by law, determine to what extent any of the rights conferred by Part III shall, in their application to (a) the members of the armed forces; (b) the members of the forces charged with the maintenance of public order; (c) persons employed in any bureau or other organization established by the State for purposes of intelligence or counter intelligence; or (d) person employed in, or in connection with the telecommunication systems set up for the purposes of any force, bureau or organization referred to in clauses (a) to (c); be restricted or abrogated so as to ensure the proper discharge of their duties and maintenance of discipline among them.

2   Section 21 of the Army Act, 1950 provides that the Central Government may make rules restricting the right of persons subject to the Army Act: (a) to be a member or associated with any trade union or labour union, or any society, institution or association; (b) to attend or address any meeting or to take part in any demonstration organised for any political purposes; and (c) to communicate with the press or to publish any book, letter or other document. These provisions have been further elaborated in the Army Rules 1954, rules 19 to 21. Similar provisions are contained in the other service Acts as well as the law relating to the paramilitary forces.

Unlike other citizens, members of the armed forces could be called upon to perform duties which may necessitate killing other people or sacrificing their own lives. They may have to serve under harsh or extreme conditions. They may have to live and serve in hostile areas, away from their family and in conditions where there may be very little separation between private life and official duties, e.g., in barracks. They must always be ready and capable of ensuring the internal security and guarding the frontiers of the country. It is true that these special factors call for placing limitations on the human rights of armed forces personnel.

The question emerges: are the members of the armed forces entitled to enjoy the Fundamental Rights subject to the limitations imposed by Article 33? Whilst taking into account the special characteristics of service life, members of the armed forces should enjoy the rights guaranteed by the Constitution of India. No derogations should be permitted in their fundamental rights which do not come in way of the discipline in the armed forces or in their effective functioning in peace and war. Some of the Fundamental Rights denied to the members of the armed forces which may not have any impact on their discipline or performance of duty are as follows.

Right to Life

The armed forces personnel while joining take a pledge that they would bear true faith and allegiance to the Constitution of India, obey all commands of superiors in peace and war and would not hesitate to sacrifice his life for the country.[3] Members of the armed forces are trained to fight a war, kill enemies and destroy property. That being so, to talk about the human rights and in particular, the 'right to life' of armed forces personnel may appear absurd to some. Let's see few recent incidents:

- In August 2018, four military personnel, including an officer of the rank of Major were killed while battling terrorists near LoC in J&K's Bandipora district. These soldiers were killed while foiling an infiltration bid near the LoC. Apparently, due to lack

---

3 The true text of the oath/affirmation administered to every person joining the Army is contained in the Army Rules, 1954, Rule 9: "I,......do swear in the name of God/ solemnly affirm that I will bear true faith and allegiance to the Constitution of India as by the law established and that I will, as in duty bound, honestly and faithfully serve in the regular Army of the Union of India and go wherever ordered by land, sea or air, and that I will observe and obey all commands of the President of the Union of India and the commands of any officer set over me even to the peril of my life." Other legislations dealing with the military and paramilitary establishment provide similar provisions.

of intelligence, they were not aware of the number of insurgents trying to infiltrate the LoC.

- In July 2018, the MiG-21 *aircraft* of Indian Air Force (IAF) took off from Punjab's Pathankot and crashed in Kangra, Himachal Pradesh, killing its pilot. Earlier in May 2018, an IAF pilot was killed when his MiG-21 fighter crashed in Jammu and Kashmir's Anantnag district. The IAF has reported 31 aircraft accidents in the last four years.

- In July 2018, at least four security forces personnel (including two policemen), who were on leave, were killed by militants in the strife-torn Valley in Kashmir.

- In November 2017, unknown gunmen killed an army soldier Irfan Ahmad Dar, who was on leave, in Wothmula village of Shopian district in Kashmir. His bullet-riddled body was found by locals in an orchard.

- In May 2017, terrorists abducted and shot dead Umar Fayaz Parray, a 22-year-old lieutenant of the Indian Army, in the Shopian district of south Kashmir. As reported, three terrorists dragged him from the wedding function in Batapora area of Shopian and later his bullet-ridden body was found in an orchard in nearby village.

A soldier knows that he may have to sacrifice his life while fighting for his country. He undergoes rigorous training, for instance, climbing cliff faces at night, rigorous swimming, jungle training, or even low flying. He is aware of these hazards to his life, but he may be not aware that he may get killed because of the recklessness of his fellow soldiers or the lack of proper equipment. A pilot may get injured or killed while flying an obsolete aircraft. A soldier may get killed by another disgruntled or mentally disturbed soldier. He might get killed in an IED explosion if the vehicle provided by the State does not have protection against such devices. A soldier who he has been provided with a faulty GPS set, may get killed for intruding into enemy territory accidentally. A soldier may get killed in an accident in mountainous terrain, if the vehicle provided to him is unfit for use on such terrain. He may die because of snake bite, if the State fails to provide him with suitable boots for jungle terrain infested with leeches, poisonous insects and snakes. While civilian casualties in an armed conflict are illegal, immoral, and unjust; could killing of an unarmed combatant, who has come home on leave will be fair? Is the government not responsible to provide security to a soldier while he is on leave in conflict-ridden area? Can a soldier be considered mere cannon fodder during the war and peace? The question which arises in such cases of negligence by the government is whether the death of a soldier in these circumstances would amount to human rights violations. Could Constitution grant greater rights to fleeing bank robbers than to soldiers who are simply trying to do their jobs? Could the next-of-kin of the deceased soldier prefer a claim against the government for human rights violations? Or, could the government can claim 'combat immunity' in such cases and refuse to pay compensation for its neglect?

While there may not be any jurisprudence on such issues in the Indian legal system, the British Supreme Court has recently decided a few such cases where the Ministry of Defence had claimed combat immunity. In 2013, the British Supreme Court held that Article 2 of the European Convention on Human Rights (ECHR)[4] places positive obligations of the UK to secure the right to life of its soldiers in the field. The Court in *Smith*[5] held that: "The extra-territorial obligation of the contracting state is to ensure the observance of the rights and freedoms that are relevant to the individual who is under its agents' authority and control, and it does not need to be more than that". The Court held that the British troops remain within the UK's jurisdiction when deployed on active service abroad, and so attract the protections of the Human Rights Act, 1998. Further, the principle of combat immunity [6] did not negate the Ministry of Defence's duty of care during the military activities in question. The Court also ruled that families of soldiers killed by 'friendly fire' could sue for negligence on

---

4   Article 2 of the European Convention on Human Rights, to which the UK is a party, provides: (1) Everyone's right to life shall be protected by law. No one shall be deprived of his life intentionally save in the execution of a sentence of a court following his conviction of a crime for which this penalty is provided by law. (2) Deprivation of life shall not be regarded as inflicted in contravention of this article when it results from the use of force which is no more than absolutely necessary: (a) in defence of any person from unlawful violence; (b) in order to effect a lawful arrest or to prevent escape of a person lawfully detained; (c) in action lawfully taken for the purpose of quelling a riot or insurrection.

5   *Smith v The Ministry of Defence; Ellis v. The Ministry of Defence* and *Allbuttv The Ministry of Defence* [2013] UKSC 41.

6   The basis of Combat Immunity in the UK came from the judgments in *Mulcahy v Ministry of Defence*[1996], building on the principle articulated in the Australian case of *Shaw Savill and Albion Company Ltd v. The Commonwealth* [1940] HCA 40. As a result of the *Smith* judgment, judicial oversight now allows inquiry into soldiers', sailors' and airmen's decisions taken in combat – unless they can prove that they should be permitted to claim Combat Immunity.

the grounds that the doctrine of combat immunity did not cover decisions "far removed from active operations against the enemy".

Combat Immunity is a defence or exemption from legal liability that applies to members of the armed forces or the Government, within the context of actual or imminent armed conflict. In general, it provides that while the armed forces are in the course of actually operating against the enemy, they are under no 'actionable' duty of care as defined by common law to avoid causing loss or damage to their fellow soldiers, or indeed to anyone who may be affected by what they do. This immunity is not limited to the presence of the enemy or when in contact with the enemy – but applies to all operations against the enemy where the armed forces are exposed to attack or the threat of attack, including planning and preparation for combat. Combat Immunity also applies to peacekeeping operations in which military personnel are exposed to attack or the threat of attack. It demarcates the parameters in which a duty of care does not arise in cases of damage to property, including personal injury or death of fellow soldiers or civilians. Combat Immunity has acted as the blanket protection for decisions taken in the confusion of battle.

There have been a number of incidents in India where military personnel have been put to risk of life without a clear and legitimate military purpose or in circumstances where the threat to life has been disregarded. In a number of cases where accidental or suspicious death of a military member has occurred, the armed forces have conducted independent inquiry but its findings have not been made public. The fundamental right to life and liberty under Article 21 of the Constitution of India occupies a transcendental position. Over the years, the right to life has been expanded to include within its fold, various facets of what is considered to be the essential facets of a life of dignity; a life that represents the minimum that the State must ensure and seek to protect. The Delhi High Court in a recent case had held: "A soldier or officer's honour and dignity is as much a part of his right to life; it is to be respected just as much, if not more, for the reason that it is offered unhesitatingly and fully in defending the borders of the nation. Unlike "hired guns" they stand guard so that the rest exercise our liberties. Denying them the right to a safe workplace with standard equipment constitutes violation of their right to life and dignity."[7]

---

7   The Delhi High Court referred to the case of *Smith v The Ministry of Defence* [2013] in awarding compensation to an Indian Air Force (IAF) pilot. On 2 May 2017, the High Court awarded Rs 55 lakh to a IAF pilot injured in 2005 MiG-21 crash. The Court was of the view that because of the nature of their profession, there was an inherent assumption of risk by fighter pilots, however, it does not extend to the acceptance of

Right Against Forced Labour

Members of the armed forces are being deprived of certain basic human rights. The democratic rights and freedoms, which should have been extended to all ranks in the armed forces, are being curtailed in particular in the case of the lower ranks in the name of 'service ethos'. The Minister of Defence responding to a question in Rajya Sabha regarding extending democratic rights and freedom to defence personnel stated: "All democratic rights and freedom are extended to all ranks.....There is no master-servant relationship of colonial days prevalent in the Army (i.e. *sahayak* or batman). The relationship is based on soldierly ethos embedded in 'leader' and 'led' values as comrades in arms."[8] The Defence Minister was perhaps not correct in making the statement as the system of *sahayak* or batsman still prevails in the Indian Army and some of the paramilitary forces.

The *Sahayak* is not a listed trade in the armed forces, but usually young combatants do this task for a few years. Their duties may include acting as a 'runner' to convey orders from the officer to subordinates; maintaining the weapons, uniform and personal equipment of the officer/JCO; carrying and operating radio sets, maps etc during exercises; and other miscellaneous tasks the officer does not have the time or inclination to do. In fact, the list of 'miscellaneous' tasks may include looking after domestic chores, taking care of children, walking dogs and cleaning vehicles. A letter addressed to the editor (*The Hindu*), describes: "I was once admitted to the military hospital for an eye injury. A jawan was in the same ward, though he appeared fit and healthy. I asked him, after a couple of days, why the hospital did not discharge him. He said innocently that although he was fit to be discharged, he had been given the duty of fetching milk for the family of the colonel (eye surgeon) every morning. He would be discharged after the colonel saheb got a *sahayak*."[9]

---

risk due to negligence in manufacturing aircraft. The Court made it clear that that it was not passing judgement on the airworthiness of the MiG-21, the workhorse of the IAF fighter fleet and an aircraft that has gained a reputation for being dangerously unreliable. *Sanjeet Singh Kalia v. Union of India* WP (C) 3414/2013, Delhi High Court, decision pronounced on 02 May 2017.The Supreme Court on 24 May 2017 has granted a stay on the order of the Delhi High Court.

8   The Minister of Defence Sri A K Antony, responding to a question in Rajya Sabha regarding extending democratic rights and freedom to defence personnel (Question No. 255, answered on 29 August 2012).

9   Available at: http://www.thehindu.com/opinion/letters/sahayak-woes/article4567611. ece, accessed 20 August 2014.

The Defence Minister in a reply to another question in the Rajya Sabha later stated, "*Sahayaks* are authorized to officers and junior commissioned officers in the Army as per their entitlement, while serving with formations functioning on war establishments.[10] These *sahayaks* are combatant soldiers who are entitled to regular pay, allowances and other benefits befitting their rank in the hierarchy. Further, as per the recommendations of the Standing Committee of Defence, the system of *sahayaks* has been taken up for review."[11] The Parliamentary Standing Committee on Defence in a 2010 report had asked the government to abolish the system of employing jawans as *sahayak*, a legacy of the British era.[12] However, the Defence Ministry had tried to justify before the Committee that *sahayaks* help officers in communications and other tasks during operations.[13]

The employment of a combatant in such duties may contribute to increasing stress levels and lowering self-esteem, resulting in incidents of suicide and fratricide. The employment of a combatant in such duties may contribute to increasing stress levels and lowering self-esteem, resulting in incidents of suicide and fratricide. Stress, overwork and poor working conditions are some factors leading to a high rate of suicide. The situation is frightful in the three defence services, which are losing more soldiers due to suicide than in action. [14] In February 2014, a soldier of Rashtriya

---

10 The scale of authorization of *sahayak* is as follows: One for every field officer and above, one for every two officers of the rank of captain and below, one for every subedar major, and one for every two junior commissioned officer of the rank of subedar and below. For more details see: Standing Committee on Defence (2008-2009) Report on Stress Management in Armed Forces, October 2008, p. 21.

11 The Minister of Defence Sri A K Antony, responding to a question in the Rajya Sabha regarding the employment of soldiers as '*sahayaks*' in the Army (Question No. 3604, answered on 3 September 2012).

12 Contrary to popular perception, the recommendations of Parliamentary Standing Committees are not binding on the government or the cabinet.

13 On 20 March 2017, the Government while debating issue in Parliament, strongly defended the *sahayak* system in the Army, holding that it provides "essential support" to the officers and junior commissioned officers fulfilling their assigned duties both in tomes of peace and war. The Union Minister of State for Defence further added that "exhaustive instructions" are repeatedly issued to all Army units to stress that *sahayak* should not be employed on menial tasks which are not in conformity with the dignity and self-respect of combatant soldiers. In Parliament, Centre defends '*sahayak*' system of the Army, *The Times of India*, March 22, 2017.

14 Replying to a question in the Rajya Sabha (Question No. 1422) on 22 July 2014, the Defence Minister said, "The armed forces lost 597 personnel to suicide in the last five years (498 from the Army, 83 from the Air Force and 16 from the Navy), while 1,349 officers quit the Army during the same period. The highest number of suicides took

Rifles in J&K shot dead five of his colleagues while they were asleep and then killed himself. During the period 2014 to 2017, the army reported a total of 270 cases of suicide/ fratricide; which includes nine officers and 19 junior commissioned officers.[15] The case of an Army man who spent five days atop a mobile phone tower in the heart of Delhi in August 2012 to highlight his grievances epitomized the crisis. [16] In India, a few studies on stress and suicide in the military have remained classified, raising serious doubts regarding the quality of the investigations and recommendations made by them.

The Indian Army has been employing civilians as casual porters in the border areas of J&K. It has been alleged that these casual porters do not get minimum wages despite long years of service in arduous conditions prevalent in a difficult terrain. These seasonal porters possess an innate knowledge of the terrain and were utilized for carriage of stores, stocking of posts, collection of water for troops, carriage and replenishment of ammunition, beating of tracks, snow clearance, conveyance of mail, and evacuation of serious casualties. In January 2017, the Supreme Court came to the aid of the casual porters and issued direction for the payment of minimum wages at the prevailing rates, regular medical facilities including in the case of injury or disability, onetime severance grant, and enhanced amount of compensation in the case of death or permanent disability. The Supreme Court was of the view that these porters provide valuable support to the Indian Army and are an integral, if not indispensable, requirement of operations in border areas. They work, albeit as casual labour, for long years with little regard of safety. Faced with disability, injury and many

---

place in the Army in 2010 when 116 troops committed suicide.

15 The incidents of fratricide and suicide in a military unit in Dharamshala in September 2018, resulting in the loss of three valuable lives, have once again proved that the issue has not been dealt with earnestly by the armed forces. Suicide is the leading cause of death in most armies during times of peace and the Indian armed forces are no exception. However, what is noteworthy in our case is that the organizational failing has been brushed aside and the entire blame has been placed on 'domestic reasons'.

16 Concerned over the rise in the number of suicides fratricidal killings in the armed forces; in 2008 the Parliamentary Standing Committee on Defence had examined the issue of stress management and recommended that (i) the Government should provide family accommodation at the station of choice for personnel deployed in counter-insurgency operations and border areas; (ii) the children of armed forces personnel should be helped in getting admission in schools and professional institutions; and (iii) the welfare organisations of the three services should be financially strengthened to enable them to extend help to distressed families. Since the denial of leave was seen to be an important factor causing stress, the Committee recommended that the issue of liberalised leave policy be examined by the Ministry of Defence with an open mind.

times death,their families have virtually no social security. The Court was of the opinion that such a situation cannot be contemplated having regard to the mandate in Articles 14 and 16 of the Constitution.[17]

Working and Living Conditions

The armed forces do not follow any specific rules on work hours, based on the premise of the permanent availability of military personnel. A research carried out by Georg Nolte and Heike Krieger (2003) shows that in Europe, the average period of work for armed forces personnel is between 36 and 50 hours per week. In Belgium, armed forces personnel generally work 38 hours per week.[18] In Denmark, working hours follow those of other civil servants with modifications for the effectiveness of the armed forces. For instance, it is normally required in Denmark to grant employees 11 hours of free time within each 24-hour period. Since military exercises sometimes last for several days, and it is not possible to comply with this provision, compensation is granted. In Italy, the regular working time is 36 hours per week. Overtime compensation can be provided in money or in time. In some European countries, the organization of working time is still based on the principle of the permanent availability of soldiers. This is true of France, for example, where a soldier can be requested to be on duty at all times in accordance with Article 12 of the General Statute on Military Personnel. Recently, however, the French Ministry of Defence adopted a system of compensation for overtime for armed forces personnel. On the basis of this regulation, armed forces personnel were granted 15 extra days of annual leave, in addition to the existing 60 days.[19] The UK follows the approach that it is necessary for a professional armed forces to make service conditions attractive, since the very existence of the military depends on the recruitment.

Restrictions on the exercise and enjoyment of social and economic

---

17 *Yash Pal v. Union of India*, WP (Civil) No. 616 of 2013 and 912 of 2013, decided on 02 January 2017. The Court also directed that the terminal benefits should be enhanced so as to provide for compensation not less than at a rate computed at fifteen days' salary for every completed year of service.

18 In Belgium, members of the armed forces have a right to annual holidays and holiday allowances. Unlike India, the regulations for the soldiers in this regard do not differ much from the other civil servants. Argent Pierre d', 'Military Law in Belgium', in Nolte George (ed.). 2003. *European Military Law Systems*, Berlin: De Gruyter Recht, p. 183-232.

19 For more details see: Nolte George (ed.). 2003. *European Military Law Systems*, Berlin: De Gruyter Recht, p. 101-103.

rights by armed forces personnel need to be specific. General restrictions should be avoided. The Ministry of Defence should take all possible measures to ensure that provisions related to working conditions are implemented in accordance with national law and international obligations. If armed forces personnel are required to work for longer than the legally defined hours, they must be monetarily compensated.

Members of the armed forces have the right to respect for their private and family life and their home. Unfortunately, after 71 years of Independence, military establishments still do not provide housing for all ranks. It may take two years or more before a person below the rank of officer is allotted family accommodation in a military station. By that time he has to be ready for the next posting. Security experts say that jawans posted far away from their native places are under tremendous stress due to the lack of contact with their families. Denial of leave adds to the stress.

Several researches have revealed that stress, overwork and poor working conditions are some of the major factors responsible for the high attrition rate and suicides among armed forces personnel. Counter insurgency operations often lead to stress-related anxiety and depression and in extreme cases, it may lead to suicide. The other reasons for the high suicide rate are domestic, and financial problems. The high attrition rate in the armed and paramilitary forces has become a cause for worry. This impelled the government to commission a study by IIM-Ahmedabad in 2012. The study cited continuous posting in difficult areas, long working hours, sleep deprivation, denial of leave, lack of healthcare facilities, delay in promotions and pay parity as causes of stress.[20] Nearly 500 armed forces personnel are discharged from service every year due to mental disorder and alcohol dependency. In the armed forces, referral for psychiatric treatment is considered a 'stigma' which may have an adverse impact on an individual's career. Thus, personnel suffering from mental health problems fight shy of seeking help. The system of referring a person specifically for psychiatric evaluation must be suitably modified and personnel of all ranks should be required to undergo such evaluation at fixed intervals of time. The Ministry of Defence, in a reply to a question in Parliament, stated recently that a large number of officers had been trained to provide psychological counselling to defence personnel and their families. Further, a psychologist visits units and formations from time to time and carries out psychological counselling, individually and

---

20 For more details see: Dixit K C, *Addressing Stress-Related Issues in Army*, IDSA Occasional Paper No 17, Institute for Defence Studies and Analyses, New Delhi, 2011.

in groups. [21] Who are these 'officers', 'where have they been trained' and what is their 'accountability' remains obscure. What is needed is adequate infrastructure for improvement in the quality of mental healthcare, and not visits by a psychologist.

Combat Role for Women

From the time of independence, women have been progressively absorbed into the main stream of economic life. They have now entered almost all walks of life which were earlier considered male bastions in our country. However, the induction of women and the progression of their careers in the armed forces in the last 25 years have been marred by controversies. Women join the armed forces with the aim of (a) job security; (b) economic independence; (c) social status; and (d) sense of achievement. However, their career profile cannot be compared to those of men. The aim of the armed forces has been to use them on a short-term basis to fill the existing gaps in the cadre. After a prolonged legal battle, women officers are now allowed permanent commission in the armed forces, albeit in select streams.

Currently, women are inducted in the accounts, administrative, education, legal, medical, signals and engineering wings of the three services. Combat roles are off limits for them due to operational concerns. The armed forces also face certain constraints in the optimum utilization of women officers. For example, postings to units performing field activities may not be suitable for women officers considering the size of such units and the nature of the task performed by them. Due to the mindset of senior officers, women generally get preferential treatment, which causes resentment among their male colleagues and results in low performance and morale. The medical category of a woman officer is lowered as soon as pregnancy is confirmed. She remains on low medical category for about 12 months and is protected from strenuous duties. This creates considerable pressure on the other officers, who have to shoulder additional workload. Posting women officers with their husbands, though a government policy, does not benefit the organization.

In 2006, when the Defence Minister had asked the Chiefs of Staff Committee to examine the feasibility of combat roles for women, the Army Headquarters, in an affidavit filed in the Delhi High Court, had ruled out any such possibility in the near future. Since then the Minister of Defence and the three service chiefs have made statements in favour of combat roles for

---

21 Lok Sabha Unstarred Question No 1782, answered on 10 March 2017.

women in the near future. Army Chief General Rawat remarked last year that the process of allowing women to play combat roles is moving fast and that initially, women would be recruited for positions in the military police. The Air Force has recently trained three women fighter pilots on an experimental basis, and the Navy is deliberating on a policy of having women onboard ships. However, women may be allowed to serve only in "combat support-related jobs", which offer fewer career advancement opportunities than hard-core combat roles in the infantry and artillery, or as fighter pilots or commanders of combat ships, because promotion to the higher ranks depends on having served in a combat unit.

Only a handful of countries, including Australia, Britain, Canada, Denmark, Finland, France, Germany, Israel, Norway, the US and Sweden allow women to have combat roles. Even in these countries, the employment of women in combat roles remains marginal. In January of 2013, the US military has lifted its blanket exclusion of women from combat.[22] However, the military commanders have right to exclude women from combat if they could assert a particular military necessity as a justification. The justification that continues to be asserted is one based on the physical differences between men and women.[23] In spite of this, on 20 August 2015, two US Army officers, Captain Kristen Griest and First Lieutenant Shaye Haver became the first two women to pass the US Army Rangers' course. Their achievement sets a precedent for the full integration of women into the ground combat arms. The culture of exclusion is deep-rooted in the armed forces and is not likely to change in the near future. Many military thinkers and senior commanders hold the opinion that employing women in combat would have devastating consequences, though there is no empirical evidence to support such an opinion.

The exclusion of women from combat seems to be based more on social mores than on practical considerations. The elimination of unnecessary gender-based discrimination would not hamper with the discipline and efficient functioning of the armed forces.[24]

---

22 Memorandum from the Chairman of the Joint Chiefs of Staff and the Secretary of Defence to the Secretaries of the Military Departments (24 January 2013), available at: http://www.defense.gov/news/WISRJointMemo.pdf.

23 Department of Defence, Report to Congress on the Review of Laws, Policies and Regulations restricting the Service of Female Members in the US Armed Forces (February 2012), available at:http://www.defense.gov/news/wisr_report_to_congress.pdf.

24 ....The (Indian) Coast Guard, after selection of women officers, takes an undertaking from such officers that they shall not get pregnant within three years of

Ex-gratia lump sum

The Central Government has been paying *ex-gratia* compensation to the next of kin of the members of the armed, para-military and central police forces personnel who died in harness in performance of their bona fide official duties. Under the Sixth Central Pay Commission (CPC), four circumstances were listed for the payment of *ex-gratia* compensation for central armed police and Assam Rifles personnel, while five were listed for such payout in the case of defence forces personnel. The amount of compensation varied from Rs 10 lakh to Rs 20 lakh. The maximum amount of Rs 20 lakh was payable for deaths occurring during enemy action in international wars or such war-like engagements, which are specifically notified by the Ministry of Defence. This clause was applicable only to defence forces personnel.

The Seventh CPC has done away with the differentiation between the defence/para-military and CAPF, and has made the recommendations for the payment of *ex-gratia* compensation under the five categories based on the circumstances under which a person has died. The circumstances are: (1) Death occurring due to accidents in the course of the performance of duties - Rs 25 lakhs; (2) Death in the course of performance of duties attribute to acts of violence by terrorists, anti-social elements etc – Rs 25 lakhs.; (3) Death occurring in border skirmishes and action against militants, terrorists, extremists and sea pirates – Rs 35 lakhs; (4) Death occurring while on duty in the specified high altitude, inaccessible border posts, on account of natural disasters, extreme weather conditions – Rs 35 lakhs; and (5) Death occurring during enemy action in war or war-like engagements, which are specifically notified by the Ministry of Defence, and death occurring during evacuation of Indian nationals from a war-torn zone in a foreign country - Rs 45 lakhs. The recommended amount of *ex-gratia* compensation is too meagre in the present circumstances as the cost of living has gone too high. [25]

---

completion of training and other such incongruous restrictions such as that they shall not get pregnant more than twice during their service careers, and if they do so, their services would be terminated. See: The Report of the Raksha Mantri's Committee of Expert constituted for the "Review of Service and Pension Matters including Potential Disputes, Minimizing Ligations and Strengthening Institutional Mechanism related to Redressal of Grievances", 2015, p. 201. Also see: Bakken Tim, A Woman Soldier's Right to Combat: Equal Protection in the Military, *Wm. & Mary J. Women & L.*, Vol. 20, 2014, p. 271-294.

25 With Rs 30-40 lakhs in hand, a person cannot afford to buy a two-bedroom flat in a Class 'C' city in India, leave apart the money required for bring up of children. Besides, there is very little difference between categories 2 to 5 and the difference in the amount

Incidentally, in its decision of 24 February 2016, the Delhi government clarified that the next of kin of deceased Delhi police personnel would continue to be eligible to receive Rs 1 crore as *ex-gratia*. In addition, it announced that the following five categories of personnel would also be covered by this scheme: (1) Defence personnel dying in operations/war, if their permanent address as recorded at the time of joining service is Delhi; (2) Para-military force personnel dying in operations/war, if their permanent address as recorded at the time of joining service is Delhi; (3) Para-military force personnel working under the government of Delhi/ Delhi police dying in the discharge of their bona fide official duty; (4) Home Guards and civil defence personnel working under the government of Delhi/Delhi police dying in the discharge of their bona fide official duty; and (5) Casualties on account of operations, calamities and disaster. The other state governments in India give varying amount of *ex gratia* which varies from Rs 5 to 10 lakhs.

The members of the armed forces work in a dangerous environment, characterized by uncertainty and unpredictability. Those who sustain injuries in service must be provided adequate healthcare facilities, while the families of those who are killed must be liberally compensated. The compensation schemes must be similar for members of the armed forces serving in similar situations. The *ex-gratia* compensation recommended by the Seventh CPC is woefully inadequate and unjustified. Why should there be discrimination in the award of *ex-gratia* compensation to the next of kin of a soldier killed in a terrorist operation from that to the next of kin of a police constable killed in Delhi?

Right to Association

The right to form associations or unions is a fundamental right under Part III of our Constitution. However, it is not available to every Indian. As discussed Article 33 gives Parliament the power to modify the fundamental rights of the members of the armed forces, intelligence services, and those employed in the telecommunication systems of these organizations 'for ensuring the proper discharge of their duties' and 'for the maintenance of discipline among them'. The legislations governing the armed forces and central police forces restrict the members' fundamental right to form a trade union, to attend or address any political demonstration and to communicate with the press. The state governments, too, have restricted these fundamental rights of police personnel.

---

of compensation recommended by the Seventh CPC appears unjustified.

In the last three decades, the armed forces of most developed democracies have been subjected to substantial reforms due to the change in the nature of perceived threat and the obligation of the armed forces to respond to a wide spectrum of tasks. The armed forces of some countries have become smaller in number, cost-effective, more lethal and civilianized. They have also become subject to greater pressure from the civil society. Equality of rights, discrimination in wages as compared to their civilian counterparts, compensation and pension have appeared on the social agenda of the armed forces. The issue of freedom of association of military personnel and the right to form trade unions has been debated in several countries. The recent solidarity amongst the retired military fraternity in our country for 'One-Rank-One-Pension' was unbelievable. A large number of serving military personnel and their families supported the movement, albeit covertly, forcing the government to take a positive decision on a long-pending grievance.

This raises a few questions. Do military personnel deserve human rights? If so, then up to what extent? Can all the rights mentioned in Part III of the Constitution be abridged or restricted for defence personnel by legislation? The Vienna Conference on Human Rights, held in 1993, emphasized that all human rights are universal, indivisible, interdependent and interrelated. It is the duty of the States to promote and protect all human rights and fundamental freedoms for everyone.

A union may offer certain advantages to its members in attaining increased wages and benefits. An effective military union can be of great service in increasing the status of a military career in the eyes of the general public, and solve the problem the Indian Army is currently facing as regards attracting officers to the service. A union can also perform a vital function in establishing a grievance process for its members in seeking an audience for their complaints and remedies to their problems. An established union, kept within reasonable bounds, could help enforce discipline in the organization.

Though not authorized to form unions or associations, few recent incidents highlights that the armed forces personnel have approached the higher court in joint petitions where their fundamental rights were at stake. In September 2017, more than 100 Army officers moved the Supreme Court, alleging "discrimination and injustice" in the promotion of officers of the Services Corps. These officers alleged that the Army Headquarter has been deploying them in operational areas but denying them due benefits. Army Headquarters had called the services cadre

32

(roughly 20 percent of the army) 'non-operational' and the officers were termed as 'non-combatants' in submission before the Supreme Court. The crux of the argument in the joint petition was that services cadre officers are deployed in operational areas, where they tackle challenges similar to combat arms corps; however, depriving them of promotional avenues was unjust, detrimental to the morale, and violative of Article 14 of the Constitution.

In an unprecedented move nearly 740 Army officers and other ranks have recently petitioned the Supreme Court challenging registration of FIR against those involved in the operations in Manipur where Armed Forces (Special Powers) Act (AFSPA) is in force. The petitioners have urged the Supreme Court to issue an appropriate writ laying down specific guidelines to protect the bonafide action of soldiers functioning under the AFSPA.[26] In July 2018, while hearing the Writ Petition filed by the Extra Judicial Execution Victim Families Association (EEVFAM), in which CBI Director was summoned, one of the judges of the Court remarked, "According to you there are 14 murderers in these cases and they are loafing around Manipur freely. You have not arrested any one of them. What happens to society? If somebody commits rape, what is there to recover, so you (CBI) will allow them to roam free?" It was feared by the members of the armed forces that spurred by comments of Supreme Court judge, the trial court would rush through procedures and convict them.[27]

The incident highlights that military personnel though not authorized to from trade unions, have resorted to such practice, albeit indirectly, whenever there has been a serious infringement of their right. In India the security forces face a great challenge not only from insurgents/ terrorists, but also from human rights activists and NGOs. Some activists portray themselves as human rights crusaders and make irresponsible statements about the functioning of the State forces in the process. The judiciary often gets influenced and places unjustified restrictions on the forces' functioning. A few judicial panels and commissions which have investigated cases of encounter killings, which took place 20-30 years ago,

---

26 Initially, 356 Army personnel moved the Supreme Court on 13 August 2018. Later in the month another 383 army personnel joined the petition, taking the number of personnel who have moved to the court to 739. In September 2018, an officer of the rank of major general also approached the Supreme Court to be impleaded in the matter. These petitions have been submitted by the military personnel on individual basis.

27 *Extra Judicial Execution Victim Families Association (EEVFAM) v Union of India* (2013) 2 SCC 493; SC Judge vitiated our trial with 'murderer' remark: Manipur cops, The Times of India, New Delhi, 15 August 2018, p. 22.

have accused the military of using disproportionate force, in particular when there were no casualties from the military during the operation. In a few cases, they have accused the security forces of not apprehending a terrorist and instead using lethal force against him. In such a situation, the US Supreme Court decision in *Orloff v. Willoughby* (1953) is quite relevant: "Judges are not given the task of running the Army. .... The military constitutes a specialized community governed by a separate discipline from that of the civilian. Orderly government requires that the judiciary be as scrupulous not to interfere with legitimate Army matters as the Army must be scrupulous not to intervene in judicial matters."

Many European countries permit military personnel to form associations to deal collectively with matters affecting their living and working conditions. For example, trade unionism is an integral part of the Dutch military. Military trade unions are allowed to promote their work at military academies from where they can recruit new members. Dutch military personnel have the right of consultation with regards to wages and pensions. However, they have limited freedom of speech and do not have the right to strike. In fact, with the exception of Sweden, none of the unions or associations of military personnel in Europe has the right to strike. In Italy, where military personnel do not have the right to join professional associations or trade unions, the Italian Constitutional Court has questioned whether the ban is in line with the European Convention on Human Rights. Discontent among the British armed forces has prompted calls for an association to represent the rights of serving personnel.

By and large unions and associations appear to have contributed to improvements in pay and benefits and to the general working and living conditions of military personnel. Military officials feel that they have improved communication and resolved personnel problems and conflicts, and not affected military discipline, efficiency, or morale. In Canada, two separate studies have shown that more than one-third of military members think positively about forming a union. In South Africa, the General Regulation of 1999 provides for the organizational rights of military trade unions.

Corruption and Human Rights

Corruption is the abuse of entrusted power for private gains. In recent years, governments and international organizations have increasingly recognized the negative impacts of corruption on the enjoyment of human rights.[28] Corruption in the armed forces, howsoever less, is a problem; though, the issue has rarely been analysed from the point of view of human rights. A military commander involved in corrupt practices of say procurement and supply of ration for troops, construction and repair of military barracks and buildings, or procurement of stores; would deprive its soldiers of authorized quality and quantity of ration, medicines and health care facilities, clothing, quality accommodation and equipments and welfare thus violating their human rights.[29] Another related issues are the misuse of regimental funds by the higher military authorities for illegitimate purposes, involvement of military units in economic activities, running of unauthorized golf courses in the name sports complex, though not visible to a common man are also sources of worrying corruption in the armed forces. In some cases, the connection between corruption and human rights may be indirect and may not violate human rights, strictly understood.[30] Corruption can also affect the enjoyment of human rights by weakening public institutions and eroding the rule of law.[31] When

---

28 Human rights are indivisible and interdependent and the consequences of corruption touch upon them all — civil, political, economic, social and cultural, as well as the right to development. For example, corruption undermines a State's human rights obligation to maximize available resources for the progressive realization of rights recognized in Article 2 of the International Covenant on Economic, Social and Cultural Rights. The corrupt management of public resources compromises the State's ability to deliver services, including health, education, and welfare, which are essential for the realization of economic, social and cultural rights. The human rights case against corruption, Office of the United Nations High Commissioner for Human Rights, Geneva.

29 The former Defenec Minster A K Anthony had tabled a list of 21 senior officers in Parliament who were facing corruption charges. The list included two lieutenant generals, four major generals, nine brigadiers, a lieutenant commander, one group captain and a coast Guard DIG. The corruption charge were related to land scam, selling military liquor in civilian markets, financial bungling in purchase of cereals and petrol in the armed forces. An officer of the rank of major general was accused of purchase of sub-standard items for a unit heading for a UN peacekeeping mission. *The Times of India*, New Delhi, 27 February 2009.

30 Corruption may be an indirect cause for violation of human rights where corrupt authorities seek to prevent the exposure of corruption. When a whistle blower (someone reporting a corruption case) is silenced by harassment, threats of posting to a far flung non-family station, or even referred for psychiatric evaluation; the rights to liberty, freedom of expression, life, and freedom from torture or cruel, inhuman or degrading treatment may all be violated. In such a case, in addition to the original act of corruption that the whistleblower was trying to denounce, it is highly probable that the acts that subsequently infringed his or her rights would also have corruption as a cause. Corruption and Human Rights: Making the Connection, International Council on Human Rights Policy & Transparency International, Switzerland, 2009, p. 26-27.

31 In March 2010, General Court Martial (GCM) held a former lady officer of the Judge

corruption is prevalent, those in positions fail to take decisions with the best interests of society in mind.

The Chief of the Army Staff (COAS) has recently issued a series of directives to root out corruption, ostentatious practices, misuse of privileges, nepotism and lackadaisical approach, among other things. Let us consider a few recent examples of corruption in the armed forces. In 2102 an officer of the rank of major general, attached to a Northern Command unit, came under investigation over the allegation of corruption for contracts that deal with the supply of rations to soldiers in Jammu and Kashmir. An officer posted at the army headquarters was arrested for allegedly running a racket of illegal transfer and postings in exchange for money; two senior officers were subjected to a CBI probe for involvement in corrupt practices and recruitment scams; and two former army chiefs and seven generals were castigated for taking flats in Adarsh Housing Society, Mumbai, meant for war widows. Unfortunately, the military's top brass has made it a practice to brush such issues under the carpet. Whenever there is an allegation of corruption, the military first denies it, then issues a statement that it was an isolated incident, and finally declares that a court of inquiry has been ordered. The proceedings, findings and recommendations of the inquiry are never made public.

Not known to many even in the military, the Regulations for the Army contain an important provision on reporting corruption. Paragraph 317 of the Regulations provides, "It is the obligatory duty of every person in military employ to bring at once to the notice of his immediate superior, or the next superior where the immediate superior officer is involved, any case of dishonesty, fraud or infringement of orders that may come to his knowledge." However, despite this obligation, very few corrupt and illegal practices are reported because the Army Act acts as a deterrent.[32] It states that any military person who makes a false accusation against anyone subject to the Act, shall be court-martialled and awarded a punishment of up to five years' imprisonment. Even if the military takes up investigation

---

Advocate General branch guilty under section 52 and 63 of the Army Act for wrongful gains. She was facing trial for allegedly demanding and accepting bribe of Rs 10,000 from an accused army man to influence court martial proceedings. She was also accused of violating good order and discipline - Section 63 of the Army Act - when she suggested a defence lawyer to military accused who was facing a GCM. She was sentenced to one year rigorous imprisonment.

32 Section 56(a) of the Army Act, 1950, provides that any person subject to the Army Act who makes a false accusation against any person subject to this Act knowing or having reason to believe such accusation to be false, shall, on conviction by court martial, be liable to suffer imprisonment for a term which may extend to five years.

of an allegation of corruption, the court is assembled by the commanding officer and his trusted subordinates. Careerism and personal gain usually prompt inquiry officers to give reports that suit the commander. In the end, it is the person who reports a case of corruption who faces the wrath of the military hierarchy.

In a society in which corruption is rampant and ethics are disregarded with impunity in the political, judicial and bureaucratic systems, there has been a concurrent erosion of values within the armed forces. This has seriously affected the functioning of the armed forces. India has ratified the United Nations Convention against Corruption on 9 May 2011.[33] Corruption undermines the fairness of institutions and processes and distorts policies and priorities, leading to disillusionment. The growing number of clashes between officers and jawans and the protests against the orderly system could be the result of such disillusionment.

Right to Promotion

The right of eligible employees to be considered for promotion is a part of their fundamental right guaranteed under Article 16 of the Constitution. The guarantee of a fair consideration in matters of promotion under Article 16 virtually flows from guarantee of equality under Article 14 of the Constitution.[34] In spite of this constitutional guarantee the issue of promotion remains marred with arbitrariness, malafides and capriciousness in the armed forces. On a number of occasions the senior officers have tried to block promotion of particular officer so as to ensure that their favourite gets the higher rank.[35] The case of *Major General H. M. Singh v. Union of India*,[36] is illustrative of malafide practices which are rotting the

---

33 The United Nations Convention against Corruption, entered into force on 14 December 2005. It has been signed by 186 states and ratified by 140.

34 Supreme Court decision in *Union of India v. Hemraj Singh Chauhan*, 2010(4) SCC 290.

35 In the armed forces, officers in the rank of lieutenant general (and their equivalents in the air force and the navy) retire two years earlier than officers at the rank of major general. In case, a major general is not promoted to the vacant post at the rank of lieutenant general before his retirement date, even if he has been approved for the promotion, he has to go out of service. This offers a lot of scope for senior officers, bureaucrats and even politicians to try to block particular officer and advance others by manipulating vacancies at senior level to make sure that positions are "open" or "closed" at the right time. Wilkinson Steven I., 2015, *Army and Nation: The Military and Indian Democracy since Independence*, Ranikhet: Permanent Black, p. 250.

36 *Major General H M Singh v. Union of India*, Civil Appeal No. 192 of 2014, decided by the Supreme Court on 9 January 2014.

system. In this case, the Supreme Court held:

> In view of the fact, that we have found the order of rejection of the appellant's claim for promotion to the rank of Lieutenant General, on the ground that he was on extended service to be invalid, we hereby set aside the operative part of the order of the Appointments Committee of the Cabinet. It is also apparent, that the Selection Board had recommended the promotion of the appellant on the basis of his record of service, past performance, qualities of leadership, as well as, vision, out of a panel of four names. In its deliberations the Appointments Committee of the Cabinet, did not record any reason to negate the aforesaid interference, relating to the merit and suitability of the appellant. We are therefore of the view, that the appellant deserves promotion to the rank of Lieutenant General, from the date due to him.

The Supreme Court in a similar case,[37] reposing full faith in the Defence Minister, referred the matter back to her to consider the entire matter in a totally dispassionate manner, with utmost objectivity and depicting total fairness. However, this is not a correct judicial approach considering that the issue has already been considered by the Ministry of Defence and the denial of legitimate promotion violates fundamental right. The Armed Forces Tribunal (AFT) in a number of cases relating to promotion has issued directions for: notional promotion where the individual had retired,[38] promotion,[39] reconsideration of the case without reference to the age bar and in case the applicant was selected to the rank of colonel, he would be given his due seniority,[40] implementation of Dynamic Assured Career Progression Scheme to AMC officers,[41] granting substantive rank to the officer and to the other similarly situated persons as given to the permanent commissioned officers,[42] promotion and related

---

37 *Union of India v. Major General Manmoy Ganguly*, Civil Appeal No. 5800 of 2018 decided on 1 August 2018.

38 *Maj Gen Devendra Nath Verma (Retd.) v. Union of India*, TA No. 255 of 2009, decided by AFT New Delhi on 22 February 2010.

39 The AFT Regional Bench Chandigarh in the case of *Ajit Singh v. Union of India*, TA No. 1292 of 2010, decided on 13 February 2012.

40 The AFT Regional Bench Lucknow in the case of *Lt Col Dharmender Singh Yadav v. Union of India*, OA No. 107 of 2011, decided on 27 July 2011.

41 The AFT Regional Bench Chandigarh in the case of *Col. Sanjeev Sehgal v. Union of India*, OA No. 488 of 2011, decided on 18 July 2011.

42 The AFT Principal Bench New Delhi in the case of *Major Nishant Gupta v. Union of India*, OA No. 330 of 2011, decided on 14 March 2012.

financial benefits to a havildar,[43] awarding compensation of Rs 50,000 to a retired havildar who was denied promotion on arbitrary grounds.[44] The AFT Principal Bench has also observed serious contradictions in the promotion/transfer of vacancy, which had seriously affected the career of the individual.[45]

The Chandigarh Bench of the Armed Forces Tribunal (AFT) in a landmark decision in August 2018 has directed the Central Government to promote an officer to the rank of Lieutenant General with all consequential benefits, 21 years after he retired from the service. The AFT observed that the government had filed a false affidavit in the High Court, from where the case was transferred, stating there were only two vacancies for the Corps of Engineers, while in reality there were three. The AFT has also imposed costs of Rs 25,000 on the government.[46]

Human Rights in the Armed Forces

Unknown to many, the Indian Army, in 1993 March, on its own and even before the enactment of the Protection of Human Rights Act, 1993 or the establishment of the National Human Rights Commission (NHRC), had established a Human Rights Cell at the Army Headquarters. This Cell is headed by an officer of the rank of Colonel and functions under the supervision of a major general who heads the Additional Directorate of Discipline and Vigilance. This cell functions in close liaison with the NHRC and NGOs. The Army has also designated officers of the rank of Colonel at its various operational headquarters to monitor and follow up reports of human rights violations by its personnel. The Army also has institutionalized human rights training both for officers and other ranks in various training programmes. It has been reported that the military training establishments like College of Combat, Infantry School, Defence Service

---

43 The AFT Principal Bench, Court No. 2 in the case of *Harish Chandra Joshi v. Union of India*, TA No. 75 of 2010, decided on 24 February 2012.

44 The AFT Principal Bench New Delhi, Court No. 2, in the case of *Vinod Kumar (Retired) v. Union of India*, OA No. 639 of 2010, decided on 10 May 2012.

45 The AFT Principal Bench New Delhi in the case of *Baljeet Singh v. Union of India*, T A No. 602 of 2009 [WP (C) No. 2755 of 2008], decided on 29 May 2012.

46 The case was a grim reminder of the ghosts of political meddling in military appointments in the 1990s. Many controversies regarding political interference had erupted in the Ministry of Defence during the tenure of Mulayam Singh Yadav as the Defence Minister. 21 years on, Maj Gen promoted, *Tribune News Service*, Chandigarh, 23 August 2018, available at: https://www.tribuneindia.com/news/nation/21-years-on-maj-gen-promoted/642056.html.

Staff College, and Institute of Military Law have included human rights in their curriculum.

Today, human rights is an extremely sensitive issue in many, probably most nations of the world. The role of the military in a democratic society is clear; it exists to ensure the security of the nation while obeying civilian authority and respecting the rights of citizens. The military authorities must develop human rights doctrine and impart training to the soldiers and officers at regular interval. The commanders must re-enforce the message that human rights is at the centre of their mission. In the US, military personnel during operations carry a card which describes the human rights policy. It focuses on "five R's" of human rights: recognize, refrain, react, record, and report. The military persons have an obligation to "recognize what a human rights violation is, refrain from committing violation, react if they see one being committed by someone else, and if they cannot prevent it, immediately record it and report it up their chain of command.[47] However, no nation has a perfect record; despite serious efforts to prevent misconduct or criminal actions violations do occur. When human rights violations take place, the organization must undertake a transparent investigation. The guilty must be punished in an exemplary manner and inquiry documents made public.

Conclusion

Every human being has human rights. Those who are soldiers are human beings. So, soldiers must have human rights. We need to give more attention to, and support for, an expanded range of the rights of soldiers. Soldiers do not have the right to life in an armed conflict, but if captured or *horse de combat*, they have the right to be treated humanely under the international humanitarian law. The idea of humane treatment during war was espoused four hundred year ago in Hugo Grotius's seminal work, *De Jure Belli ac Pacis* (1625).[48] When not engaged in war, a soldier's life can only be taken if it is practically necessary to achieve a needed military objective. Even in war, soldiers have the right, among others, not to be killed unnecessarily.[49]

---

47 The US Southern Command has developed a programme with an aim to protect human rights in its operations. A pocket-sized card used by every member of the Southern Command travelling or operating in its area of responsibility describes the command's human rights policies.

48 Hugo Grotius, *De Jure Belli ac Pacis* (1625) (On the Law of War and Peace) translated by Frances W. Kelsey, Oxford: Clarendon Press, 1925.

49 In one of the first modern international statements of the rules of war in modern times, the St. Petersburg Declaration of 1868 stated: That the progress of civilization

The crucial feature of human rights is that they attach to every human person regardless of role or situation. In the Constitutions around the world, human rights have been referred to as fundamental rights. Human rights and fundamental rights are key principles that stand at the basis of any just and equal society.[50]

The armed forces cannot stay cocooned since the personnel they recruit belong to and interact with the wider society, which has undergone significant change. An individual joining the armed forces, particularly in the ranks has a hard life. As the armed forces constitute the most powerful weapon of the executive, their internal management and other functional systems are required to be efficient, modern and in tune with the times. Article 21 of the Constitution guarantees the right to life with dignity.[51] If we respect the human rights of members of the armed forces and make them feel that they are a valued part of the society, if we protect them against misuse and oppression by the government or the by their commanders, only then we can expect them to be sensitive to the human rights of others. When the members of the armed forces function in 'aid to civil power' they are required to integrate human rights into their day-to-day operations. They would be better prepared for this if they themselves operate in an environment in which these rights are protected.[52]

---

should have the effect of alleviating as much as possible the calamities of war; That the only legitimate object which States should endeavor to accomplish during war is to weaken the military forces of the enemy; That for this purpose it is sufficient to disable the greatest possible number of men; That this object would be exceeded by the employment of arms which uselessly aggravate the sufferings of disabled men, or render their death inevitable; That the employment of such arms would, therefore, be contrary to the laws of humanity.

50 Although the two terms 'human rights' and 'fundamental rights' are often interchanged, there are key differences that cannot be overlooked. In fact, while fundamental rights are outlined and protected by the national constitution of any given state – and thus slightly vary from country to country – human rights are universal and inalienable principles guaranteed at an international level and enforced by the United Nations and other international agencies. In other words, fundamental rights are granted by individual governments and are awarded by national constitutions while human rights apply to each and every individual, regardless of their nationality, ethnicity and religion.

51 Enjoyment of a quality life by people is the essence of the guarantees right under Article 21 of the Constitution. *H L Tiwari v Kamla Devi* (2001) 6 SCC 496 : AIR 2001 SC 3215.

52 *Handbook on Human Rights and Fundamental Freedoms of Armed Forces Personnel.* (ODIHR), 2008.

Chapter – III

The Rights in Disciplinary Process

Introduction

In 1948 when the UN General Assembly adopted the Universal Declaration of Human Rights (UDHR), it proclaimed that it is a common standard of achievement for all people of all nations. The importance of UDHR can hardly be exaggerated; it has influenced the subsequent constitutional developments in most countries of the world, including India. The right to a fair trial is a norm of international human rights law, designed to protect individuals from the unlawful and arbitrary curtailment or deprivation of their basic rights and freedoms, the most prominent of which are the rights to life and to liberty. Article 10 of the UDHR declares: "Everyone is entitled in full liberty to a fair and public hearing by an independent and impartial tribunal, in determination of his rights and obligations and of any criminal charges against him." Article 11 (1) of the Declaration further states: "Everyone charged with a penal offence has the right to be presumed innocent until proved guilty according to law in a public trial at which he has had all the guarantees necessary for his defence." These two rights are further elaborated under Article 14 of the International Covenant on Civil and Political Rights,[1] which provides that "everyone shall be entitled to a fair and public hearing by a competent, independent and impartial tribunal established by law." There is also a proposal to include the right to a fair

---

1 International Covenant on Civil and Political Rights (ICCPR), UN General Assembly resolution 2200A (XXI), December 16, 1966, entered into force March 23, 1976.

trial in the non-derogable rights provided for in Article 4(2) of the ICCPR.[2]

The UN General Assembly has adopted the Basic Principles on the Independence of the Judiciary, in 1985, which provides that "everyone shall have the right to be tried by ordinary courts or tribunals using established legal procedures."[3] In addition the Commission on Human Rights resolution 2002/37, entitled "Integrity of the judicial system", also reiterates that "everyone has the right to be tried by ordinary courts or tribunals using duly established legal procedures and that tribunals that do not use such procedures should not be created to displace the jurisdiction belonging to the ordinary courts or judicial tribunals." The provisions on the right to a fair trial and judicial guarantees are also contained in regional human rights instruments like the American Convention on Human Rights (Article 8), the European Convention on Human Rights (Article 6) and the African Charter on Human and Peoples' Rights (Article 7).

The right to a fair trial is applicable both to the determination of an individual's rights and duties in a suit at law and with respect to the determination of any criminal charge against him or her. The term "suit at law" refers to various types of court proceedings, including the trials under military courts and administrative proceedings. The standards against which a trial is to be assessed in terms of fairness are numerous, complex and constantly evolving.[4] They may constitute binding obligations that are included in human rights treaties to which the State is a party. They may also be found in documents which, though not formally binding, can be taken to express the direction in which the law is evolving.[5]

---

2   *See* Draft Third Optional Protocol to the ICCPR, Aiming at Guaranteeing Under All Circumstances the Right to a Fair Trial and a Remedy, Annex I, in: "The Administration of Justice and the Human Rights of Detainees, The Right to a Fair Trial: Current Recognition and Measures Necessary for Its Strengthening," Final Report, Commission on Human Rights, Sub-Commission on Prevention of Discrimination and Protection of Minorities, 46th Session, E/CN.4/Sub.2/1994/24, June 3, 1994, at 59-62.

3   Basic Principles on the Independence of the Judiciary, UN General Assembly resolution 40/32, November 29, 1985 and resolution 40/146, December 13, 1985.

4   Dominic McGoldrick. 1994. *The Human Rights Committee, Its Role in the Development of the International Covenant on Civil and Political Rights, Oxford:* Clarendon Press, p. 415.

5   Non-binding documents of relevance to the conduct of criminal proceedings and to ascertaining fair trial standards include: the Basic Principles for the Treatment of Prisoners, UN General Assembly resolution 45/111, December 14, 1990; Standard Minimum Rules for the Treatment of Prisoners, UN Economic and Social Council resolution 663 C (XXIV), July 31, 1957 and resolution 2076 (LXII), May 13, 1977; Body of Principles for the Protection of All Persons under Any Form of Detention

The Indian Constitution and the Right to a Fair Trial

The framers of our constitution visualized the object of fundamental rights as two – fold: first, that every citizen must be in a position to claim these rights; and second, that they must be binding upon every authority. The word "authority" denoted every authority which has got power to make laws or the prerogative to have discretion vested in it. The guarantee of right to equality and equal protection of laws (Article 14), protection in respect of conviction of offence (Article 20), right to life (Article 21) and protection against arrest and detention in certain cases (Article 22) has been provided to every citizen by the Constitution as Fundamental Rights.

In the context of Indian military justice system, the right to a fair trial needs to be examined under the shadows of the Constitution. Article 33 of the Constitution provides that the rights of military personnel may be abrogated so as to ensure proper discharge of their duties and maintenance of discipline among them. Does it mean that the right to an independent and impartial justice delivery system in a democratic society would come in way of the restrictions imposed by Article 33? Certain rights relating to a fair trial as discussed below are denied to the members of armed forces on the grounds that their fundamental rights have been restricted under the Constitution.

Medieval System of Summary Trials

The summary trial, a medieval system of justice, is the principal method through which military personnel are tried. Summary trials assess the members of the armed forces members accused of minor wrongdoing more informally and expeditiously than the alternative, the court-martial, which deals with more serious infractions. It is a remnant of the British

or Imprisonment, UN General Assembly resolution 43/173, December 9, 1988; Basic Principles on the Role of Lawyers, adopted by the Eighth United Nations Congress on the Prevention of Crime and the Treatment of Offenders, Havana, Cuba, August 27-September 7, 1990; UN Standard Minimum Rules for the Administration of Juvenile Justice, UN General Assembly resolution 40/33, November 29, 1985; Code of Conduct for Law Enforcement Officials, UN General Assembly resolution 34/169, December 17, 1979; Guidelines on the Role of Prosecutors, adopted by the Eighth United Nations Congress on the Prevention of Crime and the Treatment of Offenders, Havana, Cuba, August 27-September 7, 1990; Principles on the Effective Prevention and Investigation of Extra-legal, Arbitrary and Summary Executions, UN Economic and Social Council recommended resolution 1989/65, May 24, 1989; Basic Principles on the Use of Force and Firearms by Law Enforcement Officials, adopted by the Eighth United Nations Congress on the Prevention of Crime and the Treatment of Offenders, Havana, Cuba, August 27-September 7, 1990.

military law of the colonial era and has remained unchanged in India. The process is arbitrary and needs to be updated to reflect our constitutional values of fundamental rights and freedoms.

The summary trial is usually held by the accused's commanding officer (CO) or someone delegated to act on behalf of the CO. In the case of officers up to the rank of Major (or equivalent in other two service), this power is exercised by the brigade and area commanders. This officer sits as judge, jury, prosecutor and defence. He personally decides the accused's guilt or innocence and imposes a sentence on the spot. The hierarchical nature of a military unit requires CO to know everyone under their command, including the accused and witnesses, and the details of the circumstances relating to the alleged offences before the trial begins. The military law prohibits any legal advice or legal representation for the accused.

Summary trials make up nearly 80-85 per cent of military disciplinary trials, while courts-martial are used to try the remaining disciplinary cases. Trial process may be very brief and may last few minutes only. The CO or officers trying the military person are not required to maintain an official transcript of the proceedings. The trial summary sheet records a very brief account of evidence and the sentence. Acquittals in summary trial are very few.

The summary trial process allows for significant punishments to be imposed against those found guilty. For officers up to the rank of major and junior commissioned officer, the punishment includes forfeiture of seniority or service for promotion up to 12 months, severe reprimand and stoppage of pay and allowances to recover loss or damage occasioned by the offence. For non-commissioned officers and below, the punishment includes imprisonment, detention, confinement, extra guards or duties, severe reprimand, fines up to 14 days pay, reduction in rank and penal deductions. An accused below the rank of NCO can be awarded a punishment up to 42 days of imprisonment and detention. Under the Navy Act, 1957, a CO of a ship can award imprisonment or detention up to three months summarily. The punishment awarded to an accused can have serious impact on his promotion and future growth in the services.

There is no requirement to apply the rules of evidence that apply in a civilian trial and that help an accused receive a fair trial. The accused can be compelled to testify against himself; the constitutional right to protection against self-incrimination does not apply. The accused is granted some basic rights, such as the opportunity to question witnesses and present evidence. However, under the Army Rule, 1954, as amended in 1993, the CO can deny an accused the right to cross-examine witnesses, where the charges against him were raised as a result of investigation by a court of inquiry wherein the accused had examined these witnesses.

An accused can request a review of a sentence in form of a grievance petition. The process of grievance redressal is faulty as individual remains outside the loop while decision of his petition is taken by the higher authorities and their order is not reasoned. There is no right to appeal against summary punishment, thus an accused cannot take up the matter in the Armed Forces Tribunal or the Supreme Court.

In 2005, when the Armed Forces Tribunal Bill was introduced in the Parliament, it had the provision for appeals against the summary disposals and trials (i.e., award of minor punishment). The Bill in its definition of service matters; against which armed forces personnel were to be authorized to appeal in the tribunal, included "summary disposal and trials" in sub-section 3(o)(iv). However, the Ministry of Defence subsequently informed the Standing Committee, which examined the Bill, that summary disposals and trials are proposed to be deleted from the purview of the tribunal. The reasons advanced by the Ministry of Defence were:

> Commanding Officers are authorized to award only minor punishments during summary disposal of charges under Armed Forces Act. These powers are essential for expeditiously meting out justice and maintenance of discipline of the Unit. It is apprehended that if appeals are permitted in case of summary disposal of charges, units may be embroiled in innumerable litigations. Therefore, the Ministry of Defence proposes exclusion of summary disposal and trials from the definition of 'service matters'.[6]

The Standing Committee was of the view that summary disposals and trials are important and vital issues and had long-lasting effect on career and prospects of the armed forces personnel. The Committee, in order to ensure fair dispensation of justice to armed forces personnel, strongly recommended that summary disposals and trials must be kept in

---

6   The Armed Forces Tribunal Bill, 2005 was introduced in Rajya Sabha on 20 December, 2005. The Speaker referred the bill to Standing Committee on Defence on 23 December, 2005 for examination and report. See: Tenth Report, Standing Committee on Defence (2006-2006), Ministry of Defence, Armed Forces Tribunal Bill, 2005 (presented to Lok Sabha on 23 May 2006), para 40.

the purview of the Tribunal.[7] However, the Ministry of Defence rejected the recommendations of the Standing Committee.

Coercive Grievance Redressal System

A military person who deems himself wronged by any superior/ commanding officer may complain to the higher authorities for the redress of his grievances.[8] The Regulations of the three services provide different procedures for the processing of complaints. The complaints by the officers are addressed to the Central Government, while that of the other ranks to the respective service chiefs. The intermediate authorities in the chain of command can interview the complainant, investigate the matter and forward the complaint, along with detailed paragraph-wise comments to the next superior authority. The complainant is not informed about the comments of the intermediate authorities on his grievance application. This amounts to violation of the principles of natural justice because the comments furnished by the intermediate authorities to higher authorities are essential to the complainant, so as to enable him to know what has been commented against him/her by the said military authority while forwarding the complaint.

The Regulations of the three services state that the grievance applications are to be processed expeditiously; however, the time-frame for processing is different in the case of each service. In the case of the Army, when the complaint does not contain any accusation requiring investigation, it must reach the Army headquarters (Army HQ) within 225 days. If the complainant has made an accusation requiring investigation, the complaint should reach the headquarters within 255 days. There is no time limit for the Army HQ or the Ministry of Defence (MoD) to give final decision on the petition; however, the informally this has been stated to be

---

7   Ibid, para 45.

8   Section 26 of the Army Act 1950, provides that any person below the officer rank (PBOR) who deems himself wronged by any superior or other officer may complain to the commanding officer (CO) for the redress of his grievance. When the officer complained against is the officer to whom the complaint should be preferred, the aggrieved person may complain to the officer who is next in superiority to such officer. Section 27 of the Act provides that any officer who deems himself wronged by his CO or any superior officer, and who on due application made to his CO does not receive the redress to which he considers himself entitled, may complain to the Central Government. Redress applications by the officers are to be addressed to the Central Government and by the PBORs to the Chief of the Army Staff. Similar provisions are contained in laws relating to the air force, the navy and the central paramilitary/armed police forces.

six months. In today's era of Email, fax and cell phones, a complainant has to wait for nearly 14 months (in some cases even more) to get final reply on his grievance petition is not only distressing but also worrisome. There have been instances where final decisions on the grievances relating to promotions have been delayed until the complainant retires. The delay often frustrates the complainant, leading to dissatisfaction and demoralization.

All levels of the military hierarchy are entitled to seek legal advice on a complaint. However, the aggrieved person is not provided any legal help for preferring his complaint. If the grievance is against the commanding officer or higher military authorities, the affected individual or his family may also face social seclusion and harassment. There have been allegations that those lodging complaints against their military superiors have been transferred to far-flung places, causing harassment to them and their family members.

The decision on an application is not required to be a "reasoned" order and it could be conveyed in a brief sentence, such as: "Your application has been rejected by the competent authority as being devoid of merit." Stereotype rejection orders reinforce the doubt that complaints are treated arbitrarily and against the principles of natural justice. A judgement which does not give reasons may not be, but certainly appears to be arbitrary. In case the individual affected by the decision desires to go for an appeal, he must have the opportunity to study the reasons on which the original judgement was based, so as to be able to present his counter-arguments in appeal.

In the Army, if a complainant has made an accusation, he/she is required to render a certificate, "I undertake that any false statement or false accusation made by me in this complaint will render me liable for disciplinary action."[9] In cases of the use of abusive language, misbehaviour and sexual harassment, which may take place in private, it may not be possible for a victim to support his/her accusation with any documentary proof or witness. Then the victim would be liable to disciplinary action based on the certificate rendered with his/her petition. The senior commanders and even the Defence Ministers have claimed that the armed forces have a time-tested, well established and transparent mechanism to address complaints.[10] If the grievance redressal system in the armed forces

9   Regulations for the Army, Volume I, 1987, para 364.10.

10   'Time tested mechanisms are in place for redressal of grievances of service personnel'; Minister of Defence, Shri Arun Jaitley in a written reply to Question No. 672 in

was so effective and time-tested, as claimed, the Government would not have established the benches of the Armed Forces Tribunal in 2009. The Regulation for the Army, which prescribes the procedure for the redress of grievance, is a subordinate legislation made by the government, is *mala fide* and *ultra vires* to the rights contained in the Army Act, 1950 as well as violative of natural justice.

Concerned over the increasing number of soldiers posting their complaints on social media, a new grievance redressal mechanism was started in January 2017, where in soldiers could air their grievances directly to the chief of the army staff through WhatApp messages. This ad hoc system was conditional, as soldiers had to first exhaust existing laid down grievance redressal procedure. The military bureaucracy has been claiming that the existing system is prompt and time-tested; which in reality is coercive, biased and marred with delays. No action has been taken by the government to streamline the grievance redressal system contained in the Army Act, 1950, the Air Forces Act, 1950 and the Navy Act, 1957.

Legal Aid to the Accused

Legal aid is a system in which government subsidizes the provision of legal service to the poor or to those who cannot afford to pay the normal fee.[11] It is an instrument to achieve equality before the law, enshrined in the Constitution as a Fundamental Right. Legal aid is a modern concept derived from the 'rule of law', which has the principle of 'equality before the law' as its commitment. Rule of law and equality before the law are fundamental principles of a democracy.

Under the military justice system, the rights of an accused to effective legal aid are severely restricted. The most significant is the absence of the services of an experienced legal person as counsel for the accused. The accused is not entitled to any legal help prior to the assembly of the court-martial. After the assembling officer signs convening order for assembly of a court-martial, the accused is supplied with a copy of charge-sheet and summary of evidence and explained his right to defence during the trial. The Army Rules, 1954 provides that at any general court-martial (GCM) or district court-martial (DCM), an accused person may be represented by any

---

Rajya Sabha, answered on 15 July 2014. For more details on the subject see: The Parliamentary Standing Committee on Defence (2005-2006) Tenth Report dated 25 May 2006.

11 Garner Bryan A. (ed.), *Black's Law Dictionary*, Tenth Edition, p. 1030.

officer subject to the Army Act who shall be called "the defending officer" or assisted by any person whose services he may be able to procure and who shall be called "the friend of the accused". A commissioned officer, qualified in law, is detailed by the convening authority to represent the accused as defending officer in GCM or DCM. The friend of the accused is a person belonging to the same service as that of the accused and may advise the accused on all points and suggest the questions to be put to the witnesses, but he is not authorized to examine or cross-examine the witnesses or address the court.

The Rules further provide that in a GCM or DCM civilian counsel shall be allowed to appear on behalf of the prosecutor as well as the accused. However, the convening officer may disallow the appearance of counsel at GCM/ DCM on the grounds of expediency. If an accused is charged with an offence punishable with death, he is entitled to a defence counsel at State expense. The maximum amount payable to the counsel is Rs 500/- for each day of appearance.[12] This amount is, however, inadequate for hiring the services of a counsel where an accused is charged with a serious offence.

In reality, very few of the accused can engage an experienced civilian counsel at their own expense. A service officer appointed as defending officer in a GCM or DCM remains exposed to improper command influence. Same is the case with a 'friend' provided to an accused during his trial by summary court-martial. They may belong to the same corps or unit to which the accused belongs. His prospects for future service, promotion, awards or future assignments depend upon earning the good opinion of his superiors or convening authority. He may not like to embarrass his superiors, and therefore the quality of his advise always remains doubtful. Further, the services of defending officers are not available during the appeal or post-trial period.

At the international level, there has been a growing recognition of legal aid as an important aspect of a fair trial. The ICCPR Article 14, paragraph 3 (d) guarantees the right to have legal assistance assigned to

---

12 In 1987, paragraph 479 was added in the Regulations for the Army which provides: Provision of Defence Counsel for Accused at Court Martial Trials for Offences Punishable with Death: When a person subject to the Army Act is to be tried by court martial for an offence punishable with death and such person is unable to engage a counsel for his defence at the trial owing to lack of pecuniary resources and the convening officer is satisfied about his inability, a counsel for the defence of the accused at the trial may be employed by the convening officer at Government expense in consultation with the DJAG concerned.

accused persons whenever the interests of justice so require, and without payment by them in any such case if they do not have sufficient means to pay for it. The gravity of the offence is important in deciding whether counsel should be assigned "in the interest of justice" as is the existence of some objective chance of success at the appeals stage. In cases involving capital punishment, it is axiomatic that the accused must be effectively assisted by a lawyer at all stages of the proceedings. Counsel provided by the competent authorities on the basis of this provision must be effective in the representation of the accused.[13]

The international approach to the concept of legal aid to an accused shows that it should be accepted as an essential part of the administration of justice by every nation. An accused facing a criminal trial must be provided the benefit of free legal aid and representation in non-judicial as well as judicial processes if he is unable to afford the same. The rights to life, liberty, reputation and property are fundamental and should be protected by the system of juridical administration. The necessity of legal representation in criminal trials flows from two principles: (i) the fundamental principle that an accused person is entitled to a fair trial; and (ii) equality before the law and applicability of these principles to the adversarial process.[14]

The Indian concept of legal aid is available in the provisions of its Constitution. The direct and express provision of legal aid is the most appropriate and exhaustive explanation of the Indian concept. Article 39-A, of the Constitution states:

> **Equal Justice and Free Legal Aid**—The State shall secure that the operation of the legal system promotes justice, on the basis of equal opportunity, and shall, in particular, provide free legal aid, by suitable legislation or schemes or in any other way, to ensure that opportunities for securing justice are not denied to any citizen by reasons of economic or other disabilities.[15]

Apparently, legal aid has been prescribed as an instrument for achieving equality before the law as provided under Article 14 of the

---

13 Human Rights Committee General Comment No. 32, Article 14: Right to equality before courts and tribunals and to a fair trial, CCPR/C/GC/32 dated 23 August 2007.

14 *Gideon v. Wainright* (1963) 372 US 335.

15 Article 39A puts stress upon legal justice. It ordains the state to secure a legal system which promotes justice on the basis of equal opportunity. The language of Art 39A is couched in mandatory term as is clear by the use of word 'shall' twice therein.

Constitution. Legal aid, therefore, is a form of state assistance to ensure equality before the law, the most fundamental of the Fundamental Rights guaranteed under the Indian Constitution.[16] The Supreme Court in *Hussainara Khatoon* (1980) declared, "The right to free legal service is clearly an essential ingredient of 'reasonable, fair and just' procedure for a person accused of an offence and it must be held implicit in the guarantee of Article 21.[17]

In *Khatri* (1981), the Supreme Court observed that the State cannot avoid its constitutional obligation to provide free legal services to indigent accused by pleading financial or administrative difficulties. The Court said that the right to free legal services is an essential ingredient of reasonable, fair and just procedure for a person accused of an offence. The State is under a constitutional mandate to provide a lawyer to an accused person. ......State cannot avoid its constitutional obligation to provide free legal services to a poor accused by pleading financial or administrative inability.[18]

In *Suk Das*,[19] the Supreme Court went on to the extreme position of declaring the whole trial invalid because the accused did not have the benefit of legal services and the trial court had not informed him of his right to seek free legal services. The Court even disagreed with the view of the Assam High Court that since the applicant did not ask for free legal assistance, no unconstitutionality was involved. The Supreme Court held, "If, the accused is unable to engage the services of a lawyer on account of poverty or indigence; he is entitled to obtain free legal services at the cost of the State." The Supreme Court in *Kishore Chand v. State of Himachal Pradesh*, AIR 1990 SC 2140 stated, "..... assigning an experienced defence counsel to an indigent accused is a facet of fair procedure and an inbuilt right to liberty and life envisaged under Article 14, 19 and 21 of the Constitution. Though Article 39A of the Constitution provides fundamental rights to equal justice and free legal aid and though the State provides amicus curiae to defend the indigent accused, he would be meted out with unequal defence if, as is common knowledge the youngster from the Bar who has either a little experience or no experience is assigned to defend him." Therefore, to make the people, especially those whose rights

---

16 Article 14 of the Constitution states: The State shall not deny to any person equality before the law or the equal protection of the laws within the territory of India.

17 *Hussainara Khatoon (IV) v. Home Secretary, State of Bihar*, (1980) 1 SCC 98.

18 *Khatri v. State of Bihar and others*, AIR 1981 SC 829.

19 *Suk Das v. Union Territory of Arunachal Pradesh*, AIR 1986 SC 991.

have been abridged by the Constitution for the 'security' of the nation, continue to have faith in the justice system, the provision of legal aid becomes essential.

The infrastructure required to meet the obligation of legal aid has not been developed in the armed forces. Consequently, cases before the court-martial are not adequately defended, which is in violation of the provisions of Article 22 of the Constitution. The issue of providing a defence counsel of the accused's choice at State expense was turned down in the case of *Union of India v. Ex Flt Lt G. S. Bajwa* (2003).[20] The Supreme Court held: "The Air Force Act and Rules do not oblige the State/Union of India to engage at the cost of the State a counsel for the officer who faces a trial before the court-martial. The provisions of the Act cannot be challenged on the grounds that they infringe the Fundamental Rights guaranteed to the respondent under Article 21 of the Constitution."

The concept of legal aid has not yet penetrated the primitive military justice system of India. Though legal aid has gained source and strength from the higher judiciary, the same judiciary has denied these fundamental rights to military personnel under cover of Article 33 of the Constitution.[21] The rulings of the higher courts recognizing the need for the legal aid to military personnel have been overruled by the Supreme Court, on the grounds that the Fundamental Rights of military personnel have been restricted by Parliament itself. This narrow view needs to be changed by a fresh interpretation of Article 33 by a larger Bench of the Apex Court. How can military a person whose livelihood as well as liberty is at stake, be subjected to a post-Mutiny system of justice which does not even guarantee basic safeguards?

Summary Systems of Court Martial

The Indian armed forces are following arbitrary and discriminatory systems of trial in the form of summary general court-martial (SGCM) and summary court-martial (SCM). The SGCM is prevalent in the army

---

20 *Union of India v. Ex Flt Lt G. S. Bajwa* (2003) 9 SCC 630.

21 A self-respecting serviceman going to court (against the organization) runs the risk of a heavy penalty on three counts: one, by the judiciary, if his charge or contention is found untenable; two, the service authorities may initiate disciplinary action if he could not prove allegations; and three, he also runs the risk of being labelled as *persona-non-granta* in the organization, besides going through social stigma and mental injury for having gone to the court. Singh, Brigadier K Kuldip. 1998. *Overcoming Crisis in Leadership: Indian Army*. New Delhi: Manas Publications. p. 205.

and air force, and the SCM in the army alone. These systems of trial were envisaged by the British government to govern illiterate native soldiers recruited from villages. Post-Mutiny, when a new Indian army came to be organized on the ruins of the old one, it was realized that the hands of the British commanding officer (CO) would have to be strengthened if the 'evils' which had led to the near-disappearance of the Bengal Army were to be avoided. With this objective in mind, the SGCM/SCM was established as part of the legal machinery of the Indian army. The British Indian Army Act of 1911 contains these provisions and continues to govern Indian soldiers.

The trail by SGCM was envisaged by the British commander for the filed units which were scattered and the means of communication were limited. The unit commanders were empowered to convene SGCM to punish a violator quickly. In the SGCM, any individual subject to the Army/Air Force Act can be tried by three lay officers, who can unanimously award punishment up to death. The most senior member of the SGCM should be senior in rank to the accused, while the other officers should have one year of commissioned service. The officer convening the SGCM can do away with a formal charge sheet and the statement of offence can be made briefly to disclose an offence under the Act. The provisions regarding defence of an accused during his trial by SGCM are primitive and the accused has no right to be represented by a counsel. The Army Rules, 1954 provides that the court shall ask the accused to state what he has to say in his defence. The accused shall be allowed to make his defence and may be allowed to have any person to assist him during the trial.[22]

In the case of the SCM, the CO alone constitutes the court and acts as a judge as well as prosecutor.[23] He can try accused up to the rank of Havildar. The proceedings are attended by two others, who may be officers or junior commissioned officers. They are not supposed to take any part in the proceedings and have no right to vote in determining either the

---

22 Army Rules, 1954, Rule 159.

23 Section 130 of the Army Act, 1950, makes a provision that an accused can challenge his trial by the presiding officer/any member of the general, district or summary general court-martial on the ground of bias or personal interest. However, no such right to challenge his trial by the commanding officer is available to an accused in SCM. This provision was initially made in the Indian Articles of War (Act V of 1869). Article 107 of the Indian Articles of War, 1869 makes it abundantly clear that there is no right to challenge in the case of an extraordinary court-martial i.e., summary court-martial or summary general court-martial. These provisions were followed in Section 80 of the Indian Army Act, 1911 and correspond to Section 130 of the present Army Act.

findings or the sentence. The accused has no right to engage a counsel or avail services of a defending officer. The findings and sentence of the SCM do not require to be confirmed and take effect forthwith, except in a case where the officer holding the trial is of less than five years' service. The sentence passed by such an officer is not carried out until it has been approved by an officer commanding not less than a brigade. This requirement of approval does not, however, apply where the sentence is passed by such an officer on active service.

In a SCM, the CO looks at the case from the standpoint of policy, expediency and discipline, thus violating the basic norms of natural justice. The Constitutional Bench of the Supreme Court in the case of *S M Mukherjee* [AIR 1990 SC 1984], observed, "The object underlying the rules of natural justice is to prevent miscarriage of justice and secure "fair play in action". The view gaining ground of late is that breach of the principles of natural justice renders an order or determination void. The rationale behind this view is that where there is a duty to act fairly, the principles of natural justice have to be followed as an implied statutory requirement.

In both these summary forms of court-martial, the accused has no right to defend himself through any military or civilian counsel. There is no need for a detailed judgment or even a discussion on the evidence. An accused cannot claim that he should be governed by the principles of natural justice which apply to a civil servant under Article 311 of the Constitution. The unbridled discretionary power of a CO to hold trial under SGCM/SCM is violative of Article 14.

The following example shows how the military mindset has not changed since Independence. Rules 12 of the Rules of Procedure made under the Indian Articles of War (1869) contained a provision relating to SCM. It reads: "The discipline of the native army depends in great measure on the SCM. When a soldier amenable to the Indian Articles of War has committed an offence which is ordinarily tried by SCM, commanding officer, when determining by what court the prisoner to be tried, are to bear in mind that the legislature, in conferring upon them the powers of SCM, intends that they shall exercise these powers." This provision has been reproduced as Para 447 under the 1987 Regulations for the Army substituting words "soldier amenable to the Indian Articles of War" with "a person subject to the Army Act".

The crucial requirement that is generally violated in summary systems of court-martial is that the court is predisposed to assume that the accused is guilty. A presumption of guilt undermines the whole concept of fair trial. What is even more unjust is that the accused is often under the military custody before his trial. Detention before trial is objectionable when it is used by authorities to put physical or psychological pressure on a prisoner to plead guilty to a charge.

The Supreme Court has often criticized these systems of trial as being arbitrary, awarding excessive and harsh punishments, and denying procedural rights guaranteed under the Constitution. The Court rightly commented in *Lt. Col. PPS Bedi* (1982): "The reluctance of the apex court, which is more concerned with civil law, to interfere with the internal affairs of the Armed Forces is likely to create a distorted picture in the minds of the military personnel that the persons subject to the armed forces are not citizens of India." The military hierarchy in India is reluctant to do away with these systems of trial, presumably on the grounds that they are needed to strengthen the hands of CO. This is a wrong presumption. Soldiers are no longer illiterate peasants hailing from remote areas. A number of people in the ranks are graduates or post-graduates. In fact, there would be several families in which one sibling is an officer and the other in the ranks.

The Indian Army has extensively used the summary systems of court-martial, depriving many of their livelihood, freedom and pension on the pretext of discipline. No other democratic country follows such an arbitrary system of justice.[24] The military justice systems of the UK, US, Australia, Israel, China, Russia, Canada and South Africa do not have such provisions. Continuations of summary systems of court-martial made by the British to crush the just rights of natives, which does not adhere to any of the international standards or our Constitutional norms, indicate that we are interested in continuing an antiquated system of justice against all the norms of human rights. If the presence of qualified counsel in GCM/ DCM does not affect the "discipline" and "proper function of the armed forces" then how could it affect in a trial by SGCM, where punishment of death could be pronounced by three lay military officers. Can we deny the right to a fair trial in a summary court-martial on the grounds that if allowed,

---

24 The Supreme Court has recently held that the (i) holding of an SCM is the exception and not the rule; (ii); It can only be convened where the exigencies demand an immediate and swift decision without which the situation will indubitably be exacerbated with widespread ramifications; and (iii) the decision to convene an SCM must be preceded by a reasoned order which itself will be amenable to Judicial Review. *Union of India v. Vishav Priya Singh*, civil Appeal No. 8360 of 2010, decided on 5 July 2016.

it will have an adverse impact of the discipline or performance of duty in the armed forces?

Functioning of the Judge Advocate General (JAG) Department

In the armed forces, the judge advocate general (JAG) is an executive and does not perform any functions of an advocate or of a judge.[25] The presence of judge advocate is must in a GCM, and he may attend other courts i.e., DCM and SGCM. In case an officer of judge advocate branch is not available, any person approved by the JAG may replace him. Unlike a judge in a trial by jury, the judge advocate is not a judge, except in the sense that he has to maintain an entirely impartial position. The quality of advice given by him plays a very crucial role in swaying the minds of the members of the court-martial. The department of JAG is placed under the administrative and functional control of the same executive who orders a trial by court-martial and reviews the proceedings. The officers of the JAG department are, therefore, not independent and cannot be expected to give a fair and just opinion.

In the UK, the Judge Advocates of the army and air force are civilians working full time for the civilian Judge Advocate General. They are outside the chain of command and free from command influence. In Australia, the JAG is a statutory appointment by the Governor General. He or she must be a judge of a superior court. The JAG does not sit on military tribunals, nor gives advice to the Department or the Minister. The JAG in Canadian Forces is by statute, the legal adviser to the Government of Canada, the Minister and Deputy Minister of the Department of National Defence, the Canadian Forces and Chief of Defence Staff on all issues relating to military law. The National Defence Act does not require the JAG to be an officer or other member of the Canadian Forces (CF). However, in practice, the Governor in Council has always appointed a CF officer to the position.

---

25 The department of the Judge Advocate General (JAG) in the Indian Army, Air Force and Navy represents the judiciary of the respective services. The JAG is the legal advisor to the service chief in matters of military, martial and international law. The JAG and his officers comprising the judicial branch of the armed forces are hierarchally subordinate to the convening authority, who controls their service career. He also assists the Adjutant General in matters relating to discipline involving application of military law. At the Command HQs, the department of Judge Advocate is represented by the Command Judge Advocate General (CJAG) in the Air Force and the Navy and by the Deputy Judge Advocate General (DJAG) in the Army. They are subordinate to the Commander-in-Chief of the respective command and report to him through a senior administrative executive.

In Israel, the Military Justice Law (MJL) establishes a legal apparatus headed by the Military Advocate General (MAG). The MAG and his staff operate completely independently in the areas of their operation. Members of the Military Advocate are not subject to the functional command orders of the command ranks that they serve, and the decisions that they make are in their exclusive discretion. The MAG is not subordinate to the Chief of Staff in respect of the exercise of his powers and is not under any command whatsoever—de jure or de facto. The MAG also has broad powers to intervene in the sentences imposed by disciplinary officers in cases where the officers deviate from their powers or err in imposing, activating, or failing to activate detention sentences and, in particular, in the case of conditional sentences. Not only may the MAG quash an unlawful sentence, he may also convert such a sentence to one that the disciplinary officer was authorized to impose.

The JAG plays an important role in the court-martial. His principal function at a court-martial is to sum up the evidence after the closing address of the prosecution and the defence and to advise the court on the law relating to the case. The judge advocate does not perform any function of an advocate or a judge. However, the court-martial deliberates on its findings (in the closed court) in his presence and the quality of his advice plays a crucial role in the trial. Any failure on the part of the judge advocate may cause serious prejudices to the accused. The judge advocate is in a position to sway the minds of the members of the court-martial, as the persons composing the court are untrained in law and cannot take his advice lightly.

The JAG or one of his deputies frames the charges, advises the prosecution of the accused and conducts the court-martial. Subsequently, another subordinate officer of the JAG reviews the court-martial proceedings. Thus, in a sense, the same set of officers act as the accuser/prosecutor, the judge and then also review the judgement. This in all probability would lead to a natural tendency on the part of the trial judge advocate or the officer reviewing the proceedings to willingly or unwillingly uphold the charges framed by his superior officer, who decides on his promotion and perks. In the discharge of his judicial and other functions, the JAG is subordinate to the Adjutant General, an officer who heads the prosecution in the Army. Thus, due to the organizational position of the JAG and his officers, there would always remain in the mind of the accused a lurking suspicion of bias. There has been an impression that judge advocates in India act as messengers of the prosecution in courts-martial.

The Rajasthan High Court, in the case of *Mohan Rao P. Naik*,[26] held: "If Judge Advocate is found to be biased or prejudiced, or even if there is likelihood of bias and the Judge Advocate becomes hand-in-glove with the prosecution or becomes personally interested in the trial of the case to see that the accused are convicted, it can be assumed that the Judge Advocate is biased and such a person would incur disqualification to be associated with the court in the trial." The Himachal Pradesh High Court, in the case of *Major Sansar Chand* [27] held: "The presence of a Judge Advocate, who does not seem to be impartial, will vitiate the judgement." The irony is that though an accused can object to the members constituting the court-martial, he cannot challenge the presence and authority of the Judge Advocate.

The judicial branch of the military justice system in all the countries as discussed is outside the military chain of command. India is the only exception, though independence of the judiciary is a cornerstone of the Indian Constitution. It has been repeatedly held by the Supreme Court to be a basic feature of the Constitution. The general concept of judicial independence is that an individual performing judicial function should not be under any pressure from the executive or any other authority regarding the decisions in any particular case. Ancillary to this concept is the obligation of the judiciary to provide fair trial to litigants. The independence of the judiciary and legal profession is a pre requisite for ensuring that the rule of law is upheld and for guarding against violations of human rights and freedoms. It protects the weak, the vulnerable and unpopular as well as the strong and powerful. The actions of military courts are all too often associated with miscarriage of justice and denial of human rights. Ensuring that the judge advocate are free from the military chain of command in no way would interfere with the discipline and proper functioning of the armed forces.

Unlawful Command Influence

The military commander, often called the 'convening authority' in the light of his authority to convene courts-martial, is given great latitude in dealing with disciplinary matters. He is involved in virtually every stage of the judicial process and plays a dominant role in the military justice system. He also has the lawful responsibility and authority to ensure the timely and fair disposition of charges. A convening authority has no civilian equivalent.

---

26 *Mohan Rao P. Naik*, DB Civil Petition No. 400/1988 and order dated 26 May 1988.

27 *Major Sansar Chand v. Union of India* 1980 (3) SLR (Himachal) 125.

He is not a lawyer and generally has no formal legal training. His power and discretion to make disciplinary decisions regarding his subordinates stem from his authority as a leader. The commander's fundamental duty and the need for discipline require him to communicate the organizational policy to his subordinates. This often clashes with another compelling military interest that is, maintaining a fair and impartial system of military justice.

The convening authority's power may be 'unlawfully' used to influence decisions that should be independent of command prerogatives and policy. Unlawful command influence (UCI) occurs when the convening authority influences, impedes or otherwise misdirects the administration of justice. This is quite possible in the armed forces where disobedience to command authority is itself punishable by military law and military members are conditioned from their first day to obey that authority.[28] UCI is a form of abuse of authority where rank is used to subvert a military person's right to a fair trial at court-martial, so that the senior commanders can get the result they want.

UCI results from impermissible command control where a superior substitutes (or attempts to substitute) his judgment for that of a subordinate who should be allowed to exercise independent judgment. Such unlawful influence may not only jeopardize the validity of the judicial process, but also undermines the morale of military members, their respect for the chain of command, and public confidence in the military justice system. Used interchangeably with the terms 'unlawful command control', and 'command influence', 'unlawful command influence' has been justly described as the 'mortal enemy of military justice' in military jurisprudence.[29] The excessive involvement of the commander in military justice system to influence its outcome has been a matter of concern. In reality, UCI is a malignancy that eats away at the fairness of military justice system.

The effect of UCI is twofold. In the first place, the accused may be denied a fair and impartial hearing or potentially benefit witnesses. This can have an effect on the findings. For example witnesses may be

---

28 Para 448 of the Regulations for the Army,1987, lists out punishments that could be awarded for particular offences in a summary court martial, thus leaving little scope of deviation from the general instructions. A note below Para 448 states that a copy of it will be kept in every court martial box, thus ensuring that the administrative policies contained in it are followed in a summary court-martial.

29 *United States v. Thomas* 22 MJ 388 (CMA 1986).

influenced not to give evidence in favour of the accused, or witnesses may be influenced not to provide extenuation and mitigation testimony. This can affect the accused significantly, as he may be unable to produce critical evidence and his trial may be tainted. The second issue relates to the absence of 'public confidence' in the military justice system. Due to UCI, the military justice system loses its credibility, not only within its own ranks, but also in society. The Supreme Court has held that the courts-martial have always been subject to varying degrees of 'command influence'.[30]

The notion of fair trial includes the guarantee of a fair and public hearing. Fairness of proceedings entails the absence of any direct or indirect influence, pressure or intimidation or intrusion from whatever side and for whatever motive.[31] The potential for UCI always exists in the military justice system because the system itself, unlike the civilian community, depends on effective command control. The UCI in the military justice system can occur at every level – preliminary inquiry, recording of summary of evidence, referral of charges, selection of court-martial members,[32] judge advocate, prosecutors and defending officer and even on witnesses. Although a commander's directive to the defending officer or the prosecutor normally does not cause any problem, the commander cannot direct the court members to take action which would be either illegal or unethical. When commanders and their representatives

---

30 The Supreme Court of India in *Lt. Col. Prithi Pal Singh v. Union of India* and others (1982) 3 SCC 140, commented: Courts–martial are typically *ad hoc* bodies appointed by a military officer among his subordinates. They have always been subject to varying degrees of 'command influence'. In essence, these tribunals are simply executive tribunals whose personnel are in the executive chain of command. Frequently, the members of the court-martial must look to the appointing officer for promotions, advantageous assignments and efficiency ratings—in short, for their future progress in the service.

31 Human Rights Committee General Comment No. 32, Article 14: Right to equality before courts and tribunals and to a fair trial, CCPR/C/GC/32 dated 23 August 2007.

32 In *Reid v. Covert* (1957), Justice Black observed as under: "Courts-martial are typically ad hoc bodies appointed by a military officer from among his subordinates. They have always been subject to varying degrees of 'command influence'. In essence, these tribunals are simply executive tribunals whose personnel are in the executive chain of command. Frequently, the members of the court-martial must look to the appointing officer for promotions, advantageous assignments and efficiency ratings-in short, for their future progress in the service. Conceding to military personnel that high degree of honesty and sense justice which nearly all of them undoubtedly have, the members of a court-martial, in the nature of things, do not and cannot have the independence of jurors drawn from the general public or of civilian judges."

express personal opinions regarding the result in any particular case, their opinion may affect the way the presiding officer, court members, counsel and witnesses think and act.

The Indian military justice system, though prone to unlawful command influence, is not sensitive to the issue. The convening authority's responsibilities includes determining the initial disposition of the alleged offence; deciding the charges and the type of court-martial by which an accused should be tried; selecting court-martial members; detailing prosecutors and the judge advocate for the trial; acting on the findings and sentence of the court-martial; reviewing the finding and sentence of court-martial; and considering the post-trial petition of the accused. In a number of cases, the convening authorities have used the existing provisions for the review of the findings and sentence under the Army Act to influence the court to obtain a 'desired' verdict.[33] Unfortunately, the higher courts in India have been reluctant to declare the provisions of review under the Army Act as unconstitutional.[34]

The court members, judge advocate and defending officer remain under his chain of command of the convening authority. In the Army and the Air Force, the convening authority is also authorized to return the finding and sentence for revision to the same court prior to its confirmation.[35]

The convening authority may also exercise undue command influence over the accused. The accused may be denied the opportunity to engage a reputed lawyer to defend his case. In some instances, the accused is posted to a distant place before the trial and is attached to the place of trial only later. This deprives him of administrative facilities, family support and other help in preparing his defence. During the trial, the accused is generally placed under close arrest, hampering his preparation of defence, procurement of witnesses, and so on. Under the Army Rule 96, the convening authority is empowered to deny counsel to an accused on the grounds of expediency.[36]

---

33 In *Lt Col MJ Reddy v. Union of India* WP(C) 17075/2004, decided by the Delhi HC on 31 May 2007 the proceedings were returned to the SGCM for revision. The High Court held that punishment awarded by the SGCM was outrageously disproportionate to the gravity of offence and quashed the enhanced revised punishment.

34 The Army Act, 1950, section 160.

35 The detail provisions are contained in Chapter XII of the Army Act, 1950. Under section 160, the convening authority is authorized to return the findings and sentence of a court-martial to the same court for revision.

36 In a particular general court-martial, the accused was denied a legally qualified

The Indian military justice system, designed by the British to secure obedience to the commander, has remained unaffected by the changes in the military justice systems in the other countries. The power of the convening authority to control the outcome of trials has cast an undeniable shadow of unfairness over courts-martial. The combined power of the convening authority in pre-trial and post-trial procedures permits actual unlawful command influence as well as the appearance of such interference. The perception that unlawful command influence has been at work acquires more serious dimensions because it colours the view of the civilian community as well. This is unacceptable in a society that deems the rule of law to be the bulwark of a fair justice system. In order to make the system more open and transparent, it is necessary to curtail the role of the convening authority in the Indian military justice system.

Advantage of set-off: Members of the Indian Air Force

The concept of justice evolves with time. In the Indian criminal justice system, the accused was made to languish in jail for an unspecified period until the punishment was decided. In some cases, the sentence imposed was a fraction of the time spent by the accused as an under-trial prisoner. It was considered 'unjust' and a new provision was made in the Criminal Procedure Code (Cr PC) in 1978 to ensure that the period of detention undergone by the accused is set off against the sentence of imprisonment. In order to claim benefit of set-off under section 428 of the Cr PC, two essential conditions are required to be fulfilled: (i) the accused-claimant has on conviction been sentenced to imprisonment for a term, and (ii) the claimant –accused has undergone detention during investigation, enquiry or trial before the date of conviction. In 1993, these changes were incorporated in the Army Act, 1950.[37] However, no such amendment was

---

defending officer by the convening authority, even though one was available in the station concerned, but a qualified prosecutor was appointed. This gave the prosecution an unfair edge over the defence. On the request of the prosecutor, supported by the judge advocate, the court denied a legally qualified relative of the accused permission to attend the court-martial proceedings, even as a spectator, on the grounds that he was an old man and being a civilian, a security risk. This happened, despite the fact that the said relative was a respectable citizen and a civilian government employee. According to Rule 80-A, Army Rules, 1954 a court-martial is an open court. Nobody requires permission to attend and witness the proceedings of a court-martial, except when the proceedings are held in camera. Sharma, Col. G.K. 2001. *Study and Practice of Military Law*, New Delhi: Deep & Deep Publications Pvt. Ltd., p. 768.

37 The Army HQ proposed an amendment to the Army Act to incorporate the provision of s. 428 of Cr PC. Thus in 1992, through an Amendment Act, section 169A was added in the Army Act. It provided: **Period of Custody undergone by the officer or person to**

introduced in the Air Force Act, 1950.

In India, the service HQs operate independently. The Air Force was perhaps not aware of the amendments in the army till the Army (Amendment) Act of 1992 was passed by the Parliament. The reason why the provisions of set-off have not yet been introduced in the Air Force Act is perfunctory approach of the air force officials who were responsible for taking up the issue with the government.

Plea Bargaining

Plea bargaining, according to Black's Law Dictionary (2014), means a negotiated agreement between the prosecution and the criminal defendant whereby the defendant pleads guilty in exchange for certain concessions by the prosecution. The disposal of a case by plea bargaining was introduced in the Indian criminal justice system in 2006. It is contained in sections 265A-165L of the Criminal Procedure Code, 1973.

Plea bargaining is applicable in cases where the prescribed punishment is imprisonment of seven years or less, and which are not related to the socio-economic conditions of the country or against a woman or a child below the age of 14 years. An accused has to file an application in the court to avail himself of the provision of plea bargaining. The court works out a satisfactory disposition of the case and the accused as well as the victim may participate in the process. The court may award compensation to the victim and hear the parties on the quantum of punishment. It may release the accused on probation of good conduct or may sentence the accused to one-fourth or half of the prescribed minimum punishment. The advantage of plea bargaining is not available to an accused who has been convicted of the same offence earlier or a habitual offender.

In the last two decades, plea bargaining has become a global phenomenon. Countries like Australia, Canada, Nigeria, New Zealand, South Africa, the UK and the US use plea bargaining on a regular basis. In the US plea bargaining covers more than 90 per cent of convictions at

---

be set off against the imprisonment- When a person or officer subject to this Act is sentenced by a court-martial to a term of imprisonment, not being an imprisonment in default of payment of fine, the period spent by him in civil or military custody during investigation, inquiry or trial of the same case, and before the date of order of such sentence, shall be set off against the term of imprisonment imposed upon him ,and the liability of such person or officer to undergo imprisonment on such order of sentence shall be restricted to the remainder, if any, of the term of imprisonment imposed upon him.

the state and federal level. It has also been incorporated at the international criminal tribunals. The domestic plea bargaining is generally confined to non-violent crimes; whereas the International Criminal Court (ICC) allows allow sentence negotiations for heinous offences, including genocide and crimes against humanity. One wonders, why the Government has not introduced the 'plea bargaining' in the military justice system in India.

The introduction of plea bargaining would be a step towards the humanization of our military criminal justice system. The biggest reason for people to resort to a plea bargain is to get a lesser sentence. In plea bargaining, the accused usually waives important rights and the convening authority limits the punishment it may impose. The pre-trial agreement takes on the form of a contract. The agreement must be written, and generally consists of an offer by the accused to meet certain conditions in return for ameliorative action by the convening authority, who registers his acceptance by signing the document.[38] For the armed forces, the introduction of plea bargaining would save the movements of military officers who are assembled from various stations to participate as jurors in the court-martial, reduce case load and improve efficiency in fair resolution of criminal cases. It would time and money for the armed forces and free the Armed Forces Tribunal as well as the Supreme Court of burden of entertaining appeals.

The Rule of Law

A modern and fair system of military law is as vital to operational effectiveness as having the best-trained and equipped forces. Fairness demands the application of the rule of law[39] and opportunities for individuals to be heard both in accusation and in defence. The rule of law is not merely about the maintenance and safeguarding of a legal order but also about

---

38 In a recent case, where a US soldier was awarded a punishment of 100 years in prison for rape and murder of 14-years-old Iraqi girl, the accused following plea bargaining would be eligible for parole after 10 years. GI gets 100 years in prison, *The Times of India*, 24 February 2007.

39 The rule of law is almost universally supported at the national and international level. A core definition of the rule of law as it has evolved over time appears to have three elements: (i) The power of the State may not be exercised arbitrarily—the law be prospective, accessible and clear; (ii) The law must also apply to the sovereign and instruments of the State, with an independent institution such as judiciary to apply the law to specific cases; and (iii) The law must apply to all persons equally, offering equal protection without prejudicial discrimination. These three elements of the core definition may be summarized as a government of laws, the supremacy of the law and equality before the law.

limiting the exercise of absolute power by the executive. According to Raz (1979: 224), 'The rule of law is designed to minimize the danger created by the law itself.' Further, laws must be prospective, policy-promulgated and clear; they must be relatively stable; the making of a particular legal order (such as administrative regulations) must be subject to open, stable, clear and general rules; laws must be consistently applied by an independent judiciary free from extraneous pressures; and law enforcement agencies must not pervert the law by applying it discretionarily.[40] The establishment of the rule of law is a basic prerequisite for any justice delivery system and must apply to all the organs of society and every citizen.

The rule of law provides that interactions within society be governed by the principles of fairness according to which citizens are provided meaningful opportunities to be heard, and to have disputes resolved by independent and impartial tribunals. For example, criminal proceedings, where the liberty of the accused may be at stake, require the highest degree of fairness and impartiality, while administrative processes, where the liberty of an accused is not at stake, do not have to meet as high a standard. These principles of fairness are guaranteed by the Indian Constitution to every citizen.

The military justice system has been created by a statute passed by the Parliament. It has been designed to adjudicate criminal cases efficiently. Though the system could be different from the civilian courts of law, it must adhere to the rule of law, and ensure equal rights and dignity. The three service Acts which restricts the fundamental rights of a military man to ensure his full participation in the defence of the country must also protect his rights to have a fair justice system. The Supreme Court has described a court-martial as:

> ... a specialized part of the overall mechanism by which the military discipline is preserved. It is for the special need of the armed forces that a person subject to the Army Act is tried by court-martial for an act which is an offence under the Act. Court-martial discharges judicial function and to a great extent it is a court where provisions of Evidence Act are applicable. A court-martial has also the same responsibility as any courts to protect the rights of the accused charged before it and follow the procedural safeguards. [41]

---

40 Raz, Joseph, 'The Rule of Law and Its Virtues', in *The Authority of Law: Essays on Law and Morality*, Clarendon Press, Oxford, 1979.

41 *Union of India v Hussain* AIR 1998 SC 577 at 586.

The right to a fair trial is a fundamental safeguard to ensure that individuals are protected from unlawful or arbitrary deprivation of their human rights and freedoms. The right to a fair trial applies not only to the procedures for the determination of criminal charges against individuals but also to those which determine their rights and obligations in a legal proceeding.

International standards provide for a number of guarantees at the pre-trial stage. The right to legal counsel is central to protecting the detained individual's rights at the pre-trial stage. It remains relevant throughout all stages of criminal proceedings. The summary trials under military legal system deny our armed forces personnel the freedom available to all other citizens under the Constitution. The punishment curtails liberty and causes monetary loss by way of deduction of pay and allowances. In most cases the punishments affect the prospects and the career of the service personnel adversely. In the guise of an expeditious summary justice system to maintain discipline, the armed forces personnel are neither entitled to any legal representation during their proceedings nor a right of appeal. It is a clear infringement of basic justice, desecration of fairness and a disregard for Constitutional norms. Similarly, the unscrupulous processing of a grievance petition against service conditions or award of minor summary punishments damages the effectiveness of a statutory right.

Authorizing military personnel to avail basic fundamental rights during summary trial; processing of grievance petitions in a just and democratic environment; providing effective legal aid a military person during pre-trial, trial and post-trial stages; abolition of Victorian-era summary systems of court-martial; making military-judiciary independent of command structure;   removal of unlawful command influence over court-martial; allowing advantage of set-off to the members of the air force; and incorporation of plea-bargaining in the military legal system would no way go against the spirit of Article 33 of the Constitution.

The legislation containing the military justice system is unable to meet the demands of an enlightened society and the present-day cadre of the armed forces.[42] Many advances made in the administration of military

---

42 The Tenth Report of the Parliamentary Standing Committee on Defence (2005–06), para 10, 12: The Armed Force personnel of the three services are subject to the Army Act, 1950; the Air Force Act, 1950; and the Navy Act, 1957. In this connection, several submissions have been received that the Acts suffer from inherent defects and violate the constitutional rights of a person. The Supreme Court and high courts have in their judgments in several cases taken note of harsh punishments being awarded to service personnel by commanding officers for relatively minor offences. The Committee

justice in other democracies of the world have not been reflected in the Indian system and many have been denied on the plea that their rights have been restricted by Article 33 of the Constitution.[43] How can the rights relating to an effective and impartial justice delivery system affect the discipline or effective functioning of the armed forces?

In India, the legislature and the judiciary are important institutions enjoying sovereign power to the extent assigned to them and enshrined in the Constitution. The independence of the judiciary is essential for the discharge of its plenary obligation to defend the rights of the citizen. Similarly, the legislature has vast powers of discussion, debate and law making. However, in the case of armed forces personnel, the judiciary have remained non-committal and adopted a hands-off policy. Recently, the Delhi High Court while deciding the case of *Ex Lance Naik Vishwa Priya Singh v. Union of India* 147 (2008) DLT 202 has held:

> Mindful of the fact that Article 33 of the Constitution of India confers unbridled powers on Parliament to bring into place a situation which severely abridges the Fundamental Rights of a citizen it becomes bounden duty of the Courts to ensure that the equality doctrine is not needlessly nullified. It also becomes essential that the Courts should interpret the law in a manner which will reduce to the minimum the inroads into the infrangible rights contained in Chapter III of the Constitution.

The framers of the Constitution had a positive attitude towards human rights perhaps because most of them had suffered long incarceration under the British. Accordingly, they incorporated human rights in the Constitution under the title of "Fundamental Rights" in Part III, Articles 12 to 35. Even though they may have thought it necessary to curtail certain rights of military personnel, it could never have been their intention to deprive them of the basic fundamental rights. At a time when we are enforcing rights to

---

therefore, strongly feels that it is high time that these Acts be reviewed in totality in the light of the judgments delivered by the courts to make their provisions more democratic. Available at: http://164.100.24.208/ls/Defence/10threport.pdf.

43 In Russia, military courts conduct trials independently, subordinate only to the constitution, constitutional law and statutes. The judges in military courts are independent in dispensing justice; the constitution, federal constitutional law and statute guarantee the judges independence. Their independence cannot be abrogated or diminished, and any interference with their activities is unacceptable and punishable by law. Zolotukhin, General-Lieutenant Gennady, Institutions of Military Justice of the Armed Forces of the Russian Federation, *Air Force Law Review,* Vol. 52, 2002, pp 53–80.

animals, we must be compelled to ensure that the people who protect our country are not deprived of their basic rights.

Conclusion

Respect for human rights is the essence of the philosophy of the Constitution of India. The Supreme Court has added new dimensions to various statutory provisions by the liberal interpretation of the statute, or by evolving principles of justice, equity and good conscience. Unfortunately, when it comes to the fundamental rights of military personnel, the interpretation of Article 33 by the higher judiciary has been very narrow.

There is tendency in civil society to follow the argument that number of persons affected by military law is very few and every member has voluntarily submitted himself to the existing system with all its defects. With 1.4 million serving and around 6 million retired fraternities in the country, it will be difficult to find a person who does not have a close connection with someone in the armed forces. Any unjustified action or conviction of a military person, whether or not deserved, may trigger interest not only in the immediate family but throughout ever-widening segments of the community. A lack of fairness in the administrative justice[44] and disciplinary processes can seriously undermine the cohesion, morale and discipline of the personnel and impact negatively on unit effectiveness in peace as well as war. While the government has recently done away with several colonial-era legislations, surprisingly, no efforts have been made to modernize antiquated military laws.

---

44 Administrative Justice: ….there should be a duty on bodies exercising governmental functions to act fairly, reasonably, and lawfully in decisions that materially affect an individual's rights and interests, and to ensure that individuals whose interests and livelihoods are affected by administrative decisions have a right to be heard prior to the decisions being made and a right to challenge them where appropriate. Brown Gordon (ed). 2016. *The Universal Declaration of Human Rights in the 21st Century: A Living Document in a Changing World*, Global Institute for Advanced Study.

Chapter – IV

Judicial Interpretation: Rights of the Members of the Armed Forces

---

Introduction

Present-day military personnel are more conscious of their fundamental, human and natural rights, even though they are constitutionally denied certain rights under the military law. The arbitrariness of governance in matters of promotion, posting, pay and allowances, conditions of service, and pension has been questioned in a number of cases referred to civil courts. There have also been a large number of cases in which the courts have questioned the legality, validity, and fairness of trials under the military legal system. Unfortunately, in India, judicial activism in the sphere of human rights has generally steered clear of the conditions of service of aggrieved military personnel as well as to the justice delivered by the ad hoc tribunals.

In its simple meaning Article 33 speaks of only two contingencies in which the rights of armed forces personnel can be abrogated; first for ensuring the proper discharge of duties by the Armed Forces; and secondly for the sake of maintaining discipline. Section 21 of the Army Act, 1950 and the rules related to it accordingly, place certain restrictions on the fundamental rights of military personnel which are part of Article 19 of the Constitution. The higher judiciary is yet to agree with this simple and literal interpretation of Article 33. Some of the cases relating to Article 33 are discussed as under.

Kameshwar Prasad v. State of Bihar [1962] [1]

The scope of Article 33 was for the first time was considered in this case. The Government of Bihar, by a notification dated 16 August 1957, introduced Rule 4-A into the Bihar Government Servants' Conduct Rules, 1956, which provided that no Government servant shall participate in any demonstration or resort to any form of strike in connection with any matter pertaining to his conditions of service. The appellants filed a petition before the High Court of Patna under Article 226 of the Constitution of India challenging the validity of the rule on the grounds, inter alia, that it violated Article 19, sub-clauses (a), (b) and (c) and that, in consequence, the rule was in excess of the rulemaking power conferred by Article 309. The High Court took the view that the freedom guaranteed under Articles 19 (1) (a) and 19 (1) (c) did not include a right to demonstrate or to strike so far as the government servants were concerned, and that in any case, the impugned rule was saved as imposing reasonable restrictions.

The Supreme Court held that Rule 4-A of the Bihar Government Servants' Conduct Rules, 1956, in so far as it prohibited any form of demonstration, be it however innocent or however incapable of causing a breach of public tranquility, was violative of Articles 19 (1) (a) and 19 (1)(b) of the Constitution of India, and since on the language of the rule as it stood it was not possible to so read it as to separate the legal from the unconstitutional portion, the entire rule relating to participation in any demonstration must be declared as *ultra vires*.

The Supreme court further held that the Constitution has under Article 33, selected two of the services under the State, the members of which might be deprived of the benefit of the fundamental rights guaranteed to other persons and citizens and also has prescribed the limits within which such restrictions or abrogation might take place; but the other classes of the government servants, like other persons and citizens of the country, cannot be excluded from the protection of the rights guaranteed by Part III by reason merely of their being the government servants; though on account of nature and incidents of the duties which they have to discharge in that capacity, certain restrictions on their freedoms might have to be imposed. The Court also held that Rule 4-A in so far as it prohibited strikes was valid, because there was no fundamental right to resort to a strike.

---

1   *Kameshwar Prasad v. State of Bihar* 1962 Supp (3) SCR 369 : AIR 1962 SC 1166 : 91962) 1 LLJ 294, decided on 22 February 1962 [Five Judge Bench].

O. K. Ghosh v. E.X. Joseph [1963] [2]

In this case, the respondent E.X. Joseph was serving in Audit and Accounts Department at Bombay under the service of the Government of India. He was the Secretary of the Civil Accounts Association which consists of a non-gazetted staff of the Accountant-General's Office. The said Association was affiliated to the All India Non-Gazetted Audit and Accounts Association. The latter Association had been recognized by the Government of India in December, 1956. In May, 1959, the Government withdrew recognition of the said Association. In spite of the withdrawal of the recognition of the said Association, the respondent continued to be its Secretary-General and refused to dissociate himself from the activities of the said Association, though called upon to do so. As a result of his activities, on 3 June 1960, he was served with a charge-sheet for having deliberately committed breach of Rule 4(B) of the Central Civil Services (Conduct) Rules, 1955.

The appellant O. K. Ghosh, Accountant-General (AG), Maharashtra, who held the enquiry, found the respondent guilty of the charges levelled against him. Accordingly, a show cause notice as to why he should not be removed from service was served on the respondent. On 25 July 1960, the appellant served a memo on the respondent intimating to him that it was proposed to hold an enquiry against him for having deliberately contravened the provisions of Rule 4(A) of the Rules in so far as he participated actively in various demonstrations organized in connection with the strike of Central Government employees and had taken active part in the preparations made for the said strike.

The respondent challenged the action mainly on the ground that the departmental proceedings initiated against him was that the Rules 4(A) and 4(B) were void in so far as they contravened the fundamental rights guaranteed under Article 19(1) (a), (b), (c) and (g). The Bombay High Court held that Rule 4(A) was wholly valid but quashed the proceeding under Rule 4(B) which it held to be invalid. Rule 4(A) provided that no government servant shall participate in any demonstration or resort to any form of strike in connection with any matter pertaining to his conditions of service and Rule 4(B) provided that no government servant shall join or continue to be a member of any services Association which the Government did not recognize or in respect of which recognition had been refused or withdrawn by it.

---

2   *O. K. Ghosh v. E.X. Joseph* 1963 Supp (1) SCR 789 : AIR 1963 SC 812 : 91962) 2 LLJ
     615, decided on 30 October 1962 [five Judge Bench].

Against this decision, the appellants, O. K. Ghosh and the Union of India filed a petition in the Supreme Court; whereas E. X. Joseph the respondent also preferred an appeal in the Supreme Court. The appellants contend before the Supreme Court that the high court was in error in holding that Rule 4(B) was invalid, whereas the respondent urges that Rule 4(A) was invalid and the decision of the high court to the contrary is erroneous in law. These Rules form part of a body of Rules framed in 1955 under Article 309, of the Constitution.

Rule 4-A provides that no government servant shall participate in any demonstration or resort to any form of strike in connection with any matter pertaining to his condition of service, whereas Rule 4-B lays down that no government servant shall join or continue to be a member of any Service Association of government servants: (a) which has not, within a period of six months from its formation, obtained the recognition of the government under the Rules prescribed in that behalf, or (b) recognition in respect of which has been refused or withdrawn by the government under the said Rules. The case against the respondent was that he has contravened both these Rules.

The Supreme Court held, "It is not disputed that the Fundamental Rights guaranteed by Article 19 can be claimed by government servants. Article 33, which confers power on the Parliament to modify the rights in their application to the armed forces, clearly brings out the fact that all citizens, including government servants, are entitled to claim the rights guaranteed by Article 19." Thus, the validity of the impugned rule has to be judged on the basis that the respondent and his co-employees are entitled to form Associations or Unions. It is clear that Rule 4-B imposes a restriction on this right. It virtually compels a government servant to withdraw his membership of the Service Association of Government Servants as soon as recognition accorded to the said Association is withdrawn or if, after the Association is formed, no recognition is accorded to it within six months. In other words, the right to form an association is conditioned by the existence of the recognition of the said association by the government.

If the association obtains the recognition and continues to enjoy it, government servants can become members of the said association; if the association does not secure recognition from the government or recognition granted to it is withdrawn, the government servants must cease to be the members of the said association. The Supreme Court considered the question: Can this restriction be said to be in the interests of public order and can it be said, to be a reasonable restriction? The Court held, "In our opinion, the only answer to these questions would be in the negative. It is difficult to see any direct or proximate or reasonable connection between the recognition by the government of the association and the discipline amongst, and the efficiency of, the members of the said association. Similarly, it is difficult to see any connection between recognition and public order. Thus, the validity of the impugned rule has to be judged on the basis that the respondent and his co-employees are entitled to form associations or unions. It is clear that Rule 4-B imposes a restriction on this right. It virtually compels a government servant to withdraw his membership of the Service Association of Government Servants as soon as recognition accorded to the said association is withdrawn or if, after the association is formed, no recognition is accorded to it within six months. In other words, the right to form an association is conditioned by the existence of the recognition of the said association by the government." The Supreme Court, referring to its decision in the case of *Kameshwar Prasad*, quashed the departmental proceedings instituted against the respondent for the alleged contravention of Rules 4-A and 4-B.

Ram Sarup v. Union of India [1964] [3]

In *Ram Sarup v. Union of India* [32], the petitioner was a sepoy in Defence Security Corps (DSC). On 13 June 1962, he shot dead three DSC personnel and was charged on three counts under Section 69 of the Army Act read with Section 302 IPC. He was tried by a general court martial (GCM). On 12 January 1963, the GCM found him guilty of the three charges and sentenced him to death. The findings and sentence awarded by the court-martial was confirmed by the Central Government. Thereafter, the petitioner filed a writ petition in the Supreme Court praying for the issue of a writ of habeas corpus and a writ of certiorari setting aside the order dated 12 January 1963 of the GCM and the order of the Central Government confirming the sentence and his release from the jail.

The contentions raised for the petitioner were: (1) That the provisions of section 125 of the Army Act are discriminatory and contravene the provisions of Article 14 of the Constitution inasmuch as it is left to the unguided discretion of the officer mentioned in that section to decide whether the accused person would be tried by a Court Martial or by a Criminal Court. (2) Section 127 of the Act [4] which provides for successive

---

3   *Ram Sarup v. Union of India* (1964) 5 SCR 931 : AIR 1965 SC 247 : (1965) Cr LJ 236, decided on 12 December 1963 [Five Judge Bench].

4   Section 127 of the Army Act, 1950 has been omitted by Act No. 37 of 1992.

trials by a Criminal Court and a Court Martial, violates the provisions of Article 20 of the Constitution as it provides for the prosecution and punishment of a person for the same offence more than once. (3) The petitioner was not allowed to be defended at the GCM by a legal practitioner of his choice and therefore there had been a violation of Article 22(1) of the Constitution. (4) The procedure laid down for the trial of offences by the GCM had not been followed inasmuch as the death sentence awarded to the petitioner was not passed with the concurrence of at least two-thirds of the members of the Court. (5) Section 164 of the Act provides two remedies, one after the other, to a person aggrieved by any order passed by a GCM. Sub section (1) allows him to present a petition to the officer or authority empowered to confirm any finding or sentence of the court-martial and sub-section (2) allows him to present a petition to the Central Government or to any other authority mentioned in that sub-section and empowers the Central Government or the other authority to pass such order on the petition as it thinks fit. The petitioner could avail of only one remedy as the finding and sentence of the GCM was confirmed by the Central Government. He, therefore, could not go to any other authority against the order of the Central Government by which he was aggrieved.

It was urged by the petitioner that in the exercise of the power conferred on Parliament under Article 33 of the Constitution to modify fundamental rights guaranteed by Part III, in their application to the armed forces, it enacted Section 21 of the Army Act which empowers the Central Government, by notification, to make rules relating to such extent and in such manner as may be necessary. That these matters do not cover the Fundamental Rights under Article 14, 20 and 22 of the Constitution and this indicates the intention of Parliament not to modify any other Fundamental Right.

The Attorney-General has urged that the entire Army Act has been enacted by Parliament and if any of the provisions of the Act is not consistent with the provisions of any of the articles in Part III of the Constitution, it must be taken that to the extent of the inconsistency Parliament had modified the fundamental rights under those articles in their application to the person subject to that Act. Any such provision in the Act is as much law as the entire Act. The Supreme Court agreed with submission of the Attorney-General that each and every provision of the Act is a law made by Parliament and that if any such provision tends to affect the fundamental rights under Part III of the Constitution, that provision does not, on that account, become void, as it must be taken that Parliament has thereby, in the exercise of its power under Article 33 of the Constitution, made the requisite modification to affect the respective fundamental right.

This was perhaps the first case where Supreme Court incorrectly relied upon the submission of the Attorney General in the interpretation of Article 33.

Ous Kutilingal Achudan Nair v. Union of India, [1976] [5]

The appellants were office-bearers of the Civil Employees Unions in the various Centers of the Defence Establishments of Secunderabad and Hyderabad. They filed a writ petition in the High Court to impugn the authority of the Commandants in declaring the Unions, represented by the appellants as unlawful associations. The Registrar of Trade Unions had issued Certificates of Registration to the four Unions represented by the appellants between 1954 and 1970. The General Secretary of Class IV, Civil Employees Union, Secunderabad was informed, per letter dated 12 May 1971, by the Under Secretary of the Government of India, Ministry of Defence that their Unions could not be granted recognition as these employees being in the Training Establishments, were not entitled to form Unions. The Commandant also issued a notice to the appellants to show cause why disciplinary action should not be taken against them for forming this unlawful association. The main ground taken in the petition was that the impugned action was violative of their fundamental right to form associations or Unions conferred by Art. 19(1)(c) of the Constitution.

The Union of India, in reply averred that the Civilian Non-Combatants in the Defence Establishments were governed by the Army Act and were duly prohibited by Rules framed thereunder from joining or forming a Trade Union; that the associations in question were formed in breach of that prohibition, and were, therefore validly declared illegal.

The High Court has held that the right of the appellants to form associations given by Article 19(1) (c) of the Constitution had been lawfully taken away. The High Court accordingly dismissed the petition. The appellants carried an appeal to the Appellate Bench of the High Court. The Bench dismissed the appeal holding that the impugned action was not without jurisdiction.

---

5   Ous Kutilingal Achudan Nair v. Union of India, (1976) 2 SCC 780 : AIR 1976 SC 1179 : 1976 SCR (2) 769, [4 Judge Bench], decided on 20 November 1975. Appeal by special leave from the judgment and order dated the 18th June 1974 of the Andhra Pradesh High Court at Hyderabad in Writ Appeal No. 460 of 1974.

The main contention of the appellants before the Supreme Court was that the members of the Unions represented by the appellants, though attached to the Defence Establishments, are 'civilians', designated as "Non-Combatants Un-Enrolled". They include cooks, chowkidars, laskars, barbers, carpenters, mechanics, boot-makers, tailors, etc. They are governed by the Civil Service Regulations for purposes of discipline, leave, pay, etc. and are also eligible to serve up to the age of 60 years unlike that of the members of the Armed Forces. In view of these facts, these categories of civilian employees attached to the Defence Establishments, could not be validly called "members of the Armed Forces" covered by Article 33 of the Constitution.

The points sought to be made out were: that the members of the appellants' Unions are not subject to the Army Act as they do not fall under any of the categories enumerated in sub-clauses (a) to (i) of section 2 of the Army Act, 1950, and that the impugned notifications are *ultra vires* the Army Act and are struck by Article 19(1)(c) and 33 of the Constitution.

The Supreme Court held that Article 33 of the Constitution provides an exception to the preceding Articles in Part III including Article 19(1)(c). By Article 33, Parliament is empowered to enact law determining to what extent any of the rights conferred by Part III shall in their application to the members of the armed forces or forces charged with the maintenance of public order, be restricted or abrogated so as to ensure the proper discharge of their duties and the maintenance of discipline among them.

In enacting the Army Act, 1950, in so far as it restricts or abrogates any of the fundamental rights of the members of the Armed Forces, Parliament derives its competence from Article 33 of the Constitution. Section 2(1) of the Act enumerates the persons who are subject to the operation of this Act. According to sub-clause (i) of this section, persons governed by the Act, include "persons not otherwise subject to military law who, on active service, in camp, on the march or at any frontier post specified by the Central Government by notification in this behalf, are employed by, or are in the service of, or are followers of, or accompany any portion of the regular army."

The Supreme Court held that the members of the Unions represented by the appellants fall within this category. It is their duty to follow or accompany the armed personnel on active service, or in camp or on the march. Although they are non-combatants and are in some matters governed by the Civil Service Regulations, yet they are integral to the

Armed Forces. They answer the description of the "members of the Armed Forces" within the contemplation of Article 33. Consequently, by virtue of section 21 of the Army Act, the Central Government was competent by notification to make rules restricting or curtailing their fundamental rights under Article 19 (1) (c).

Further, Rule 19 (ii) of the Army Rules, 1954, imposes a restriction on the fundamental rights, stating, "No persons subject to the Army Act shall, without the express sanction of the Central Government be a member of, or be associated in any way with, any trade union or labour union, or any class of trade or labour unions." In exercise of its powers under section 4 of the Defence of India Act, the Government of India has by notification dated 11 February 1972, provided that all persons not being members of the Armed Forces of the Union, who are attached to or employed with or following the regular Army shall be subject to the military law. The Army Act, 1950, has also been made applicable to them. By another notification dated 23 February 1972, under Section 9 of the Army Act, civilian employees of the training establishments and Military Hospitals have been taken out of the purview of the Industrial Disputes Act. Section 9 of the Army Act further empowers the Central Government to declare by notification, persons not covered by section 3 (i) of the Act, also as persons on active service. In view of these notifications issued under section 4 of the Defence of India Act and the Army Rules, the appellants can no longer claim any fundamental right under Article 19 (1) (c) of the Constitution.

Lt Col PPS Bedi v. Union of India [1982] [6]

In this case, three Writ Petitions [WP No. 4903/81, WP No. 1513/79 and WP No. 5930/80] were filed by military personnel who were to be tried by GCM for breach of army discipline. They questioned the legality and validity of the order convening the general court-martial, more particularly its composition. In their petitions under Article 32 of the Constitution it was contended that (1) to satisfy the requirements of Article 33 the law must be a specific law enacted by Parliament in which a specific provision imposing restriction or even abrogation of fundamental rights should be made; (2) Rule 40 of the Rules should be so construed as to subserve the mandate of Article 21 that the Army with its total commitment to national security against foreign invasion must be assured the prized liberty of individual members against unjust encroachment and the court

---

6   *Lt Col PPS Bedi v. Union of India* (1982) 3 SCC 140 : AIR 1982 SC 1413 decided on
     25 August 1982 [Three Judge Bench].

should strike a just balance between military discipline and individual personal liberty; and (3) principles of natural justice should be observed even in respect of persons tried by the army tribunals. In each petition legality and validity of the order convening the GCM, more particularly the composition of the court-martial in respect of each petitioner was questioned.

In this case, the web of argument was woven round the true construction and intendment underlying Rule 40 of the Army Rules. It was said that the grammatical construction must accord with the underlying intendment of Rule 40 and that the approach must be informed by the expanding jurisprudence and widening horizon of the subject of personal liberty in Article 21 because in the absence of Article 33 the procedure prescribed for trial by the GCM under the Act would have been violative of Article 21. Approach, it was urged, must be to put such liberal construction on Rule 40 as to sub-serve the mandate of Article 21. Army, with its total commitment to national independence against foreign invasion must equally be assured the prized liberty of individual member against unjust encroachment. It was said that the court should strike a just balance between military discipline and individual personal liberty. And door must not be bolted against principles of natural justice even in respect of Army tribunal. An unnatural distinction or differentiation between a civilian offender and an offender subject to the Act would be destructive of the cherished principle of equality, the dazzling light of the Constitution which illumines all other provisions.

The Supreme Court referred to Article 33 of the Constitution which reads as under:

"33. **Power to Parliament to modify the rights confer red by this Part in their application to forces**: Parliament may by law determine to what extend any of the rights conferred by this Part shall, in their application to the members of the Armed Forces or the Forces charged with the maintenance of public order, be restricted or abrogated so as to ensure the proper discharge of their duties, and the maintenance of discipline among them."

The contention, in this case, was that in order to satisfy the requirement of Article 33, Parliament must enact specific law specifying therein the modification of the rights conferred by Part III and that a restriction or abrogation of fundamental rights cannot be left to be deduced or determined by implication. In other words, the submission was that the law to satisfy the requirement of Article 33 must be a specific law enacted by Parliament in which a specific provision imposing restriction or even abrogation of fundamental rights should be made and when such provisions are debated by the Parliament it would be clear as to how far restriction is imposed by Parliament on the Fundamental Rights enacted in Part III in their application to the members of the Armed Forces or the forces charged with the maintenance of public order. The submission was that a conscious and deliberate Act of Parliament may permit erosion of Fundamental Rights in their application to the members of armed forces. Such a serious inroad on Fundamental Rights cannot be left to Central Government to be done by delegated legislation. Article 33 permits Parliament by law to not merely restrict but abrogate the Fundamental Rights enacted in Part III in their application to the members of Armed Forces. The Act was enacted in 1950 and was brought into force on 22 July 1950. Thus the Act was enacted after the Constitution came into force on 26 January 1950. When power to legislate is conferred by Constitution, and Parliament enacts a legislation, normal inference is that the legislation is enacted in exercise of legislative power and legislative craftsmanship does not necessitate specifying the powers. Since the Constitution came into force, Parliament presumably was aware that its power to legislate must be referable to Constitution and therefore it would be subject to the limitation prescribed by the Constitution. Whenever a legislation is being debated for being put on the statute book, Articles 12 and 13 must be staring into the face of that body. Consequently when the Act was enacted not only Articles 12 and 13 were hovering over the provisions but also Article 33 which to some extent carves out an exception to Articles 12 and 13 must be present to the corporate mind of Parliament which would imply that Parliament by law can restrict or abrogate Fundamental Rights set out in Part III in their application to Armed Forces.

The Supreme Court dismissed all the three petitions; but made following caustic remarks against the prevalent military justice system:

> Reluctance of the apex court more concerned with civil law to interfere with the internal affairs of the Army is likely to create a distorted picture in the minds of the military personnel that persons subject to Army Act are not citizens of India. It is one of the cardinal features of our Constitution that a person by enlisting in or entering armed forces does not cease to be a citizen so as to wholly deprive him of his rights under the Constitution. ... In the larger interest of national security and military discipline Parliament in its wisdom

may restrict or abrogate such rights in their application to the Armed Forces but this process should not be carried so far as to create a class of citizens not entitled to the benefits of the liberal spirit of the Constitution. Persons subject to Army Act are citizens of this ancient land having a feeling of belonging to the civilized community governed by the liberty-oriented constitution. Personal liberty makes for the worth of human being and is a cherished and prized right. Deprivation thereof must be preceded by an enquiry ensuring fair, just and reasonable procedure and trial by a judge of unquestioned integrity and wholly unbiased. A marked difference in the procedure for trial of an offence by the criminal court and the court-martial is apt to generate dissatisfaction arising out of this differential treatment.... Ours is still an antiquated system.

In concluding paragraph of the judgement, the Supreme Court said, "The wind of change blowing over the country has not permeated the close and sacrosanct precincts of the Army. If in civil courts the universally accepted dictum is that justice must not only be done but it must seem to be done, the same holds good with all the greater vigour in case of court-martial where the judge and the accused done the same dress, have the same mental discipline, have a strong hierarchical subjugation and a feeling of bias in such circumstances is irremovable. We, therefore, hope and believe that the changes all over the English speaking democracies will awaken our Parliament to the changed value system. In this behalf, we would like to draw pointed attention of the Government to the glaring anomaly that courts-martial do not even write a brief reasoned order in support of their conclusion, even in cases in which they impose the death sentence. This must be remedied in order to ensure that a disciplined and dedicated Indian Army may not nurse a grievance that the substance of justice and fair play is denied to it."

R. Viswan v. Union of India [1983] [7]

The petitioners who belonged to the General Reserve Engineering Force (GREF) were charged under section 63 of the Army Act, 1950 on allegations that they had assembled in front of the Chief Engineer and shouted slogans demanding release of personnel placed under arrest, participated in a black flag demonstration and associated themselves with an illegal association. They were tried by court-martial in accordance with

---

7 *R. Viswan v. Union of India* 1983 SCR (3) 60 : 1983 SCC (3) 401 : 1983 SCALE (1)497, decided on 6 May 1983 [Five Judge Bench].

the prescribed procedure and, on being convicted, were dismissed from service. The petitioners submitted that their convictions by court-martial were illegal and raised the following contentions in support of their plea that:

(i) The GREF was a civilian construction agency and not a 'force' raised and maintained under the authority of the Central Government and consequently, the members of GREF were not "members of Armed Forces or the Forces charged with the maintenance of public order" within the meaning of Article 33 of the Constitution and therefore the application of section 21 of the Army Act read with Rules 19 to 21 of the Army Rules to them was unconstitutional since it restricted their fundamental rights in a manner not permitted by the Constitution;

(ii) SROs 329 and 330 which were notifications having the effect of applying the provisions of the Army Act and the Army Rules to the members of the GREF were *ultra vires* the powers of the Central Government under Section (1) and (4) of section 4 of the Army Act;

(iii) Section 21 of the Army Act was unconstitutional as it was not justified by the terms of Article 33 since under that Article it was Parliament alone which was entrusted with the power to determine to what extent any of the fundamental rights shall, in application to the members of the Armed Forces or Forces charged with the maintenance of public order, be restricted or abrogated and Parliament could not have left it to the Central Government to determine the extent of such restriction or abrogation as was sought to be done under section 21;

(iv) The petitioners were entitled to exercise their fundamental rights under clause (a), (b) and (c) of Article 19 (1) without any of the restrictions imposed by Rules 19 to 21 of the Army Rules and therefore they could not be charged under section 63 of the Army Act on the facts alleged against them;

(v) Their trial was not in accordance with law; and that the application of the provisions of the Army Act and the Army Rules to the members of GREF for purposes of discipline was discriminatory and violative of Article 14 inasmuch as the members of the GREF were governed both by the Central Civil Services (Classification Control and Appeal) Rules,

1965 and the provisions of the Army Act and the Army Rules in matters of discipline.

The Supreme Court held that the functions and duties of GREF are integrally connected with the operational plans and requirements of the Armed Forces. There can be no doubt that without the efficient and disciplined operational role of GREF the military operations in border areas during peace as also in times of war will be seriously hampered and a highly disciplined and efficient GREF is absolutely essential for supporting the operational plans and meeting the operational requirements of the Armed Forces. The members of the GREF answer the description of "members of the Armed Forces" within the meaning of Article 33 and consequently the application of section 21 of the Army Act to the members of GREF is protected by that Article and the fundamental rights of the members of GREF must be held to be validly restricted by section 21 read with Rules 19 to 21 of Army Rules. The petitioners were therefore liable to be charged under section 63 of the Army Act for the alleged violations of Rules 19 to 21 and their convictions and subsequent dismissals must be held to be valid.

The question whether the members of GREF can be said to be members of the Armed Forces for the purpose of attracting the applicability of Article 33 must depend essentially on the character of GREF, its organisational set up, its functions, the role it is called upon to play in relation to the armed forces and the depth and intimacy of its connection and the extent of its integration with the Armed Forces. The history, composition, administration, organization and role of GREF clearly show that GREF is an integral part of the armed forces and that the members of GREF can legitimately be said to be members of the armed forces within the meaning of Article 33. It is undoubtedly a departmental construction agency as contended on behalf of the petitioners but it is distinct from other construction agencies such as the Central Public Works Department in that it is a force intended primarily to support the Army in its operational requirement.

The Central Government is empowered under sub-section (1) of section 4 of the Army Act to apply any of the provisions of that Act to any force raised or maintained in India under the authority of that Government. When the provisions of the Army Act are applied to any force under sub-section (1) of section 4, the Central Government can, by notification issued under sub-section (4) thereof, direct by what authority, the jurisdiction, powers and duties incident to the operation of those provisions shall be exercised or performed in respect of that force. The word 'force' is not defined anywhere in the Army Act but sub-section (2) of section 4 clearly contemplates that 'force' referred to in sub-section (1) of section 4 must be a force organised on similar lines as the army with rank structure. There can be no doubt that GREF is a force organised on army pattern with units and sub-units and rank structure. It is clear from the letter dated 16 June 1960 addressed by the Secretary, Border Roads Development Board to the Director General Border Roads that GREF is a force raised and maintained under the authority of the Central Government. The Central Government therefore had the power under sub-sections (1) and (4) of section 4 to issue notifications SRO 329 and SRO 330 applying some of the Army Act and the Army Rules to the GREF.

Section 21 of the Army Act empowers the Central Government to make rules restricting "to such extent and in such manner as may be necessary" three categories of rights of any person subject to the Army Act. These rights are part of the Fundamental Rights under clauses (a), (b) and (c) of Article 19(1) and under the constitutional scheme, they cannot be restricted by executive action unsupported by law. But section 21 is saved by Article 33 which carves out an exception in so far as the applicability of fundamental rights to members of the armed forces and the forces charged with the maintenance of public order is concerned. On a plain grammatical construction of its language, Article 33 does not require that Parliament itself must by law restrict or abrogate any of the fundamental rights in order to attract the applicability of that Article. There is no substance in the contention that applying the provisions of the Army Act and the Army Rules to the members of GREF for purpose of discipline is discriminatory and violative of Article 14.

The Supreme Court that once the Central Government has imposed restrictions in exercise of this power, the Court will not ordinarily interfere with the decision of the Central Government that such restrictions are necessary because that is a matter left by Parliament exclusively to the Central Government which is best in a position to know what the situation demands. Section 21 must, in the circumstances, be held to be constitutionally valid as being within the power conferred under Article 33. The provisions of the Army Act 1950 and the Army Rules 1954 as applied to the members of GREF are protected by Article 33 against invalidation on the ground of violation of Article 14.

The Supreme Court made it clear the members of GREF are members of the armed forces within the meaning of Article 33. As regards, casual labour employed by GREF were concerned, the Supreme Court did not express any opinion whether they too are members of the armed forces or not, as this question was not taken up for consideration before the Court.

Delhi Police Non-Gazetted Karmchari Sangh v. Union of India [1987] [8]

The non-gazetted members of the Delhi Police Force wanted to form an association of their own and for that purpose constituted the Karmachari Union in 1966 and applied for its registration under the Trade Union Act, 1926 and this was refused. After the coming into effect from 2 December 1966 of the Police Force (Restriction of Rights) Act, 1966, another application for recognition was made on 9 December 1966 which was granted on 12 December 1966. The non-gazetted members of the Delhi Police Force were permitted to become members of the Sangh.

The Police Force (Restriction of Rights) Rules, 1966 made by the Central Government on 12 December 1966 were amended by the Amendment Rules of 1970. Rule 11 thereof provides for revocation of the recognition granted to an association if the said associations' articles are not in conformity with the Rules or are not brought in conformity with the provisions of the amended Rules within a period of 30 days. Since the Articles of Association of the appellant Sangh contained a number of provisions not in conformity with the rules and since the Sangh failed to bring the same in conformity, its recognition was revoked by circular dated 1 April 1971. The appellants, therefore, filed a writ petition before the Delhi High Court challenging the constitutional validity of the Act, Rules and the impugned circular. The writ petition was rejected and the appellant approached the Supreme Court by way of special leave.

The Supreme Court while dismissing the petition, held:

> Before considering the rival contentions urged before us, it would be useful to refer to the salient features of the Police Forces (Restriction of Rights) Act, 1966 to appreciate its ambit and the restrictions imposed by its provisions. The Act was enacted to delineate the restrictions imposed of the rights conferred by Part III of the Constitution, in their application to the members of the forces charged with the maintenance of public order so as to ensure the

---

8 *Delhi Police Non-Gezetted Karmchari Sangh v. Union of India* AIR 1987 SC 379 : 1987 SCC (1) 115 : 1986 SCALE (2)872, date of Judgement 20 November 1986 [Two Judge Bench].

proper discharge of their duties' and the maintenance of discipline among them. The Parliament obviously has this power under Article 33 of the Constitution of India. The provisions of the Act seek to place certain restrictions on members of the police force in exercise of their fundamental rights guaranteed by Article 19(1)(c) to form Association or Unions. Section 3 of the Act reads as follows:

"3(1). No member of a police force shall without the express sanction of the Central Government or of the prescribed authority:

(a) be a member of, or be associated in any way with, any trade union, labour union, political association or with any class of trade unions, labour unions or political associations; or

(b) be a member of, or be associated in any way with, any other society, institution, association or organization that is not recognized as part of the force of which he is a member or is not of a purely social, recreational or religious nature; or

(c) communicate with the press or publish or cause to be published any book, letter or other document except where such communication or publication is in the bona fide discharge of his duties or is of a purely literary, artistic or scientific character or is of a prescribed nature.

Explanation: If any question arises as to whether any society, institution, association or organization is of a purely social, recreational or religious nature under clause (b) of this subsection, the decision of the Central Government thereon shall be final.

(2) No member of a police force shall participate in or address, any meeting or take part in any demonstration organized by any body of persons for any political purposes or for such other purposes as may be prescribed."

The Supreme Court was of the opinion that the Police Force (Restriction of Rights) Act, 1966, the Police Force (Restriction of Rights) Rules 1966 (as amended by the 1970 Rules) and the circular dated 1 April 1971 are all constitutionally valid. They do not offend the provisions of Articles 14 and 19(1)(c) of the Constitution. Further, the right under Article 19(1)(c) of the Constitution is not absolute. Article 19(4) specifically empowers the State to make any law to fetter, abridge or abrogate any of the fights under Article 19(1)(c) in the interest of public order and other considerations. While the right to freedom of association is fundamental, recognition of such association is not a fundamental fights and the Parliament can by law regulate the working of such associations by imposing conditions and restrictions on such functions. The Fundamental Rights guaranteed by Article 19(1)(c) can be claimed by the government servants. A government servant may not lose his right by joining government service. Article 33 which confers power on the Parliament to abridge or abrogate such rights in their application to the Armed Forces and other similar forces shows that such fights are available to all citizens, including government servants. What has happened in this case is only to impose reasonable restrictions in the interest of discipline and public order.

According to Supreme Court, Rule 11 read with Rule 3(c) of the Amended Police Force (Restriction of Rights) Rules, 1966 has to be judged keeping in mind the character of the employees to whom it applies. It is true that the rules impose a restriction on the right to form an association. It virtually compels a government servant to withdraw his membership of the association as soon as recognition accorded to the said association is withdrawn or if, after the association is formed, no recognition is accorded to it within six months. In other words, the right to form an association is conditioned by the existence of the recognition of the said association by the government. If the association obtains recognition and continues to enjoy it, government servants can become members of the said association, if the said association does not secure recognition from the government or recognition granted to it is withdrawn, government servants must cease to be members of the said association. That is the plain effect of the impugned role. These rules are protected by Articles 33 and 19(4) of the Constitution. Besides, it is settled law that the right guaranteed by Article 19(1)(c) to form associations does not involve a guaranteed right to recognition also.

The Court held, "It cannot be disputed that the Fundamental Rights guaranteed by Article 19(1)(c) can be claimed by Government servants. A Government servant may not lose its right by joining government service. Article 33 which confers power on the Parliament to abridge or abrogate such rights in their application to the armed forces and other similar forces shows that such rights are available to all citizens, including government servants. But it is, however, necessary to remember that Article 19 confers fundamental rights which are not absolute but are subject to reasonable restrictions. What has happened in this case is only to impose reasonable restrictions in the interest of discipline and public order. Section 3 of the Police Force (Restriction of Rights) Act permits the rulemaking authority to define any group of Police Force that can form an Association. It also gives power to prescribe the nature of activity that each such association

87

of members can indulge in. It, therefore, follows that if rules can be framed defining this aspect, a rule can also be framed enabling the authorities to revoke or cancel recognition once accorded, if the activities offended the rules. Besides the classification based on ranking has its own rationale behind it. The Court is dealing with a Force in which discipline is the most important prerequisite. Non-gazetted officers consist of men of all ranks; the lowest cadre and officers who are superior to them. If all the non-gazetted officers are grouped together irrespective of rank, it is bound to affect discipline. It was perhaps, realizing the need to preserve discipline that the changes in the rule were affected.

Intelligence Bureau Employees' Association v. Union of India [1997] 9

The writ petitions filed under Article 32 of the Constitution relate to functioning of the Intelligence Bureau Employees' Association (the petitioner Association), a society registered under the Societies Registration Act, 1860. The petitioner Association was claimed to be an association of the employees working in the Intelligence Bureau (IB) of the Government of India. It was registered as a society on 23 June 1979. On 3 May 1980, the Joint Director of IB issued a circular memorandum wherein it was stated that the Government has now made it clear that in a security organization like the IB there is no scope for an employees' association. In the said circular it was also stated that the grievances of the employees would be the basic concern of all members of the organization. The petitioners challenged the validity of the said circular memorandum on the ground that it is violative of the fundamental rights of the petitioners guaranteed under Articles 14 and 19 of the Constitution.

During the pendency of the writ petition, Article 33 of the constitution has been amended by the Constitution (Fiftieth Amendment) Act, 1984 which received the assent of the President of India on 11 September 1984. As a result of the said amendment Article 33 was substituted by the following provision:

> 33. Power of Parliament to modify the rights conferred by this Part in their application etc.—Parliament may, by law, determine to what extent any of the rights conferred by this Part shall, in their application to,—

---

9 *Intelligence Bureau Employees' Association v. Union of India* (1997) 11 SCC 348, decided on 24 April 1996 [Two Judge Bench].

(a)   The members of the Armed Forces; or

(b)   The members of the Forces charged with the maintenance of public order; or

(c)   Persons employed in any bureau or other organisation established by the State for purposes of intelligence or counter-intelligence; or

(d)   Persons employed in, or in connection with, the telecommunication systems set up for the purposes of any Force, bureau or other organization established by the State for purposes of any Force, bureau or organization referred in clauses (a) to (c),

be restricted or abrogated so as to ensure the proper discharge of their duties and the maintenance of discipline among them.

Under the un-amended Article 33 the rights conferred by Part III could be restricted or abrogated by a law made by Parliament in respect of members of the Armed Forces and members of Forces charged with maintenance of public order. As a result of the Fiftieth Amendment the scope of the provision has been enlarged and persons employed in any bureau or other organization established by the State for the purpose of intelligence or counter-intelligence, which could include the IB, and persons employed in or in connection with the telecommunication system set up for the purpose of any force, bureau or organization referred to in the preceding clauses have been brought within the ambit of Article 33. The said amendment in the Constitution was followed by the Intelligence Organizations (Restriction of Rights) Act, 1985, which received the assent of the President of India on 6 September 1985. Section 3 of the said Act makes the following provisions:

3. (1) No member of an Intelligence Organization shall,—

Be a member of, or be associated in any way with, any trade union, labour union, political association or with any class of trade unions, labour unions or political associations; or

Be a member of, or be associated in any way with, or raise funds for, or hold office in, or function in any other manner for, any other society, institution, association or organization that is not recognised by the Central Government as part of the Intelligence Organization of which he is a member or is not of a purely social, recreational or religious nature; or

(a) Communicate with the press or publish or cause to be published any book, letter, pamphlet, poster or other document except with the prior permission of the head of the Intelligence Organization; or

(b) Except for purposes of official duty, contact or communication with any person or any matter relating to functioning, structure, personnel or organizational affairs of the Intelligence Organization of which he is a member;

(c) Use the name of the Intelligence Organization of which he is a member for purposes not authorized by the head of the Intelligence Organization or in any other manner except for purposes relating to the official work and functioning of the Organization itself.

Explanation.—If any question arises as to whether any society, institution, association or organization is of a purely social, recreational or religious nature under clause (b) of this sub-section, the decision of the Central Government thereon shall be final.

(2) No member of an Intelligence Organization, shall participate in, or address, any meeting or take part in any demonstration organized by any body of persons for any political purposes or for such other purposes as may be prescribed.

The counsel for the petitioner Association challenged the validity of the Fiftieth Amendment in the Constitution but was not been able to show how the said amendment which enlarged the scope of Article 33 so as to include persons engaged in activities connected with the activities of the Armed Forces and Forces charged with the maintenance of public order referred to in the un-amended Article 33 was destructive of the basic structure of the Constitution so as to transgress the limitations placed on the amending power under Article 368 of the Constitution.

The Supreme Court held that a perusal of the provisions of Section 3 of the Act of 1985 shows that there is no complete prohibition in respect of employees of an Intelligence Organization becoming a member of an association. The prohibition is only in respect of associations specified in clause (a) of sub-section (1) of section 3, i.e, trade unions, labour unions, political associations or with any class of trade unions, labour unions or political associations. Under clause (b) of sub-section (1) it is permissible to form associations which are purely social, recreational or religious in nature. It is also permissible to form any other association or organisation provided it is so recognised by the Central Government. It is thus open to the petitioner Association, if it so chooses, to move the Central Government for recognition and if it fulfils the requirements laid down by the Central Government for such recognition, the said request shall be given due consideration by the Central Government.

According to Supreme Court, after the amendment of Article 33 by the Fiftieth Amendment and enactment of Act No. 58 of 1985 the circular memorandum has lost its significance and no purpose would be served by going into the validity of the same. The writ petitions have, therefore, become infructuous and are accordingly dismissed as having become infructuous.

Union of India v. L D Balam Singh [2002] [10]

In this case, the petitioner was serving the Army and residing with his family in a government married accommodation in Patiala Cantt. On 28 December 1991 a search of his residence was conducted by Army Officers and allegedly opium weighing 4.900Kgs was recovered from his family quarter. He was tried by the GCM under Section 69 of the Army Act for an offence punishable under Section 18 of the Narcotic Drugs and Psychotropic Substances Act, 1985 (NDPS Act). After the trial was over, the petitioner was convicted and sentenced by the GCM. The NDPS Act admittedly contains certain procedural safeguards, which were allegedly violated in this case by the army authorities.

The Supreme Court held that army personnel are as much a citizen as any other individual citizen of this country. Incidentally, the provision as contained in Article 33 does not by itself abrogate any rights and its applicability is dependent on Parliamentary legislation. The language used by the framers is unambiguous and categorical and it is in this perspective Article 33 may be noticed at this juncture. A plain reading [of Article 33] thus would reveal that the extent of restrictions necessary to be imposed on any of the fundamental rights in their application to the armed forces and the forces charged with the maintenance of public order for the purpose of ensuring proper discharge of their duties and maintenance of discipline among them would necessarily depend upon the prevailing situation at a given point of time and it would be inadvisable to encase it in a rigid

---

10 *Union of India v. L D Balam Singh* (2002) 9 SCC 73: [2002] 3 SCR 385: 2002 (2) LC 790(SC), decided on 24 April 2002 [Two Judge Bench].

statutory formula. The Constitutions makers were obviously anxious that no more restrictions should be placed than are absolutely necessary for ensuring proper discharge of duties and the maintenance of discipline amongst the armed force personnel and therefore Article 33 empowered the Parliament to restrict or abridge within permissible extent, the rights conferred under Part III of the Constitution in so far as the armed force personnel are concerned.

The Supreme Court referred to its decisions in *R Viswan, PPS Bedi* as well as the Calcutta High Court decision in the case of *Amal Sankar Bhaduri*.[11] The Court held that the NDPS Act admittedly contains certain safeguards and the law reports are replete with case laws pertaining to these safeguards. Dilution of the safeguards as prescribed in the statute has strongly been criticised and negated and the same were ascribed to be strictly mandatory in nature. The issue thus: whether by reason of the respondent being a member of the armed forces would stand denuded of such a safeguard in the event the GCM takes note of an offence under a specific statute. Article 33 of the Constitution though conferred a power but has not been taken recourse to put a bar or restraint as regards the non-availability of the statutory safeguards in terms therewith.

The charge leveled against the respondent was under the NDPS Act. The Court clarified that when a particular statute is taken recourse to, question of trial under another statute without taking recourse to the statutory safeguards would be void and the entire trial would stand vitiated unless, there are existing specific provisions in the particular statute. Needless to record that there were two other civilian accused who were tried by the Court at Patiala but were acquitted of the offence for non-compliance of the mandatory requirements of the NDPS Act.

According to Supreme Court, once the petitioner was put on trial for an offence under the NDPS Act, the GCM and the army authorities cannot state that though the petitioner would be tried for an offence under Section 18 of the NDPS Act, yet the procedural safeguards as contained in the statutory provision would not be applicable to him being a member of the armed forces. The Act applies in its entirety irrespective of the jurisdiction of the GCM or other courts and since the army authorities did not take into consideration the procedural safeguards as is embodied under the Statute, the question of offering any credence to the submissions of Union of India in support of the appeal does not and cannot arise. The Supreme Court did

---

11 *Lt Col Amal Sankar Bhaduri v. Union of India* 1987 CLT 1.

not find any infraction of any law in the judgment of the High Court and thus dismissed the appeal.

Union of India v. Ex Flt Lt GS Bajwa [2003] [12]

Flt Lt Bajwa, the respondent was tried by GCM on the charge of disobeying the lawful command given by his superior officer and also for improper conduct prejudicial to the good order and Air Force discipline. According to the respondent the proceedings before the GCM were conducted illegally and improperly and in breach of law and he was denied legal assistance in the court-martial proceedings even though he was charged of a serious offence which, on proof, entailed a sentence of imprisonment for a term which could extend to 14 years under section 41(2) and 7 years under Section 65 of the Air Force Act. The GCM ultimately found him guilty by its verdict pronounced on 21 June 1983 and imposed the sentence of dismissal from service.

The Delhi High Court placed reliance on the Supreme Court decision in *Suk Das* [13] to support the view that the accused has a Fundamental Right under Article 21 of the Constitution to obtain free legal service at the cost of the State, if he is unable to engage the services of a lawyer on account of poverty or indigence. The High Court on 3 August 1995 allowed the writ petition filed by the respondent and while setting aside the order of dismissal passed by the GCM directed his reinstatement in the same post which he held when he was dismissed.

In Supreme Court, the Additional Solicitor General submitted that the finding recorded by the high court that the failure of the appellant to provide a counsel to the respondent at State expense resulted in breach of the Fundamental Right of the respondent guaranteed under Article 21, was recorded by the high court in ignorance of the provisions of Article 33 of the Constitution which expressly empowers the Parliament to modify the rights conferred by Part III in their application to the members of the armed forces. The high court, therefore, erred in not considering the provisions of the Act, as a law made by Parliament under Article 33 of the Constitution modifying and restricting the right conferred by Article 21 of the Constitution. In a court-martial trial the appellant was not required to provide a counsel at State expense to the respondent, whose rights were governed by the provisions of the Air Force Act and the Rules.

---

12 *Union of India v. Ex Flt Lt GS Bajwa* (2003) 9 SCC 630 : (2003) 3 SCR 1092 decided on 2 May 2003, Two Judge Bench.

13 *Suk Das v. Union Territory of Arunachal Pradesh* AIR 1986 SC 991.

They provided that the appellant may be represented by an officer called "the defending officer" or assisted by any person whose services he may be able to procure who shall be called "the friend of the accused." The respondent was in fact permitted to engage a counsel at his own expense but he failed to do so.

The Supreme Court held, "It is indeed surprising that while considering the submissions urged on behalf of the respondent alleging the breach of his Fundamental Right under Article 21 of the Constitution, the high court neither noticed the provisions of Article 33 nor does it appear to have been brought to its notice. Article 33 expressly empowers the Parliament to determine by law the extent to which any of the rights conferred by Part III of the Constitution, in their application, inter alia, to the members of the armed forces, shall be restricted or abrogated to ensure the proper discharge of their duties and the maintenance of discipline among them. The Parliament can, therefore, in exercise of powers conferred by Article 33 of the Constitution of India restrict or abrogate the Fundamental Rights guaranteed under Part III of the Constitution in their application to the members of the armed forces. It, therefore, follows that if any provision of the Act or the Rules restricts or abrogates any right guaranteed under Part III of the Constitution of India, it cannot be challenged on the ground that it is violative of the Fundamental Right as guaranteed under Part III. It is no doubt true that the restriction or abrogation is dependent on Parliamentary legislation and only a law passed by virtue of Article 33 can override Articles 21 and 22 of the Constitution of India.

The Supreme Court referred to the ruling of Constitutional Bench in *Ram Sarup* and its observations in *PPS Bedi*, ".....every provision of the Army Act enacted by the Parliament, if in conflict with the Fundamental Rights conferred by Part III, shall have to be read subject to Article 33 as being enacted with a view to either restricting or abrogating other Fundamental Rights to the extent of inconsistency or repugnancy between Part III of the Constitution and the Army Act."

The Court also held that its judgement in *Suk Das v. Union Territory of Arunachal Pradesh* (supra) related to free legal service at the cost of the State if the accused was unable to engage the services of a lawyer on account of poverty or indigence. That was not a case dealing with a member of the armed forces governed by a law enacted by Parliament, which restricted or abrogated the right with a view to ensure the proper discharge of duties and the maintenance of discipline among members of the armed forces, and which the Parliament was authorized to enact by virtue of Article 33 of the Constitution. The Supreme Court also did not find any anomaly in the procedural being followed by the GCM and set aside the Delhi High Court order of 3 August 1995.

[**Note**: The Constitution Bench of the Supreme Court in *Chandra Bhawan Boarding and Lodging, Bangalore[14]* has held, "While rights conferred under part III are fundamental, the directives given under part IV are fundamental in the governance of the country. We see no conflict on the whole between the provisions contained in Part III and Part IV. They are complementary and supplementary to each other." It is now fairly settled that the right to legal aid and speedy trial are part of the guarantee of human rights envisaged by Article 21 of the Constitution of India. The failure to provide free legal aid to an accused at the cost of the State unless refused by the accused would vitiate the trial. [15] Further, while upholding the death sentence handed out in the of case of *Mohammed Ajmal Mohammad Amir Kasab* [16] the Supreme Court held, "the right to access to legal aid, to consult and to be defended by a legal practitioner, arises when a person arrested in connection with a cognizable offence is first produced before a magistrate and, in case he has no means to engage a lawyer of his choice, that one would be provided to him from legal aid at the expense of the State. The right flows from Articles 21 and 22(1) of the Constitution and needs to be strictly enforced.]

F. R. Jesuratnam v. Chief of the Air Staff [1976][17]

The appellant, a Squadron Leader in the Indian Air Force (IAF), was placed under close arrest under the Air Force Act on 9 November 1974. He was tried by a GCM which sentenced him to six months rigorous imprisonment on 4 March 1975. The sentence duly concurred under Section 152 of the Act by the Chief of the Air Staff on 8 April 1975 and the petitioner was thereafter sent to jail for serving the sentence. Section 164 of the Act provided, "sentence shall, whether it has been revised or not, be reckoned to commence on the day on which the original proceedings were signed by the presiding officer." The sentence, therefore, commenced to run on 4 March 1975. The petitioner contended that the period of his detention from 9 November 1974 to 4 March 1975 be set off against the sentence

---

14 *Chandra Bhawan Boarding and Lodging, Bangalore v. State of Mysore* AIR 1970 SC 2042.

15 *State of Maharashtra v. Manubhai Pragaji Vashi* 1996 AIR 1: 1995 SCC (5) 730.

16 *Mohammed Ajmal Mohammad Amir Kasab v. State of Maharashtra* (2012) 9 SCC 1.

17 *F. R. Jesuratnam v. Chief of the Air Staff* (1976) Cri LJ 65.

awarded to him. It was stated that the benefit of pre-trial detention, which is given to a civilian by reasons of Section 428 of the Code of Criminal Procedure, 1973 should be applicable to the petitioner.

In 1973 the Criminal Procedure Code (Cr PC) replaced the Act of 1898. A new section 428 stating that the period of detention undergone by the accused to be set off against the sentence of imprisonment was incorporated in it. This provision was made on the recommendations of the Joint Committee of Parliament which was of the view that in many cases an accused person is made to suffer jail life for a period out of proportion to the gravity of offence or to the punishment provided by a statute. This provision allowed setting-off of the period of detention undergone as an under-trial prisoner against the sentence of imprisonment was meant to mitigate suffering of an accused. The Amendment Act of 1978 further amended section 428 with a view to making it clear that it did not apply to imprisonment in default of payment of fine. However, no such amendment was introduced in the three services Acts (i.e. the Army Act, 1950, the Air Force Act, 1950 and the Navy Act, 1957).

There was a divergence of opinion between various High Courts whether the provision of set-off contained in section 428 of the Cr PC was applicable to persons sentenced to undergo imprisonment by a court-martial under the services Acts. The High Courts of Madras (*PP Chandrasekharan v. Union of India* 1977), Delhi (*Sqn Ldr F R Jesuratnam v Chief of the Air Staff*, 1976) and Punjab & Haryana (*RL Sharma v. Union of India* 1975) had taken a view that the benefit of s. 428 of the Cr PC cannot be claimed by persons convicted by court-martial. A single judge of the Kerala HC (*S Subramanian v. Union of India* 1979) and a Division bench of the Calcutta HC (*AS Bhisht v Union of India*, 1986) had taken a contrary view. Finally the Supreme Court in *Ajmer Singh v. Union of India* [1987 SC 1646] resolved the conflict by holding that the three service Acts (Army Act, 1950, Air Force Act, 1950 and the Navy Act 1957) constitute special law conferring special jurisdiction and powers on court martial and prescribing a special form of procedure for trial of offences under these Acts. Section 428 of the Cr PC contains an intrinsic indication that the provision of set-off cannot be claimed by persons convicted and sentenced by court-martial. The reason being that section 5 of the Cr PC renders the provisions of the Code inapplicable in respect of all matters covered by a special law. In *Ajit Kumar v Union of India* 1988, the provision of set-off was reaffirmed by the Supreme Court.

The Supreme Court held that the Air Force Act, 1950, is a special law to which the Criminal Procedure Code, 1973, does not apply by virtue of Section 5 of the Code. The non-extension of the benefit of Section 428 of the Code to sentences under the Air Force Act is not only discriminatory and is also violative of Articles 14 and 21 of the Constitution.

[**Note**: The Army HQ proposed an amendment to the Army Act to incorporate the provision of section 428 of Cr PC. Thus in 1992, through an Amendment Act, section 169A was added in the Army Act. It provided:

> **Period of Custody undergone by the officer or person to be set off against the imprisonment** - When a person or officer subject to this Act is sentenced by a court-martial to a term of imprisonment, not being an imprisonment in default of payment of fine, the period spent by him in civil or military custody during investigation, inquiry or trial of the same case, and before the date of order of such sentence, shall be set off against the term of imprisonment imposed upon him, and the liability of such person or officer to undergo imprisonment on such order of sentence shall be restricted to the remainder, if any, of the term of imprisonment imposed upon him.

The amended section now is in tune with the provisions of Section 428 of the Cr PC. The Navy Act incorporated the provision of set-off through Amendment Act of 2005 [(section 151 (3)].[18]

Opinion of High Courts

The High Courts in India have also dealt with cases referring to Article 33 of the Constitution. In *R Chatterjee*[19] the petitioner had been appointed as a short service commissioned officer from 6 July 1949 to 5 July 1950. He had applied for extension for one more year but had not been given extension. On 1 June 1950, he was arrested on the charge of having absented himself

---

18 In India, there service HQs operate independently. The reason why the provisions of set-off have not yet been introduced in the Air Force Act is perfunctory approach of the officials and their superiors who are expected to take up the amendment with the government. The Chief Justice of India had taken a note of this anomaly in a case in 2013 and had urged the Central Government to amend the law, but nothing has moved since then. He has recently requested the Attorney General to update the law for extending a similar provision to air force personnel. CJI Dipak Misra seeks Attorney General's aid to tweak court-martial laws for IAF, *The Economic Times*, New Delhi, 16 February 2018.

19 *R. Chatterjee v. Sub Area Commander HQ Madras* AIR 1951 Mad 777, (1951) 1 MLJ 258, decided by the Madras High court on 4 January 1951.

from the station for one month without proper authorization. On 22 June 1950 the new Army Act, 1950 came into force. Until then the Indian Army Act, 1911 was in force. The petitioner contended that his detention after 5 July 1950 was illegal since it was in violation of Article 20, 21 and 22 of the Constitution. The Madras High Court held that though Article 33 gave power to Parliament to modify the rights conferred by Part III in their application to the Armed forces, unless Parliament determined to what extent such rights could be modified, the law which stood before the conferment of the fundamental rights (in this case the Indian Army Act of 1911) would apply so far as the armed forces personnel are concerned. The Act of 1911 was modeled upon the English Army Act and in England, it has been held that a commissioned officer cannot at his own sweet will and pleasure resign his appointment. The Court held that the detention of the petitioner for the purpose of bringing him to trial before a court-martial was not illegal.

In *Major C M Sayanakar* [20] the applicant was engaged to a US citizen [Overseas Citizen of India]. Under the Army Order 14/2004-MI dealing with "Marriage with Foreign Nationals" an individual subject to the Army Act is required to obtain prior permission of the higher authorities for marriage with a foreign national. However, his application for permission to marry was rejected by the military authorities because his prospective spouse refused to renounce her US citizenship.[21] His subsequent request for resignation from the military in order to marry her was also turned down by the competent authority.[22]

---

20 *Major C M Sayanakar v. The Chief of the Army Staff* (WP No 289 of 2011), decided by the Bombay High Court on 25 March 2011.

21 The Army Order 14/2004 lays down guidelines and rules/procedure governing marriage of serving service personnel with foreign nationals. Application for such prior sanction is required to be given through proper channels 120 days prior to the proposed date of marriage. Application is to accompany a written undertaking from the foreign national to the effect that she/he will renounce her/his original nationality and accept Indian Citizenship as soon as the Indian Citizenship Act, 1955 permits her/ him to do so, duly countersigned by the Judicial Magistrate or notary or equivalent of the concerned country. Where the Army officer proposes to resign in order to be able to marry a foreign national and submits an application for resignation, the concerned authority will obtain Government sanction in consultation with military intelligence (from security point of view and refund of costs) and process the application as per Government's sanction (paragraph 20 of Army Order read with paragraph 17).

22 Under Rule 16C of Army Rules, 1954, an officer has no right to resign but has only a right to make an application for resignation. The Government of India has laid down Instructions dated 20th January 1979 for seeking premature retirement/resignation of defence service officers, which provide that such request is to be granted only

The petitioner placed reliance on Article 16.1 of the Universal Declaration of Human Rights (UDHR), Article 23(2) of the International Covenant on Civil and Political Rights, 1966 (ICCPR) and Article 33 of the Constitution. Article 16 (1) of the UDHR states: "Men and women of full age, without any limitation due to race, nationality or religion, have the right to marry and to found a family." Further, Article 23(2) of the ICCPR provides that the right of men and women of marriageable age to marry and to found a family shall be recognized. The petitioner claimed that the restrictions imposed by Section 21 of the Army Act, 1950 and Rules 19 to 21 of the Army Rules, 1954 are only in respect of certain fundamental rules (right to form associations, right to participate in political or non-military activities, right to communicate to press or publish), but there is no restriction on the rights of the petitioners to life and liberty under Article 21 of the Constitution. The Mumbai High Court, though did not referred to Article 33 of the Constitution in its decision, but directed the government to accepting application for resignation from the applicant with effect from the date of marriage with foreign national subject to proof of the marriage being furnished.

The Jammu & Kashmir High Court in the case of *Vinayak Daulatrao Nalawade* [23] has taken the view that non-compliance of Army Rule 180 in a court of inquiry would be fatal. The Court pointed out that in accordance with Article 33 of the Constitution the army personnel have been provided with a special procedure under the Army Act and the Rules. The vires of these Act and Rules are not challengeable because of Article 33 of the Constitution. However, further derogation in the rights of army personnel would be violative of Articles 21 and 14 of the Constitution.

The Madhya Pradesh High Court in the case of *Lt Col Jitendra Singh Sahi* commented: "Compared with civil servants the members of defence services suffer disadvantage in fully defending themselves, as they have less constitutional protection of fairer procedure against disciplinary action because of the provisions contained in Article 33 of the Constitution of India." Further, "The members of the defence services, subject to the Army Act have only statutory protection under the Act and the Rules.

---

on the following grounds: (a) Supersession; (b) Extreme compassionate grounds; (c) Low medical category; and (d) Failure to acquire technical qualifications. Since the application of petitioner for resignation does not fall under any of the aforesaid categories, his request was rejected.

23 *Vinayak Daulatrao Nalawade v. Corps Commander, 15 Corps* (an unreported judgment in WP No. 490 of 1985, decided on 5 May 1986).

Even outside the provisions of the Act and the Rules, they cannot bring to aid principles of natural justice."[24]

Rajasthan High Court in *Roop Singh* [25] considered seven petitions against trial by summary court-martial. The Court held: "having regard to the constitutional mandate of Article 33 as explained by the Supreme Court in *Ram Sarup* (1965) and *Lt Col PPS Bedi* (1982), the grievance as to the provisions relating to a summary court-martial being discriminatory and therefore violative of Article 14 cannot be entertained." The High Court further held, "…. having gone through various provisions of the Act and the Rules with respect to the trial of offences by summary court-martial we are firmly of the view that provisions are not discriminatory and they do not infringe Article 14 of the Constitution. The Army Act and Rules in our opinion, contain sufficient safeguards and the offender need have no apprehension about any arbitrary decision at the hands of officers constituting the summary court-martial." However, the Rajasthan High Court was wrong in referring *Ram Sarup case*, because the petitions under consideration related to trial under summary court-martial, where in *Ram Sarup*, the accused was tried by General Court Martial where procedure similar to a trial under Cr PC is followed.

The Calcutta High Court in *Lt Col Amal Sankar Bhaduri* [26] considered an interesting question as regards the jurisdiction of the Writ Court in matters of court-martial in general. The Court held that while it is true that army personnel ought to be subjected to strictest form of discipline and Article 33 of the Constitution has conferred powers on to the Parliament to abridge the rights conferred under Part III of the Constitution in respect

---

24 *Lt Col Jitendra Singh Sahi v. Union of India* [1993 (O) MPLJ 951, decided on 17 December 1992]. In this case, the MP High Court considered the competence of the Chief of the Army Staff, to take recourse to the procedure of termination of services under Rule 14 of the Rules, when the court martial for the alleged misconduct amounting to offence, was barred by limitation. The Court was of the opinion that provisions of the Army Act have to be construed strictly and any interpretation which takes away or curtails substantially the right of effective opportunity of defence to an Army Officer should not be readily accepted unless the provision of law by its language plainly warrants the same. The word 'impracticable' used in Army Rule 14, has therefore, to be given a legal meaning to understand it as conveying that 'which is possible but not practicable' and not 'which is impossible to accomplish'. In the present case the court martial was barred by law of limitation and it was impossible to hold it.

25 *Roop Singh v. Union of India* CWP No. 2490 of 1987, Rajasthan High Court, decided on 31 August 2006 [Two Judge Bench].

26 *Lt Col Amal Sankar Bhaduri v. Union of India*, (1987) Cal LT 1 (HC), 91 CWN 631,decided on 24 December 1985, Kolkata High Court.

of the members of the Armed Forces, but does that mean and imply that the army personnel would be denuded of the Constitutional privileges as guaranteed under the Constitution. Can it be said that the army personnel form a class of citizens not entitled to the Constitution's benefits and are outside the purview of the Constitution. To answer above in the affirmative in my view, would be a violent departure to the wishes of the framers of our Constitution. Army personnel are as much citizen as any other individual citizen of this country. At this juncture it would be worthwhile to refer to Article 33 of the Constitution. Article 33 has been engrafted in the Constitution to enable the Parliament by law to restrict the rights as contained in Part III of the Constitution. The extent of restrictions necessary to be imposed on any of the fundamental rights in their application to the armed forces and the forces charged with the maintenance of public order for the purpose of ensuring proper discharge of their duties and maintenance of discipline among them would necessarily depend upon the prevailing situation at a given point of time and it would be inadvisable to encase it in a rigid statutory formula.

The Delhi High Court while deciding the case of *Lance Naik V.P. Singh* has held:

> Mindful of the fact that Article 33 of the Constitution of India confers unbridled powers on Parliament to bring into place a situation which severely abridges the Fundamental Rights of a citizen it becomes bounden duty of the Courts to ensure that the equality doctrine is not needlessly nullified. It also becomes essential that the Courts should interpret the law in a manner which will reduce to the minimum the inroads into the infrangible rights contained in Chapter III of the Constitution......A Summary Court-Martial (SCM) must be an exception and not the rule. It can only be convened where the exigencies demand an immediate and swift decision without which the situation will indubitably be exacerbated with widespread ramifications....The decision to convene an SCM must be preceded by a reasoned order which itself will be amenable to judicial review.[27]

Analysis of Article 33

The Supreme Court in *Ram Sarup* relied on the submission made by the Attorney General that, "the entire [Army] Act has been enacted by Parliament and if any of the provisions of the Act is not consistent with the

---

27 *Lance Naik V.P. Singh v. Union of India,* (2008) WP (C) 2511/1992 decided on 25 January 2008, along with six other petitions.

provisions of any of the articles in Part III of the Constitution, it must be taken that to the extent of the inconsistency Parliament had modified the fundamental rights under those articles in their application to the person subject to that Act. Any such provision in the Act is as much law as the entire Act." The Supreme Court agreed with the submission made by the Attorney General and commented, "We agree that each and every provision of the Act is a law made by Parliament and that if any such provision tends to affect the fundamental rights under Part III of the Constitution, that provision does not, on that account, become void, as it must be taken that Parliament has thereby, in the exercise of its power under Article 33 of the Constitution, made the requisite modification to affect the respective fundamental right."

In *Ram Sarup*, the accused was a sepoy in the Defence Security Corps, and was arraigned on serious charge of murder of three military persons. He was tried by general court-martial and sentenced to the death. He was denied the right to engage a civilian counsel for his defence. In every criminal justice system an accused is given an opportunity to make his defecne before he is condemned. The Supreme Court was satisfied with the affidavit by the military authorities that the accused had made no such grievance during the trial. The Supreme Court in its judgment in *Ram Sarup* has not made any reference to two qualifications expressly provided in Article 33. The Constitution permits encroachments on fundamental rights in their application to the members of the armed forces only in so far as such restriction or abrogation is necessary for the 'maintenance of discipline' or the 'proper discharge of duties by them'. This was perhaps the first occasion where the Supreme Court went wrong in relying the submission of Attorney General. The Court followed an incorrect approach as placing complete ban on the judicial review of court-martial or actions of the military authorities allowing absolute and arbitrary power to the government on the rights of the members of the armed forces.

In *Viswan* case the Supreme Court held, "The guideline for determining as to which restrictions should be considered necessary by the Central Government within the permissible extent determined by Parliament is provided in Article 33 itself, namely, that the restrictions should be such as are necessary for ensuring the proper discharge of their duties by the members of the Armed Forces and the maintenance of discipline among them. The Central Government has to keep this guideline before it in exercising the power of imposing restrictions under Section 21 though, it may be pointed out that once the Central Government has imposed restrictions in exercise of this power, the court will not ordinarily interfere with the decision of the Central Government that such restrictions are necessary because that is a matter left by Parliament exclusively to the Central Government which is best in a position to know what the situation demands." The Court held that the power of the Central Government to restrict or abrogate fundamental rights is unanalysed and unrestricted, permitting violations of the constitutional limitations. Article 33 carves out an exception in so far as the applicability of Fundamental Rights to members of the Armed Forces are concerned. It is elementary that a highly disciplined and efficient armed force is absolutely essential for the defence of the country."

The Supreme Court has always been guided by the Latin maxim *boni judicis est ampliare jurisdictiomen,* that law must keep pace with society to retain its relevance, for if society moves but the law remains static, it would be bad for both. It has zealously protected the human rights of individuals and has interpreted Article 21 of the Constitution liberally and given it more content, meaning and purpose. It has evolved contemporary jurisprudence and implemented international conventions and treaties. The judicial fraternity has added new dimensions to various statutory provisions by the liberal interpretation of the statute, or by evolving principles of justice, equity and good conscience. In the case of *Charanjit Singh Gill*, the Supreme Court has held: "Even today the law relating to the armed forces remains static which requires to be changed keeping in view the observations made by the Supreme Court in *Prithi Pal Singh Bedi* case, the constitutional mandate and the changes effected by other democratic countries. The time has come to allay the apprehension of all concerned that the system of trial by court-martial is not the archetype of summary and arbitrary proceedings. In the absence of effective steps taken by Parliament and the Central Government, it is the constitutional obligation of the courts in the country to protect and safeguard the constitutional rights of all citizens including those enrolled in the armed forces to the extent permissible under law by not forgetting the paramount need of maintaining the discipline in the armed forces of the country."[28]

In interpreting Constitution, the Supreme Court is not bound to accept an interpretation which retards the progress and impedes social integration; it adopts such interpretation which would bring about the ideas set down in the Preamble aided by Part III and IV of the Constitution.[29] Interpretation

28 *Union of India v. Charanjit Singh Gill* (2000) 5 SCC 742.

29 *Ashok Kumar Gupta v. State of UP* (1997) 5 SCC 201.

of the flexible provisions of the Constitution can be accompanied by dynamism and lean; in case of conflict, in favour of the weaker or the one who is needier. Therefore, a purposive rather a strict literal approach to interpretation should be adopted. A constitutional provision must be construed not in a narrow and constricted sense but in a wide and liberal manner so as to anticipate and take account of changing conditions and purposes so that a constitutional provision does not get fossilized but remains flexible enough to meet the emerging problems and challenges. This principle of interpretation is particularly apposite to the interpretation of fundamental rights. A constitution, and in particular that of it which protects and which entrenches fundamental rights and freedoms to which all persons in the state are to be entitled is to be given a generous and purposive construction. The content of a right is defined by the court. Parliament while enacting a law does not provide content to the right. The final word on the content of the right is Supreme Court. [30] The Constitution is a living document. Constitutional provisions have to be construed having regard to the march of time and the development of law.[31]

Justice Bhagwati in the case of *State of Rajasthan v Union of India*[32], observed that the Supreme Court is the 'ultimate interpreter' of the Constitution: "It is for this court to uphold the constitutional values and to enforce the constitutional limitations. That is the essence of the rule of law." In the case of *Pathumma v State of Kerala* [33], the Supreme Court stated; "This Court while acting as a sentinel on the *qui vive* to protect the fundamental rights guaranteed to the citizens of the country must try to strike a just balanced between the fundamental rights and the larger and broader interests of the society". *In Maneka Gandhi* [34] the court observed, "The attempt of the court should be to expend the reach and ambit of the fundamental rights, rather than to attenuate their meaning and content by a process of judicial construction." As the interpreter of the fundamental rights enshrined in the Constitution, the Supreme Court has interpreted these provisions in a liberal manner. The Supreme Court has in the case *Ajay Hasia v. Khalid Mujib Sehravardi* declared that it has a special responsibility, "to enlarge the range and meaning of the fundamental

---

30 *M Nagraj v. Union of India* (2006) 8 SCC 212.

31 *I R Caelho v. State of Tamil Nadu* (2007) 2 SCC 1.

32 *State of Rajasthan v Union of India* AIR 1977 SC 1361.

33 *Pathumma v State of Kerala* AIR 1978 SC 771.

34 *Maneka Gandhi v. Union of India* AIR 1978 SC 597.

rights and to advance the human rights jurisprudence."[35] However, when it comes to the fundamental rights or human rights of military personnel, the interpretation of the Constitutional provision by the Supreme Court has been very narrow.

Conclusion

The Constitution should be so interpreted so to afford all Fundamental Rights to the members of the armed forces except those which by their nature are inapplicable. The list of inapplicable rights may be shortened as the society advances and the horizon of human rights expands. May be in time to come, the members of the armed forces be allowed to form trade unions or associations, with the limitation that they will not have the right to go on strike. The Indian soldier is perhaps the most neglected person today. The judiciary fails to understand the difficult circumstances under which he has to use lethal force; political leaders fails to appreciate his work in protecting the nation and pay lip service in times of crisis.

---

35 *Ajay Hasia v. Khalid Mujib Sehravardi* AIR 1981 SC 487.

Chapter – V

Constitutional Restrictions on the Fundamental Rights : Examples from Democratic States

Introduction

The functions of a constitution, according to Bulmer (2017),[1] are: (i) to declare and define the boundaries (territorial and personal) of the political community; (ii) to declare and define the nature and authority of the political community; (iii) to express the identity and values of a national community; (iv) to declare and define the rights and duties of citizens; (v) to establish and regulate the political institutions of the community; (vi) toshare power between different layers of government; and (vi) to commit states to particular social, economic or developmental goals. The vast majority of contemporary constitutions describe the basic principles of the state, the structures and processes of government, accountability mechanism and the fundamental rights and duties of citizens[2] that cannot

---

1 Bulmer Elliot, 2017, *What is a Constitution? Principles and Concepts*, International Institute for Democracy and Electoral Assistance (International IDEA), Sweden. Available   at: https://www.idea.int/sites/default/files/publications/what-is-a-constitution-primer.pdf.

2 Most constitutions include a declaration of fundamental rights applicable to citizens. At a minimum, these will include the basic civil liberties that are necessary for a democratic society (e.g. the freedoms of thought, speech, association and assembly; due process of law and freedom from arbitrary arrest or unlawful punishment). Many constitutions go beyond this minimum to include social, economic and cultural rights or the specific collective rights of minority communities. Further, some rights may apply to both citizens and non-citizens, such as the right to be free from torture or physical abuse.

106

be unilaterally changed by an ordinary legislative act. The armed forces are legitimate institutions created under the constitutions in nearly every country. They are to safeguard the national boundaries against external aggression and maintain its integrity and sovereignty. The use of force by the armed forces must be in support of the constitutional mandate. In conditions of extreme disorder, the constitution may give emergency powers to the armed forces and have provisions to indemnify them for their legitimate acts during emergent situations.[3] The constitution may deal with the prerequisites for engaging in armed conflict and specific powers or duties during a state of emergency. Many constitutions restrict the rights and freedoms, which are available to other citizens in the country.

In this chapter the constitution of few states has been analyzed to ascertain the way it restricts fundamental rights and freedoms of the members of the armed forces.

Australia

The Australian Constitution[4] has been described as 'the birth certificate of

---

3   There is no express provision in the Indian Constitution for the declaration of martial law. Article 355 of the Constitution places a duty upon the Government of India to protect every state not only from external aggression but also from internal disorder. The power to legislate with regard to martial law falls within Entry I, List I, which provides for the defence of the whole or part of the territory of India. However, it is implicit in the text of Article 34 that the government may declare martial law within the territory of India. Article 34 provides that Parliament may be law indemnify any person.... in respect of any act done by him in connection with the maintenance or restoration of order in any area within the territory of India where martial law was in force or validate any sentence passed, punishment inflicted under martial law.

4   The Australian Constitution was drafted at a series of conventions held during the 1890s and attended by representatives of the colonies. Before the Constitution came into effect, its terms were approved, with one small exception, by the people of New South Wales, Victoria, Queensland, Western Australia, South Australia, and Tasmania. The Australian Constitution was then passed as part of a British Act of Parliament in 1900, and took effect on 1 January 1901. A British Act was necessary because before 1901 Australia was a collection of six self-governing British colonies and ultimate power over those colonies rested with the British Parliament. In reality, however, the Constitution is a document which was conceived by Australians, drafted by Australians and approved by Australians. Since that time, Australia has become an independent nation, and the character of the Constitution as the fundamental law of Australia is now seen as resting predominantly, not on its status as an Act of the British Parliament, which no longer has any power over Australia, but on the Australian people's decision to approve and be bound by the terms of the Constitution. What has been judicially described as 'the sovereignty of the Australian people' is also recognized by section 128 which provides that any change to the Constitution must be approved by the people

a nation'. It also provides the basic rules for the government of Australia. The Australian Constitution is the fundamental law binding everybody including the Commonwealth Parliament and the Parliament of each State. Accordingly, even an Act passed by a Parliament is invalid if it is contrary to the Constitution. The legislative powers of the Parliament are contained in Article 51 of the Australian Constitution. It provides that the Parliament shall have power to make laws for the peace, order, and good government of the Commonwealth with respect to the naval and military defence of the Commonwealth and of the several States, and the control of the forces to execute and maintain the laws of the Commonwealth.[5] The executive power of the Commonwealth is vested in the Queen and is exercisable by the Governor-General as the Queen's representative, and extends to the execution and maintenance of this Constitution, and of the laws of the Commonwealth.[6]

Freedom of association is not expressly protected in the Australian Constitution. There is also no free-standing right to association implied in the Constitution. Generally, Australian Parliaments may make laws that encroach on freedom of association. In practice, Australians are generally free to associate with whomever they like, and to assemble to participate in activities including, for example, a protest or demonstration. However, freedom of association and assembly are less often discussed, and their scope at common law less clear than related freedoms, such as freedom of speech.[7]

The Australian system of government presupposes that defence personnel,[8] when carrying out their official duties, are politically neutral and obedient to lawful direction from the government of the day, whatever

---

of Australia.

5   Article 51(vi) of the Australian Constitution.

6   Article 61 of the Australian Constitution.

7   The commander of Australian forces in Afghanistan in 2010, General Cantwell was quoted in the newspaper of 17 April 2012. He said: 'at the human level [operations in Afghanistan] were not worth it'. Rejecting 'the dirty ugly world of international relationships, where 'it's you scratch my back, I'll scratch yours ... [where] lives become less important', the General said it was wrong to forfeit the life of any soldier for ill-conceived political purpose. Michelle Grattan, 'Most Troops Home by Next Year's End', *The Age*, 17 April 2012, Melbourne edition, p. 4.

8   The term 'defence personnel means all defence employees, defence members and External Service Providers. Defencemembermeans a member of the Permanent Navy, the Regular Army, the Regular Army Supplement or the Permanent Air Force, or a Reserve member who is rendering continuous full-time service.

its political complexion. This does not mean that defence personnel are precluded from engaging in political activities,[9] as it is recognised that they have a right, as citizens, to participate in the political life of Australia. At the same time, so that the political neutrality of defence is not in doubt, certain restrictions have been imposed on defence personnel concerning their participation in political activities.

In participating in any political activity, the ability of defence personnel to properly serve the government of the day, whatever political party is in office, must not be called into question. The defence personnel may: (a) join a political party or organisation and take an active part in its affairs provided they do not identify any part of defence with any political activity; (b) attend political meetings provided they do not identify any part of defence with any political activity; (c) write letters to newspapers expressing their personal views about public issues, subject to compliance with the provisions of certain document[10] and provided they do not identify any part of Defence with any political activity; and (d) express their personal opinions on a political party, candidate or an issue, but not as defence personnel. Where defence personnel do engage in such political activities, they must avoid giving the impression that such activities are being undertaken in other than a private capacity.

As regards participation in local government, the defence members must not, without the permission of the appropriate Service Chief or the Service Chief's delegate, be nominated for election to a local government body or accept office in a local government body. In giving permission, the Service Chief may consider it appropriate that the defence member transfers to the appropriate Reserve, is discharged, or has their full-time duty terminated. Similarly, the defence employees and External Service Providers must not, without the permission of a three-star level defence employee or their authorised delegate or a three-star level Defence member or their authorised delegate, be nominated for election to a local government body or accept office in a local government body. Where Defence personnel are permitted to accept office in a local government body, they are subject to the instructions and restrictions applicable to Defence personnel taking part in political activities.

---

9   Political activity means all activity carried out for, and on behalf of, or in connection with: (1)elections to any State or Federal Parliament, Territory Legislature or Local Government body; (2)any political party; or (3)any group or organisation seeking to gain political advantage. Voting is not considered a political activity.

10 DI(G) ADMIN 08–1—Public comment and dissemination of information by DefenceMembers.

Article 44 of the Australian Constitution restricts who can be a Federal parliamentary candidate. Specifically, it provides that any person who holds any office of profit under the Crown shall be incapable of being chosen or of sitting as a senator or as a member of the House of Representatives. However, it further provides that this restriction does not apply to officers or members of the naval or military forces of the Commonwealth whose services are not wholly employed by the Commonwealth. Therefore, defence personnel cannot be candidates if they hold any office of profit at the time of their nomination to the Divisional Returning Officer (for the House of Representatives) (DRO), or the Australian Electoral Officer (for the Senate) (AEO), of the Australian Electoral Commission. Similar limitations apply in most States and Territories. The defence members may resign, elect to be discharged, or transfer to the appropriate inactive Reserve in order to become a candidate for election. A current member of the Reserve Forces may become a parliamentary candidate provided they cease any continuous full-time or part-time service in which they are engaged.

In order to ensure that the political activities of the defence employees remain compatible with their public service obligations and that defence's impartiality in political matters is preserved, certain restrictions apply to the defence employees and External Service Providers. The Defence employees and External Service Providers must not take part in activities of a political nature on Defence premises, for the purposes of furthering the interests of a political party or a person's candidature for election to political office. This prohibition does not extend to the use on polling days of an area which may be set aside as a polling place in accordance with section 80 of the Commonwealth Electoral Act 1918. Further, the defence employees and External Service Providers must not, in any activity of a political nature: (a) use, without the approval of a three-star level Defence employee or their authorised delegate or a three-star level Defence member or their authorised delegate, any information gained by or conveyed to them through their connection with Defence; (b) Allow such activity to interfere with the functioning of Defence in the performance of its roles, or prejudice performance of their duties as Defence employees or External Service Providers; (c)speak in public, or publish or have published, any book, article, letter or other material (electronically or otherwise) unless in accordance with instructions contained in DI(G) ADMIN 08–1; (d) engage in conduct in such a manner as to identify Defence with a political activity; and (e) use any Defence property or facilities except in accordance with instructions contained in DI(G) PERS 01–1. The defence employees and External Service Providers must not take a leading or publicly prominent part in the affairs of a political organisation or party where such would identify any part of the defence with a political activity and/or impair their ability to adequately fulfil their obligations to the defence.

In order to be able to contest an election for Federal parliament, the defence employees must resign before the date of their nomination.[11] A defence employee who resigns to contest an election is entitled to be re-engaged as a defence employee under section 32 of the Public Service Act 1999, provided that the resignation took effect not earlier than six-months before the closing date for nominations and the defence employee was a candidate in the election but failed to be elected.

In order to ensure that the political activities of the defence members remain compatible with their service position and thereby preserve the defence's impartiality in political matters, the following restrictions apply: (a) The defence members must not take part in political activities in Service establishments or on board Navy ships, for the purposes of furthering the interests of any political party or any person's candidature for election to political office. The defence members must not, in any activity of a political nature: (a) use their rank when identifying, describing, or referring to themselves; (b) wear their uniform; (c) wear party ribbons or emblems or other political badges while on duty or in uniform; (d) use, without the consent of a three-star level Defence member or their authorised delegate or a three-star level defence employee or their authorised delegate any information gained by or conveyed to them through their connection with Defence; (e) allow such activity to interfere with the functioning of the defence in the performance of its roles, or prejudice performance of their duties as defence members; (f) speak in public, or publish or have published, any book, article, letter or other material (electronically or otherwise) unless in accordance with DI(G) ADMIN 08–1; (g) engage in conduct in such a manner as to identify Defence with a political activity; and (i) use any defence property or facilities except in accordance with DI(G) PERS 01–1. The defence members on continuous full-time duty must not take a leading or publicly prominent part in the affairs of a political organisation or party where such would identify any part of defence with a political activity and/or impair their ability to adequately fulfil their obligations to

---

11 The defence employee must have resigned in writing clearly stating that the reason for their resignation was for the purposes of contesting an election. The defence employee's manager must forward the defence employee's resignation letter to the appropriate personnel section for inclusion on the Defence employee's personal file. Defence Instructions (General), Political Activities of Defence Personnel, the Department of Defence, Canberra Act 2600, 4 October 2007, para 23.

Defence.[12]

The Defence Force Discipline Act of 1982 provides certain specific offences like the disobeying a lawful command,[13] failing to comply with a general order,[14] negligence in performance of a duty,[15] unauthorized disclosure of information,[16] and prejudicial conduct meaning an act that is likely to prejudice the discipline of, or bring discredit on the Defence Force.[17] A recent statutory burden of the freedom of the speech is encompassed within Australia's revised terrorism laws. Section 35P(2) of the National Security Legislation Amendment Act of 2014 (NSAA) makes it a criminal offence punishable for up to 10 years imprisonment, if a person discloses information relating to special intelligence operations.[18] However, the phrase 'special intelligence operations' contained in the NSAA is loosely defined. It could have an extensive meaning that may impede upon people's ability to inform the public about governmental affairs.[19]

Belgium

Belgium is a Parliamentary Monarchy. Under the Belgian Constitution, the King commands the armed forces.[20] A founding member of the North Atlantic Treaty Organization (NATO), Belgium has consistently supported the alliance with manpower and financial contributions. Although the king is technically commander in chief of the armed forces, they are under the operational authority of the Ministry of National Defence and a joint ministerial committee composed of the ministers of national defence; foreign affairs; the interior and public office; justice and institutional

---

12 Defence Instructions (General), Political Activities of Defence Personnel, the Department of Defence, Canberra Act 2600, 4 October 2007.

13 Section 27, the Defence Force Discipline Act, 1982.

14 Section 29, the Defence Force Discipline Act, 1982.

15 Section 35, the Defence Force Discipline Act, 1982.

16 Section 58, the Defence Force Discipline Act, 1982.

17 Section 60, the Defence Force Discipline Act, 1982.

18 *National Security Legislation Amendment Act (No1) 2014* (Cth) section 35P(2)(ii).

19 Australia has a narrow and fragile right to free expression, which is limited to political matters. This freedom in its present form is insufficient to protect and facilitate the requisite transparency and accountability in Australia's public institutions. Buckingham Jake, Current trends surrounding the constitutional freedom of political communication, *Bond University Student Law Review*: Vol. 4, Issue 1/2, 2016, pp. 1-12.

20 Article 167, the Belgian Constitution.

reform; and communications posts, telephones, and telegraphs. This committee collectively oversees the three conventional military services—the army, navy, and air force—as well as the *gendarmerie*. [21] The Ministry of National Defence and the General Staff provide centralized logistic support, major policy direction and planning, and the allocation of tasks among the services, which nevertheless train separately and retain distinct individuality. Approximately two-thirds of the armed forces are a volunteer or career military personnel.

In 2004, new Legislation on military recruitment and selection became operative in Belgium. One of the objectives of this legislation was to enlarge the applicant population. Accordingly minimum age for induction in the armed forces was raised from 31 years to 34 years. The new legislation dictates that military service is no longer a privilege of Belgian citizenship, but as from 2004 EU-citizens are also admitted to the Belgian Armed Forces.

Belgium follows the French tradition of considering the armed forces as *"la Grande Muette"*, meaning the armed forces obey the orders of politicians and have no political role to play. Armed forces are seen as public service.

According to Article 14 of the Disciplinary Regulation of the Armed Forces (RDF) of 1975, the members of the armed forces enjoy all basic rights as other citizens of Belgium. However, some of these rights have been regulated by the Parliamentary Act. The members of the armed forces may join any political party they choose and enjoy the rights associated with the membership. They are not permitted to participate in any political activities. They only function that they are allowed to exercise within the political party are those of expert, council, or members of a research centre. Any other activity or public participation in political activities is prohibited even outside the duty hours. While engaging in political activities, the members of the armed forces must abstain from wearing a

---

21 The gendarmerie is one of the armed forces of Belgium but is not part of the army. Apart from having a general headquarters and a training school, it is organized into territorial groups, mobile groups, and criminal investigation detachments. Its main functions are the investigation of crimes, the escorting of prisoners, preventive police work, the restoration and maintenance of public order, the enforcement of traffic laws, and military police duties. The gendarmerie is under the command of the Ministry of National Defense, but its officers are also answerable to the Ministry of the Interior and Public Office for the enforcement of certain laws and for public order matters. They are also answerable to the Ministry of Justice and Institutional Reform for criminal and investigative matters.

military uniform and from giving publicity to their military status.[22]

The members of the armed forces are permitted to join a professional military trade union or a trade union affiliated to a union represented at the National Work Council. A detailed regulation exists on the control and approval of the trade unions considered as representative, as well as on the different consultation procedure. Belgian laws forbid the members of the armed forces to go on strike.[23] According to Article 9 of the RDF, members of the armed forces must at all times: accomplish all service duties which the Constitution, the law, the regulations, instructions, and orders applicable to the armed forces places on them; show respect to the Head of the State, the constitutional powers and the institution of the State; avoid compromising the honour or the dignity of their status and their function; and avoid any activity which contradicts the Constitution and the laws of the Belgian people. The members of the armed forces are not to reveal any information classified as secret or confidential, even after their term of service has ended.[24] Any breach of the rights and duties of a member of the armed forces is a disciplinary offence.

The armed forces adhere to the national criminal code but have an additional list of purely military offences, such as absence without leave, desertion, sleeping on guard duty, misuse of weapons and equipment, and breaches of military discipline. Belgium has no separate military justice system. It has been abrogated in 2003.

Denmark

The general freedom of association is documented in the Danish Constitution since 1849. The freedom of assembly is separated from the freedom of association in the Constitution, as is the freedom of speech.[25]

---

22 Article 15, the Disciplinary Regulation of the Armed Forces (RDF), 14 January 1975.

23 Article 16, the Disciplinary Regulation of the Armed Forces (RDF), 14 January 1975.

24 Argent Pierre d', 'Military Law in Belgium', in Nolte George (ed.), 2003, *European Military Law Systems*, Berlin: De Gruyter Recht, pp. 183-232.

25 In practice, the freedom of association of trade unions was first secured through the conclusion of the so-called September Compromise in 1899 (also referred to as the Danish Labour Market Constitution). This 'constitution' determines the rules of the regulation of the labour market by the labour market organisations and is still in force. It was revised in 1960 under the name of the Basic Agreement. The freedom of trade union association was settled together with the managerial prerogative; the employers' right to manage and divide the work including the right to hire the at any time necessary labour force. Jorgensen, Carsten, Freedom of association of trade unions in Denmark, May 2004, available at: https://faos.ku.dk/pdf/forskningsnotater/

The general freedom of association in relation to the state is recognized in general in Article 78 of the Constitution. It states that all able citizens have the constitutional right to form organizations as desired. All Danish employees are eligible for membership of a trade union; including the police and armed forces, and other statutory civil servants. The right to strike is encompassed by collective law, which means that the unions and not the workers have the right to strike. Unlawful strikes in a Danish context are defined as breaches on the peace obligation according to the collective agreement.[26]

Denmark is a nation of organizations and associations. In Denmark, the military association is a trade union and has had a long track record of successfully bargaining on behalf of its members.[27] The head of the association has direct access to the Minister of Defence in order to be able to lobby on behalf of association members. The association is responsible for acting reasonably in line with all of the freedoms and responsibilities it has been empowered with. For example, its collective bargaining does not interfere with active operations. There is a relationship of mutual trust between the association and the armed forces in Denmark. If it were to abuse its freedoms and status, the union would risk losing its communication line with the military leadership. In Denmark, trade unions contribute positively to military efficiency.[28]In Denmark, the government has issued guidelines on permissible speech and modes of communication, as well as personal use of social media.

France

France has strong military traditions. The link between the French nation

---

forskningsnotater_2004/fnotat52.pdf.

26 Jorgensen, Carsten, Freedom of association of trade unions in Denmark, May 2004, available at: https://faos.ku.dk/pdf/forskningsnotater/forskningsnotater_2004/fnotat52. pdf.

27 Three military trade unions are of significance in the Danish armed forces. Together they organize all military personnel. Their division is based on education, rather than rank and service. The HOD represents all commissioned officers of the three service; CS organizes the non-commissioned officers and all regulars except the army; and the HKKF has about 4.300 members from the regular army. Sorensen Henning, Danish military trade unions nad their political role, in Bartle Richard and Lindy Heinecken (ed.), 2006, *Military Unionism in the Post-Cold War Era: A future reality?* London: Routledge, pp. 197-211.

28 Sorensen Henning, Danish military trade unions nad their political role, in Bartle Richard and Lindy Heinecken (ed.), 2006, *Military Unionism in the Post-Cold War Era: A future reality?* London: Routledge, p. 210.

and its armed forces has traditionally been very close at least since the French Revolution. Article 12 of the Declaration of 1789 states that: The guarantee of the rights of humans and citizen requires a public force: this force is therefore established for the advantage of all, and for the particular ability of those to whom it attributed." Further, according to the Constitution from 1848, "The public force is, in essence, obedient; no armed corps may be deliberate." The principle of subordination of the army to the civilian authorities was considered to be fundamental. Restrictions of the right of political expression of the soldiers in the field have been accepted as necessary. The armed forces are meant to exercise their profession without discussion.[29] The French Constitution from 1958 does not deal with the role of the armed forces either in terms of democratic legitimacy or in terms of soldier's rights.

The statutory position of soldiers in France is qualified as "*cantonnementjuridique*", meaning legal containment. This means that soldiers serve as volunteers and agree to be submitted to special duties and service obligations which come with their status. Article 1 of the General Statute of the Military (Statute of 13 July 1972 – SGM), provides, "Military status requires under all circumstances discipline, loyalty, and a spirit of sacrifice. The duties which it involves and the submissions which it implies deserve the respect of the citizens and the consideration of the nation." The article further states that the soldiers' rights and freedom may be restricted by law. According to Article 6 of SGM, soldiers enjoy all the rights and liberties granted to citizens, but the same article adds: "the exercise of some of them is either forbidden or restrained under the conditions of this law".[30] Soldiers in active service are not allowed to enrol in political parties, or in any association of political character (Article 9- SGM). In addition, Article 10 of the General Regulation on Discipline in the Armed Forces (RDGA) adds a general duty of the military not to compromise the neutrality of the armed forces in philosophical, religious, political and trade union activities. The military personnel under Article 10(3) of RDGA are also forbidden to organize or participate in demonstrations and propaganda in the above fields. However, military personnel may attend

---

29 The French soldiers are, therefore, commonly known in French as "*la grandemuette*". Gerkrath Jorg, Military Law in France, in Nolte George (ed.), 2003, *European Military Law Systems*, Berlin: De Gruyter Recht, p. 278.

30 There has not been any significant public discussion or criticism as regard to the restrictions on soldiers' rights. The only issue which seems to raise discussion is the soldiers' right to free expression. GerkrathJorg, Military Law in France, in Nolte George (ed.), 2003, *European Military Law Systems*, Berlin: De Gruyter Recht, p. 302.

a political meeting in civil dress and their military status is not disclosed.

Article 7 of SGM guarantees the freedom of opinion and belief to a soldier. However, opinion and beliefs may be expressed only when off-duty. After due authorization from the authorities, a soldier may express himself in public on political questions [Article 7(2) SGM].

In France, the right to association for the soldiers is strictly limited. Article 10 of SGM prohibits the exercise of "professional groupings with trade union character", and considers membership of such unions as being incompatible with military discipline. In two recent cases of October 2014, the European Court of Human Rights (ECtHR) lifted the French blanket ban on military trade unions.[31] The Court considered the French ban a violation of Article 11 of the European Convention on Human Rights (ECHR), which established the right to form trade unions as a specific aspect of freedom of association. Previously, the ECtHR has held that under Article 11, restrictions, even significant ones, could be imposed on the forms of action and expression of an occupational association and of the military personnel who joined it, provided that such restrictions did not deprive them of the general right of association in defence of their occupational and non-pecuniary interests. A blanket ban on forming or joining a trade union encroached on the very essence of freedom of association, could not be considered proportionate and necessary in a democratic society; thus violation of Article 11.[32]

Article 10 of the RDGA strongly restricts the right of free assembly.

---

31 If these judgments are extended to military personnel, this will have substantial impact on the existing – or lacking – "bargaining" structures set out for military personnel. ECtHR 2 October 2014, 20609/10 (Matelly/France); ECtHR 2 October 2014, 32191/09 (ADEFDROMIL/France). In December 2014 President François Hollande announced a Billgranting French military personnel the right to join a military association, but not a "trade union" in the French sense of the word.

32 In *Matelly v. France* (application no. 10609/10), an officer in the French gendarmerie which forms in France a part of the military, was forced to resign from an association named *Forum gendarmes et citoyens*. The forum was considered by the Director General of the National Gendarmerie as a trade-union-like occupational group, which was prohibited under Article L. 4121-4 of the Defence Code. In *Adefdromil v. France* (application no. 32191/09) the *Association de Defence des Droits des Militaires (ADEFDROMIL)*, a professional organization for servicemen, complained about its denial of access to justice, as it was considered to be in breach of the same provisions of Article L. 4121-4 of the Defence Code. This article L 4121-4 declares the existence of occupational organizations for military personnel as well as the membership of such organizations incompatible with the prescriptions of the military discipline.

Article 13(8) of the RDGA prohibits any kind of collective demonstration. According to Article 11 of SGM, the right to strike is incompatible with military status.[33]

Germany

The Constitution or Basic Law for the Federal Republic of Germany contains Basic (Fundamental) Rights in Part I from Article 1 to 19. All fundamental rights are, as a general rule applicable to German soldiers also. Accordingly, section 6 of the German Law on the Rights and Duties of Soldiers (*Soldatengesetz* [SG]) provides that soldiers are entitled to the same rights as every other citizen. All restrictions which apply to the normal citizen are also applicable to soldiers also. Conscription is permitted by article 12a of the Constitution which states that men who have attained the age of 18 may be required to serve in the Armed Forces. Women are exempted from the draft but allowed to perform volunteer service.

Conscription in the German Federal Republic which began on 21 July 1956 has been suspended since 1 July 2011. The German Parliament has now decided to transform the German Armed Forces into an army of professional and volunteer soldiers. Instead of compulsory military service, the law now provides for voluntary military service of up to 23 months for both men and women. Conscription is limited to times when the parliament declares that Germany is under attack or imminently threatened by armed force. Because conscription has only been suspended and not abolished, there was no need to amend the Constitution, which also means that it could be reactivated at any time.

Article 17a (1), which is contained in Part I of the Constitution, makes provision for restriction of basic rights of the members of the armed forces. It provides:

Restriction of basic rights in specific instances

Laws regarding military and alternative service may provide that the basic right of members of the Armed Forces and of alternative service freely to express and disseminate their opinions in speech, writing and pictures (first clause of paragraph (1) of Article 5), the basic right of assembly (Article 8), and the right of petition (Article 17) insofar as it permits the submission of requests or complaints jointly with others, be restricted during their period of military or

---

33 GerkrathJorg, Military Law in France, in Nolte George (ed.), 2003, *European Military Law Systems*, Berlin: De Gruyter Recht, pp. 305-306.

alternative service.

Under Article 17a (1) of the Constitution the fundamental rights which can be further restricted by an Act of Parliament re: freedom of expression, freedom of peaceful assembly, and the right to collective petition. So far, special restrictions on the freedom of assembly have not been enacted. Apart from the fundamental rights which are enumerated in Article 17a of the Constitution, no other fundamental rights may be subject to specific limitations. Soldiers have a special status of subordination vis-à-vis the state, meaning that there are restrictions imposed on them which are not imposed on civilians. German doctrine describes the status of a soldier as a *"Sonderstatusverhaltmis"* meaning special status relationship. The restrictions on fundamental rights are permissible only if they are necessary and appropriate to fulfil the aim of contributing to the effectiveness of the armed forces. The courts use the concept of "citizen in uniform" or its corollary *"Inner Fuhrung"* [34] while interpreting the soldier's constitutional rights. In their double role as civilian citizens and citizens in uniform, German soldiers and officers are expected to be knowledgeable and even participate in political discussions, which are officially organized within military units. They are expected to participate in discussions on military matters, security and peace. Grievance procedures are closely related to the democratic principles of participation and co-determination.[35]

Section 15 of the German Law on the Rights and Duties of Soldiers (SG) demands political neutrality of the soldier. Section 15 SG distinguishes between political activities while on duty, in the barracks, and off-duty. A

---

34 The concept *"Innere Fuhrung"* is the manifestation of the political will to reconcile the soldier's civil rights with his military obligations. In its basic dimensions the concept was designed prior to the establishment of the German armed forces. By *"Innere Fuhrung"* three major objectives should be achieved: (i) the legal, political and ethical justification for having armed forces and the citizens' obligation to do military service; (ii) the integration of the armed forces and the individual soldier into state and society, as well as into the NATO and the Western European Union; and (iii) the willingness of the individual soldier to serve with conviction, to fulfill his duties to the best of his ability, and thereby to be prepared to accept the restrictions of some of his basic rights by special legislation concerning military service. These objectives in turn require the military to be receptive to social, political and technical developments taking place in society. The principle of *Innere Fuehrung* balances the need for an efficient, mission-ready military against the need to uphold society's democratic values. Schiebold Kurt Helmut (1995), The German Model of Democratic Control over the Armed Forces, available at: *Teorija in praksa*, Vol. 5/6, 2005, pp. 421-425..

35 Callaghan Jean, "Unions and the German Armed Forces: The Citizens in Uniform", in Bartle Richard and Lindy Heinecken (ed.), 2006, *Military Unionism in the Post-Cold War Era: A future reality?* London: Routledge, pp. 165-176.

soldier, while on duty, is not allowed to engage in political activity. He is free to express his political opinion during conversations with his comrades on duty, but he may not work for a particular political party. Section 15 (2) SG restricts political activities like distribution of leaflets, working as a representative, etc, within the barracks during leisure time. It has been confirmed by the German Constitutional Court that section 15 (1) and (2) of SG are in conformity with the Article 5 of the Constitution relating to the freedom of expression.[36] During off-duty hours a soldier may engage in political activities under the accepted concept of the "citizen-in-uniform." He may be even granted special leave to participate in political activities; however, it is prohibited to wear a uniform at public political assemblies.

Section 25 SG authorizes the legislator to lay down criteria of ineligibility and incompatibility for soldiers on their right to be elected.[37] A soldier is required to notify his superiors of a nomination to stand for political office. He will be granted special leave for the time of his elected term, and his duties as a member of the armed forces are suspended for the period of mandate. The freedom of assembly enshrined in Article 8 of the Constitution has not been restricted under Article 17a. German soldiers also enjoy the freedom of association, which is enshrined in Article 9 of the Constitution. This includes right to form special interest groups for soldiers, such as German Federal Armed Forces Association. The Association formed in 1956 claims to represent the interest of all service-members and is considered to be an expression of the concept of the "citizen-in-uniform". *Innere Fuehrung*, with its vital corollary of "citizen in uniform," ensures that the *Bundeswehr* serves as a democratically structured and operated armed force that remains acceptable to the majority of the German people.[38]

Article 45b of the Constitution has created the office of Parliamentary

---

36 Nolte Georg and heike Krieger, 'Military Law in Germany', in Nolte George (ed.), 2003, *European Military Law Systems*, Berlin: De Gruyter Recht, p. 371.

37 The Constitution expressly authorizes the legislature to restrict soldiers' rights—as long as they are in uniform and on duty; for instance the right to freedom of assembly, the right to petition in joint actions and the basic right to freely express and spread one's own opinion in words, writing and image. The Legal Status of Military Personnel Act also puts limits on soldiers' freedom of speech, for instance they should not talk publicly about official matters. Callaghan Jean, Unions and the German Armed Forces, in Bartle Richard and Lindy Heinecken (ed.), 2006, *Military Unionism in the Post-Cold War Era: A future reality?* London: Routledge, p. 169.

38 Koltermann Jens O., Citizen in Uniform: Democratic Germany and the Changing *Bundeswehr, Parameters*, Summer 2012, p.108-126.

Commissioner for the Armed Forces to safeguard basic rights and to assist the Bundestag in exercising parliamentary oversight over the Armed Forces.[39] The Parliamentary Commissioner enjoys a special status within Germany's parliamentary system. He acts as an advocate for service personnel and assists the Bundestag in exercising parliamentary oversight over the armed forces. [40]

Malaysia

Part II of the Malayan Constitution[41] contains "Fundamental Liberties" from Articles 5 to 13 which includes the rights relating to liberty; freedom from slavery and forced labour; protection against retrospective criminal laws and repeated trials; the equality; prohibition of banishment and freedom of movement; freedom of speech, assembly and association; freedom of religion; and the rights in respect of education and property.[42] Article 10(1) relating to the "Freedom of speech, assembly and association" provides that every citizen has the right to freedom of speech and expression; the right to assemble peaceably and without arms; and the right to form associations. However, restrictions may be imposed on these rights as it deems necessary or expedient in the interest of the security of the Federation or public order.[43] In imposing restrictions in the interest of the security of the Federation, the Parliament may pass law prohibiting the

---

39 The Constitution of Germany, Article 45b. The Office of Parliamentary Commissioner for the Armed Forces:A Parliamentary Commissioner for the Armed Forces shall be appointed to safeguard basic rights and to assist the Bundestag in exercising parliamentary oversight over the Armed Forces.

40 The German Basic Law entrusts the Parliamentary Commissioner with the task of safeguarding the basic rights of service personnel. He scrutinizes the services' compliance with the principles of leadership development and civic education, and reports to Parliament on conditions within the *Bundeswehr*. Every member of the forces is able to contact the Parliamentary Commissioner directly – and to do so without going through official channels, which means their submissions do not have to be passed on by superiors who have often contributed to the difficulties brought to the Parliamentary Commissioner's notice. No member of the services may be discriminated against because they have contacted the Parliamentary Commissioner. The Parliamentary Commissioner for the Armed Forces has the right to request reports about the exercise of disciplinary power in the armed forces and to attend criminal or disciplinary proceedings in court. The work done by the Parliamentary Commissioner for the Armed Forces, his special status, his rights and his duties have an impact on the leadership behaviour of many military superiors.

41 As amendment by Act A1320 which came into operation on 27 December 2007.

42 The Constitution of the Federation of Malaysia as on 1 November 2010.

43 Article 10(2) of the Malayan Constitution.

questioning of any matter, right, status, position, privilege, sovereignty or prerogative established or protected by the Constitution. [44]Article 137 of the Constitution established an Armed Forces Council, which is responsible for the command, discipline and administration of the members of the armed forces, other than matters relating to their operational use.

The Armed Forces are listed as being part of the Public Services in the Malayan Constitution.[45] The restrictions on fundamental rights applying to the other Public Services also apply to the Armed Forces. Thus, the fundamental rights relating to the freedom of speech and expression; assembly; and to form an association, which is available to every citizen could be restricted by the Parliament for the members of the Armed Forces on the grounds of security or public order. There is no explicit provision in regard to restrictions on the fundamental rights in the Armed Forces Act of 1972. However, the Armed Forces are bound by restrictions vis-a-vis participation in politics, freedom to form associations, etc, in keeping with the British and Commonwealth traditions relating to the Armed Forces. Insubordinate behaviour,[46] disobedience to superior officer,[47] disobedience to standing orders,[48] unauthorized disclosure of information,[49] and conduct prejudice to service discipline[50] are listed as an offence under the Armed Forces Act of 1972.

The Netherlands

In the Netherlands,[51] the constitutional provisions regarding the armed

---

44 Article 10(4) of the Malayan Constitution.

45 The Malayan Constitution, Part X, Article 132(1)(a)].

46 Section 49, the Armed Forces Act of 1972.

47 Section 50, the Armed Forces Act of 1972.

48 Section 51, the Armed Forces Act of 1972.

49 Section 79, the Armed Forces Act of 1972.

50 Section 87, the Armed Forces Act of 1972.

51 The Kingdom of the Netherlands consists of four countries: the Netherlands, Aruba, Curacao and Sint Maarten. Within this Kingdom, the Charter for the Kingdom of the Netherlands is the highest regulation. Article 14 of the Charter states that rules on the affairs of the Kingdom can be laid down in Kingdom Acts of Parliament or in Orders in Council of the Kingdom. Article 42 of the Charter states that the Dutch Constitution regulates the model of government of the Netherlands. Regulations regarding only the Netherlands are to be found in Acts of Parliament. In principle, therefore, the Dutch Constitution concerns only the Netherlands. However, on account of Article 5 of the Charter, articles of the Dutch Constitution can deal with affairs of the Kingdom.

forces date back to the first Constitution of the Kingdom on1815. During that time the army's character used to be that of a conscript body led by a volunteer cadre of professional officers. In 1995/1997, the Constitution was amended on the issue of the composition of the armed forces. The task of the armed forces, as stated in Article 97 is as follows: "There shall be armed forces for the defence and protection of the interests of the Kingdom, and in order to maintain and promote the international legal order. The Government shall have supreme authority over the armed forces."[52] The conscription in the armed forces has not been abolished in the Netherlands, but the calling into active service of conscripts has been suspended. Article 98 of the Constitution, as amended of 22 June 2000, provides, "(1) The armed forces shall consist of volunteers and may also include conscripts; and (2) Compulsory military service and the power to defer the call-up to active service shall be regulated by Act of Parliament." The Minister of Defence has primary responsibility with regards to the armed forces. In 1976 the office of the Chief of Defence Staff was created, who holds the highest rank in the armed forces. The Military Discipline Code (MDC) contains both the 34 disciplinary offences a soldier can commit and also the rules regarding the disciplinary procedures. These offences relate to misconduct which is not that serious that it constitutes a military crime. The commanding officer is able to make use of military disciplinary law to correct small problems with light sanctions with a normative material or physical character, like reprimands, fines, extra duties and confinement to barracks.

The fundamental rights as contained in the constitution are primarily concerned with securing the rights of citizens as against public authorities. In principle, soldiers exert public authority; therefore, their acts and legal positions are entirely covered by the public law. Soldiers enjoy fundamental rights in principle as contained in the Constitution and in human rights treaties. In this respect, there is no difference between "professional" soldiers and conscripts.

The Dutch Constitution allows restrictions on fundamental rights only on the basis of an Act of Parliament. Under the Dutch laws, for soldiers, engaging in political activities is an offence under Article 35 of the

---

52 The armed forces consist of the Royal Army (de *Koninklijke Landmacht*), the Royal Navy (de *Koninklijke Marine*), the Royal Air Force (de *Koninklijke Luchtmacht*) and the Royal Military Police (de *Koninklijke Marechaussee*). The main duties of the armed forces are to defend the territory of the Kingdom and NATO-Member States and to make a worldwide contribution to peace, security and stability by crisis management, humanitarian aid and disaster relief.

Military Disciplinary and Military Criminal Code (WMT). The freedom of association is guaranteed by Article 8 of the Constitution and Article 11 of the European Convention on Human Rights (ECHR).[53] The soldiers have the right to vote and to stand for election. Special leave must be granted to soldiers who wish to vote. If a soldier is elected or appointed to a public organ for which the activities cannot be undertaken simultaneously with the functions in the armed forces, he will be suspended from the service or may be given special leave to attend the session of the public organ and participate in the related activities. If a person has been appointed minister or state secretary, he is dismissed from the service.

Article 7 of the Constitution of the Netherlands and Article 10 of the ECHR deal with the freedom of expression. Article 10(2) of the ECHR provides that restrictions on the freedom of expression 'necessary in a democratic society' can be imposed. Under the military code, special restrictions on the freedom of expression can be imposed on volunteers as well as conscripts. It also imposes a duty of secrecy with regard to providing any information concerning the service to anyone who is not competent to receive it. Both, the Military Criminal Code (WMSr) and the Military Disciplinary Act (WMT) limit the exercise of the freedom of expression for active duty service personnel and make it a criminal/disciplinary offence.[54]

The Constitution of the Netherlands in Article 9 and the ECHR, Article 11, deal with the freedom of demonstration and assembly. However, under Article 11 (2) of the ECHR, "lawful restrictions" can be imposed with regards to the members of the armed forces. Article 33 (1) of WMT makes it a disciplinary offence to organize or participate in demonstrations on military premises, if no prior permission has been sought from the competent authority or has been refused for reasons of traffic or is against the regular service order. Article 33 (2) prohibits participation in uniform in a demonstration or assembly outside military premises unless it exclusively concerns the working conditions for soldiers. Participation in demonstrations abroad is prohibited. Provisions contained in the military

---

53 The European Convention on Human Rights became part of the Dutch legal system in 1954.

54 Article 6 of the Military Disciplinary Act (WMT) and Article 12a of the *Militaire Ambtenarenwet* (MAw) provide that anyone who passes on information concerning the service to someone who is not competent to receive it, which from the nature appears that the information is secret, acts contrary to military discipline. Besselink Leonard F.M., 'Military Law in the Netherlands', in Nolte George (ed.), 2003, *European Military Law Systems*, Berlin: De Gruyter Recht, p. 589.

disciplinary and military criminal code make it an offence not to obey a service regulation. These provisions are in a sense 'unspecific' and cannot be considered a lawful basis for restricting fundamental rights by service regulations.[55]

The European Convention on Human Rights became part of the Dutch legal system in 1954. From 1970 onwards, the European Court on Human Rights (ECtHR) has delivered more than 60 rulings in which it has concluded that the Netherlands has been guilty of a violation of the convention. The Court has held that certain aspects of the way in which the legal action against the conscripts had been executed were in contradiction with the right to a fair hearing, as safeguarded by Article 6 ECHR. The ruling in the few cases led to the modernization of the Dutch system of military criminal law and military disciplinary law. Now, the jurisdiction over soldiers has been transferred to civil court and a civil servant instead of a military officer decides to initiate the prosecution of soldiers.

Spain

Spain has a long tradition of military intervention over weak civilian governments and direct military dictatorship. The Spanish Constitution Article 62(h) states that the King is to exercise supreme command of the Armed Forces. However, this function is symbolic in nature. The fundamental rights are contained in Part I of Constitution from sections 10 to 54 of soldiers. The Spanish Constitution is tied directly to international treaties on human rights. Section 10 of the Constitution guarantees fundamental rights stating:

(1) The dignity of the person, the inviolable rights which are inherent, the free development of the personality, the respect for the law and for the rights of others are the foundation of political order and social peace.

(2) Provisions relating to the fundamental rights and liberties recognized by the Constitution shall be construed in conformity with the Universal Declaration of Human Rights and international treaties and agreements thereon ratified by Spain.

The derogation of fundamental rights in Spain is subject not only

---

55 Besselink Leonard F.M., 'Legal and Constitutional Position of the Netherlands Armed Forces and International Military Cooperation, 2011, available at:https://dspace.library. uu.nl/handle/1874/214157.

to the rules, but also to the requirement of necessity, reasonableness, and proportionality.[56]

The Spanish Constitution contains some specific provisions limiting certain rights and freedoms for military personnel. For instance, standing for the office of deputy or senator is constitutionally excluded under section 70 of the Constitution. Section 22 of the Constitution recognizes the rights to the association; however, section 22 (5) prohibits the formation of associations of secret and paramilitary character. As regard the right of the military personnel to join trade union, the right is restricted under Section 28, which provides that the law may restrict or except the exercise of this right in the Armed Forces or Institutes or other bodies subject to military discipline, and shall lay down the special conditions of its exercise by civil servants. Section 29 (1) states that all Spaniards shall have the right to individual and collective petition, in writing, in the manner and subject to the consequences to be laid down by law. However, this right is restricted under section 29(2) which states: "Members of the Armed Forces or Institutes or bodies subject to military discipline may only exercise this right individually and in accordance with statutory provisions relating to them.

The regulation of soldiers' rights and freedom is contained in the following Acts: 85/1978, approving the Royal Ordinance of the Armed Forces (OR); Organic Act 7/1980 on religious freedom; Organic Act 4/1981, complementing Section 116(1) of the Constitution on alert, exception and siege;[57] Organic Act 11/1985 on freedom to form trade unions, Organic Act 13/1985 approving the Military Criminal Code; Organic Act 2/1989 on Military Jurisdictional Procedure; Organic Act 13/1991 regulating military service; and Organic Act 8/1998 on the Disciplinary Regulations of the Armed Forces (RDFA) and Act 17/1999 on the Regulations Concerning Professional Soldiers.

The following provisions of the RDFA dealing with freedom of speech provide:

---

56 Section 53 (1) of the Spanish Constitution provides: The rights and freedoms recognized in Chapter 2 are binding on all public authorities. Only by an act which in any case must respect their essential content, could the exercise of such rights and freedoms be regulated, which shall be protected in accordance with the provisions of section 161(1) (a). Section 161(1) (a) states that the Constitutional Court has jurisdiction over the whole Spanish territory and is entitled to hear appeals against the alleged unconstitutionality of acts and statutes having the force of an act.

57 Section 116 (1) of the Constitution states: "An organic act shall make provision for the states of alarm, emergency and siege (martial law) and the powers and restrictions attached to each of them."

Section 178: Military personnel have the right to freedom of expression, but must acquire prior authorization for the exercise thereof when their statement concern issues which could harm or interfere with the protection of the national security (i.e., information that is known only because of the individual's position or duties in the armed forces) are involved.

Section 179: Members of the armed forces have the right to the possession and use of social mass media within military enclosures. However, when reasons of national security or exigencies of discipline or defence of the unit requires it, the Minister of Defence -- or, in case of emergency, the competent military authority, with the Minister's countersignature – may limit the exercise of this right.

In Spain, professional soldiers are not allowed to become members of a political party. Section 182 of the RDFA according provides:

Section 182: Member of the armed forces may take advantage of any political or association options which are allowed to them by the Constitution. Soldiers, must, however, maintain their neutrality by not participating in significant political or union activities, and by not tolerating those who encourage or disseminate information encouraging participation in significant party or union activity within military enclosures. Soldiers may not be affiliated with any type of political or union organization, attend their meetings, or publicly express opinions on them. Conscripts and short-term soldiers' may maintain any affiliations previously held, but must abstain from party or union activity during the time of service.

However, it is possible for a soldier to be elected to position like councillor or regional deputy. Section 141 of Law 17/1999 on Military Personnel regulates the situation of soldiers who run for election. These soldiers are placed in the administrative situation of "voluntary leave"; meaning that the soldier is not active during the period and is not under the military legal system until he comes back to the military active duty. If he is elected, he is suspended from the military service; in case not elected, he returns to his previous status.

Restrictions of freedom of Association are contained in the Royal Ordinance. It provides:

Section 181 OR: Members of the armed forces, whose interest are guarded by the State, shall not have the option of participating in unions or associations with [any] protest purpose. They shall not, under any circumstances, have the option of placing conditions on the fulfilment of their duties with a view to better satisfying their personal or professional interest; neither shall they have any recourse to any for – direct or indirect – of strike. Soldiers may belong to other type of legally authorized associations such as those of a religious, cultural, sporting, or social character.[58]

South Africa

Before the emergence of democracy in South Africa in 1994, members of the Defence Force were prohibited from becoming members of trade unions. Section 126 B (1) of the Defence Act, 1957, provided: "A member of the Permanent Force shall not be or become a member of any trade union as defined in section 1 of the Labour Relations Act, 1956 (Act 28 of 1956): provided that this provision shall not preclude any member of such Force from being or becoming a member of any professional or vocational institute, society, association or like body approved by the Minister."

On 27 April 1994, the new South African Defence Force (SANDF) came into being. It immediately faced a challenge of transforming the forces from the pre-1994 all-white male conscription force to an all-volunteer force representative of the broader society. This major restructuring led to the need for some form of collective representation. Just four months after the establishment of SANDF the South African National Defence Union (SANDU) was created.

The new Constitution of the Republic of South Africa South Africa[59] makes provision of defence forces that is structured and managed as a disciplined military.[60]The Constitution contains 'Bill of Rights' from Section 7 to 35. The rights listed in the 'Bill of Rights', as provides in Section 7(3), are subject to the limitations contained or referred to in section 36, or elsewhere in the Bill. Section 36 of the Constitution dealing with limitation of rights, provides that the rights contained in the 'Bill' may be limited only in terms of law of general application to the extent that the limitation is reasonable and justifiable in an open and democratic society

---

58 The Spanish Constitutional Court in its judgment 219/2001 of 31 October 2001 has held that there is a constitutional distinction between the prohibition of military trade unions and the permission for military personnel to form associations.

59 The Constitution of the Republic of South Africa of 1996.

60 Section 200(1), the Constitution of the Republic of South Africa South Africa.

based on human dignity, equality and freedom, taking into account all relevant factors, including (a) the nature of the right; (b) the importance of the purpose of the limitation; (c) the nature and extent of the limitation; (d) the relation between the limitation and its purpose; and (e) less restrictive means to achieve the purpose.

The new South African Constitution guarantees the right of every worker, including the members of the defence forces, to form and join a trade union and to participate in the activities and programmes of a trade union and to strike. With the new democratic dispensation and the coming into existence of the Constitution, the members of the Defence Force were allowed to form and join trade unions.

Chapter 8 of the South African Defence Act, 2002[61] which applies to all members of armed forces and civilian employees, contains limitations on their rights. Article 50 of the Act states that subject to the Constitution, the rights of members or employees may be restricted in the manner and to the extent set out in subsections (2) to (7). Sub section (2) provides that for the purposes of military security and safety of members of the armed forces and employees, such members and employees may be subjected to: (a) searches and inspections; (b) screening of their communications with people in or outside the department; (c) security clearances which probe into their private lives; and (d) shared accommodation or privation in accordance with the exigencies of military training and operations. Sub-section (3) provides that for security and the protection of information, members of the armed forces and employees may be subjected to restrictions in communicating any kind of information, and where appropriate, may be subjected to prohibition of communication of information. Further under sub-para (4), the right of members of the Regular Force, serving members of the Reserve Force and members of auxiliary service to peaceful and unarmed assembly, demonstration, picketing and petition, may be restricted. Sub-para (6) stipulates that in order to maintain the armed forces as a structured and disciplined military force, the rights of member of the Regular Force, serving members of the Reserve Force and members of auxiliary force to join and participate in the activities of trade unions and other organizations may be subjected to such restrictions as may be prescribed. In addition, under sub-para (7), the access to information in the department may be restricted. Under sub-para (8), there is a prohibition on the member of the Regular Force to serve as a Member of Parliament or any other legislative body.

---

61   The South African Defence Act of 2002 (Act No. 42 of 2002).

In 1999, the Constitutional Court in *South African National Defence Force Union v. Minister of Defence* 1999 (6) BCLR 615, interpreted the word 'worker' in section 23(2) of the Constitution to include members of the Defence Force. The Court ruled, "Soldiers like any other citizens have the right to freedom of expression and to form and join military unions". The Court decided that the requirement of strict discipline would not necessarily be undermined by permitting Defence Force members to join a trade union, as the structure and scope of such a trade union might differ given the military environment. As a result, the right to form and join a trade union was extended to members of the South African National Defence Force (SANDF) and military trade unions received full recognition in the Defence Force.

On 26 August 2009, certain members of the Defence Forces marched to the Union Buildings in Pretoria, which led to the destruction of public property.[62] This incident undermined military discipline and it was felt that the trade union activities amongst the armed forces could adversely affect the national security. There are demands in certain fractions of the armed forces to de-unionize the SANDF.[63]

Sweden

Like most other democratic countries, Sweden has a written constitution. It regulates the manner in which the Swedish Parliament (the Riksdag) and the Government are appointed and sets out the way in which these State bodies shall work. In most countries, statutes are assembled in a single

---

62 On 26 August 2009 many members of the South African National Defence Force gathered at the precincts of the Union Buildings in Pretoria to demonstrate their grievances. In doing so they contravened military orders and a court order that had been issued that morning. Some amongst them were armed with pistols, pangas, knobkerries and petrol bombs. The conduct of at least some of them provoked a confrontation with the police, who found themselves compelled to use a water cannon, and to fire rubber bullets, in an attempt to bring things under control, and police and military vehicles were damaged.

63 This can be done by amending section 200 of the Constitution by inserting a new subsection (2) which, in the interest of national security, will forbid members of the Defence Force from forming or joining military trade unions. Instead of military trade unions, South Africans might consider allowing soldiers to form or join professional associations, which will represent soldiers' interests related to working conditions. The professional associations should not have any political objectives and should not engage in any industrial action. Mnisi, Eric Z., National Security and the Constitutional Right to Join Military Trade Unions: Is Constitutional Amendment an Imperative, *Scientia Militaria, South African Journal of Military Studies*, Vol. 45, No. 2, 2017, p. 129-139.

document. Sweden, however, has four fundamental laws: the Instrument of Government (IG), the Act of Succession (AS), the Freedom of the Press Act (FPA), and the Fundamental Law on Freedom of Expression (FLFE). Freedom of opinion and other rights and freedoms enjoy special protection under the Constitution.

The basic principles of the form of government are expressed in Chapter 1 of the Instrument of Government. Article 1 states: "All public power in Sweden proceeds from the people. Swedish democracy is founded on the free formation of opinion and on universal and equal suffrage. It is realised through a representative and parliamentary form of government and through local self-government. Public power is exercised under the law." The rights and freedoms which can be limited by means of law and are covered by qualified procedure rules are as follows:[64]

1. Freedom of expression: freedom to communicate information and express thoughts, views and opinions and sentiments, pictorially, in writing or in any other way [Constitution Chapter 2, Article 1(1)].

2. Freedom of assembly: freedom to organize and attend meetings for information, expression of opinion or other similar purposes or to present artistic work [Constitution Chapter 2, Article 1(3)].

3. Freedom to demonstrate: freedom to organise and take part in demonstrations in a public place [Constitution Chapter 2, Article 1(4)].

4. Freedom of association: freedom to associate with others for public or private purposes [Constitution Chapter 2, Article 1(5)].

Sweden has a long tradition of military unionism. Sweden's first association for military personnel was established almost a hundred years ago. One of the main reasons for Swedish military officers to organize themselves in trade unions was to get the opportunity to have an influence on their working conditions and to be treated like any other citizen. As a result of the establishment of military trade unions, the employee's isolation from the rest of society was avoided. The Swedish military personnel are, and have traditionally been, organized in three different

---

64 The Constitution of Sweden, Published by Sveriges Riksdag, 2016, SE-100 12, Stockholm, Sweden.

unions: POF—The Non-Commissioned Officers' (including their civil-military equals) Union); KOF—The Warrant Officers' Union; and SOF—The Commissioned Officers' Union.

The military association promotes the interests of military officers by taking part in the process of decision-making, which influences the working conditions for officers. It also focuses on training for its members and other areas of interest. Collective agreements on all issues affecting military personnel are negotiated every 1-3 years. Strikes or other offensive actions are only allowed during the negotiation period and not while an agreement is still valid. The most important advantage of the Swedish model is that officers feel more satisfied with their work because of the knowledge that their concerns are being addressed. Furthermore, discussions take place before decisions are made, reducing the possibility of disagreement and conflict. The involvement all parties in the decision-making creates a sense of ownership and shared responsibility. In Sweden, there has been no contradiction between membership of a trade union and the military chain of command. Sweden It affords military personnel the right to strike. Sweden has never expressed concerns regarding the effectiveness of their militaries as a result of unionization and maintains that military unions have a positive effect as they intend to lead to a "satisfied soldier". In the case of (the threat of) war, legislation grants the government the right to ban industrial action. It leads to the conclusion that, although no legal restrictions for the right to strike relating to the armed forces apply, this right is in fact limited, in particular by the (military) unions' constructive approach. So far, no Swedish military union has ever been involved in a strike.[65]

The UK

In the case of the United Kingdom, fundamental rights are not out in the constitutional form. A soldier remains liable to the criminal law of England wherever he is based, whether in the UK or abroad. A soldier is free to discuss political issues or to distribute political leaflets, whether on or off duty, in the same way as a civilian. He is, however, subject to any restrictions on this freedom imposed by military law. The main military offences relevant in this case are: threatening or disrespectful conduct towards a superior officer (Armed Forces Act, 2006, section 11) disobedience to a lawful command (section 12), contravention of a

---

65 Brickman Annika, Military Trade Unionism in Sweden, *Armed Forces and Society*, Vol. 2, No. 4, August 1976, pp. 529-538.

standing order or any other routine order of a continuing nature, or any of Her Majesty's forces (section 13), or conduct prejudicial to good order and discipline (section 19). In addition, the disclosure of restricted material would also constitute a criminal offence.[66]

As regard, freedom to peaceful assembly, British soldiers may conduct peaceful protests, for example against taking part in the military operation provided they do not infringe provisions of the Armed Forces Act like mutiny (section 6), desertion (section 7) and absent without leave (section 9 of the Act). In *R v. Arrowsmith* (1975) QB 678, the accused was convicted as a result of distributing leaflets to soldiers suggesting that they should leave the army or desert rather than serve in Northern Ireland.

In relation to political activities, Regular Service personnel are not to take active part in the affairs of any political organization, party or movement. They are not to participate in political marches or demonstrations. A soldier may be or a prospective or adopted parliamentary candidate. No restriction is placed upon the attendance at political meetings of such personnel provided that uniform is not worn, Service duties are not impeded, and no action is taken which would bring the Service into disrepute.[67]

The members of the armed forces in the UK are not permitted to establish trade unions for military purposes, although they may be members of appropriate civilian trade unions and professional associations to enhance their trade skills and professional knowledge and as an aid to resettlement into civilian life. They are not to participate in industrial action or in any form of political activity organized by civilian trade unions or professional associations. No restriction is to be placed upon the attendance at meetings of civilian trade unions or professional associations or at courses of instruction run by such organizations where attendance at

---

66 The Queen's Regulation (1975) state that it can be an offence against the Official Secrets Acts for a person to divulge, whether during or after a period of service with the armed forces, official information acquired by such a person during such service unless expressly authorized to do so. All personnel are forbidden to communicate any official information, including information about to be made public, to any person other than one to whom they are authorized to communicate it or one to whom it is their official duty to communicate it. The use of such information for personal controversy or for any private purpose during or after completion of service without due authority may be a breach of the Official Secrets Acts. Any information of a professional or technical nature that all members of the armed forces may acquire in the performance of their duty, or in the course of their official studies, is the property of the Crown and is not to be published in any form without the prior approval of the Ministry of Defence. Queen's Regulations for the Army (1975), para J12.003 and 004.

67 Queen's Regulations for the Army (1975), para J5. 581-J5.583.

such a meeting or course is intended to enhance trade skills and professional knowledge.[68] Attendance at such meetings is to be subject to the proviso that uniform is not to be worn, Service duties are not impeded, and no action is taken which would bring the Service into disrepute. In addition, service facilities, including military aircraft and motor transport, are not to be used at, or in connection with, any function the purpose of which is to further the interests of a trade union or professional association. In case of any uncertainty about the nature of any organization, the Ministry of Defence remains the final authority.[69]

The United States

In the US, Congress adopted the Uniform Code of Military Justice (UCMJ) in its modern form in 1950. The UCMJ and military policies implemented under it exist to promote justice, to assist in maintaining good order and discipline in the armed forces. The UCMJ governs all active duty military members, reservists, and, in certain circumstances, retired members. There are four UCMJ articles which either directly restrict free speech or serve as a means to enforce organizational policies that limit free speech. These restrictions traditionally go unnoticed during times of relative peace but receive more scrutiny during conflicts. The articles are:

Article 88: Contempt toward officials

Any commissioned officer who uses contemptuous words against the President, the Vice President, Congress, the Secretary of Defence, the Secretary of a military department, the Secretary of Homeland Security, or the Governor or legislature of any State, Commonwealth, or possession in which he is on duty or present shall be punished as a court-martial may direct.

Article 92: Failure to obey order or regulation

---

68 The Select Committee on the Armed Forces Bill 1985-86 considered the right of servicemen to join trade union. The Assistant Under Secretary explained the position to the Committee as follows: "The services are disciplined body. An individual serviceman clearly retains his rights as a citizen in a democratic society. He must avoid actively participating in an organization which has aims which are not supportive of his own function, or what he is there for. His duty is to defend the nation. Therefore, it has long been the policy that the Services as whole should not form associations within themselves or join external bodies such as trade unions, except in circumstances which are designed to assist the eventual resettlement of Servicemen to civilian life." *Special Report from the Select Committee on the Armed Forces Bill, 1985-86*, at p. 192.

69 Queen's Regulations for the Army (1975), para J5.588 and J5.589.

Any person subject to this chapter who (1) violates or fails to obey any lawful general order or regulation; (2) having knowledge of any other lawful order issued by a member of the armed forces, which it is his duty to obey, fails to obey the order; or (3) is derelict in the performance of his duties;shall be punished as a court-martial may direct.

Article 133: Conduct unbecoming an officer and a gentleman

Any commissioned officer, cadet, or midshipman who is convicted of conduct unbecoming an officer and a gentleman shall be punished as a court-martial may direct.

Article 134: General article

Though not specifically mentioned in this chapter, all disorders and neglects to the prejudice of good order and discipline in the armed forces, all conduct of a nature to bring discredit upon the armed forces, and crimes and offences not capital, of which persons subject to this chapter may be guilty, shall be taken cognizance of by a general, special, or summary court-martial, according to the nature and degree of the offence, and shall be punished at the discretion of that court.[70]

---

70 Levy, a doctor in the US military, was drafted and commissioned as captain in the Army Medical Corps in 1966. When assigned to train Special Forces medical personnel, he refused, saying that he considered Special Forces personnel to be "liars and thieves and killers of peasants and murderers of women and children." When Levy's superior directly ordered him to train Special Forces personnel, he refused to obey the order. During this time, Levy made several statements to enlisted men to the effect that he would refuse orders to go to Vietnam, that black soldiers should disobey such orders, and that he had disobeyed orders to train Special Forces members. For his statements to enlisted men, Levy was convicted by court-martial of "conduct unbecoming an officer and a gentleman" in violation of Article 133 of the UCMJ and "conduct prejudicial to good order and discipline in the Armed Forces" in violation of Article 134 of the UCMJ. The Third Circuit overturned Levy's convictions under Articles 133 and 134 on the ground that the excessively vague language and overbroad sweep of the "General Articles", as they are known, violated the fifth and first Amendments. In a 5-3 decision the Supreme Court reversed, and reinstated Levy's conviction. To uphold Levy's conviction, the Court first had to determine that Articles 133 and 134 were neither unconstitutionally vague nor overbroad. The Court ruled against Levy on all three points, expressly applying different constitutional standards than it would have used to review a civilian conviction. Levy was also convicted of refusal to obey a direct order, in violation of Article 90(2) of the UCMJ. The Supreme Court held that the military is a unique organization. Justice Rehnquist referred to the military as a "specialized society separate from civilian society ... with laws and traditions of its own", "a specialized community governed by a separate discipline," and "a society apart from civilian society." Further, the military officer holds "a particular position

Article 88 applies only to commissioned officers and includes comments made during off-duty hours as well as comments made while in uniform. The application of Article 88 is so broad that even an expression of personal opinion by an officer to his spouse, while in their home, regarding, for example, his thoughts that the President made a poor decision in a specific military operation could lead to prosecution. Only one officer has been convicted at general court-martial under Article 88.The court in *United States v. Howe* [71] found Army Lieutenant Henry Howe guilty of violating Article 88 when he participated in a peace rally. Howe went to the rally while off-duty. He wore civilian clothes and carried a sign that advocated withdrawal of troops from Vietnam and voting out President Johnson. Howe was sentenced to hard labour for a year, required to forfeit all pay and allowances, and discharged from the Army.

Article 92 dealing with the failure to obey order or regulation, is not a direct prohibition of speech but covers any situation where a service member knowingly violates a lawful general order. Orders to perform military duties or acts are presumed lawful. The UCMJ qualifies that an order may not, without such a valid military purpose, interfere with private rights or personal affairs. Articles 133 and 134 are general articles to catch-all charge because they include "conduct unbecoming an officer and a gentleman" and "all conduct of a nature to bring discredit upon the armed forces." These articles are effective for prosecuting speech or conduct not specifically prohibited under Articles 88 or 92 but that a local military command feels is inappropriate and thus "discrediting".[72] In addition to its legal framework, the military also curtails free speech rights with certain organizational policies.[73] Military regulations permitting the commander

---

of responsibility and command." Disciplinary standards may "regulate aspects of the conduct of members... which in the civilian sphere are left unregulated." Congress is allowed greater flexibility when prescribing the rules by which the [military] shall be governed even where first amendment rights are involved. While the first amendment protects servicemen, the "different character of the military community and of the military mission requires a different application of those protections." This difference is justified by the "fundamental necessity for obedience and the consequent necessity for imposition of discipline." *Parker v. Levy*, 417 US 733 (1974).

71 *United States v. Howe*, 37 CMR 555 (A.B.R. 1966).

72 Reuter Emily, Second Class Citizen Soldiers: A Proposal for Greater First Amendment protections for America's Military Personnel, *Wm. & Mary Bill Rts. J.*, Vo. 16, issue 1, 2007, pp. 315-344.

73 For instance, the Department of Defence Directive 1344.10 includes a list of prohibited political speech, including participating in partisan political campaigns, soliciting votes or doing research for a partisan organization, and participating in any radio, television,

to restrict speech posing a clear danger to loyalty, discipline and morale have been upheld by civilian courts.[74]

The membership in military unions, organizing of military unions, and recognition of military unions prohibited.[75] It is also unlawful for any person to organize or participate in any strike or demonstration involving members of the armed forces that is directed against the Government of the US. Further, the use of any military installation, facility, vessel, or other property of the US is prohibited for any meeting, demonstration or prohibited activity. The members of the armed forces or civilian officer are prohibited from any negotiation or bargain concerning the terms or conditions of military service of members of the armed forces with any person. The commanders are permitted to consider the views of the member of the armed forces presented individually or as a result of participation on command-sponsored or authorized advisory councils, committees, or organizations. The members of the armed forces are permitted to present complaints or grievances concerning the terms or conditions of the service to authorized member of the armed forces in accordance with established military procedures.[76] Any violation of these norms is punishable with

---

or other program or group discussion as an advocate ... of a partisan political party, candidate, or cause. The regulations allow for a member to express a personal opinion on political candidates and issues, but such expressions cannot include contemptuous words against the officeholders prohibited by Article 88 of the UCMJ. This caveat pressures military members to express only those personal political views that support incumbent politicians. Reuter Emily, Second Class Citizen Soldiers: A Proposal for Greater First Amendment protections for America's Military Personnel, *Wm. & Mary Bill Rts. J.*, Vo. 16, issue 1, 2007, p. 324.

74 *Carlson v. Schlesinger*, 511 F.2d, 1327 (DC Cir. 1975). For more details see: Morris Lawrence J., Free Speech in the Military, *Marquette Law Review*, Vol. 65, issue 4, Summer 1982, pp. 660-695.

75 The US Code 10, Article 976 states that membership in military unions, organizing of military unions, and recognition of military unions prohibited. The term "member of the armed forces" means (i) an active duty member of the armed forces, (ii) a member of the National Guard who is serving on full-time National Guard duty, or (C) a member of a Reserve component while performing inactive-duty training. It is unlawful for a member of the armed forces to join or maintain membership in such organization. No member of the armed forces and civilian employee may negotiate or bargain on behalf of the United States concerning the terms or conditions of military service of members of the armed forces with any person who represents or purports to represent members of the armed forces.

76 The Court of Military Review has held that there must be a certain amount of 'breathing room' for speech by military personnel. For example, a service-member who told his commander that he would issue a press release if the commander kept pressuring him not to complain to his congressman about food and living conditions was found not

fine, imprisonment up to five year or both; and in the case of organization with minimum fine of $25,000.[77]

The South Asian Countries

Bangladesh: Bangladesh emerged as a sovereign state on 16 December 1971. A parliamentary form of government was introduced in Bangladesh according to the Provisional Constitution Order of 1972, and the political elite became the supreme policymakers. The 1972 constitution, which was passed by the Constituent Assembly on 4 November 1972, essentially continued the process. Article 45 of the Bangladesh Constitution declares: "Nothing in this Part (Part III dealing with fundamental rights) shall apply to any provision of a disciplinary law relating to members of a disciplined force, being a provision limited to the purpose of ensuring the proper discharge of their duties or the maintenance of discipline in that force."

Nepal: Part III of the 2015 Constitution of Nepal, contains Fundamental Rights and Duties from Articles 16 to 48. Article 17(2) dealing with the "Right to Freedom" lists various rights relating to the freedom of opinion and expression; freedom to assemble peacefully without arms; freedom to form unions and association, etc. Clause (1) of Article 17 states that except as provided for by law no person shall be deprived of her/his personal liberty and does not expressly makes any direct restrictions on fundamental rights of military personnel. Section 19 of the Nepal Army Act, 2006, however, lays restrictions on the activities of persons subject to the Act. It states:

19. Restriction on establishing and operating organization or association:

(1) A person who falls under the jurisdiction of this Act shall not do the following acts:

(a) To establish, operate, accept membership or assist to a union, association or organization, or participate in a programme organized by such union, association or organization.

(b) To participate or deliver speech to any assembly or to

---

guilty of 'wrongful communication of a threat'. The court said the man should be free to speak without being subject to adjudication as a blackmailer. *United States v. Schmidt*, 16 CMA 57, 61, 36 CMR 213, 217 (1966).

77   Title 10, United States Code Armed Forces, Article 976.

participate in any demonstration organized by any person or groups for a political or other similar purpose.

(c) To publish a leaflet, pamphlet or similar documents.

(2) Notwithstanding anything contained in Clause (a) of Sub-section (1), nothing shall be deemed to prevent a person who falls under the jurisdiction of this Act from assisting a religious, social, cultural and entertainment union, association or organization or participating in a programme of such union, association or organization upon receiving an approval of the Government of Nepal and subject to the provision of this Act.

Pakistan: The Constitution of the Islamic Republic of Pakistan, 1973, Part II deals with Fundamental Rights and Principles of Policy in Articles 7 to 28. Article 8(1) states that any law, or any custom or usage having the force of law, in so far as it is inconsistent with the rights conferred by this Chapter, shall, to the extent of such inconsistency, be void. Sub clause (2) further clarifies that the State shall not make any law which takes away or abridges the rights so conferred and any law in contravention to this clause, be void. However, the next clause (3) states that provision of Article 8, "shall not apply to any law relating to members of the Armed Forces, or of the police or of such other forces as are charged with the maintenance of public order, for the purpose of ensuring the proper discharge of their duties or the maintenance of discipline among them."

Sri Lanka: Chapter III of the Constitution of Sri Lanka contains fundamental Rights from Articles 10-17. Article 14 (1) specifically provides that every citizen is entitled to the rights relating to the freedom of speech and expression including publication; the freedom of peaceful assembly; the freedom of association; the freedom to form and join a trade union; the freedom to engage by himself or in association with others in any lawful occupation, profession, trade, business or enterprise; etc. Article 14 (8) of the Sri Lankan Constitution is similar to Article 33 of the Indian Constitution. It specifies that the exercise and operation of the fundamental rights declared and recognized by Articles 12(1), 13 and 14 shall, in their application to the members of the Armed Forces, Police Force and other Forces charged with the maintenance of public order, be subject to such restrictions as may be prescribed by law in the interests of the proper discharge of their duties and the maintenance of discipline among them.

There are legal barriers to the unionization of the armed forces in most countries. Wherever unions exist, they are prohibited to interfere in grievances of an operational or organizational nature. Their activities are constrained by rules or regulations pertaining to military discipline, and in most cases, the military unions cannot represent their members directly. In Europe, the European Organization of Military Associations (EUROMIL) is the umbrella organization of 43 military associations and trade unions from 28 countries. It was founded in 1972 and represents approximately 500,000 soldiers and their families. It is the primary forum for cooperation among military associations on issues of common concern. Its mission is to represent human rights and fundamental freedoms of military personnel in Europe. EUROMIL has consultative status at the United Nations Economic and Social Council (ECOSOC). EUROMIL play an important role to enhance the well-being and performance of individual service members in the armed forces. There are well-regulated negotiation systems whereby military associations exercise collective bargaining over the course of many years with authorities in Austria, Belgium, Denmark, Finland, Germany, Hungary, Ireland, the Netherlands, Norway, Switzerland, and Sweden.[78]

---

78 Office for Democratic Institutions and Human Rights, Report of the Fourth Meeting in the ODIHR Human Rights, Discussion Series for Representatives of the Forum for Security Co-operation, Civil and Political Rights of Armed Forces Personnel (23 October 2014, Vienna), available at: https://www.osce.org/odihr/135696?download=true.

Chapter VI

Conclusion and Recommendations

Article 33 of the Constitution is an exception to the Fundamental Rights contained in Part III. A military person does not lose his Fundamental Rights *ipso facto* by joining the armed forces, but under Article 33, Parliament is endowed with power to restrict or abrogate the Fundamental Rights of the military personnel. Article 33 does not by itself abrogate any rights, but its applicability depends upon Parliamentary legislation. The term military includes certain categories of civilian personnel also who are non-combatant; but who on active service, in camps, on the march or at any frontier posts are employed by or are in service of the regular army. [1]

The freedom of association is a basic human right which should apply to all groups in society, including the armed forces personnel. However, most of the Western and Asian Constitutions discussed in the previous chapter, deny military personnel the right to unionize under the apprehension that this might impair combat effectiveness and national security. In their view military trade unions might lead to a breakdown of military discipline and threaten the chain of command. Unionization is prohibited, for example, in the UK, the USA, India, Pakistan, Bangladesh, Sri Lanka, Nepal, Spain, Portugal, Italy, France, Turkey, Greece, and Canada. The legal prohibition is expressed either in Acts of Parliament or in the military manuals.[2] In case of the United Kingdom, fundamental rights are not set

---

1   *O Kutilingal Achudan Nair v. Union of India,* (1976) 2 SCC 780 : AIR 1976 SC 1179 : 1976 SCR (2) 769.

2   For instance, Israeli Basic Law on Human Dignity and Liberty (1992) provides,"There shall be no restriction of rights under this Basic Law held by persons serving in the Israel

out in constitutional form. A soldier is free to discuss political issues in the same way as a civilian; however certain restrictions on this freedom have been imposed by military law. In the US, the Uniform Code of Military Justice (UCMJ) governs all active duty military members, reservists, and, in certain circumstances, retired members. However, Articles 88, 92, 133 and 134 restrict free speech or serve as a means to enforce organizational policies that limit free speech. These restrictions traditionally receive more scrutiny when the armed forces are operationally deployed. The political as well as military leaders emphasized the unique nature of military service – captured by the phrase "it's a service, not a job" – while pointing out the ultimate sacrifice required by the "military way of life". With the exception of Austria and Sweden, no country allows military unions to strike and limitations are placed on the scope of collective bargaining.[3]

India is a signatory to several international treaties protecting individuals from arbitrary or improper treatment, including the International Covenant on Civil and Political Rights (ICCPR), the International Convention on the Prevention and Punishment of the Crime of Genocide, and the International Convention on the Elimination of All Forms of Racial Discrimination, the International Convention against Torture and Other Cruel, Inhuman or Degrading Treatment or Punishment, and the four Geneva Conventions of 1949. As a UN member state, India is bound by the UN Charter, which pledges member states to "promote and encourage respect for human rights and for fundamental freedoms for all without distinction," and by the Universal Declaration of Human Rights, which protects the rights to liberty, freedom of expression and opinion, peaceful assembly, an effective remedy for acts violating fundamental rights, and a "fair and public hearing by an independent and impartial tribunal."

The ICCPR explicitly provides that the rights to life, freedom from torture or cruel, inhuman, or degrading treatment, freedom from prosecution under retroactive legislation, and freedom of thought,

---

Defense Forces, the Israel Police, the Prisons Service and other security organizations of the State, nor shall such rights be subject to conditions, except by virtue of a law, or by regulation enacted by virtue of a law, and to an extent no greater than is required by the nature and character of the service. Basic Law: Human Dignity and Liberty (1992), Article 9: Reservation regarding security forces.

3 For more details see: Mittelstadt J., "The Army is a Service, Not a Job": Unionization, Employment, and the Meaning of Military Service in the Late-Twentieth Century United States', *International Labour and Working-Class History*, 2011, No. 80, pp. 29-52.

conscience, and religion are non-derogable. The right to equality before the courts and tribunals and to a fair trial is a key element of human rights protection and serves as a procedural means to safeguard the rule of law. Article 14 of the ICCPR aims at ensuring the proper administration of justice, and to this end guarantees a series of specific rights. Article 14 is of a particularly complex nature, combining various guarantees with different scopes of application. The first sentence of paragraph 1 sets out a general guarantee of equality before courts and tribunals that applies regardless of the nature of proceedings before such bodies. The second sentence of the same paragraph entitles individuals to a fair and public hearing by a competent, independent and impartial tribunal established by law, if they face any criminal charges or if their rights and obligations are determined in a suit at law. Article 14 contains guarantees that the States parties must respect, regardless of their legal traditions and their domestic law. Deviating from fundamental principles of fair trial, including the presumption of innocence, is prohibited at all times. The provisions of Article 14 apply to all courts and tribunals within the scope of that article whether ordinary or specialized, civilian or military.[4]

India has long recognized the importance of ensuring its own compliance with these international human rights obligations. The Constitution provides, as a Directive Principle of State Policy, that the government "shall endeavour to foster respect for international law and treaty obligations in the dealings of organized people with one another," and also authorizes the central government to enact legislation implementing its international law obligations. The Supreme Court has frequently emphasized that constitutional and statutory provisions should be interpreted in light of India's international law obligations. The development of Fundamental Rights is a continuous process. It has to be re-interpreted at regular intervals and the judicial authorities have to play important role in their progressive development.

In India, the Parliament, instead of imposing the restrictions in the law itself, has empowered the Central Government to impose the restrictions as contemplated by Article 33. Section 21 of the Army Act, 1950, enacted under the authority of Article 33 gives the Central Government power to make rules restricting the three of the fundamental rights conferred by Article 19 of the Constitution. The Army Rules, 1954 framed by the Central Government under the authority of section 191 of the Army Act,

---

4 Human Rights Committee General Comment No. 32, Article 14: Right to equality before courts and tribunals and to a fair trial, CCPR/C/GC/32 dated 23 August 2007.

1950 contain Rules 19-21 which restricts the right of military personnel (i) to be part of any organization, association, or society or associated with any trade union activities; (ii) to attend, address or take part in any demonstration held for any political purpose, and (iii) to publish in any form or communicate with press in relation to a political question, or deliver any lecture related to political activities, etc. These restrictions are necessary for ensuring the discipline and proper discharge of duty by the members of the armed forces.[5] The restrictions thus imposed, so long cover the purpose specified by Article 33, the courts cannot examine the propriety or suitability of the restrictions.[6]

Reforms in Justice Delivery System

Despite our obsession with latest technology, armament and best soldiery, our justice system remains the most conservative. Military justice is a national issue, like the development of weapons, the size of our military, employment of women in combat roles in the armed forces, and so on. We need to address this strategic question: "What type of military justice system should we have to maintain the morale and discipline of the armed forces?" We can no longer leave it to the military to decide this. It has to be viewed from the perspectives of the politician and the people. Once the people, the politicians and the military agree on the strategic aspects of military justice, the other related issues can be evolved. So far we have considered the military justice system in a very narrow sense and left it to the armed forces.

Only a few minor changes were made in the British Indian Army Act, 1911, before being adopted by independent India. The military justice systems of the US, Australia, Canada and the South Africa also originated from the British Articles of War. However, they have undergone substantial changes in the last 15-20 years. The impetus came from changing international human rights concepts and criticism of the system by the judiciary. The British military justice system has itself undergone a series of amendments and modification in the last 15 years, culminating in the adoption of a single system of permanent Court-Martial under the tri-service Armed Forces Act, 2006.

The convening authority under the Indian military justice system holds an authoritative and influential position. He is responsible for: making the decision to prosecute; deciding the charges against the accused; deciding

---

5   R. *Viswan v. Union of India* 1983 SCR (3) 60 :AIR 1983 SC 658: 1983 SCC (3) 401.

6   Ibid.

about the type of court martial to try accused; appointing the prosecutor and the court members; detailing a judge advocate for trial (the judge advocate, the prosecutor and the court members come under his authority in the chain of command); can deny the service of a defence counsel on the ground of expediency; reviewing the sentence awarded by the court-martial; referring the proceedings back to the court for reconsideration (enhancing the punishment) even if an accused is acquitted by the court; considering the pre-confirmation petition of the accused; confirming the sentence awarded by the court-martial; and considering the post-confirmation petition of the convicted person.

Other nations, such as the UK, Australia, Canada, Israel, South Africa and the US have restricted the role of commanders in their military justice systems in order to limit actual bias as well as accusations and perceptions of unlawful command influence in judicial proceedings. An effective judicial review system also balances the power of the convening authority in the USA. It is essential that the military justice system responds to the evolving norms of human rights and the Indian Constitution. It must meet the expectations of serving military personnel. The Supreme Court *Re Union of India v Charanjit S Gill* has commented:

> In the absence of effective steps taken by the Parliament and the Central Government, it is the constitutional obligation of the courts in country to protect and safeguard the constitutional rights of all citizens including the personnel enrolled in the armed forces to the extent permissible under law by not forgetting the paramount need of maintaining the discipline in the armed forces of the country.[7]

The Constitution Bench of the Supreme Court in *Ram Sarup v. Union of India*,[8] with reference to Article 33 of the Constitution, has laid down limitations provided on the applicability of fundamental rights guaranteed to the military personnel under Articles 14, 16 and 21 of the Constitution and under Section 21 of the Army Act. In this case, the main contention raised for the petitioner based on the violation of fundamental rights was that the petitioner was not allowed to be defended at the general court

---

7 *Union of India v Charanjit S Gill* AIR 2000 SC 3425, at para 10.

8 In *Ram Sarup v. Union of India, Ram Sarup v. Union of India* AIR 1965 SC 247, the petitioner was charged on three counts under Section 69 of the Army Act read with Section 302 IPC. He was tried by a general court martial (GCM). On 12 January 1963, the GCM found him guilty of the three charges and sentenced him to death. The findings and sentence awarded by the GCM were confirmed by the Central Government. Thereafter, the petitioner filed a writ petition in the Supreme Court.

martial by a legal practitioner of his choice which was in violation of Article 22 (1) of the Constitution.[9] It was urged by the petitioner that in the exercise of the power conferred under Article 33 of the Constitution to modify fundamental rights guaranteed by Part III, the Parliament has enacted the Army Act, 1950. Section 21 of the Army Act empowers the Central Government to make rules relating to such extent and in such manner as may be necessary. That the restrictions imposed under Section 21 do not cover the fundamental rights under Articles 14, 20 and 22 of the Constitution and this indicates the intention of Parliament not to modify any other fundamental right.

However, the Supreme Court relied on the submission of the Attorney General that the entire Army Act has been enacted by Parliament and if any of the provisions of the Act is not consistent with the provisions of any of the Articles in Part III of the Constitution, it must be taken that to the extent of the inconsistency, Parliament has modified the fundamental rights under those articles in their application to persons subject to that Act. Any such provision in the Act is a law made by the Parliament and that --any such provision does not, on that account, become void. In fact in this case, the Supreme Court incorrectly relied upon incongruous submission of the Attorney General in the interpretation of the true and simple meaning of Article 33.

Article 14 of the Constitution deals with equality before law and provides, "The State shall not deny to any person equality before the law or equal protection of the laws within the territory of India." The concept of equality and equal protection of laws guaranteed by Article 14 in its proper spectrum encompasses social and economic justice in a political democracy.[10] Equality before law is co-relative to the concept of rule of law for all round evaluation of healthy social order. A basic postulate of the rule of law is that "justice should not only be done but it must also be seen to be done." Credibility in the functioning of justice delivery system and the reasonable perception of the affected parties are the relevant

---

9 Article 14 of the ICCPR explicitly addresses the guarantee of legal assistance in criminal proceedings in paragraph 3 (d). The States are obliged to provide free legal aid in cases where to individuals who do not have sufficient means to pay for it. Where a person sentenced to death seeks available constitutional review of irregularities in a criminal trial but does not have sufficient means to meet the costs of legal assistance in order to pursue such remedy, the State is obliged to provide legal assistance in accordance with Article 14, paragraph 1, in conjunction with the right to an effective remedy as enshrined in Article 2, paragraph 3 of the ICCPR.

10 *Dalmia Cement (Bharat) Ltd v. Union of India* (1996) 10 SCC 104.

considerations to ensure the continuance of public confidence in the credibility and impartiality of the judiciary.[11] Constitutional principle of equality is inherent in the rule of law. Every State has a constitutional obligation and duty to protect the life and liberty of its citizens; that is a fundamental requirement for observance of the rule of law. The Supreme Court in *Delhi Development Authority v. Joint Action Committee*[12] has held that reasonableness and fairness is the heart and soul of Article 14 of the Constitution. Therefore, the decision of the army to deny an accused the right to be tried by a defending officer of his choice in a court martial on capital charges (in *Ram Sarup*), demonstrates that the decision of the army authorities was neither 'reasonable' nor 'fair'. In fact, in subsequent amendment, a new provision has been inserted in the Regulations for the Army which provides for a counsel to a military person at state expense, if he is charges with an offence punishable with death.[13]

The right to be defended by person of choice was violated in *Ram Sarup*; which in fact is a serious violation of Article 14 of the Constitution. To put is differently, if *Ram Sarup* was defended by a counsel of his choice in court martial, it would have not affected the 'discipline' and the 'effective functioning' of the military. The Supreme Court has held that law which authorizes the trial of any class of persons by Special Court or by a procedure which differs substantially from the ordinary procedure to the prejudiced of the accused,[14] offends against Article 14.[15]

The Army Act was enacted in 1950 and was brought into force on 22 July 1950. Thus, the Act was enacted after the Constitution came into force on 26 January 1950. However, there was no clause-by-clause tread-bare discussion when the three services Acts (i.e. the Air Force Act 1950 and the Navy Act 1957) were passed by the Parliament. Let us consider

---

11 *P K Ghosh v. J G Rajput* (1995) 6 SCC 744.

12 *Delhi Development Authority v. Joint Action Committee* (2008) 2 SCC 672.

13 The Regulations for the Army, Volume I, 1987, paragraph 479 (a); Provision of Defence Counsel for Accused at Court-Martial Trials for Offences Punishable with Death: When a person subject to the Army Act is to be tried by court martial for an offence punishable with death and such person is unable to engage a counsel for his defence at the trial owing to lack of pecuniary resources and the convening officer is satisfied about his inability, a counsel for the defence of the accused at the trial may be employed by the convening officer at Government expense in consultation with the DJAG concerned.

14 *Rayala Corporation v. Director of Enforcement* (1970) 1 SCR 639.

15 *K R Rawat v. State of Saurashtra* (1952) SCT 435: AIR 1952 SC 123.

the case of *PPS Bedi v Union of India*,[16] wherein the Supreme Court for the first time critically analysed the laws governing the three services. The Court held, "Army, with its total commitment to national independence against foreign invasion must equally be assured the prized liberty of individual member against unjust encroachment. It was said that the court should strike a just balance between military discipline and individual personal liberty. And door must not be bolted against principles of natural justice even in respect of Army tribunal. An unnatural distinction or differentiation between a civilian offender and an offender subject to the Army Act would be destructive of the cherished principle of equality, the dazzling light of the Constitution which illumines all other provisions."

It was argued in the Bedi's case that the law to satisfy the requirement of Article 33 must be a specific law enacted by Parliament in which a specific provision imposing restriction or even abrogation of fundamental rights should be made and when such provisions are debated by the Parliament it would be clear as to how far restriction is imposed by Parliament on the fundamental rights enacted in Part III in their application to the members of the Armed Forces or the forces charged with the maintenance of public order. Submission is that a conscious and deliberate Act of Parliament may permit erosion of fundamental rights in their application to Armed Forces. Such a serious inroad on fundamental rights cannot be left to Central Government to be done by delegated legislation. Article 33 permits Parliament by law to not merely restrict but abrogate the fundamental rights enacted in Part III in their application to the members of Armed Forces. The Army Act, Section 21 confers power on the Central Government to make Rules restricting to such extent and in such manner as may be necessary to modify the fundamental freedom conferred by Article 19 (a) and (c) in their application to Armed Forces and none other meaning that Armed Forces would enjoy other fundamental freedoms set out in part III. Armed with this power, Rules 19, 20 & 21 have been framed by the Central Government.

The Supreme Court held, "While investigating and precisely ascertaining the limits of inroads or encroachments made by legislation enacted in exercise of power conferred by Article 33, on the guaranteed fundamental rights to all citizens of this country without distinction, in respect of armed personnel, the court should be vigilant to hold the balance between two conflicting public interests; namely necessity of discipline in

---

16 *Lt Col PPS Bedi v. Union of India* (1982) 3 SCC 140 : AIR 1982 SC 1413 decided on
    25 August 1982

armed personnel to preserve national security at any cost, because that itself would ensure enjoyment of fundamental rights by others, and the denial to those responsible for national security of these very fundamental rights which are inseparable adjuncts of civilized life."

In concluding part of the Bedi's judgement, the Supreme Court commented, "Reluctance of the apex court more concerned with civil law to interfere with the internal affairs of the Army is likely to create a distorted picture in the minds of the military personnel that persons subject to Army Act are not citizens of India. It is one of the cardinal features of our Constitution that a person by enlisting in or entering armed forces does not cease to be a citizen so as to wholly deprive him of his rights under the Constitution. .... In the larger interest of national security and military discipline Parliament in its wisdom may restrict or abrogate such rights in their application to the Armed Forces but this process should not be carried so far as to create a class of citizens not entitled to the benefits of the liberal spirit of the Constitution. Persons subject to Army Act are citizens of this ancient land having a feeling of belonging to the civilized community governed by the liberty-oriented constitution. Personal liberty makes for the worth of human being and is a cherished and prized right. ... Absence of even one appeal with power to review evidence, legal formulation, conclusion and adequacy or otherwise of punishment is a glaring lacuna in a country where a counterpart civilian convict can prefer appeal after appeal to hierarchy of courts. ..... Ours is still an antiquated system. The wind of change blowing over the country has not permeated the close and sacrosanct precincts of the Army..... We, therefore, hope and believe that the changes all over the English-speaking democracies will awaken our Parliament to the changed value system. In this behalf, we would like to draw pointed attention of the Government to the glaring anomaly that Courts Martial do not even write a brief reasoned order in support of their conclusion, even in cases in which they impose the death sentence."

This decision led to a few amendments in the Army Act in 1992 and the establishment of the Armed Forces Tribunal as an appellate forum for the members of the armed forces in 2007. The Minister of State in the Ministry of Defence, while introducing the Army (Amendment) Bill of 1992 in Parliament has stated, "The .... objective is to do away with the harsh, archaic and obsolete provisions which have somehow been carried forward in the Act from 1911, which were no longer in conformity with the

149

modern jurisprudence."[17] The main question here is that if the submission of the Attorney General in *Ram Sarup* case was justified, where was the need for the Parliament to amend the military law and create an appellate forum for the armed forces?

The Supreme Court in *Union of India v LD Balam Singh*[18] has said: "A plain reading [of Article 33] thus would reveal that the extent of restrictions necessary to be imposed on any of the fundamental rights in their application to the armed forces and the forces charged with the maintenance of public order for the purpose of ensuring proper discharge of their duties and maintenance of discipline among them would necessarily depend upon the prevailing situation at a given point of time and it would be inadvisable to encase it in a rigid statutory formula. The Constitutions makers were obviously anxious that no more restrictions should be placed than are absolutely necessary for ensuring proper discharge of duties and the maintenance of discipline amongst the Armed Force Personnel and therefore Article 33 empowered the Parliament to Forces, but does that mean and imply that the Army restrict or abridge within permissible extent, the rights conferred under Part III of the Constitution in so far as the Armed Force Personnel are concerned."

The Court further held that Article 33 of the Constitution though conferred a power but has not been taken recourse to put a bar or restraint as regards the non-availability of the statutory safeguards in terms therewith. While it is true that Army personnel ought to be subjected to

---

17 During the discussion on the Army (Amendment) Bill, 1992 in Parliament, the Minister of State in the Ministry of Defence stated, "There was a certain opinion expressed at certain time in the Defence Ministry consequent on a Supreme Court judgement or Supreme Court obiter dictum or opinion that a separate judicial review mechanism can be considered. But, since then the Ministry has examined this issue in great detail. The opinion of the armed forces is that any system of such judicial review over the court martial will considerably at any rate distract from the sacrosanct discipline of the army. Even the Founding Fathers of our Constitution have insulated court martial from the power of Superintendent of High Courts under Article 227(4) and also from the extraordinary powers conferred on the Supreme Court for grant of special leave to appeal, etc. So, the founders of our Constitution have taken this into consideration and in their wisdom very rightly insulated the discipline working of the armed forces. So, we do not want that the court martial decisions are immediately taken to court whether at the end of the court martial or while the proceedings are still on. That will take away from the powers of the Commanding Officer and it will violate the principles of army discipline in actual working." Available at:https://parliamentofindia.nic.in/ls/lsdeb/ls10/ses4/2218089207.htm.

18 *Union of India v. L D Balam Singh* (2002) 9 SCC 73: [2002] 3 SCR 385: 2002 (2) LC 790(SC).

strictest form of discipline and Article 33 of the Constitution has conferred powers on to the Parliament to abridge the rights conferred under Part III of the Constitution in respect of the members of the Armed Personnel would be denuded of the Constitutional privileges as guaranteed under the Constitution."

The Delhi High Court while deciding the case of *Lance Naik V.P. Singh v. Union of India,* (2008) held:

> Mindful of the fact that Article 33 of the Constitution of India confers unbridled powers on Parliament to bring into place a situation which severely abridges the Fundamental Rights of a citizen it becomes bounden duty of the Courts to ensure that the equality doctrine is not needlessly nullified. It also becomes essential that the Courts should interpret the law in a manner which will reduce to the minimum the inroads into the infrangible rights contained in Chapter III of the Constitution.

The Supreme Court in *Yash Pal v. Union of India* (2017) [19] came to rescue of porters hired by the army as casual labourers in the border areas of J&K. These porters were issues identity cards by the competent authority in the army. However, they were not treated as regular employees and denied the benefits of minimum pay despite having served for long years in the Army. The Court directed for payment of minimum wages at the prevalent rates; payment of allowances for working in high risk/active service areas; regular medical services in the case of injury or disability; compensation in the case of permanent disability; interim relief of Rs 200,000 as applicable under the Workmen's Compensation Act, 1923; and one-time severance grant of Rs 50,000, for those who have rendered ten years of service.

The Indian judiciary has played a creative role in enlarging and protecting human rights. Fundamental rights which are not specifically mentioned have been spelt out and deduced on the reasoning that certain un-enumerated rights are implicit in the enumerated guarantees. The Supreme Court in *Pathumma v. State of Kerala*[20] has held: "In interpreting the constitutional provisions for judging the impact of an enactment on the fundamental rights of the citizens the approach of the Courts is to interpret the constitutional provisions against the social setting of the country so as to show a complete consciousness and deep awareness

---

19 WP (Civil) No. 616 of 2013 and No. 912 of 2013, decided on 2 January 2017.

20 *Pathumma v. State of Kerala*, AIR 1978 SC 771 : 1978 SCR (2) 537.

of the growing requirements of the society, the increasing needs of the nation, the burning problems of the day and the complex issues facing the people which the legislature in its wisdom, through beneficial legislation, seeks to solve. The judicial approach should be dynamic rather than static, pragmatic rather than pedantic and elastic rather than rigid. It must take into consideration the changing trends of economic thought, the temper of the times and the living aspirations and feelings of the people. This Court must strike a just balance between the fundamental rights and the larger and broader interests of society."

In order to lessen the burden on trials, and ensure speedy disposal of cases, the Criminal Law (Amendment) Act, 2005 has introduced the concept of Alternate Dispute Resolution—plea bargaining--into the criminal arena.[21] The plea-bargaining agreement has become widespread due to the advantages it offers to both the accused and the prosecution. The success of plea bargaining as a procedure leading to high convictions has been proven in the United States, where its constitutionality has been upheld.[22]While implementing the concept of plea bargaining in the Indian military justice system, few safeguards must be kept in mind: (i) plea must be voluntary and an accused must be made aware of circumstances and likely consequence by a law qualified officer, (ii) the officers of the judge advocate general branch should play a greater role in the process, for which they need to be independent from the existing chain of command, and (iii) complete record of disposition to be maintained to ensure transparency and consistency.

Importance of Human Rights

In India, the enjoyment of human rights by the members of the armed forces is disproportionately restricted, not by the Constitution, but by the law passed by the Parliament or subordinate legislations, i.e., made by the government. For instance, an Act of Parliament has bestowed on them the right to make complaints seeking the redress of their grievances. The Regulations of the three services, made by the Government, provide different procedures for the processing of complaints.[23] The unscrupulous

---

21 Criminal Law (Amendment) Bill 2005 was passed by both the Houses of Parliament vide Notification No. S.O. 990 (E) dt. 03.7.06 and came into force from July 05, 2006. It added a new Chapter XX-A to the Criminal Procedure Code, 1973.

22 *Santobello v. New York* 404 US 257 (1971).

23 The Army Act, 1950, sections 26 and 27; the Air Force Act, sections 26 and 27; and the Navy Act, Section 23 deal with the redress of grievance. The Regulations for the

processing of a grievance petition damages the effectiveness of a statutory right; often frustrates the complainant, leading to dissatisfaction and demoralization. The framers of the Constitution had a positive attitude towards human rights perhaps because most of them had suffered long incarceration under the British. Accordingly, they incorporated human rights in the Constitution under the title of 'Fundamental Rights' in part III, Articles 12–35. Even though they may have thought it necessary to curtail certain rights of 'men in uniform', it could never have been their intention to deprive them of the basic fundamental rights. The Supreme Court has held: 'It is a fallacy to regard Fundamental Rights as a gift from the State to its citizens. Individual possess basic human rights independently of any constitution by reasons of basic fact that they are members of human race. These Fundamental Rights are important as they possess intrinsic value.'[24] At a time when our civil society and the honourable members of Parliament are fighting for the rights of animals, we must be compelled to ensure that the people who protect our country are not deprived of their rights.

In our country even prisoners deprived of personal liberty are not wholly denuded of their fundamental rights. In the larger interest of national security and military discipline Parliament in its wisdom may restrict or abridge such rights in their application to the Armed Forces but this process should not be carried so far as to create a class of citizen not entitled to the benefits of liberal spirit of the Constitution. Military personnel are citizens of this ancient land having feeling of belonging to the civilized community governed by the liberty-oriented Constitution. They are as much a citizen as any other individual citizen of this country. By virtue of being citizens, members of the armed forces should enjoy the same human rights and fundamental freedoms as other citizens. Respect for human rights has a positive impact and can help to improve cohesiveness and operational effectiveness. Respect for rights also contributes to trust and good working relations between peers, and between soldiers and their commanders.[25] Ensuring that soldiers enjoy a broad range of human

---

Army (1987), para 364 (as amended in 1992); the Regulations for the Air Force (1964), para 621 and 622; and the Regulations for the Navy (1991), Part II, para 238 and 239 prescribe procedure for submission and processing of the redress complaints.

24 *M Nagraj v Union of India* AIR 2007 SC 71.

25 In the last seven year there have been nine reported incidents of officers-soldiers clash in the army. In one of the most serious such incident in May 2012, the court of inquiry, chaired by the deputy chief of the Infantry Division recommended disciplinary action against the 168 personnel of the Field Artillery Regiment, including the unit

rights can also foster a positive public image of armed forces in society. Human rights are not merely a matter of high-sounding aspirations written in manuals, they must also be fully implemented in daily practice in the armed forces.

There have been a number of instances where the military authorities have curtailed Fundamental Right to life and liberty of members of the armed forces in an unjust and malicious way. The State must be held responsible for the unlawful acts of its officers and it must repair the damages to the citizens by its officers for violating their right of personal liberty without any authority of law in an absolute high-handed manner. [26] The award of compensation against the state is an appropriate and effective remedy; such provisions need to be introduced in the military legal system.

The Supreme Court in *Kumari Shrilekha Vidyarthi v. State of UP*[27] has remarked that decision maker invested with the wide discretion in administrative action is expected to exercise that discretion in accordance with the general principles governing exercise of power in a constitutional democracy unless of course the statute under which such power is exercised indicates otherwise. One of the most fundamental principles of rule of law recognized in all democratic systems is that the power vested in any competent authority shall not be exercised arbitrarily and if the power is exercised it should not lead to any unfair discrimination.[28] The basic requirement of Article 14 is fairness in action by the State and it is difficult to accept that the State can be permitted to act otherwise in any field of its activity, irrespective of the nature of its function, when it has the

---

commanding officer, after finding them prima facie guilty for the face-off, breakdown of discipline, abject failure of command and control, violence and other lapses. In July 2017, an army officer of the rank of major was shot dead by a jawan of his unit after he reportedly rebuked him for using his mobile phone at a forward position in Uri sector of Kashmir. A few senior retired officers are of the view that the growing number of clashes between officers and jawans indicate a serious crisis in the Indian Army which has resulted from the prolonged apathy of the military and political leadership. For more details see: Unhappy Army, *Frontline*, 15 November 2013.

26 *Dhananjay Sharma v. State of Haryana*, (1995) 3 SCC 757.

27 *Kumari Shrilekha Vidyarthi v. State of UP* 1991 AIR 537, 1990 SCR Supl (1) 625.

28 There is no precise statutory or other definition of the term "arbitrary". The term 'Arbitrary/ arbitrariness' has been defined in the following words, "Depending on individual discretions; a determination made without determination of or regards for facts, circumstances, fixed rules or procedure; a (judicial decision) funded upon prejudice or preference rather than on reason of fact; this type of decision is often termed arbitrary and capricious. Garner Bryan A., *Black's Law Dictionary*, Tenth Edition, 2014, Thomson Reuters, p. 125.

uppermost duty to be governed by the rule of law. The Constitution does not envisage or permit unfairness or unreasonableness in State actions in any sphere of its activity contrary to the professed ideals in the Preamble.

A large number of Indians have been subject to the military justice system in the past 71 years and more will do so in the future. This makes it all the more necessary to examine the extent of applicability of Article 33 of the Constitution to this section of the population and to protect their Fundamental Rights. Encroachment of the Fundamental Rights of the members of the armed forces is not permissible in matters which do not relate to the discharge of their duties or to the maintenance of discipline. The models followed in the US, the UK, Australia, Canada and South Africa, could be examined to see how these countries have resolved the issues related to the applicability of individual rights and constitutional guarantees to military personnel.

Fundamental Rights: Members of the Armed Forces

The members of armed forces must be entitled to every Fundamental Right contained in the Constitution, subject to certain restrictions inherent to military service in conformity with international human rights law. For example, freedom to form association and freedom of expression may be limited to prevent the armed forces personnel from publicizing legitimate military official classified documents. We need to consider how the following Fundamental Rights come in the way of military discipline and their effective functioning during the peacetime.

- **The right to life**: for example, investigations into unexplained deaths while performing military tasks or in military camps and placing investigation reports in public domain.

- **The right to equality**: for example, differences in treatment to women officers; payment of *ex gratia* at par with Delhi police personnel who die while performing official duty.

- **The right not to be subjected to torture, cruel, inhuman, or degrading treatment or punishment**: for example, not be awarded any cruel punishment or treatment and not subjected to forced labour.

- **The freedom of peaceful assembly and the freedom of association**: for example, allowing limited right to form associations and take up matters with the government relating to their pay and promotions.

- **The right to humane conditions of work and wages**: for example, payment of remuneration for extra work; right to suitable service accommodation, respect for their private and family life and their home.

- **The right to a fair trial and fair hearing and the right to an effective remedy**: for example right to fair hearing in the case of award of minor punishments, trial under summary systems of court martial like SCM and SGCM; provision of free legal aid during disciplinary trials and making appeals; streamlining the power of convening authority in military justice system; the processing of grievance redressal applications keeping applicant in loop, similar to those being followed in a number of other democratic countries; and introduction of plea bargaining in the military justice system.

In Indian armed forces women experience discrimination in terms of the positions open to them and their career progression. Discrimination, harassment, bullying and abuse not only violate the rights of victims but are detrimental to discipline and morale within armed forces, and thus to operational effectiveness. The full integration of both women and men is necessary for armed forces to draw upon all the available skills and talents of service personnel. Military disciplinary and justice systems need to be sensitive to these issues and must develop the necessary expertise to deal with them appropriately. The integration of women into combat role is most likely to improve troop performance and motivation. The armed forces need to change their organizational culture and the attitudes of male soldiers towards women. It may be useful to define female soldiers not primarily as women but, on the contrary, in the first instance as fellow professionals. It implemented properly, the accession of women to the combat arms is likely to enhance military's combat effectiveness.[29]

Ensuring respect for the Fundamental Rights of armed forces personnel is not merely a legal obligation on states. It is also crucial in raising awareness and creating a professional culture within the military that includes respect for human rights as part of a commitment to democratic values. When this is achieved, the armed forces are not just defenders of a state's territorial integrity; they also defend and embody its values.

---

29 King Anthony, Women in Combat, *The Three Sword Magazine*, Vol. 29, 2015, pp. 22-26. Also see: Bastick Megan, *Integrating a Gender Perspective into Internal Oversight within Armed Forces*, Geneva: DCAF, OSCE, OSCE/ODIHR, 2014, pp. 64.

Any restriction on Fundamental Rights must be related to the maintenance of discipline, morale and efficiency of the armed forces. In the absence of such a connection, there is no reason why a military person would not enjoy the same rights as any other citizens. Indeed, it would be ironic for those who have the ultimate responsibility of protecting freedom, justice and social equality, at the risk of their lives, to not enjoy the same Fundamental Rights.

The Government must appoint an expert committee headed by a Member of Parliament to review the three-service legislation and bring out a new common code for the armed forces. The new system should limit command authority, and balance it with procedure established by law and judicial authority. This system must be based on two basic principles: (a) every soldier, sailor or airman, regardless of rank, must be responsible and accountable for his actions, and (b) every soldier, sailor or airman, regardless of circumstance, must be entitled to being treated fairly and with dignity and respect. Such a study and reform is long overdue.

Present-day military personnel in India are more conscious of their fundamental, human and natural rights. The members of the armed forces cannot be expected to respect humanitarian law and human rights in their operations unless respect for human rights is guaranteed within the military ranks. The morale and discipline of the armed forces are enhanced when the troops feel that they are being treated with dignity, fairness and equality under the law. The soldiers whose human rights are protected within the organization are more likely to prevent human rights violations during deployment.[30]

The arbitrariness of governance in service matter and justice delivery systems has been questioned in a large number of cases. The Ministry of Defence in place of providing relief to the members of the armed forces has been infamous for filing appeals in every case which has been decided

---

30 Under international human rights laws, the obligations of the military while deployed in internal security duties are as follows: (i) The duty to respect, i.e. the duty not to violate human rights and not to impose more restrictions of rights than necessary to fulfil its obligations and to protect the rights of others; (ii) The duty to protect, i.e. to protect, to the extent possible, all persons against violations of rights by others or by otherwise dangerous situations; (iii) The duty to ensure and to fulfil human rights, i.e. to provide, to the extent possible, all persons with basic services and living circumstances that allow them full enjoyment of their rights; and (iv) The duty not to discriminate, i.e. the duty to ensure at all times equal treatment of all persons before the law. They are required to promote, protect and respect the human rights of all people without any adverse distinction.

against them by the courts or tribunal.[31] A recent report submitted to the Minister of Defence has made scathing remarks on the ministry's attitude calling it a "compulsive litigant" rather than a "responsible litigant". It pointed out that most litigations were "ego-fuelled", further observing that the "cost incurred in litigation, by litigants and the exchequer, and the wastage of man-hours and other intangible aspects such as movement of files and personnel, surpasses the amount involved in redressing the issue itself." The report also highlighted that "the duty of the Government was not to win cases by hook or crook or to trample down weaker parties or to score advantage over litigants."According to report, "The times have changed and there would have to be an attitudinal shift towards flexibility, transparency and a progressive and proactive outlook by rationalizing the rights of individuals with those of the State."[32]

The law relating to the armed forces in India remains static and requires to be changed keeping in view the changes effected by other democratic countries. We can no longer ignore the challenges of remodelling the governance of the armed forces and protecting the fundamental rights of its personnel. There is a need for a more authentic projection of the military as it cannot be disconnected from the civilian realm. The government must redefine the rights and duties of military personnel to ensure that the military as an employer is capable of attracting and retaining the best talent.

---

31 The Armed Forces Tribunal, Chandigarh Regional Bench has recently commented on the pitiable attitude of the Ministry of Defence in granting war injury pension to entitled military personnel. The Bench commented, "The Armed Forces Tribunal Act has been established for the welfare of the Army personnel who are generally not so literate and are villagers. This is a welfare step and in such matters (war injuries), the rule of technicalities cannot be allowed to invoke to take away a just cause as the one in the present case. .... we are of the view that closing the door for ex-serviceman whose leg was amputated on line of control due to Mortar blast injury, if denied the benefit which is due to him under law, would be very harsh and will not meet the expectation of individual who are serving the nation." Further, "We are constrained to point out that, the non-grant of War Injury Pension to the petitioner and similarly placed soldiers are a gross miscarriage of justice. See: *Inder Singh v. Union of India*, CWP 8653 of 2009) decided on 18 April 2011 and *Chattar Singh v. Union of India* (OA No. 4590 of 2013) decided on 17 December 2015.

32 The Raksha Mantri's Committee of Expert constituted for the "Review of Service and Pension Matters including Potential Disputes, Minimizing Ligations and Strengthening Institutional Mechanism related to Redressal of Grievances" submitted it report to the Minister of Defence in November 2015. The Report hasbrought out that a total of 16,138 (Army 14,411, Navy 437, Air Force 1,241, and Coast Guard 49) cases related to the uniformed services were pending before various Courts and Tribunals in the country. Report available at: https://mod.gov.in/sites/default/files/Reportcc_0.pdf.

A. Constituent Assembly Debates

(Debated on 9 December 1948)[1]

The Constituent Assembly of India met in the Constitution Hall, New Delhi, at Ten of the Clock, Mr. Vice-President (Dr. H. C. Mookherjee) in the Chair.

Mr. Vice-President: We then come to article 26. The motion before the House is:

That article 26 form part of the Constitution.

The Honourable Dr. B. R. Ambedkar: Sir, I move:

> "That in article 26 for the words 'guaranteed in' the words 'conferred by' be substituted."

This part does not guarantee but only confers these rights. Therefore to bring the language in conformity, I propose this amendment.

Mr. Vice-President: The question is:

> "That in article 26 for the words 'guaranteed in' the words 'conferred by' be substituted."

The amendment was adopted.

Mr. Vice-President: The question is that:

That Article 26, as amended stand part of the Constitution.

The motion was adopted.

Article 26, as amended was adopted to the Constitution.[2]

---

1 CONSTITUENT ASSEMBLY OF INDIA Debates - VOLUME VII, p. 995, Thursday, the 9th December, 1948.

2 Article was renumbered and appeared as Article 33, as adopted by the Constituent Assembly:

> **33: Power of Parliament to modify the rights conferred by this part in their application to Forces**:- Parliament may by law determine to what extent any of the rights conferred by this Part shall, in their application to the members of the Armed Forces or the Forces charged with the maintenance of public order, be restricted or abrogated so as to ensure the proper discharge of their duties and the maintenance of discipline among them.

AMENDMENT

Clause 2 of the Constitution (Fifty-Second Amendment) Bill, 1984

2. Substitution of Article 33. For Article 33 of the Constitution, the following article shall be substituted, namely:-

> "33. Power of Parliament to modify the rights conferred by this Part in their application to Forces, etc.- Parliament may, by law, determine to what extent any of the rights conferred by this Part shall, in their application to,-
>
> (a)   the members of the Armed Forces; or
>
> (b)   the members of the Forces charged with the maintenance of public order; or
>
> (c)   the members of the Forces charged with the protection of property belonging to, or in the charge of or possession of the state; or
>
> (d)   persons employed in any bureau or other organisation established by the State for purposes of intelligence or counter intelligence; or
>
> (e)   persons employed in, or in connection with, the telecommunication systems set up for the purposes of any Force, bureau or organisation referred to in clauses (a) to (d)
>
> be restricted or abrogated so as to ensure the proper discharge of their duties and the maintenance of discipline among them."

B.   Lok Sabha Debates

(Introduced, debated and adopted –22 August, 23 August 1984)

The Minister of Home Affairs (Shri P.V. Narasimha Rao): I beg to move for leave to introduce a Bill further to amend the Constitution of India.

Mr. Speaker: I have got notices from the members who want to oppose the introduction of this Bill.

Shri Sunil Maitra: (Calcutta North-East): Sir, this is another piece of pernicious legislation that has been brought by the government in order not to extend the democratic rights, but in order to abridge the rights already conferred on us. Sir the policies of the Government have been creating resentment among the masses. The Armed Forces, para-military forces, Government employees, semi-Government employees and the vast mass of the people are the targets of certain ruthless policies of the government of India. The net result of it is the enormous mass of the people are becoming restless. If the government had been serious, then it would have devised some way in order to hear the grievances of the people, in order to listen to the resentment of the people in various segments and tried to find some avenues whereby some mutual discussion would have taken place and the grievances would have been redressed. But instead of finding avenues, the Government are trying to amend the Constitution for the 52nd time to see to it that the rights already conferred on the people are abridged.

Sir, Article 33 was only limited to the Armed Forces. Now, its scope is being expanded. Now, not only the Armed Forces, but also the Government employees working in the telecommunication system and working in other government institutions are being sought to be brought under the purview of the Amendment of the Constitution. But, Sir, let this Government understand that this will not solve the problems. Sir, this government till today is not realizing that it is sitting on the top of a live volcano.

Shri Sudhir Giri (Cont.): Mr. Deputy Speaker, Sir, I oppose the introduction of this Bill.

Please go through Article 33 of the Constitution which says:

> "Parliament may, by law, determine to what extent any of the rights conferred by this part (i.e., Part III) shall, in their application to the members of the Armed Forces or the Forces charged with the maintenance of public order, be restricted or abrogated so as to ensure the proper discharge of the duties and the maintenance of discipline among them."

Sir, the founding fathers while including this provision in the Constitution had in their mind that the restrictive law should be applicable only to the Armed Forces and the Forces charged with the maintenance of public order. That is, I think, the police forces. But this Bill is going to expand the ambit of this provision.

Sir, our forefathers had to fight a long battle to achieve these Fundamental Rights. They sacrificed their life and after this battle and sacrifices these rights had been achieved, the Government is going to curb these rights. What are the causes? I feel the capitalist system of our country is facing a crisis. Every capitalist system of development in any country has its own inherent inconsistencies which leave the Government or the Administration to face the crisis in every way. In our country also I find that the crisis has deepened. For this reason the people of the country are agitating. While the people have been conscious of their rights and preserving those rights in their favour, the Government is going to curb those rights. I think the Government feels that it will not be possible for it to maintain law and order in the country by application of CRP Forces. That is why the Government is expanding the ambit of the Constitution so that in respect of the people who will voice their demands for the realization of their rightful gains, the Government is going to sack them. I therefore, oppose the introduction of this Bill at this stage.

Shri Harikesh Bahadur (Gorakhpur): This Government came into power in 1980. Since then have been continuously bringing several measures to abrogate fundamental rights of the citizens of various sections of society. Their fundamental rights are being attacked by several legislations which have been brought before this House. This is another attack on the fundamental rights of our people, a section of them. That is why I strongly oppose it at the introduction stage.

There are several other points which I would like to make here. Whatever may be the intention, the entire country will feel that this bill has been brought before the House with the criminal intention of the Government. By abrogating the fundamental rights of the citizens, the Government is not going to serve the purpose basically. They are going to attack the democratic fabric. The Government has already misused military, para-military and police forces. We have been observing it. By this amendment in the Constitution they want to make it very legitimate. Now, through this process they will misuse it very badly. It is a danger for every citizen of this country. That is why I oppose it. Whatever assurance is given by the Home Minister, I would like to say Government has lost its credibility completely. We are not going to accept any of his assurances.

Shri Satyasadhan Chakraborty (Calcutta South): The Constitution has given certain fundamental rights to the people. They enjoy many other rights. But some rights are regarded as fundamental because, without these rights, the democracy cannot function; the individuals cannot function. That is why these rights are enshrined in Part III of the Constitution so that these cannot be changed easily by any Government, by the whims of any Government. What is the Government doing today? They are trying to take away these fundamental rights from Part III of the Constitution and making them subjected to the Parliamentary law passed by an ordinary majority, at the whims of any Government. So, I oppose this very strongly.

Take, for example, the member of the Armed Forces. What are the reasons for taking away their rights? I am in favour of discipline; I am in favour of order. The hon. Minister will have to explain what he actually understands by discipline and order. Is it the old British idea of law and order? I oppose this because some categories of persons who enjoy certain freedoms which this Constitution guarantees, those persons are going to be deprived of those rights.

I oppose this because of other reasons also. The Government are taking these powers but they will not specify when they bring forward a Bill like this, what rights they are going to abrogate, what rights they are going to abridge. Certain categories of people, not even directly connected with law and order are going to be deprived of their rights. This is a dangerous thing. The hon. Minister should have mentioned in the Statement of Objects and Reasons that these are the rights they want to curtail or abrogate. They are taking a sweeping power and, in future, in an ordinary Bill they will enunciate all these things and pass it. That is why I feel it is a dangerous thing.

In conclusion, I thank you for your patience and I would only say that all the amendments and the laws have reference to certain things. There must be a cause of action. What is the cause of their action? What has happened in the country? Why are the raising para-military forces and also taking away the rights of the people? Have you declared emergency anywhere? Is the country passing through emergency? In an emergency certain things can be done. But without declaring emergency, they are taking all the steps that emergency in the country warrants and that too when there is no attack from outside.

I oppose this Bill as undemocratic, unconstitutional and against all the fundamental laws of the country."[1]

The Minister of Home Affairs (Shri P.V. Narasimha Rao): Mr. Speaker, Sir, I beg to move:

> "That the Bill further to amend the Constitution of India, be taken into consideration."

Sir, by Article 33 of the Constitution, Parliament is empowered to enact

---

1   Thereafter leave was granted to introduce the Bill and the Parliament proceeded to take the Bill into consideration.

laws determining to what extent any of the rights conferred by Part III of the Constitution shall, in their application to the members of the banned forces or the forces charged with the maintenance of public order be restricted or abrogated so as to ensure the proper discharge of their duties and the maintenance of discipline among them.

There are certain other organizations whose charter of duties is akin or complementary to that of the forces charged with the maintenance of public order. These organizations are meant for collection of intelligence and for transmission and reception of messages relating to law and order. The maintenance of discipline among personnel working in these organizations is as vital in the national interest as maintaining of discipline by members of armed forces or police forces. It is, therefore proposed to amend Article 33 of the Constitution to bring within its ambit personnel working in the aforesaid categories of organizations.

Sir, I would like to add at this stage that with the hope that my reasonableness will be matched by the reasonableness from the other side, I have tabled an amendment to delete (c) which is not really related to security. It is important in itself but we thought that it will be reasonable to delete it. So, all the other items are directly related to security and that is why I expect from the Opposition that the same reasonableness would be shown and there will be no difficulty in accepting this amendment.

Mr. Speaker: Motion moved:

"That the Bill further to amend the Constitution of India, be taken into consideration."

Shri Somnath Chatterjee (Jadavpur):

Sir, we are told that in view of the supposedly great concessions made by him in proposing the deletion of Clause-C from the proposed amendments we should be reasonable and by being reasonable, he thinks, he assumed that we ought to support this Bill. I am afraid, Madam, we cannot oblige my right hon. friend. Madam, in a sense, I welcome this Bill because it will accelerate the process of the final eclipse of this anti-people Government. This Bill exposes once again, once more the authoritarian character of this Government during these last days when it is fighting to stop disintegration of its party, gasping for breath for survival. Madam, I feel it is political impropriety and moral perversity to assume more and more draconian powers by amendment to the Constitution. Of course, we are not surprised that such types of anti-people laws should be brought forward in this House by this Government because enforcement of the people's Fundamental Rights, even though minimal --as they are in our Constitution—is always considered to be an abuse of the powers by this Government. That is why we find greater and greater restraint, greater and greater control by the executive on the exercise of the minimal Fundamental Rights. Madam, you are aware that Fundamental Rights which are contained in Article 19 of the Constitution there are exceptions provided on the ground or reasonable restrictions, almost all the Fundamental Rights as provided in Article 19 of the Constitution are subject to control, subject to restriction and subject to curb and greater and greater use of this restrictive clause have been taken recourse to for the purpose of reducing the ambit of the Constitutional and Fundamental Rights of the people of this country. We consider that it is unfortunate that our founding fathers did not repose faith in the people of this country, who fought for the emancipation of the country from the British foreign rule, foreign domination, and the whole Constitution in some aspects has assumed that the people of this country will misuse the very limited power that has been given to them under the Constitution. Unfortunately, what has been done during the last 34 years, since the Constitution came into force? What we find is no enlargement of the rights of the people. No amendment has been brought by this Government or the earlier Government for the enlargement of the rights of the people. Workers' rights have been restricted, common peoples' rights have been restricted; preventive detention law is now a permanent feature of this country. I would like the Home Minister to show if they have brought about any changes either in the law or in the Constitution where they have conceded any greater right to the people.

What our Constitution-makers thought to be sufficient, we feel that it was unfortunate even then, that the Parliament in the exercise of its legislative power can impose restrictions on the exercise of the Fundamental Rights--by whom--by members of the Armed Forces or the Forces charged with maintenance of public order which includes the police. It was thought sufficient and, of course, I consider it unfortunate.

These are some of the provisions which are the black spots on our Constitution like Article 22(4) which permits preventive detention. These are the black spots, and we should have changed them as we have changed so many other provisions of the Constitution. We have changed those provisions of the Constitution which perpetuated privy purses and princely system in this country, because it was found that it went against the very concept of a democratic society, egalitarian society; it perpetuated vested interests. This is why this Parliament in its constituent power has changed these provisions, obliterated them. We have obliterated provisions like Article 31 (B) where Zamindari was, in a sense, perpetuated. By experience, people have changed those provisions of the Constitution which were standing in the way of the country's progress, although many other provisions still remain. This government ought to have a commitment to the rights of the people, but we find that somehow, their whole attitude is that the people should have least rights and their rights should be as minimal as possible. That is why one such law has been passed which takes away the people's rights. What is ESMA, Essential Services Maintenance Act? This is nothing but what takes away very very limited rights which the working class in this country has been enjoying. Article 19, with its various sub-Articles, makes the exercise of Fundamental Rights possible not in a very wide manner but in a restricted manner. Now in the name of security of the country---it is always easy to mention security of the country---what is being proposed to be done is to confer powers on the Parliament to make laws to take away the rights of any and every so-called security force in this country. Why? Are the people in the Security services of the country all anti-nationals? Do they not have any sense of patriotism? For the sake of their service conditions, for the improvement of their service conditions, or for removal of certain grievances, can they not be allowed to form associations or be permitted to project their grievances before the authorities? Can they not be expected to act with a sense of responsibility? Why do you distrust them? You are creating a chasm between them and the Government. How do you help in the instilling in them a spirit of service to the country and the people? You are alienating them from the Government by putting greater and greater restraints on their minimal rights.

This is our opposition, in principle, to the Bill. I would like to know one very significant fact: the Hon Minister has not stated in what manner he wants to exercise this power. What are the rights affected? Kindly see the Constitution, and what is being proposed to be done.

It says here that the fundamental rights "... can be restricted or abrogated so as to ensure the proper discharge of their duties and maintenance of discipline among them. That is what you say. If so, you have to make a law. It cannot be done by a mere amendment...

Sir, you want to issue ordinances, taking away rights. What are the rights which you will take away? The Army Act is an illustration. Under Article 33 of the Constitution, rules have been framed, taking away their trade union rights. Even the civilian employees of the Defence Services are not being considered fit to have the right to form associations. How, then, do they project their views? Do you want to make them deaf and dumb, and to stifle their views, even if they have a reasonable demand?

I would like to tell the Hon Minister: In a part of this country, *viz.*, West Bengal, police have been given all trade union rights. Has that affected the efficiency of the police?

Shri Sontosh Mohan Dev (Silchar): Definitely.

Shri Somnath Chatterjee: Let there be a serious discussion. Don't always be flippant.

Shri Sontosh Mohan Dev: It has been said so by one of your Ministers.

Shri Somnath Chatterjee: If, in a particular case, our police had been inefficient, our Minister is honest enough to admit it. Not like you. I can cite cases where the Supreme Court has passed strong strictures against the police in States ruled by Congress (I) Governments. Therefore, you should educate yourself first.

Sir, I am proud to say that in West Bengal which is a part of this country, we have conceded the minimum right of the police to form trade unions, to participate in the process of consideration of their rights as responsible citizens of India, and as responsible members of the police force. It has not created any difficulty. Therefore, I say that the Government of India thrives on authoritarianism. This government excels in taking away the rights of the people. I am sorry I cannot support this Bill. We shall oppose it in spite of this proposed amendment of the hon. Minister. We think this is another piece of draconian legislation; and this type of legislation will do nothing but denude the rights of the people, which means it is an anti-people legislation. I oppose it.

Shri Ravindra Varma (Bombay North): I have profound respect for the Rt. Hon Home Minister. In fact his ardent and effective manner in which he advocated the cause of human rights in the United Nations has enhanced the respect in which he is held all over the country. It is, therefore, a sad conspiracy of circumstances that has occasioned the sight of the Rt. Hon. Gentleman coming before the House with four Bills in succession aimed at restricting the fundamental rights of the citizens in this country. Article 33 of the Constitution does confer the right on Parliament to enact laws to restrict and abridge the Fundamental Rights of certain categories of citizens. Rt. Hon. friend from Jadhavpur has also pointed out to the fact that once this amendment is adopted, the Government will be empowered to bring in Bills to the House and use the authority or abuse the authority to bring proposals before the House which can be adopted with a simple majority, which therefore, will not require the majority needed to amend a constitutional provision. Though there are many Fundamental Rights enumerated in Part III, the target of Article 33 — as my hon. friend from Jadhavpur [would] bear me out — is the Fundamental Rights in Article Number 19 which deals with the freedom of speech, freedom of association, etc. The target of attack is the Fundamental Right in Article 19, which is the freedom of association and freedom of speech to which my hon. friend has referred. Any restriction imposed on the Fundamental Right of a citizen can be justified only if it can be proved that it is in the interest of Collective the society and the State and only if the restriction imposed is minimal. Unfortunately, I beg to submit for your consideration what my Rt. Hon. Friend has brought before the House enlarges the area, the number of categories which are affected by this restriction or abridgement of the Fundamental Rights. Moreover, the Bill as it is now before the House leaves the criteria for justification vague.

The enlargement is not a minimal enlargement. My hon. friend knows very well that 33 (a) and (b) as they are today in the existing Article of the Constitution cover about three million people.

Shri Ravindra Varma: ...

The rationale of the restriction has been put down in the Article as it is. There are two objectives that have been mentioned, one is the proper discharge of their duties and the other is the maintenance of discipline. These are impeccable, these are understandable but we do not grudge these, we do not cavil at them. We agree specially because of the special nature of these services, their relation to security and public order, to which we are as committed as the Right hon. gentleman, the need for immediate and implicit obedience of orders of superiors, the need for full-hearted and earnest compliance, even at the cost of one's life and limb, there must be a special consideration to the Forces and some other categories that have already been listed by the founding fathers of the Constitution.

But are these additional restrictions necessary? What are the restrictions that are necessary? I would like to submit for the consideration of my Right hon. friend that this Bill itself is unnecessary. Why? Because the Army, the Air Force and the Navy are covered by Sections 20 and 21 of the Army Act, to which my hon. friend from Jadavpur referred. It very clearly says that:

> The Central Government, by notification, can make rules restricting to such extent and in such manner as may be necessary, the right of any person subject to this Act-
>
> (a) to be a member of, or to be associated in any way with, any trade union or labour union or any class of trade or labour unions, or any society, institution or association, or any class of institutions or associations;
>
> (b) to attend or address any meeting to take part in any demonstration organized by anybody of persons for any political or other purposes;
>
> (c) to communicate with the press or to publish or cause to be published any book, letter or other document.
>
> This applies to the army, navy and air force.

Now I want to point out to the right hon. friend from Hanamkonda that, besides this, there is a piece of legislation, passed by the House, which is called the Police Forces (Restriction of Rights) Act, 1966. This is very germane to the point that I am trying to make and I would like even the Home Minister to lend his ears to what I am saying. What is that? Madam, this Police Forces (Restriction of Rights) Act, section 3, imposes similar restrictions, exactly similar restrictions.

Mr. Chairman: He should conclude soon. I am giving the first bell.

Shri Ravindra Varma: Section 3 of the Act, is a virtual repetition with annotation of these very restrictions, imposed by section 20 of the Army Act. The Police Forces (Restriction of Rights) Act, 1966 has a long Schedule, which contains 23 Acts, some of the States and some of the Centre. Madam, if you will permit me, I will read out to you section 3 of that Act, which says...

Mr. Chairman: Do not go into the details.

Shri Ravindra Varma: It is not the details; it is very important. My case is that the right which he is seeking from the House is already with him. He has come here in a somnolent mood, or in a fit of amnesia. You must permit me to take this case. It says:

> "No member of the police force shall, without the express sanction of

169

Central Government, or of the prescribed authority:

(a) be a member of, or be associated in any way with, any trade union, labour union, political association or with any class of trade union....

(b) A member of, or be associated in any way with, any other society, institution, association, or organization that is not recognized as part of the force, of which he is a member, or is not purely social, recreational or religious in nature; or

(c) communicate with the press or publish...."

What arises from that? The question of the nature of the organization or association whether it is banned or not allowed is decided by the Central Government.

Added to section 3, comes another section, section 5, which is very important. It says:— (Interruption) The hon. Member from Bhilwara must always rush in where angels fear to tread. Section 5 reads:

"The Central Government may, by notification in the Official Gazette, amend the Schedule by including therein any other enactment relating to a force charged with the maintenance of public order, or by omitting there from any enactment already specified therein..."

It means that any of these forces covered by your clause, can be included in the schedule by a notification.

The CRPF was created by an Act of this House in 1949, the Border Security Force by an Act of 1968, the Territorial Army by an Act of 1948. Section 9 of the Territorial Army Act says that the Army Act is applicable to the members of the Territorial Army. The Railway Protection Force was created by an Act in 1957 and the Central Industrial Security Force by an Act of 1968. Therefore, it can be seen that all these forces were created by Acts passed by this House and there is already power vested in this Government, vested by the Act that I have referred to, by sheer notification, by mere notification, to include these forces within the purview of the restrictions which I have referred to.

Here comes the main question. If these are the restrictions which my hon. friend, who is now whispering elsewhere, has in mind...

Mr. Somnath Chatterjee: Or whispered to.

Mr. Chairman: He will reply to it.

Shri Ravindra Varma: I do not want him to read my speech tomorrow. He is not listening to me. This is downright disrespect to the House... (Interruptions)

Mr. Chairman: Others are listening to you.

Mr. Ravindra Varma: Madam, I must be on your right side; otherwise, you would not allow me to continue.

Therefore, if these are all the restrictions we have in mind, then he has the powers already. Therefore, an apprehension arises in our mind, an inference arises in our mind that perhaps these are not the restrictions that he has in mind.

Shri P.V. Narasimha Rao: Mr. Speaker, Sir, when I said that I expected reasonableness from the Opposition, I thought that my expectation was well-founded when I made it, but now I see that whatever reasonableness I have shown is unreciprocated....

Prof. Maldhu Dandavate: Are you withdrawing your Amendment?

Shri P.V. Narasimha Rao: That is precisely what I was going to say: in spite of the fact that I do not find any echo, any reciprocation, from the other side, I stick to the amendment which I have tabled because, as I said, I found on a second, third, reading of the amendment that clause (c) could be deleted since it does not really fit into this scheme of Constitutional Amendment. So, I have to conclude that the Government will have to go ahead with it on its own steam. As has been pointed out, clauses (a) and (b) are already there. This Amendment has been put in the form of the whole article as amended being incorporated and not in the form of an amendment which is in addition to, or deletion of, what is contained in the original proviso.

(a) and (b) are already covered. In effect what we have now done is to add 'person employed in any bureau of other organization established by the State for the purpose of intelligence or counter intelligence and persons employed in...set up for the purpose of any force or organization referred to in clauses (c) and (d). I would like to submit that...more or less provisions which flow from the original provisions. Actually the... telecommunication system is something which is absolutely vital to the working of the... organizations whether it is the Army or the....Police or the Bureau or organizations established for the purpose of intelligence

171

or counter intelligence. No intelligence work can be done without telecommunications. Clauses (d) and (e) which now after amendment... become (c) and (d) go together because without (e), (d) cannot work and (a) cannot work. When it comes to telecommunications...not consider it as a positive addition. It is consequential and operational in nature and not substantive. So I do not see what objection there can be to this. Of course, objections on principles, so on and so forth have been aired...

Prof. Madhu Dandavate: Regarding telecommunication, so long as its relations with the other forces are concerned, I think it would be covered even without that.

Shri P.V. Narasimha Rao: I do not know whether it would be covered. The wording is quite clear—'Persons employed in or in connection with the telecommunications system set up for the purpose of any force, bureau or organisation referred to in clauses (a) to (d)'. I am not sure whether this is covered and even if it is covered, it is covered once again here and you cannot have any objection.

This is the scheme of the constitutional amendment. Now about human rights much was said. I would like to submit that the Government is as much wedded to human rights as anyone else. These laws that have been made——the Army Act, etc. have been made with the security of the country in view and whatever rules have been made, have been upheld by the Supreme Court and there is no question of abridging the rights of these people for consideration which are not eminently connected with the security of the country. This is the scheme of the law and I do not think there can be any objection to that.

We have heard certain experiences. Mr. Indrajit Gupta referred to some of them. I do not have to go into details. But I would like to assure the House that based on these experiences this constitutional amendment is being brought.

The other important aspect which was raised at the time of introduction of the Bill is the redressal of grievances. I already stated that there is a machinery in respect of redressal of grievances. I already stated that there is machinery in respect of redressal of grievances and if there are any suggestions to strengthen it, to streamline it and to make it more effective, I am prepared to consider them. I have not gone into all the details of what machinery exists. I can read out whatever note I have got from the authorities concerned, but I would like to go deeper into the ramification of that machinery and I would again like to state that I believe in the redressal of grievances. I believe in the contentment of these forces, I do not believe in suppressing them or bottling up their dissatisfaction. I am one with the hon. Members who have raised these points.

Now, that will come, as Mr. Indrajit Gupta pointed out, by law, by rules and by making these organizations become useful, positive and strengthened. That is a different process altogether and I would like to say that I entirely believe in that process and we shall see to it that that process is strengthened.

Shri Ravindra Varma's amendment---my hon. friend from Bombay-North—does not belong here. I would like to respectfully submit to him that this is a Constitutional amendment. The Constitutional amendment, within the framework of Article 33, has to have certain parameters. His amendment does not fit in here. This can come only later either by law or by exercise of powers vested in the Government. That would be seen. I would respectfully submit to him that he should withdraw this amendment which just does not fit into this context at all.

So, Sir, with these few words, I would like to commend this to the unanimous, if possible acceptance of the House.

Upon an amendment moved by the Minister of Home Affairs, sub-clause (c) was deleted and consequential changes were made in sub-clause (d) and (e). Section 2 of **the Constitution (Fiftieth Amendment) Act, 1984** was adopted as follows:

2. Substitution of Article 33.- For Article 33 of the Constitution, the following article shall be substituted, namely:-

"33. Power of Parliament to modify the rights conferred by this Part in their application to Forces, etc.- Parliament may, by law, determine to what extent any of the rights conferred by this Part shall, in their application to,-

(a)   the members of the Armed Forces; or

(b)   the members of the Forces charged with the maintenance of public order; or

(c)   persons employed in any bureau or other organisation

established by the State for purposes of intelligence or counter intelligence; or

(d)   persons employed in, or in connection with, the telecommunication systems set up for the purposes of any Force, bureau or organisation referred to in clauses (a) to (c) be restricted or abrogated so as to ensure the proper discharge of their duties and the maintenance of discipline among them."

Cases

Supreme Court

High Court

1

Kameshwar Prasad v. State of Bihar 1962 Supp (3) SCR 369 : AIR 1962 SC 1166 : 91962) 1 LLJ 294, decided on 22 February 1962 [Five Judge Bench].

JUDGMENT:

This appeal comes before us by virtue of a certificate of fitness granted under Article 132 of the Constitution by the High Court of Patna. The question involved in the appeal is a short one but is of considerable public importance and of great constitutional significance. It is concerned with the Constitutional validity of Rule 4-A, which was introduced into the Bihar Government Servants' Conduct Rules, 1956, by a notification of the Governor of Bihar dated 16 August 1957 and reads:

> "4-A. **Demonstrations and strikes.**-No Government servant shall participate in any demonstration or resort to any form of strike in connection with any matter pertaining to his conditions of service."

Very soon after this rule was notified the six appellants, the first of whom is the President of the Patna Secretariat Ministerial Officers' Association and the others are Assistants or Clerks under the Bihar State Government, filed on 26 August 1957, a petition before the High Court of Patna under Article 226 of the Constitution challenging the validity of the rule on various grounds including inter alia that it interfered with the rights guaranteed to the petitioners by sub-clauses (a), (b) and (c) of clause (1) of Article 19 of the Constitution of India and that in consequence the rule was in excess of the rulemaking power conferred by Article 309 of the Constitution which was the source of the authority enabling service-rules to be framed. They prayed for an order restraining the respondent-State from giving effect to the rule and to desist from interfering with the petitioners' right to go on strike or to hold demonstrations. The learned Judges of the High Court who heard the petition were of the opinion that the freedom guaranteed under Article 19(1)(a) and 19(1)(c) of the Constitution did not include a right to resort to a strike or the right to demonstrate so far as servants of Government were concerned. The learned Judges however, further considered the validity of the rule on the assumption that the freedoms enumerated in sub-clauses (a) and (c) of Article 19(1) did include those rights. On this basis they held that the rule impugned was saved as being reasonable restraints on these guaranteed freedoms.

The learned Judges therefore directed the petition to be dismissed, but on application by the appellants they granted a certificate under Article 132 of the Constitution to enable them to approach this Court.

At this stage it is necessary to mention that a similar conclusion as the one by the High Court of Patna now under appeal was reached by the learned Judges of the High Court of Bombay before whom the constitutional validity of Rule 4A of the Bihar Rules was impugned. The correctness of that decision is under challenge in this Court in SLPs (Civil) Nos 499 and 500 of 1961 and the appellants in that appeal sought leave to intervene in this appeal and we have permitted them to do so, and we heard Mr Chari -learned Counsel for the interveners in further support of the appeal.

Before entering on a discussion of the arguments advanced before us it might be convenient to state certain matters which are common ground and not in controversy:

(1) The impugned Rule 4-A was framed under Article 309 of the Constitution which enacts, to quote the material words:

> "309. Subject to the provisions of this Constitution, Acts of the appropriate Legislature may regulate the recruitment, and conditions of service of persons appointed, to public services ..... and provision is made by the proviso to the Article for the Governors of States to make rules until, provision in that behalf is made by or under an Act of the appropriate Legislature."

We are' drawing attention to the Article under which the rule is made for the purpose of pointing out that the rulemaking power being subject to the Constitution, the validity of the rule would have to be tested by the same criteria as are applicable to all laws and subordinate legislation. In other words, if there are any constitutional limitations upon lawmaking, such of them as are appropriate to the subject dealt with by the rule would be applicable to them.

(2) It would be seen that the rule prohibits two types of activities, both in connection with matters pertaining to the conditions of service (i) the holding of demonstrations, and (ii) resort to strikes to achieve the purpose indicated. This Court had, in *All India Bank Employees' Association v. National Industrial Tribunal* [1962] 3 SCR 269, to consider the question as to whether the right to form an association guaranteed by Article 19(1) (c) involved or implied the right to resort to a strike and answered it in the negative. In view of this decision learned Counsel for the appellants, as also Mr. Chari for the interveners confined their arguments to the

question of the legality of the provision as regards the right ..... to hold demonstrations." The validity of the rule therefore in so far as it prohibits strikes, is no longer under challenge. The argument addressed to us on behalf of the appellants may be shortly stated thus: The service rule being one framed under Article 309 is a "law" within the definition of Article 13(3) of the Constitution and it would have to be pronounced invalid to the extent that it is inconsistent with the provisions of Part III of the Constitution Article 13(2). Article 19(1) confers on all citizens the right by sub-clause (a) to freedom of speech and expression, and by sub-clause (b) to assemble peacefully and without arms, and the right to "demonstrate" would be covered by these two sub-clauses. By the mere fact that a person enters Government service, be does not cease to be "a citizen of India", nor does that disentitle him to claim the freedoms guaranteed to every citizen. In fact, Article 33 which enacts: "Parliament may by law determine to what extent any of the rights conferred by this Part shall, in their application to the members of the Armed Forces or the Forces charged with maintenance of public order, be restricted or abrogated so as to ensure the proper discharge of their duties and the maintenance of discipline among them."

Obviously proceeds on the basis of persons in the service of Government being entitled to the Protection of the fundamental rights guaranteed by Part III of the Constitution and is inserted to enable special provision being made for the abrogation, if necessary, of the guaranteed freedoms in the case of two special services only, viz., the army and the police force. The approach to the question regarding the constitutionality of the rule should be whether the ban that it imposes on demonstrations would be covered by the limitation of the guaranteed rights contained in Article 19(2) and 19(3). In regard to both these clauses the only relevant criteria which has been suggested by the respondent-State is that the rule is framed in the interest of public order. A demonstration may be defined as "an expression of one's feelings by outward signs". A demonstration such as is prohibited by, the rule may be of the most innocent type- peaceful orderly such as the mere wearing of a badge by a Government servant or even by a silent assembly say outside office hours-demonstrations which could in no sense be suggested to involve any breach of tranquility, or of a type involving incitement to or capable of leading to disorder. If the rule had confined itself to demonstrations of type which would lead to disorder then the validity of that rule could have been sustained but what the rule does is the imposition of a blanket-ban on all demonstrations of whatever type-innocent as well as otherwise-and in consequence its validity cannot be upheld.

Before considering these arguments of learned Counsel it is necessary to deal with the submission by Mr Sen who appeared for the Union of India who intervened in this appeal which, if accepted, would cut at the root of the entire argument for the appellant. He endeavoured to persuade us to hold that though the power to frame Service Rules under Article 309 was subject to the Constitution with. the result that the rules so framed ought not to –be contrary to any constitutional provision, still it did not follow that every one of the fundamental rights guaranteed by Part III could be claimed by a Government servant. He urged that as a person voluntarily entered Government service he must by that very act be deemed to have consented to enter that service in such reasonable conditions as might be framed for ensuring the proper working of the administrative machinery of the Government and for the proper maintenance of discipline in the Service itself. Under Article 310 every office is held, subject to the provisions of the Constitution, at the pleasure of the President or of the Governor as the case may be, and provided a rule regulating the conditions of service was reasonable and was calculated to ensure the purposes above named he submitted that its reasonableness and validity could not be tested solely by reference to the criteria laid down in clauses (2), (3) or (4) of Article 19.

In this connection we were referred to a few decisions of the American Courts for the proposition that the constitutionality of special rules enacted for the discipline of those in the service of Government bad to be tested by criteria different from those applicable to ordinary citizens. Thus in *Ex Parte: Curtis* (1) the constitutionality of a law prohibiting officers or employees of the United States from' (requesting, giving to or receiving from any other officer or employee of the government any money or property or other thing of value for political purposes," under a penalty of being discharged and, on conviction fined, was upheld. In the majority judgment which was delivered by Waite, C.J., the reasonableness of such a rule is pointed out. It is however manifest that no fundamental right could be claimed to have been infringed by the provision there impugned. In *United Public Workers v. Mitchell*, which was another case to which our attention was invited, one of the questions raised related to the validity of an Act of Congress (The Hatch Act, 1940) making it unlawful for the employees in the Executive Branch of the Federal Government to take part in political campaigns and making the same the basis for disciplinary departmental action. It was contended that this was an interference with the right of free speech as well as with political rights. Keed, J., who spoke for the majority observed:

> "The interference with free expression has to be seen in comparison with the requirements of orderly management of administrative personnel....... .... We accept appellant's contention that the nature of political rights reserved to the people is involved. The right claimed as inviolate may be stated as the right of a citizen to act as a party official or worker to further his own political views. Thus we have a measure of interference by the Hatch Act and the Rules with what otherwise would be the freedom of the civil servant under the First Amendment. And, if we look upon due process as a guarantee of freedom in those fields, there is a corresponding impairment of that right under the Fifth Amendment................ We do not find persuasion in appellants' argument that such activities during free time are not subject to regulation even though admittedly political activities cannot be indulged in during working hours. The influence of political activity by government employees, if evil in its effects on the service, the employees or people dealing with them, is hardly less so because that activity takes place after hours............ It is accepted constitutional doctrine that these fundamental human rights are not absolutes........... The essential rights of the First Amendment are subject to the elemental need for order without which the guarantees, of civil rights to others would be a mockery."

Mr Sen also referred us to *Mc Auliffe v. New Bedford* (1892) 155 Mass 216, in support of the position that servants of Government formed a class and that conditions of service imposed upon them which are reasonable and necessary to ensure efficiency and discipline cannot be questioned on the ground of their contravening any constitutional guarantees. Mr Sen drew our attention in particular to the following passage in the judgment of Holmes, J.:

> "There is nothing in the Constitution or the statute to prevent the city from attaching obedience to this rule as a condition to the office of policeman, and making it part of the good conduct required. The petitioner may have a constitutional right to talk politics, -but he has no constitutional right to be a policeman. There are few employments for hire in which the, servant does not agree to suspend his constitutional right of free speech, as well as of idleness, by the-implied terms of his contract. The servant cannot complain, as he takes the employment on the terms which are offered him. On the same principle, the city may impose any reasonable condition upon holding offices within its

control. This condition seems to us reasonable, if that be a question open to revision here (The Police Regulation prohibiting members of the department from soliciting money etc. for political purposes)."

As regards these decisions of the American Courts, it should be borne in mind that though the First Amendment to the Constitution of the United State reading "Congress shall make no law......... abridging the freedom of speech..........." appears to confer no power on the Congress to impose any restriction on the exercise of the guaranteed right, still it has always been understood that the freedom guaranteed is subject to the' police power --the scope of which however has not been defined with precision or uniformly. It is on the basis of the police power to abridge that freedom that the constitutional validity of law a penalizing libels, and those relating to sedition, or to obscene publications etc., has been sustained. The resultant flexibility of the restrictions that could be validly imposed renders the American decisions inapplicable to and without must use for resolving the questions arising under Article 19(1)(a) or (b) of our Constitution wherein the grounds, on which limitations might be placed on the guaranteed right are set out with definiteness and precision.

Learned Counsel invited our attention also to the decision of this Court in *Balakotaiah v.Union of India* [1958] SCR 1052 to a similar effect. But it must however, be noted that in *Balakotaiah's* case the validity of the rule was not challenged.

In further support of his submission that the freedoms guaranteed to citizens by Article 19 cannot in their very nature, be applied to those who are employed in government service out attention was invited to sub-clauses (d), (e) and (g) of Clause (1). It was said that a Government servant who was posted to a particular place could obviously riot exercise the freedom to move throughout the territory of India and similarly, his right to reside and settle in any part of India could be said to be violated by his being posted to any particular place. Similarly, so long as he was in government service he would not be entitled to practicise any profession or trade and it was therefore urged that to hold that these freedoms guaranteed under Article 19 were applicable to government servants would render public service or administration impossible. This line of argument, however, does not take into account the limitations which might be imposed on the exercise of these rights by clauses (5) and (6) under which restrictions on the exercise of the rights conferred by sub-clauses (d) and (g) may be imposed if reasonable in the interest of the general public.

In this connection he laid stress on the fact that special provision had been made in regard to service under the State in some of the Articles in Part III - such as for instance Articles 15, 16 and 18(3) and (4) - and he desired us there from to draw the inference that the other Articles in which there was no specific reference to Government servants were inapplicable to them. He realised however, that the implication arising from Article 33 would run counter to this line of argument but as regards this Article his submission was that it was concerned solely to save Army Regulations which permitted detention in a manner which would not be countenanced by Article 22 of the Constitution. We find ourselves unable to accept the argument that the Constitution excludes Government servants as a class from the protection of the several rights guaranteed by the several Articles in Part III save in those cases where such persons were specifically named.

In our opinion, this argument even if otherwise possible has to be repelled in view of the terms of Article 33. That Article- selects two of the Services under the State-members of the armed forces charged with the maintenance of public order and saves the rules prescribing the conditions of service in regard to them-from invalidity on the ground of violation of-any of the fundamental rights guaranteed by Part III and also defines the purpose for which such abrogation or restriction might take place, this being limited to ensure the proper discharge of duties and the maintenance of discipline among them. The Article having thus selected the Services members of which might be, deprived of the benefit of the fundamental rights guaranteed to other persons and citizens and also having prescribed the limits within which such restrictions or abrogation might take place, we consider that other classes of servants of Government in common with other persons and other citizens of the country cannot be excluded from the protection of the rights guaranteed by Part III by reason merely of their being Government servants and the nature and incidents of the duties which they have to discharge in that capacity might necessarily involve restrictions of certain freedoms as we have pointed out in relation to Article 19 (1) (e) and (g).

The first question that falls to be considered is whether the right to make a "demonstration" is covered by either or both of the two freedoms guaranteed by Article 19(1)(a) and 19(1)(b). A "demonstration" is defined in the Concise Oxford Dictionary as "an outward exhibition of feeling, as an exhibition of opinion on political or other question especially a public meeting or procession". In Webster it is defined as "a public exhibition by a party, sect or society......... as by a parade or mass-meeting". Without going very much into the niceties of language it might be broadly stated that a demonstration is a visible manifestation of the feelings or sentiments of an individual or a group. It is thus a communication of one's ideas to others to whom it is intended to be conveyed. It is in effect therefore a form of speech or of expression, because speech need not be vocal since signs made by a dumb person would also be a form of speech. It has however to be recognised that the argument before us is confined to the rule prohibiting demonstration which is a form of speech and expression or of a mere assembly and speeches therein and not other forms of demonstration which do not fall within the content of Article 19(1)(a) or 19(1)(b). A demonstration might take the form of an assembly and even then the intention is to convey to the person or authority to whom the communication is intended the feelings of the group which assembles. It necessarily follows that there are forms of demonstration which would fall within the freedoms guaranteed by Article 19(1)(a) and 19(1) (b). It is needless to add that from the very nature of things a demonstration may take various forms; It may be noisy and disorderly, for instance stone throwing by a crowd may be cited as an example of a violent and disorderly demonstration and this would not obviously be within Article 19(1)(a) or (b). It can equally be peaceful and orderly such as happens when the members of the group merely wear some badge drawing attention to their grievances.

If thus particular forms of demonstration fall within the scope of Article 19(1)(a) or 19(1)(b), the next question is whether r. 4-A, in so far as it lays an embargo on any form of demonstration for the redress of the grievances of Government employees, could be sustained as falling within the scope of Article 19(2) and (3). These clauses run:

> "19. (2) Nothing in sub-clause (a) of clause (1) shall affect the operation of any existing law, or prevent the State from making any law in so far as such law imposes reasonable restrictions on the exercise of the right conferred by the said sub-clause in the interests of the security of the State, friendly relations with foreign States, public order, decency or morality or in relation to contempt of court defamation or incitement to an offence.
>
> (3) Nothing in sub-clause (b) of the said clause shall affect the operation of any existing law in so far as it imposes, or prevent the State from making any law imposing, in the interests of public order' reasonable restrictions on the exercise Of the right conferred by the said sub-clause."

The learned Judges of the High Court have, as stated earlier, upheld the validity of the rule by considering them as reasonable restrictions in the interest of public order. In coming to this conclusion the learned Judges of the High Court did not have the benefit of the exposition of the meaning of the expression in the interest of public order in these two clauses by this Court in *Superintendent, Central Prison, Fatehgarh v. Ram Manohar Lohia* (1960) 2 SCR 821. Speaking for the Court Subba Rao, J., summarised his conclusion on the point in these terms:

> "Public order (Article 19(2) and (3)) is synonymous with 'public safety and tranquility. It is the absence of disorder involving breaches of local significance in contradistinction to national upheavals such as revolution, civil strike, war affecting the security of the State."

The learned Judge further stated that in order that a legislation may be "in the interests of public order" there must be a proximate and reasonable nexus between the nature of the speech prohibited and public order. The learned Judge rejected the argument that the phrase "in the interests of public order" which is wider than the words', for the maintenance of public order" which were found in the Article as originally enacted-thereby sanctioned the enactment of a law which restricted the right merely because the speech had a tendency however remote to disturb public order. The connection has to be intimate, real and rational. The validity of the rule now impugned has to be judged with reference to tests here propounded.

If one had to consider the propriety of the rule as one intended to ensure proper discipline apart from the limitations on law-making, in a Government servant and in the context of the other provisions made for the making of representations and for the redress of services, grievances, and apart from the limitations imposed by the Constitution there could be very little doubt nor would it be even open to argument that the rule now impugned was both reasonable and calculated to ensure discipline in the Services and in that sense conducive to ensure efficiency in the Service.

Based on this aspect of the function of the rule the argument as regards Article 19(2) & (3) was put on a twofold basis: (1) that the maintenance of public order was directly dependent upon the existence of a body of Government servants who were themselves subject to strict discipline. In other words, the maintenance of discipline among Government servants not only contributed to the maintenance of public order but was a sine qua non of public order. (2) The other aspect in which it was presented was the negative of the one just now mentioned that if Government servants were ill disciplined and were themselves to agitate in a disorderly manner for the redress of their service grievances, this must lead to a demoralization of the public and would be reflected in the disappearance of public order.

We find ourselves unable to uphold this submission on behalf the State. In the first place we are not here concerned with any rule for ensuring discipline among the police, which is the arm of the law primarily charged with the maintenance of public order. The threat to public order should therefore arise from the nature of the demonstration prohibited. No doubt, if the rule were so framed as to single out those types of demonstration which were likely to lead to a disturbance of public tranquility or which 'Would fall under the other limiting criteria specified in Article 19(2) the validity of the rule could have been sustained. The vice of the rule, in our opinion, consists in this that it lays a ban on every type of demonstration--be the same however innocent and however incapable of causing a breach of public tranquility and does not confine itself to those forms of demonstrations which might lead to that result.

Learned Counsel for the respondent and those who supported the validity of the rule could not suggest that on the language of the rule as -it stood, it was possible to read it as to separate the legal from the unconstitutional portion of the provision. As no such separation is possible the entire rule has to be struck down as unconstitutional.

We have rejected the broad contention that persons in the service of government form a class apart to whom the rights guaranteed by Part III do not, in general, apply. By accepting the contention that the freedoms guaranteed by Part III and in particular those in Article 19(1)(a) apply to the servants of government we should not be taken to imply that in, relation to this class of citizen, the responsibility arising from official position would not by itself impose some limitations on the exercise of their rights as citizens. For instance, section 54(2) of the Income-tax Act, 1922, enacts:

> "If a public servant discloses any particulars contained in any such statement, return, accounts, documents, evidence affidavit, deposition or record, he shall be punishable with imprisonment which may extend to six months, and shall also be liable to fine."

Section 128(1) of the Representation of the People Act, 1951, enjoins on every officer, clerk, agent etc. Who performs any duty in connection, with the recording or counting of votes at an election shall maintain the secrecy of the voting and shall not communicate to any person any information calculated to violate such secrecy, and visits the breach of the rule by punishment with imprisonment for a term which may extend to three months or with fine. It cannot be contended that provisions on these or similar lines in these or other enactments restrict the freedom of the officers etc. merely because they are prohibited from communicating information which comes to them in the course of the performance of the duties of their office, to others. The information having been obtained by them in the course of their duties by virtue of their official position, rules or provisions of the law prescribing the circumstances in which alone such information might be given out or used do not infringe the right of freedom of speech as is guaranteed by the Constitution.

We would therefore allow the appeal in part and grant the appellants a declaration that r. 4A in the form in which it now stands prohibiting "any form of demonstrations is violative of the appellants" rights under Article 19(1)(a) & (b) and should therefore be stuck down. It is only necessary to add that the rule, in so far as it prohibits a strike, cannot be struck (own since there is no fundamental right to resort to a strike. As the appellants have succeeded only in part, there will be no order as to costs in the appeal.

Appeal allowed in part.

2

O. K. Ghosh v. E.X. Joseph 1963 Supp (1) SCR 789 : AIR 1963 SC 812 : 91962) 2 LLJ 615, decided on 30 October 1962 [five Judge Bench].

HEADNOTE:

The respondent, a Central Government servant, who was the Secretary of the Civil Accounts Association of Non-Gazetted Staff, was departmentally proceeded against under Rule 4(A) and 4(B) of the Central Civil Services (Conduct) Rules, 1955, for participating in demonstrations in preparation of a general strike of Central Government employees and for refusing to dissociate from the Association after the Government had withdrawn its recognition of it. He impugned the validity of the said rules on the ground that they infringed his fundamental rights under Article 19 of the Constitution. The High Court held that Rule 4(A) was wholly valid but quashed the proceeding under Rule 4(B) which it held to be invalid. Rule 4(A) provided that no Government servant shall participate in any demonstration or resort to any form of strike in connection with any matter pertaining to his conditions of service and Rule 4(B) provided that no Government servant shall join or continue to be a member of any services Association which the Government did not recognise or in respect of which recognition had been refused or withdrawn by it.

Held, that in view of the decision of this Court that Rule 4(A) of the Central Civil Services (Conduct) Rules, 1955, in so far as it prohibited any form of demonstration was violative of the Government servants' fundamental rights under Article 19(1) (a) and (b), the High Court was in error in holding that the rule was wholly valid.

Participation in demonstration organised for a strike and taking active part in preparation for it cannot, either in law or fact, mean participation in the strike. The respondent could not, therefore, be said to have taken part in a strike as such and the proceeding against him under s. 4(A) being based on that part of it which was invalid must also be invalid. It was clear that Rule 4(B) of the said Rules imposed restriction on the undoubted right of the Government Servants under Article 19 which were neither reasonable nor in the interest of public order tinder Article 19(4). The rules clearly showed that in the granting or withdrawing, of recognition, the Government right be actuated by considerations other than those of efficiency or discipline amongst the services or public order. The restriction imposed by Rule 4 (B), therefore, infringed Article 19(1) (c) and must be held to be invalid.

Appeals by special leave from the judgment and order dated 18 January 1961 of the Bombay High Court in Miscellaneous petition No. 255 of 1960.

JUDGMENT:

1. The respondent E.X. Joseph is in the service of the Government of India in the Audit and Accounts Department at Bombay. He was the Secretary of the Civil Accounts Association which consists of non-gazetted staff of the Accountant-General's Office. The said Association was affiliated to the All India Non-Gazetted Audit and Accounts Association. The latter Association had been recognized by the Government of India in December, 1956. In May, 1959, the Government withdrew recognition of the said Association. In spite of the withdrawal of the recognition of the said Association, the respondent continued to be its Secretary General and refused to dissociate himself from the activities of the said Association, though called upon to do so. As a result of his activities, on or about 3 June 1960, he was served with a charge-sheet for having deliberately committed breach of Rule 4(b) of the Central Civil Services (Conduct) Rules, 1955 (hereinafter called the Rules). Appellant No. 1, O. K. Ghosh, Accountant-General (AG), Maharashtra, who held the enquiry, found the respondent guilty of the charges levelled against him. Accordingly, a notice to show cause why he should not be removed from service was served on the respondent. On 25 July 1960, appellant No. 1 served a memo on the respondent intimating to him that it was proposed to hold an enquiry against him for having deliberately contravened the provisions of Rule 4(A) of the Rules in so far as he participated actively in various demonstrations organised in connection with the strike of Central Government employees and had taken active part in the preparations made for the said strike.

On 8 August 1960, the respondent filed a writ petition on the original side of the Bombay High Court under Article 226 of the Constitution and prayed that a writ of certiorari should be issued to quash the charge-sheets issued against him by appellant No. 1 in respect of the alleged contravention of Rules 4 (B) and 4 (A) and a writ of prohibition should be issued prohibiting a appellant No. 1 from proceeding further with the departmental proceedings against the respondent. In his petition, the respondent asked for other incidental reliefs. The main ground on which the respondent challenged the validity of the departmental proceedings initiated against him was that Rules 4(A) and 4(B) were void in so far as they contravened the fundamental rights guaranteed to the respondent under Article 19(1) (a), (b), (c) and (g). This contention was resisted by appellant No. 1 and appellant No. 2, the Union of India, who had been impleaded as respondents to the said petition. It was urged on their behalf that the impugned Rules were valid and so, the claim for a writ of certiorari or writ of prohibition was not justified.

The writ petition was heard by a Division Bench of the Bombay High Court. On January 18, 1961, the High Court rejected the petition in so far as the respondent had claimed writs in regard to the enquiry for breach of Rule 4(A); the Court held that the said Rule was valid and so, the departmental proceedings initiated against the respondent in respect of the breach of the said Rule could not be successfully impeached. In respect of the proceedings under Rule 4(B), however, the High Court held that the said Rule was invalid and so, the departmental proceedings in respect of the breach of the said Rule have been quashed. It is against this decision that the appellants, the AG and the Union of India, have come to this Court by Appeal No. 378/1962; whereas E. X. Joseph the respondent, has preferred Appeal No. 379/1962: Both the- appeals have been brought to this Court by special leave.

The appellants contend that the High Court was in error in holding that Rule 4(B) was invalid, whereas the respondent urges that Rule 4(A) was invalid and the decision of the High Court to the contrary is erroneous in law. Before dealing with the contentions of the parties, it is necessary to set out the two impugned Rules. These Rules form part of a body of Rules framed in 1955 under Article 309, of the Constitution.

Rule 4-A provides that no Government servant shall participate in any demonstration or resort to any form of strike in connection with any matter pertaining to his condition of service,. whereas Rule 4-B lays down that no Government servant shall join or continue to be a member of any Service Association of Government servants: (a) which has not, within a period of six months from its formation, obtained the recognition of the Government under the Rules prescribed in that behalf, or (b) recognition in respect of which has been refused or withdrawn by the Government under the said Rules. The case against the respondent is that he has contravened both these Rules.

The question about the validity of Rule 4-A has been the subject-matter of a recent decision of this Court in *Kameshwar Prasad v. The State of Bihar* [1962] Supp 3 SCR 369 (1). At the hearing of the said appeal, the appellants and the respondent had intervened and were heard by the Court.

189

In that case, this Court has held that Rule 4-A in the form in which it now stands prohibiting any form. of demonstration is violative of the Government servants' rights under Article 19(1)(a) & (b) and should, therefore, be struck down. In striking down the Rule in this limited way, this Court made it clear that in so far as the said Rule prohibits a strike, it cannot be struck down for the reason that there is no fundamental right to resort to a strike. In other words, if the Rule was invoked against a Government servant on the ground that be had resorted to any form of strike specified by Rule 4- A, the Government servant would not be able to contend that the Rule was invalid in that behalf. In view of this decision, we must hold that the High Court was in error in coming to the conclusion that Rule 4-A was valid as a whole.

That takes us to the question about the validity of Rule 4-B. The High Court has held that the impugned Rule contravenes the fundamental right guaranteed to the respondent by Article 19 (1) (c). The respondent along with other Central Government servants is entitled to form Associations or Unions and in so far as this right is prejudicially Rule, the said Rule is invalid. The learned Solicitor General contends that in deciding the question about the validity of the Rule, we will have to take into account the provision of clause (4) in Article 19. This clause provides that Article 19(1) (c) will not affect the operation of any existing law in so far as it imposes, in the interests of public order or morality, reasonable restrictions on the exercise of the right conferred by the said sub-clause. The argument is that the impugned Rule does nothing more than imposing a reasonable restriction on the exercise of the right which is alleged to have been contravened and, therefore, the provision of the rule is saved by clause (4).

This argument raises the problem of construction of clause (4). Can it be said that the Rule imposes a reasonable restriction in the interests of public order? There can be no doubt that Government servants can be subjected to rules which are intended to maintain discipline amongst their ranks and to lead to an efficient discharge of their duties Discipline amount Government employees and their efficiency may, in a sense, be said to be related to public order. But in considering the scope of clause (4), it has to be borne in mind that the rule must be in the interests of public order and must amount to a reasonable restriction. The words "public order" occur even in clause (2), which refers, inter alia, to security of the State and public order. There can be no doubt that the said words must have the same meaning in both clauses (2) and (4). So far as clause (2) is concerned, security of the State having been expressly and specifically provided for, public' order cannot include the security of State, though in its widest sense it may be capable of including the said concept. Therefore, in clause (2), public order is virtually synonymous with public peace, safety and tranquility. The denotation of the said words cannot be any wider in clause (4). That is one consideration which it is necessary to bear in mind. When clause (4) refers to the restriction imposed in the interests of public order, it is necessary to enquire as to what is the effect of the words "in the interests of". This clause again cannot be interpreted to mean that even if the connection between the restriction and the public order is remote and indirect, the restriction can be said to be in the interests of public order. A restriction can be said to be in the interests of public order only if the connection between the restriction and the public order is proximate and direct. Indirect or far-fetched or unreal connection between the restriction and public order would not fall within the purview of the expression "in the interests of public order."

This interpretation is strengthened by the other requirement of clause (4) that, by itself, the restriction ought to be reasonable. It would be difficult to hold that a restriction which does not directly relate to public order can be said to be reasonable on the ground that its connection with public order is remote or far-fetched. That is another consideration which is relevant. Therefore, reading the two requirements of clause (4), it follows that the impugned restriction can, be said to satisfy as the test of clause (4) only if its connection with public order is shown to be rationally proximate and direct. That is the view taken by this Court in *The Superintendent Central Prison, Fatehgarh v. Dr Ram Manohar Lohia* AIR 1960 SC 633. In the words of Patanjali Sastri .T., in *Rex v. Basudev,* [1949] SCR 657,661, "the connection contemplated between the restriction and public order must be real and proximate, not far-fetched or problematical." It is in the light of this legal position that the validity of the impugned rule must be determined.

It is not dispute that the fundamental rights guaranteed by Article 19 can be claimed by Government servants. Article 33 which confers power on the parliament to modify the rights in their application to the Armed Forces, clearly brings out the fact that all citizens, including Government servants, are entitled to claim the rights guaranteed by Article 19.

Thus, the validity of the impugned rule has to be judged on the basis that the respondent and his co-employees are entitled to form Associations or Unions. It is clear that Rule 4-B imposes a restriction on this right. It virtually compels a Government servant to withdraw his membership of the Service Association of Government Servants as soon as recognition accorded to the said Association is withdrawn or if, after the Association is formed, no recognition is accorded to it within six months. In other words, the right to form an Association is conditioned by the existence of the recognition of the said Association by the Government.

If the Association obtains the recognition and continues to enjoy it, Government servants can become members of the said Association; if the Association does not secure recognition from the Government or recognition granted to it is withdrawn, Government servants must cease to be the members of the said Association. That is the plain effect of the impugned rule. Can this restriction be said to be in the interests of public order and can it be said, to be a reasonable restriction? In our opinion, the only answer to these questions would be in the negative. It is difficult to see any direct or proximate or reasonable connection between the recognition by the Government of the Association and the discipline amongst, and the efficiency of, the members of the said Association.

Similarly, it is difficult to see any connection between recognition and public order. A reference to Rule 5 of the Recognition of Service Association Rules recently made in 1959 would clearly show that there is no necessary Connection between recognition or its withdrawal and public order. Rule 5 enumerates different conditions by clauses (a) to (1) which every Service Association must comply with; and Rule 7 provides that if a Service Association recognized under the said Rules has failed to comply with the conditions set out in Rule 4, 5, or 6, its recognition may be withdrawn. One of the conditions imposed by Rule 5(1) is that communications addressed by the Service Association or by any office bearer on its behalf to the Government or a Government authority shall not contain any disrespectful or improper language.

Similarly, Rule 5(g) provides that the previous permission of the Government shall be taken before the Service Association seeks affiliation with any other Union, Service Association or Federation; and Rule 5 (h) prohibits the Service Association from starting or publishing any periodical, magazine or bulletin without the previous approval of the Government. It is not easy to see any rational, direct or proximate connection between the observance of these conditions and public order. Therefore, even without examining the validity of all the conditions laid down by rule 4, 5 or 6, it is not difficult to hold that the granting or withdrawing of recognition may be based on considerations some of which have no connection whatever either with the efficiency or discipline amongst the Services or with public order. It might perhaps have been a different matter if the recognition or its withdrawal had been based on grounds which have a direct, proximate and rational connection with public order. That however cannot be said about each one of the conditions prescribed by Rule 4, 5 or 6. Therefore, it is quite possible that recognition may be refused or withdrawn on grounds which are wholly unconnected with public J. order and it is in such a set-up that the right to form Associations guaranteed by Article 19(1)(c) is-made subject to the rigorous restriction that the Association in question must secure and continue to enjoy recognition from the Government. We are therefore, satisfied that the restriction thus imposed would make the guaranteed right under Article 19(1)(c) ineffective and even illusory. That is why we see no reason to differ from the conclusion of the High Court that the impugned Rule 4-B is,' invalid. In the result, appeal No. 378/1962 fails and is dismissed.

In regard to appeal No. 379/1962, though we have partly reversed the conclusion of the High Court in respect of the validity of the whole of Rule 4-A. it appears that the departmental proceedings initiated against the respondent in respect of, the alleged breach of rule 4-A have to be quashed, because the alleged contravention of the said Rule on which the said proceedings are based is contravention of that part of Rule 4-A which has been held to be invalid by this Court.

The material charge against the respondent in that behalf is that he had deliberately contravene the provisions of Rule 4-A in so far as he has participated actively in the various demonstrations organised in connection with the strike of Central Government employees and took part in the preparations made for the said strike.

It will be noticed that the result of the decision of this Court in *Kameshwar Prasad's* case [1962] Supp. 3 SCR 369, is that in so far as the rule prohibits any form of demonstration, it is invalid. It is not invalid in so far as it may prohibit participation in strikes. The charge against the respondent is not that he participated in any strike; the charge is that he participated in the various demonstrations; and that is a charge based upon that part of the rule which prohibits demonstrations all-together. It is true that the demonstrations in which he is alleged to have participated actively were organised in connection with the strike; but that does not mean either in fact or in law that he participated in the strike itself. Similarly, the charge that he took active part in the preparations made for the said strike, also does not mean in fact or in law that he participated in the strike. If he joined demonstrations organised in connection with the strikes, or if he took part in the preparations for the strike, it cannot be said that he took part in the strike as such, and so, the charge cannot be reasonably construed to mean that his conduct amounted to a contravention of the rule which prohibits strikes. Therefore, though Rule 4-A is partly, and not wholly, invalid as held by this Court in the case of *Kameshwar Prasad*, the particular charge against the respondent being on the basis of that part of the rule which is invalid, it must follow that the departmental proceedings based on that charge are also invalid. That is why appeal No. 379/1962 must be allowed and the departmental proceedings instituted against the respondent for the alleged contravention by him of rules 4-A and 4-B must be quashed.

There would be no order as to costs.

Appeal 378/62 dismissed.

Appeal 379/62 allowed.

3

Ram Sarup v. Union of India (1964) 5 SCR 931 : AIR 1965 SC 247 : (1965) Cr LJ 236, decided on 12 December 1963 [Five Judge Bench].

The General Court Martial sentenced the petitioner, a sepoy, to death under section 69 of the Army Act read with section 302 of the Indian Penal Code (IPC) for shooting dead two sepoys and a Havildar. The Central Government confirmed the sentence. The petitioner filed writs of habeas corpus and certiorari for setting aside the orders of the Court Martial and the Central Government and for his release.

HELD:

(i) The petitioner made no request for being represented at the court martial by a counsel of his choice; consequently no such request was refused, and that there has been no violation of the fundamental right of the petitioner to be defended by a counsel of his choice.

(ii) There has been no non-compliances of the provisions of section 132(2) of the Army Act. In view of the provisions of Rules 45, 46, 61(2) and 62 of the Army Rules, 1954, the petitioner's statement, that the death sentence was voted by an inadequate majority of the members of the Court which can be considered to be a mere allegation, cannot be based on any definite knowledge as to how the voting went at the consideration of the finding in pursuance of Rule 61.

(iii) Section 164 does not lay down that the correctness of the order or sentence of the Court Martial is always to be decided by two higher authorities; it only provides for two remedies. The further petition can only be made to the authority superior to the authority which confirms the order of the Court Martial, and if there be no authority superior to the confirming authority, the question of remedy against its order does not arise.

(iv) Each and every provision of the Army Act is a law made by Parliament and that if any such provision tends to affect the fundamental rights under Part III of the Constitution, that provision does not, on that account, become void, as it must be taken that Parliament has in exercise of its power under Article 33 of the Constitution made the requisite modification to affect the respective fundamental right.

(v) The provisions of section 125 of the Act are not discriminatory and do not infringe the provisions of Article 14 of the Constitution.

(vi) The discretion to be exercised by the military officer specified in section 125 of the Act as to the trial of accused by Court Martial or by an ordinary court, cannot be said to be unguided by any other policy laid down in the Act or uncontrolled by any authority. There could be a variety of circumstances which may influence the decision as to whether the offender be tried by a Court Martial or by ordinary criminal court and therefore becomes inevitable that the discretion to make the choice as to which court should try the accused be left to responsible Military officers under whom the accused is serving. Those officers are to be guided by considerations of the exigencies of the service maintenance of discipline in the army, speedier trial, the nature of the offence and the person against whom the offence is committed. This discretion is subject to the control of the Central Government.

(vii) According to section 549 of the Code of Criminal Procedure (of 1898) and the rules thereunder, the final choice about the forum of the trial of a person accused of a civil offence rests with the Central Government, whenever there be difference of opinion between a Criminal Court and Military authorities about the forum. The position under sections 125 and 126 of the Army Act is also the same.

JUDGMENT:

1. Ram Sarup, petitioner, was a sepoy in 131 Platoon DSC, attached to the Ordnance Depot, Shakurbasti. As a sepoy, he is subject to the Army Act, 1950 (XLVI of 1950), hereinafter called the Act.

2. On 13 June 1962 he shot dead two sepoys, Sheotaj Singh and Ad Ram and one Havildar Pala Ram. He was charged on three counts under section 69 of the Act read with section 302 IPC and was tried by the General Court Martial. On 12 January 1963 the General Court Martial found him guilty of the three charges and sentenced him to death.

3. The Central Government confirmed the findings and sentence awarded by the General Court Martial to the petitioner. Thereafter, the petitioner has filed this writ petition praying for the issue of a writ in the nature of a writ of order dated January 12, 1963 of the General Court Martial and the order of the Central Government confirming the said findings and sentence and for his release from the Central Jail, Tihar, New Delhi, where he is detained pending execution of the sentence awarded to him.

4. The contentions raised for the petitioner are: (1) That the provisions of

section 125 of the Act are discriminatory and contravene the provisions of Article 14 of the Constitution inasmuch as it is left to the unguided discretion of the officer mentioned in that section to decide whether the accused person would be tried by a Court Martial or by a Criminal Court. (2) Section 127 of the Act[1] which provides for successive trials by a Criminal Court and a Court Martial, violates the provisions of Article 20 of the Constitution as it provides for the prosecution and punishment of a person for the same offence more than once. (3) The petitioner was not allowed to be defended at the General Court Martial by a legal practitioner of his choice and therefore there had been a violation of the provisions of Article 22(1) of the Constitution. (4) The procedure laid down for the trial of offences by the General Court Martial had not been followed inasmuch as the death sentence awarded to the petitioner was not passed with the concurrence of at least two-thirds of the members of the Court. (5) Section 164 of the Act provides two remedies, one after the other, to a person aggrieved by any order passed by a Court Martial. Sub section (1) allows him to present a petition to the officer or authority empowered to confirm any finding or sentence of the Court Martial and sub-section (2) allows him to present a petition to the Central Government or to any other authority mentioned in that sub-section and empowers the Central Government or the other authority to pass such order on the petition as it thinks fit. The petitioner could avail of only one remedy as the finding and sentence of the Court Martial was confirmed by the Central Government. He, therefore, could not go to any other authority against the order of the Central Government by which he was aggrieved.

5. It will be convenient to deal with the first point at the end and take up the other points here.

6. The petitioner has not been subjected to a second trial for the offence of which he has been convicted by the General Court Martial. We therefore do not consider it necessary to decide the question of the validity of section 127 of the Act in this case.

7. With regard to the third point, it is alleged that the petitioner had expressed his desire, on many, occasions, for permission to engage a practicing civil lawyer to represent him at the trial but the authorities turned down those requests and told him that it was not permissible under the Military rules to allow the services of a civilian lawyer and that, he would have to defend his case with the counsel he would be provided by

---

1   Section 127 of the Army Act, 1950 has been omitted by Act No. 37 of 1992.

the Military Authorities. In reply, it is stated that this allegation about the petitioner's requests and their being turned down was not correct, that it was not made in the petition but was made in the reply after the State had filed its counter affidavits in which it was stated that no such request for his representation by a legal practitioner had been made and that there had been no denial of his fundamental rights. We are of opinion that the petitioner made no request for his being represented at the Court Martial by a counsel of his choice, that consequently no such request was refused and that he cannot be said to have been denied his fundamental right of being defended by a counsel of his choice.

8. In paragraph 9 of his petition he did not state that he had made a request for his being represented by a counsel of his choice. He simply stated that certain of his relatives who sought interview with him subsequent to his arrest were refused permission to see him and that this procedure which resulted in denial of opportunity to him to defend himself properly by engaging a competent civilian lawyer through the resources and help of his relatives had infringed his fundamental right under Article 22 of the Constitution. If the petitioner had made any express request for being defended by a counsel of his choice, he should have stated so straight-forwardly in para 9 of his petition. His involved language could only mean that he could not contact his relations for their arranging a civilian lawyer for his defence. This negatives any suggestion of a request to the Military Authorities for permission to allow him representation by a practicing lawyer and its refusal.

9. We therefore hold that there had been no violation of the fundamental right of the petitioner to be defended by a counsel of his choice, conferred under Article 22(1) of the Constitution.

10. Further, we do not consider it necessary to deal with the questions, raised at the hearing, about the validity of Rule 96 of the Army Rules, 1954, hereinafter called the rules, and about the power of Parliament to delegate its powers under Article 33 of the Constitution to any other authority.

11. The next point urged for the petitioner is the sentence of death passed by the Court Martial was against the provisions of' section 132(2) of the Act inasmuch as the death sentence was voted by an inadequate majority. The certificate, signed by the presiding officer of the Court Martial and by the Judge-Advocate, and produced as annexure 'A' to the respondent's counter to the petition, reads:

"Certified that the sentence of death is passed with the concurrence of at least Two-third of the members of the Court as provided by Army Act section 132(2)."

It is alleged by the petitioner that this certificate is not genuine but was prepared after his filing the writ petition. We see no reason to accept the petitioner's allegations. He could not have known about the voting of the members of the General Court Martial. Rule 45 gives the Form of Oath or of Affirmation which, is administered to every member of a Court Martial. It enjoins upon him that he will not on any account at any time whatsoever disclose or discover the vote or opinion of any particular member of the Court Martial unless required to give evidence thereof by a Court of Justice or Court Martial in due course of law. Similar is the provision in the Form of Oath or of Affirmation which is administered to the Judge-Advocate, in pursuance of rule 46. Rule 61 provides that the Court shall deliberate on its finding in closed Court in the presence of the Judge-Advocate. It is therefore clear that only the members of the Court and the Judge-Advocate can know how the members of the Court Martial gave their votes. The votes are not tendered in writing. No record is made of them. Sub-rule (2) of rule 61 provides that the opinion of each member of the Court as to the finding shall be given by word of mouth on each charge separately. Rule 62 provides that the finding on every charge upon which the accused is arraigned shall be recorded and, except as provided in the rules, shall be recorded simply as a finding off 'guilty' or of 'not guilty'. In view of these provisions, the petitioner's statement, which can be considered to be a mere allegation, cannot be based on any definite knowledge as to how the voting went at the consideration of the finding in pursuance of rule 61.

12. Further, there is no reason to doubt what is stated in the certificate which, according to the counter-affidavit, is not recorded in pursuance of any provision governing the proceedings of the Court Martial, and does not form part of any such proceedings. It is recorded for the satisfaction of the confirming authority. The certificate is dated 12 January 1963, the date on which the petitioner was convicted. The affidavit filed by Colonel N S Bains, Deputy Judge-Advocate General, Army Headquarters, New Delhi, contains a denial of the petitioner's allegation that the certificate is a false and concocted document and has been made by the authorities after the filing of the writ Petition. We see no reason to give preference to the allegations of the petitioner over the statement made by Col Bains in his affidavit, which finds support from the contents of Exhibit A signed by the presiding officer of the Court Martial and the Judge-Advocate who could

possibly have no reason for issuing a false certificates We therefore hold that there had been no noncompliance of the provisions of section 132(2) of the Act.

13. Next we come to the fifth point. It is true that section 164 of the Act gives two remedies to the person aggrieved by an order, finding or sentence of a Court Martial, they being a petition to the authority which is empowered to confirm such order, finding or sentence and the petition to the Central Government or some other officer mentioned in sub-section (2), after the order or sentence is confirmed by the former authority. The final authority to which the person aggrieved by the order of the Court Martial can go is the authority mentioned in sub-section (2) of section 164 and if this authority happens to be the confirming authority, it is obvious that there could not be any further petition from the aggrieved party to any other higher authority against the order of confirmation. The further petition can only be to the authority superior to the authority which confirms the order of the Court Martial and if there be no authority superior to the confirming authority, the question of a remedy against its order does not arise. Section 164, does not lay down that the correctness of the order or sentence of the Court Martial is always to be decided by two higher authorities. It only provides for two remedies.

14. Section 153 of the Act provides inter alia that no finding or sentence of a General Court Martial shall be valid except so far as it may be confirmed as provided by the Act and section 154 provides that the findings and sentence of a General Court Martial may be confirmed by the Central Government or by any officer empowered in that behalf by warrant of the Central Government. It appears that the Central Government itself exercised the power of confirmation of the sentence awarded to the petitioner in the instant case by the, General Court Martial. The Central Government is the highest authority mentioned in sub-section (2) of section 164. There could therefore be no occasion for a further appeal to any other body and therefore no justifiable grievance can be made of the fact that the petitioner had no occasion to go to any other authority with a second petition as he could possibly have done in case the order of confirmation was by any authority subordinate to the Central Government. The Act itself provides that the Central Government is to confirm the findings and sentences of General Courts Martial and therefore could not have contemplated, by the provisions of section 164, that the Central Government could not exercise this power but should always have this power exercised by any other officer which it may empower in that behalf by warrant.

15. We therefore do not consider this contention to have any force.

16. Lastly, Mr. Rana, learned counsel for the petitioner, urged in support of the first that in the exercise of the power conferred on Parliament under Article 33 of the Constitution to modify the fundamental rights guaranteed by Part III, in their application to the armed forces, it enacted section 21 of the Act which empowers the Central Government, by notification, to make rules restricting to such extent and in such manner as may be necessary, the right of any person with respect to certain matters, that these matters do not cover the fundamental rights under Articles 14, 20 and 22 of the Constitution, and that this indicated the intention of Parliament not to modify any other fundamental right. The learned Attorney-General has urged that the entire Act has been enacted by Parliament and if any of the provisions of the Act is not consistent with the provisions of any of the articles in Part III of the Constitution, it must be taken that to the extent of the inconsistency Parliament had modified the fundamental rights under those articles in their application to the person subject to that Act. Any such provision in the Act is as much law as the entire Act. **We agree that each and every provision of the Act is a law made by Parliament and that if any such provision tends to affect the fundamental rights under Part III of the Constitution, that provision does not, on that account, become void, as it must be taken that Parliament has thereby, in the exercise of its power under Article 33 of the Constitution, made the requisite modification to affect the respective fundamental right.** We are however of opinion that the provisions of section 125 of the Act are not discriminatory and do not infringe the provisions of Article 14 of the Constitution. It is not disputed that the persons to whom the provisions of section 125 apply do form a distinct class. They apply to all those persons who are subject to the Act and such persons are specified in section 2 of the Act. The contention for the petitioner is that such persons are subject to be tried for civil offences i.e., offences which are triable by a Criminal Court according to section 3 (ii) of the Act, both by the Courts Martial and the ordinary Criminal Courts, that section 125 of the Act gives a discretion to certain officers specified in the section to decide whether any particular accused be tried by a Court Martial or by a Criminal Court, that there is nothing in the Act to guide such officers in the exercise of their discretion and that therefore discrimination between different persons guilty of the same offence is likely to take place inasmuch as a particular officer may decide to have one accused tried by a Court Martial and another person, accused of the same offence, tried by a Criminal Court, the procedures in such trials being different.

17. We have been taken through the various provisions of the Act and the Rules with respect to the trial of offences by a Court Martial. The procedure to be followed by a Court Martial is quite elaborate and generally follows the pattern of the procedure under the Code of Criminal Procedure. **There are, however, material differences too. All the members of the Court Martial are Military Officers who are not expected to be trained Judges, as the presiding officers of Criminal Courts are. No judgment is recorded. No appeal is provided against the order of the Court Martial. The authorities to whom the convicted person can represent against his conviction by a Court Martial are also non-judicial authorities. In the circumstances, a trial by an ordinary Criminal Court would be more beneficial to the accused than one by a Court Martial.** The question then is whether the discretion of the officers concerned in deciding as to which Court should try a particular accused can be said to be an unguided discretion, as contended for the appellant. Section 125 itself does not contain anything which can be said to be a guide for the exercise of the discretion, but there is sufficient material in the Act which indicates the policy which is to be a guide for exercising the discretion and it is expected that the discretion is exercised in accordance with it. Magistrates can question it and the Government, in case of difference of opinion between the views of the Magistrate and the army authorities, decide the matter finally.

18. Section 69 provides for the punishment which can be imposed on a person tried for committing any civil offence at any place in or beyond India, if charged under section 69 and convicted by a Court Martial. Section 70 provides for certain persons who cannot be tried by Court Martial, except in certain circumstances. Such persons are those who commit an offence of murder, culpable homicide not amounting to murder or of rape, against a person not subject to Military, Naval or Air-Force law. They can be tried by Court Martial of any of those three offences if the offence is committed while on active service or at any place outside India or at a frontier post specified by the Central Government by notification in that behalf. This much therefore is clear that persons committing other offences over which both the Courts Martial and ordinary Criminal Courts have Jurisdiction can and must be tried by Courts Martial if the offences are committed while the accused be on active service or at any place outside India or at a frontier post. This indication of the circumstances in which it would be better exercise of discretion to have a trial by Court Martial, is an index as to what considerations should guide the decision of the officer concerned about the trial being by a Court Martial or by an ordinary Court.

Such considerations can be based on grounds of maintenance of discipline in the army, the persons against whom the offences are committed and the nature of the offences. It may be considered better for the purpose of discipline that offences which are not of a serious type be ordinarily tried by a Court Martial, which is empowered under section 69 to award a punishment provided by the ordinary law and also such less punishment as he mentioned in the Act. Chapter VII mentions the various punishments which can be awarded by Courts Martial and section 72 provides that subject to the provisions of the Act a Court Martial may, on convicting a person of any of the offences specified in sections 34 to 68 inclusive, award either the particular punishment with which the offence is stated in the said sections to be punishable or in lieu thereof any one of the punishments lower in the scale set out in section 71, regard being had to the nature and degree of the offence.

19. The exigencies of service can also be a factor. Offences may be committed when the accused be in camp or his unit be on the march. It would lead to great inconvenience if the accused and witnesses of the incident, if all or some of them happen to belong to the army, should be left behind for the purpose of trial by the ordinary Criminal Court.

20. The trials in an ordinary court are bound to take longer, on account of the procedure for such trials and consequent appeals and revision, then trials by Courts Martial. The necessities of the service in the army require speedier trial. Sections 102 and 103 of the Act point to the desirability of the trial by Court Martial to be conducted with as much speed as possible. Section 120 provides that subject to the provisions of sub-section (2), a Summary Court Martial may try any of the offences punishable under the Act and sub-section (2) states that an officer holding a Summary Court Martial shall not try certain offences without a reference to the officer empowered to convene a district court martial or on active service a summary general court martial for the trial of the alleged offender when there is no grave reason for immediate action and such a reference can be made without detriment to discipline. This further indicates that reasons for immediate action and detriment to discipline are factors in deciding the type of trial.

21. Such considerations, as mentioned above, appear to have led to the provisions of section 124 which are that any person, subject to the Act, who commits any offence against it, may be tried and punished for such offence in any place whatever. It is not necessary that he be tried at a place which be within the jurisdiction of a criminal court having jurisdiction

over the place where the offence be committed.

22. In short, it is clear that there could be a variety of circumstances which may influence the decision as to whether the offender be tried by a Court Martial or by an ordinary Criminal Court, and therefore it becomes inevitable that the discretion to make the choice as to which court should try the accused be left to responsible military officers under whom the accused be serving. Those officers are to be guided by considerations of the exigencies of the service, maintenance of discipline in the army, speedier trial, the nature of the offence and the person against whom the offence is committed.

23. Lastly, it may be mentioned that the decision of the relevant military officer does not decide the matter finally. Section 126 empowers a criminal court having jurisdiction to try an offender to require the relevant military officer to deliver the offender to the Magistrate to be proceeded against according to law or to postpone proceedings pending reference to the Central Government, if that criminal court be of opinion that proceedings be instituted before itself in respect of that offence. When such a request is made, the military officer has either to comply with it or to make a reference to the Central Government whose orders would be final with respect to the venue of the trial. The discretion exercised by the military officer is therefore subject to the control of the Central Government.

24. Reference may also be made to section 549 of the Code of Criminal Procedure [of 1898] which empowers the Central Government to make rules consistent with the Code and other Acts, including the Army Act, as to the cases in which persons subject to military, naval or air-force law be tried by a court to which the Code applies or by Court Martial. It also provides that when a person accused of such an offence which can be tried by an ordinary criminal court or by a Court Martial is brought before a Magistrate, he shall have regard to such rules, and shall, in proper cases, deliver him, together with a statement of the offence of which he is accused, to the Commanding Officer of the Regiment, Corps, Ship or detachment to which he belongs, or to the Commanding Officer of the nearest military, naval or air-force station, as the case may be, for the purpose of being tried by Court Martial. This gives discretion to the Magistrate, having regard to the rules framed, to deliver the accused to the military authorities for trial by Court Martial.

25. The Central Government framed rules by SRO 709 dated 17 April 1952 called the Criminal Courts and Court Martial (Adjustment of

Jurisdiction) Rules, 1952, under section 549 Cr PC. It is not necessary to quote the rules in full. Suffice it to say that when a person charged is brought before a Magistrate on an accusation of offences which are liable to be tried by Court Martial, the Magistrate is not to proceed with the case unless he is moved to do so by the relevant military authority. He can, however, proceed with the case when he be of opinion, for reasons to be recorded, that he should so proceed without being moved in that behalf by competent authority. Even in such a case he has to give notice of his opinion to the Commanding Officer of the accused and is not to pass any order of conviction or acquittal under sections 243, 245, 247 or 248 of the Code of Criminal Procedure, or hear him in defence under section 244 of the said Code; is not to frame any charge against the accused under section 254 and is not to make an order of committal to the Court of Session or the High Court under section 213 of the Code, till a period of 7 days expires from the service of notice on the military authorities. If the military authorities intimate to the Magistrate before his taking any of the aforesaid steps that in its opinion the accused be tried by Court Martial, the Magistrate is to stay proceedings and deliver the accused to the relevant authority with the relevant statement as prescribed in section 549 of the Code. He is to do so also when he proceeds with the case on being moved by the military authority and subsequently it changes its mind and intimates him that in its view the accused should be tried by Court Martial. The Magistrate, however, has still a sort of control over what the military authorities do with the accused. If no effectual proceedings are taken against the accused by the military authorities within a reasonable time, the Magistrate can report the circumstances to the State Government which may, in consultation with the Central Government, take appropriate steps to ensure that the accused person is dealt with in accordance with law. All this is contained in Rules 3 to 7. Rule 8 practically corresponds to section 126 of the Army Act and rule 9 provides for the military authorities to deliver the accused to the ordinary courts when, in its opinion or under the orders of the Government, the proceedings against the accused are to be before a Magistrate.

26. According to section 549 of the Code and the rules framed there under, the final choice about the forum of the trial of a person accused of a civil offence rests with the Central Government, whenever there be difference of opinion between a Criminal Court and the military authorities about the forum where an accused be tried for the particular offence committee by him. His position under section 125 and 126 of the Act is also the same.

27. It is clear therefore that the discretion to be exercised by the military officer specified in of the Act as to the trial of accused by Court Martial or by an ordinary court, cannot be said to be unguided by any policy laid down by the Act or uncontrolled by any other authority. Section 125 of the Act therefore cannot, even on merits, be said to infringe the provisions of Article 14 of the Constitution.

28. The writ petition therefore fails and is dismissed.

4

Ous Kutilingal Achudan Nair v. Union of India, (1976) 2 SCC 780 : AIR 1976 SC 1179 : 1976 SCR (2) 769, [4 Judge Bench], decided on 20 November 1975. Appeal by special leave from the judgment and order dated the 18th June 1974 of the Andhra Pradesh High Court at Hyderabad in Writ Appeal No. 460 of 1974.

JUDGMENT :

This is an appeal by special leave against a judgment of the High Court of Andhra Pradesh. The appellants are office-bearers of the Civil Employees Unions in the various Centers of the Defence Establishments of Secunderabad and Hyderabad. They filed a writ petition in the High Court to impugn the authority of the Commandants in declaring the Unions, represented by the appellants as unlawful associations. The Registrar of Trade Unions had issued Certificates of Registration to the four Unions represented by the appellants between 1954 and 1970. The General Secretary of Class IV, Civil Employees Union, Secunderabad was informed, per letter dated 12 May 1971, by the Under Secretary of the Government of India, Ministry of Defence that their Unions could not be granted recognition as these employees being in the Training Establishments, were not entitled to form Unions. The Commandant also issued a notice to the appellants to show cause why disciplinary action should not be taken against them for forming this unlawful association. The main ground taken in the petition was that the impugned action was violative of their fundamental right to form associations or Unions conferred by Art. 19(1)(c) of the Constitution.

In their reply-affidavit, the respondents averred that the Civilian Non-Combatants in the Defence Establishments were governed by the Army Act and were duly prohibited by Rules framed thereunder from joining or forming a Trade Union; that the associations in question were formed in breach of that prohibition, and were therefore, validly declared illegal.

The learned Judge of the High Court, who tried the petition, held that the right of the appellants to form associations given by Art. 19(1) (c) of the Constitution, had been lawfully taken away. He accordingly dismissed the petition. The appellants carried an appeal to the appellate Bench of the High Court. The Bench dismissed the appeal holding that the impugned action was not without jurisdiction.

The main contention of Mr. K R Nambiyar, appearing for the appellants is that the members of the Unions represented by the appellants, though attached to the Defence Establishments, are 'civilians', designated as "Non- Combatants Un-Enrolled". They include cooks, chowkidars, laskars, barbers, carpenters, mechanics, boot makers, tailors, etc. They are governed by the Civil Service Regulations for purposes of discipline, leave, pay, etc. and are also eligible to serve up to the age of 60 years unlike that of the members of the Armed Forces. In view of these admitted facts, proceeds the argument, these categories of civilian employees, attached to the Defence Establishments, could not be validly called "members of the Armed Forces" covered by Article 33 of the Constitution. The points sought to be made out are: that the members of the appellants' Unions are not subject to the Army Act as they do not fall under any of the categories enumerated in sub-clauses (a) to (i) of section 2 of the Army Act, 1950, and that the impugned notifications are *ultra vires* the Army Act and are struck by Article 19(1)(c) and 33 of the Constitution. For reasons that follow, the contentions must be repelled.

Article 33 of the Constitution provides an exception to the preceding Articles in Part III including Article 19(1)(c). By Article 33, Parliament is empowered to enact law determining to what extent any of the rights conferred by Part III shall in their application to the members of the armed forces or forces charged with the maintenance of public order, be restricted or abrogated so as to ensure the proper discharge of their duties and the maintenance of discipline among them.

In enacting the Army Act, 1950, in so far as it restricts or abrogates any of the fundamental rights of the members of the Armed Forces, Parliament derives its competence from Article 33 of the Constitution. Section 2(1) of the Act enumerates the persons who are subject to the operation of this Act. According to sub-clause (i) of this section, persons governed by the Act, include "persons not otherwise subject to military law who, on active service, in camp, on the march or at any frontier post specified by the Central Government by notification in this behalf, are employed by, or are in the service of, or are followers of, or accompany any portion of the regular army."

The members of the Unions represented by the appellants fall within this category. It is their duty to follow or accompany the Armed personnel on active service, or in camp or on the march. Although they are non-combatants and are in some matters governed by the Civil Service Regulations, yet they are integral to the Armed Forces. They answer the description of the "members of the Armed Forces" within the contemplation of Article

33. Consequently, by virtue of section 21 of the Army Act, the Central Government was competent by notification to make rules restricting or curtailing their fundamental rights under Article 19 (1) (c).

Rules 19 (ii) of the Army Rules, 1954, imposes a restriction on the fundamental rights in these terms:

> **Unauthorised Organisation**:--No persons subject to the Act shall, without the express sanction of the Central Government:-
>
> (i)   xxx.
>
> (ii)   be a member of, or be associated in any way with, any trade union or labour union, or any class of trade or labour unions."

In exercise of its powers under section 4 of the Defence of India Act, the Government of India has by notification dated 11 February 1972, provided that all persons not being members of the Armed Forces of the Union, who are attached to or employed with or following the regular Army shall be subject to the military law. The Army Act, 1950, has also been made applicable to them. By another notification dated 23 February 1972, under Section 9 of the Army Act, civilian employees of the training establishments and Military Hospitals have been taken out of the purview of the Industrial Disputes Act. Section 9 of the Army Act further empowers the Central Government to declare by notification, persons not covered by section 3 (i) of the Act, also as persons on active service.

In view of these notifications issued under section 4 of the Defence of India Act and the Army Rules, the appellants can no longer claim any fundamental right under Article 19 (1) (c) of the Constitution.

5

Lt Col PPS Bedi v. Union of India (1982) 3 SCC 140 : AIR 1982 SC 1413 decided on 25 August 1982 [Three Judge Bench].

HEADNOTE:

The petitioner in each of the three writ petitions [Writ Petition No. 4903/81, Writ Petition No. 1513/79 and Writ Petition No. 5930/80] who was to be tried by general court martial for breach of army discipline questioned the legality and validity of the order convening the general court martial, more particularly its composition. In their petitions under Article 32 of the Constitution it was contended on behalf of the petitioners (1) that to satisfy the requirements of Article 33 the law must be a specific law enacted by Parliament in which a specific provision imposing restriction or even abrogation of fundamental rights should be made; (2) that Rule 40 of the Rules should be so construed as to subserve the mandate of Article 21 that the Army with its total commitment to national security against foreign invasion must be assured the prized liberty of individual members against unjust encroachment and the court should strike a just balance between military discipline and individual personal liberty; and (3) that principles of natural justice should be observed even in respect of persons tried by the Army Tribunals.

JUDGMENT:

1. Validity and legality of an order made against each petitioner convening General Court Martial to try each petitioner in respect of the charges framed against each of them is questioned on diverse grounds but principally the composition in each of these petitions under Article 32 of the Constitution. In Writ Petition No. 4903/81 the petitioner has also challenged the constitutional validity of Rules 22, 23, 24 and 40 of the Army Rules, 1954 ('Rules' for short) as being violative of the fundamental rights of the petitioner guaranteed under Articles 14 and 21 of the Constitution. As certain contentions were common to all the three petitions they were heard together and are being disposed of by this common judgment Facts alleged on which legal formulations were founded may be briefly set out in respect of each petitioner.

Re: Writ Petition No. 4903/81:

2. Petitioner Lt Col Prithipal Singh Bedi was granted permanent regular

commission in the Regiment of Artillery in 1958 and in course of his service he came to be promoted as Captain, then as Major and at the relevant time he was holding the rank of Lt Colonel and in that capacity he was designated as Commanding officer, 226, Medium Regiment of 43 Artillery Brigade. As part of his duty he had to write interim confidential reports (ICR) of five officers of the rank of Major subordinate to him. One Major R S Sehgal was one of the subordinate officers whose interim confidential report was written by the petitioner. Under the relevant Rules the officer whose confidential report is written by his superior has to be shown the confidential report and in token of his having seen the same his signature is to be obtained, the purpose underlying this procedure being that the attention of the subordinate officer is drawn to the counselling remark in the confidential report which may encourage him to remedy the defect pointed out and to improve in his efficiency. The confidential reports prepared by the petitioner were to be reviewed by the Brigadier. It is alleged that Brig N Sondhi, AVSM who held the office of the Brigadier and under whom the petitioner was working as Lt Colonel at the time of writing reports had already been transferred on 8 January 1980 and therefore, the confidential reports submitted by the petitioner were required to be reviewed by the officer who occupied the of office of Brigadier consequent upon the transfer of Brig N Sondhi. It is admitted that petitioner had also received his order of transfer dated 6 February 1980 but he left the charge on 26 February 1980, after completing the formality of handing over charge and also writing the interim confidential reports which he was bound to complete before proceeding on transfer. It is alleged that Major R S Sehgal in respect of whom petitioner wrote the confidential report on 20 February 1980, which contained a counselling remark adverse to the officer was a near relation of Brig N Sondhi. It is further alleged that even though Brig Sondhi had already been transferred and had left charge, yet on 25 February 1980, the confidential reports were forwarded by the Headquarters 43 Artillery Brigade to Brig Sondhi for reviewing the same. While so reviewing the confidential reports, Brig Sondhi addressed a query with respect to the last sentence in para 27 in the confidential report of Major Sehgal: "that the last sentence appears to have been written possibly at a different time. It is suggested that a confirmation may be asked for from the officer as to whether he was aware of the complete para prior to signing. The ICR may thereafter be returned for onward dispatch." Suspicion underlying this query is that adverse entry reflected in the last sentence of para 27 was interpolated after the confidential report was signed by Major Sehgal. The suspicion arose on the visual impression that: (a) there is change in ink

211

of last line; (b) last line appears to have been written over the signature of the officer reported upon; (c) size of lettering of the last line is smaller than the rest of the para. It may be mentioned that ultimately this alleged interpolation in the interim confidential report after the same having been initialled by the officer reported upon is the gravamen of the charge under section 45 of the Army Act on which the petitioner is called upon to face a trial by the General Court Martial convened under the impugned order dated 11 April 1981.

Re: Writ Petition No. 1513/79:

3. The first petitioner Captain Dharampal Kukrety and second Petitioner Naik Bhanwar Singh were both attached at the relevant time to 2 Rajput Regiment but since the order to try them before a General Court Martial both of them are attached to 237 Engineer Regiment of 25 Infantry Division which is a part of the 16th Corps of the Indian Army. Petitioner 1 was promoted as Acting Major but because of the direction to try him before a Court Martial he has been reverted to the substantive rank of Captain. Petitioner 2 holds the substantive rank of Naik. In the year 1978 one Lt Col S N Verma was the Commanding officer of the 2 Rajput Regiment and the 1st petition was directly under him being second in command. One Major V K Singh belonging to the 2 Rajput Regiment was a Company Commander under Lt Col Verma. He applied for casual leave for seven days and Lt Col Verma granted the same. In the meantime on 14 October 1978, Lt Col Verma proceeded on leave. First petitioner being the second in command was officiating Commanding officer when Lt Col Verma proceeded on leave. On 16 October 1978, the 1st petitioner informed Maj V K Singh that he could proceed on leave with effect from 17 October 1978, for a period of seven days. Maj V K Singh, however, overstayed his leave and returned after 10 days. Petitioner contends that he being a strict disciplinarian, he did not approve of the default of Major Singh and, therefore, he reported the matter to Lt Col Verma on his return from leave who in turn asked the 1st petitioner to make investigation and submit report. On the 1st petitioner making the report, Lt Col S N Verma ordered abstract of evidence to be recorded by framing some charge against Major V K Singh. The allegation is that the father-in-law of Major V K Singh is Deputy Speaker of Haryana State Legislative Assembly and a man of powerful political influence who appears to have contacted third respondent Lt General Gurbachan Singh to assist his son-in-law Major V K Singh. It is alleged that when Major V K Singh was produced before 7th respondent Brigadier P N Kacker, the latter appeared reluctant to proceed

against Major V K Singh. First petitioner sought an interview with 7th respondent and insisted that disciplinary action should be initiated against Major V K Singh. First petitioner sought an interview with 5th respondent on 16 December 1978. Major V K Singh was awarded 'displeasure' which appears to have infuriated the first petitioner because according to him punishment was disproportionately low compared to default. It is alleged that 5th respondent suggested that 1st petitioner be put on AFMS-10 for psychiatric investigation. 1st petitioner sought attachment to other unit, certain very untoward incidents followed which are detailed in the report of Court of Inquiry set up for ascertaining the facts which are not necessary to be detailed here. First petitioner has set out in his petition chronology of events leading to his being charge-sheeted. Ultimately, an order was made to try him by a General Court Martial and a General Court Martial was convened as per the order dated 7 October 1979. The legality and validity of the order constituting the General Court Martial is impugned in this petition.

Re: Writ Petition No. 5930/80:

4. Petitioner Captain Chander Kumar Chopra joined the Army as 2nd Lieutenant on 12 January 1969, and in course of time came to be promoted as Captain and at the relevant time he belonged to 877 AT BN ASC under 20 Mountain Division which is one of the Divisions in 33 Corps. Petitioner was second-in-command. On 12 February 1979, the petitioner sought a personal interview with commanding officer Lt Col R M Bajaj to report against Major S K Malhotra for the irregularities committed in the Company disclosing misappropriation of funds, pilferage of petrol and stores, furnishing of false information and certificates in official documents resulting in loss to the State, misuse of transport and misuse of power and property. As Lt Col Bajaj did not possibly take any action on this report, the petitioner on 7 March 1979, submitted an application to the Chief of Staff, Headquarters, 33 Corps c/o 99 APO to bring to the notice of Chief of Staff the irregularities going on in 'A' Coy 877 AT BN ASC and seeking an interview at an early date. The petitioner's request for a personal interview was turned down whereupon the petitioner made an application for casual leave for 13 days wef 26 February 1979, which appears not to have been granted. On 16 March 1979, the petitioner was summoned by Lt Col Bajaj at his residence and he was assured that justice would be done but the petitioner should cancel the letter dated 7 March 1979, and surrender the demi-official letter addressed to Chief of Staff, 33 Corps in the interest and name of the Unit. Thereafter the petitioner was

taken to office by Lt Col Bajaj and it is alleged that under pressure, letter dated 16 March 1979, written in the petitioner's own hand as dictated by Lt Col Bajaj was taken and at the same time a number of certificates were also taken from the petitioner. A Court of Inquiry was set up to inquire into the allegations made against Major Malhotra by the petitioner. The Court of inquiry commenced investigation on 27 August 1979. The petitioner submitted a request to summon 15 witnesses to substantiate his allegation against Major Malhotra. Probably this request did not find favour and the petitioner entertained a suspicion that the members constituting the Court of Inquiry were highly prejudiced against him. The Court of Inquiry submitted its report. It is not necessary to recapitulate the findings of the Court of Inquiry save and except that not only the Court of inquiry negatived all the allegations of petitioner against Major Malhotra but on the contrary found that the petitioner had taken some store items unauthorisedly on 30 January 1979, which were returned on 31 January 1979. Pursuant to the findings of the Court of inquiry a charge-sheet was drawn up against the petitioner for having committed offences under sections 56 (a) and (b), and 63 of the Army Act. Direction was given for recording summary of evidence. Subsequently the impugned order convening the General Court Martial was issued. The petitioner thereupon filed the present petition.

5. In each petition legality and validity of the order convening the General Court Martial more particularly the composition of the Court Martial in respect of each petitioner is questioned. The challenge up to a point proceeds on grounds common to all the three petitions and they may be dealt with first.

6. The contention is that the constitution of General Court Martial in each case is illegal and contrary to Rule 40 of the Army Rules and, therefore the order constituting the General Court Martial in each case must be quashed.

7. The web of argument is woven round the true construction and intendment underlying Rule 40. It was said that the grammatical construction must accord with the underlying intendment of Rule 40 and that the approach must be informed by the expanding jurisprudence and widening horizon of the subject of personal liberty in Article 21 because in the absence of Article 33 the procedure prescribed for trial by the General Court Martial under the Act would have been violative of Article 21. Approach, it was urged, must be to put such liberal construction on Rule 40 as to sub-serve the mandate of Article 21. Army, with its total commitment to national independence against foreign invasion must equally be assured the prized liberty of individual member against unjust encroachment.

It was said that the court should strike a just balance between military discipline and individual personal liberty. And door must not be bolted against principles of natural justice even in respect of Army tribunal. An unnatural distinction or differentiation between a civilian offender and an offender subject to the Act would be destructive of the cherished principle of equality, the dazzling light of the Constitution which illumines all other provisions.

8. The dominant purpose in construing a statute is to ascertain the intention of the Parliament. One of the well recognised canons of construction is that the legislature speaks its mind by use of correct expression and unless there is any ambiguity in the language of the provision the Court should adopt literal construction if it does not lead to an absurdity. The first question to be posed is whether there is any ambiguity in the language used in Rule 40. If there is none, it would mean the language used, speaks the mind of Parliament and there is no need to look somewhere leers discover the intention or meaning. If the literal construction leads to an absurdity, external aids to construction can be resorted to. To ascertain the literal meaning it is equally necessary first to ascertain the juxtaposition in which the Rule is placed, the purpose for which it is enacted and the object which it is required to subserve and the authority by which the Rule is framed. This necessitates examination of the broad features of the Act.

9. The Act as its long title would show was enacted to consolidate and amend the law relating to the governance of the regular Army and it came into force on July 22, 1950. Section 2 sets out the persons subject to the Act. Section 3 provides the dictionary clause. Sub-section (2) of section 3 defines 'civil offence' to mean an offence which is triable by a criminal court. Expression 'corps' is defined in section 3 (vi) to mean any separate body of persons subject to the Act which is prescribed as a corps for the purpose of all or any of the provisions of the Act. 'Department' has been defined in placitium (ix) to include any division or branch of a department. Chapter III deals with the commission, appointment and enrollment of Army personnel. Chapter IV sets out the statutory conditions of service and Chapter V deals with service privileges. Chapter VI sets out various offences made punishable by the Act. Section 69 provides that subject to the provisions of section 70 any person subject to the Act who at any place in or beyond India commits any civil offence shall be deemed to be guilty of an offence against the Act and if charged therewith under the section, shall be liable to be tried by a court-martial and, on conviction, be punishable in the manner therein prescribed. This provision would show

that if any person subject to the Act commits any offence triable by ordinary criminal court which for the purpose of the Act would be a civil offence, is liable to be tried for the same, though not an offence under the Act, by the court martial and be punishable in the manner prescribed in section 69. Section 70 carves out an exception in respect of certain civil offences which cannot be tried by a court martial. In view of the provision prescribed in section 69, a situation is bound to arise where an ordinary criminal court and the court martial both will have jurisdiction to try a person for having committed a certain civil offence. To avoid conflict of jurisdiction, section 125 is enacted conferring a discretion on the officer commanding the army, army corps, division or independent brigade in which the accused person is serving or such other officer as may be prescribed to decide before which court the proceeding shall be instituted and if that officer decides that it should be instituted before a court-martial, to direct that the accused person shall be detained in military custody. Section 126 confers power on the criminal court to require the officer who has decided to use his discretion in favour of court-martial under section 125, to deliver the accused to the nearest magistrate to be proceeded against according to law, or he may direct the officer to postpone proceedings pending a reference to the Central Government. On such a reference being made, the Central Government will have power to determine whether the person should be tried by an ordinary criminal court or by a Court Martial and the decision of the Central Government in this behalf is rendered final. A successive trial by a court-martial and the ordinary criminal court is distinctly possible in view of the provision contained in section 127. Chapter VII sets out the various punishments which can be imposed under the Act. Chapter VIII deals with penal deductions that can be made from the pay and allowances of an officer. Chapter IX provides for arrest and proceedings before trial. Section 108 in Chapter X provides that there shall be four kinds of court-martial: (a) general courts-martial; (b) district courts-martial, (c) summary general courts-martial; and. (d) summary courts-martial. Sections 109 to 112 confer power on various authorities to convene one or other kind of court- martial. Section 113 provides for composition of General Court-Martial and it may be extracted:

> "113. A general court-martial shall consist of not less than five officers, each of whom has held a commission for not less than three whole years and of whom not less than four are of a rank not below that of captain."

Section 118 confers power on general or summary general court martial to try any person subject to the Act for any offence punish able therein and to pass any sentence authorized thereunder. Chapter XI prescribes procedure of court-martial. Section 129 provides that every court-martial shall, and every district or Summary general court martial may, be attended by a judge-advocate, who shall be either an officer belonging to the department of the Judge-Advocate General, or any of his deputies. Section 130 of the Act is important and it may be extracted:

> "130. (1) At all trials by general, district or summary 1 general court-martial, as soon as the court is assembled, the names of the presiding officer and members shall be read over to the accused, who shall thereupon be asked whether he objects to being tried by any officer sitting on the court.
>
> (2) If the accused objects to any such officer, his objection and also the reply thereto of the officer objected to, shall be heard end recorded, and the remaining officers of the court shall, in the absence of the challenged officer decide on the objection.
>
> (3) If the objection is allowed by one-half or more the votes of the officers entitled to vote, the objection shall be allowed, and the member objected to shall retire, and his vacancy may be filled in the prescribed manner by another officer subject to the same right of the accused to object.
>
> (4) When no challenge is made, or when challenge has been made and disallowed, or the place of every officer successfully challenged has been filled by another officer to whom no objection is made or allowed, the court shall proceed with the trial."

Section 133 provides that the Indian Evidence Act, 1872, shall, subject to the provisions of the Act, apply to all proceedings before a court-martial. Chapter XII provides for confirmation of the finding and sentence and revision thereof. Chapter XIII deals with the execution of sentence awarded by court-martial. Chapter XIV deals with pardons, remissions and suspensions of sentence. Section 191 in Chapter XV confers power to make Rules for the purpose of carrying into effect the provisions of the Act and without prejudice to the generality of the power so conferred by sub-section (1), the rules made inter alia may provide for convening and constituting of court-martial and the appointment of prosecutors at trials by courts-martial, adjournment, dissolution and sitting of court-martial and the procedure to be observed in trials by courts-martial and the appearance of legal practitioners thereat.

10. Armed with these powers Army Rules, 1954 have been framed. To begin with, the Rules in Chapter V may be noticed. Rule 22 prescribes procedure for hearing of charge at a stage anterior to the convening of court-martial. After this preliminary hearing of the charge, if further action is contemplated, Rule 23 prescribes procedure for recording summary of evidence. After recording summary of evidence, Rule 24 enables the commanding officer either to remand the accused for trial by a court-martial or refer the case to the proper superior military authority or if he thinks it desirable, re-hear the case and either dismiss the charge or dispose of it summarily. Rule 25 provides procedure for inquiry of charge against an officer, the salient feature of it is that the procedure prescribed in Rule 22 and 23 is required to be followed in the case of an officer if he so requires.

11. Rule 28 sets out the general format of charge-sheet and Rule 30 prescribes contents of charges. Rule 33 enacts detailed provisions for preparation for defence by the accused which amongst others confer a right on the accused person to interview any witness he wishes to call for his defence and an embargo on censoring his correspondence with his legal advisers as also a prohibition on interviewing the witnesses whom the accused wishes to call in his defence. Rule 34 provides for assistance to the accused to summon his witnesses. Rule 37 provides for convening of general and district courts-martial. Rule 37(1) and (2) were relied upon in support of a submission by Mr Sanghi, which provides that the convening officer before convening court martial has to satisfy himself that the charges to be tried by the court are for offences within the meaning of the Act and that the evidence justifies a trial of those charges and if not so satisfied, he is entitled to order the release of the accused or refer the case to the superior military authority.

12. Rule 41 provides that on the Court assembling, the order convening the court shall be laid before it together with the charge-sheet and the summary of evidence or a true copy thereof and also names, ranks and corps of the officers appointed to serve on the Court. A duty is cast on the court to satisfy itself that it is legally constituted and one such duty being that the court, as far as it can ascertain, shall satisfy itself that it has been convened in accordance with the provisions of the Act and the Rules and that each of the officer composing the court-martial is eligible and not disqualified for serving on that court-martial and further in case of a general court-martial, the officers are of the required rank. After the court has satisfied itself about its constitution, it shall cause the accused to be brought before

it as provided in Rule 43. Rule 44 enables the accused as required by section 130 of the Act to state whether he has any objection to be tried by any officer sitting on the Court. A detailed procedure is prescribed for disposing of the objection. Elaborate trial procedure is prescribed in the event the accused pleads not guilty and barring minor situational variants the procedure prescribed is analogous to the one prescribed in the Code of Criminal Procedure [Cr PC] for trial of an accused by the Court of Sessions. A reference to Rule 95 is advantageous. It enables an accused person to be represented by any person subject to the Act who shall be called the defending officer or assisted by any person whose services he may be able to procure and who shall be called the friend of the accused. Rule 96 confers power subject to the Rules on the Chief of the Army Staff to permit counsel to appear on behalf of the prosecutor and the accused at general and district courts-martial, if the Chief of the Army Staff or the convening officer, declares that it is expedient to allow the appearance of counsel thereat, and such declaration may be made as regards all general and district court-martial held at any particular place, or as regards any particular general or district court martial, and may be made subject to such reservation as to cases on active service, or otherwise, as seems expedient. In case of a general court-martial where it is obligatory to associate a Judge-Advocate, Rule 105 provides for powers duties and obligations of the Judge Advocate, one such being that both the prosecutor and the accused are entitled to his opinion on any question of law relating to the charge or trial. Rule 177 provides for setting up of a Court of Inquiry, its composition and the subsequent Rules provide for the procedure to be followed by a Court of Inquiry. Rule 180 provides that whenever an inquiry affects the character or military reputation of a person subject to the Act, full opportunity must be afforded to such person of being present throughout the inquiry and of making any statement and of giving any evidence he may wish to make or give and of cross-examining any witness whose evidence in his opinion affects his character or military reputation and producing any witnesses in defence of his character or military reputation This Rule was relied on by Mr Sanghi to urge that whenever character or military reputation of a person subject to the Act is involved it is obligatory to set up a Court of Inquiry. On a plain reading of Rule 180, the submission is without merits but that would come later. Rule 187 has reference to section 3 (vi). It prescribes that bodies of persons subject to the Act are to be treated a 'Corps' for the purpose of Chapter III and section 43(a) of the Act and Chapters II and III of the Rules.

13. At this stage it would be profitable to refer to Article 33 of the

Constitution which reads as under:

> "33. **Power to Parliament to modify the rights confer red by this Part in their application to forces**: Parliament may by law determine to what extend any of the rights conferred by this Part shall, in their application to the members of the Armed Forces or the Forces charged with the maintenance of public order, be restricted or abrogated so as to ensure the proper discharge of their duties, and the maintenance of discipline among them."

Chapter IV in the Rules specifies restrictions on the fundamental rights. Rule 19 prescribes restrictions on the fundamental freedom under Article 19(1)(c), to wit, to form associations or unions. Similarly Rules 20 and 21 prescribe restrictions on the freedom of speech and expression guaranteed under Article 19(1)(a). No contention was advanced before us in respect of restrictions prescribed by Rules 19, 20 and 21 on the freedom of speech and expression and the freedom of forming associations and unions. The contention was that a trial by a court-martial would result in deprivation of personal liberty and it can only be done in view of Article 21, by procedure established by law and the law prescribing such procedure must satisfy the test prescribed by Articles 14 and 19. It was contended that in view of the decision in *Maneka Gandhi v. Union of India* (1978) 2 SCR 621: (1978) 1 SCC 248, the law to satisfy the test of Article 21 must be just, fair and reasonable and if the procedure prescribed by the Cr PC for trial of offences is just, fair and reasonable, any deviation there from in the procedure prescribed for trial by court-martial would neither be just, fair nor reasonable and it would be violative of Article 21. The question really is, how far this contention about violation of Article 21 is available in view of the provision contained in Article 33. **The contention is that in order to satisfy the requirement of Article 33, Parliament must enact specific law specifying therein the modification of the rights conferred by Part III and that a restriction or abrogation of fundamental rights cannot be left to be deduced or determined by implication. In other words, the submission is that the law to satisfy the requirement of Article 33 must be a specific law enacted by Parliament in which a specific provision imposing restriction or even abrogation of fundamental rights should be made and when such provisions are debated by the Parliament it would be clear as to how far restriction is imposed by Parliament on the fundamental rights enacted in Part III in their application to the members of the Armed Forces or the forces charged with the maintenance of public order. Submission is that a conscious**

220

and deliberate Act of Parliament may permit erosion of fundamental rights in their application to Armed Forces. Such a serious inroad on fundamental rights cannot be left to Central Government to be done by delegated legislation. **Article 33** permits Parliament by law to not merely restrict but abrogate the fundamental rights enacted in Part III in their application to the members of Armed Forces. The Act was enacted in 1950 and was brought into force on 22 July 1950. Thus the Act was enacted after the Constitution came into force on 26 January 1950. When power to legislate is conferred by Constitution, and Parliament enacts a legislation, normal inference is that the legislation is enacted in exercise of legislative power and legislative craftsmanship does not necessitate specifying the powers. Since the Constitution came into force, Parliament presumably was aware that its power to legislate must be referable to Constitution and therefore it would be subject to the limitation prescribed by the Constitution. Whenever a legislation is being debated for being put on the statute book, Articles 12 and 13 must be staring into the face of that body. Consequently when the Act was enacted not only Articles 12 and 13 were hovering over the provisions but also Article 33 which to some extent carves out an exception to Articles 12 and 13 must be present to the corporate mind of Parliament which would imply that Parliament by law can restrict or abrogate fundamental rights set out in Part III in their application to Armed Forces. But it was said that by contemporanea exposition Section 21 of the Act clearly sets out the limits of such restriction or abrogation and no more. Section 21 confers power on the Central Government to make Rules restricting to such extent and in such manner as may be necessary to modify the fundamental freedom conferred by Article 19 (a) and (c) in their application to Armed Forces and none other meaning that Armed Forces would enjoy other fundamental freedoms set out in part III. Armed with this power, Rules 19, 20 & 21 have been framed by the Central Government. Taking cue from Section 21 and Rules 19, 20 and 21, it was submitted that while Article 33 enables the Parliament by law to abrogate or restrict fundamental rights in their application to Armed Forces, Parliament exercised the same power limited to what is prescribed in Section 21 and specified the restrictions in Rules 19, 20 and 21 and, therefore, the remaining fundamental rights in Part III are neither abrogated nor restricted in their application to the Armed Forces. Consequently it was urged that the Act prescribing the procedure of court-martial must satisfy the requirement of Article 21.

14. **While investigating and precisely ascertaining the limits of inroads or encroachments made by legislation enacted in exercise of power**

conferred by Article 33, on the guaranteed fundamental rights to all citizens of this country without distinction, in respect of armed personnel, the court should be vigilant to hold the balance between two conflicting public interests; namely necessity of discipline in armed personnel to preserve national security at any cost, because that itself would ensure enjoyment of fundamental rights by others, and the denial to those responsible for national security of these very fundamental rights which are inseparable adjuncts of civilized life.

15. Article 33 confers power on the Parliament to determine to what extent any of the rights conferred by part III shall, in their application to the members of the Armed Forces, be restricted or abrogated so as to ensure the proper discharge of duties and maintenance of discipline amongst them. Article 33 does not obligate that Parliament must specifically adumbrate each fundamental right enshrined in part III and to specify in the law enacted in exercise of the power conferred by Article 33 the degree of restriction or total abrogation of each right. That would be reading into Article 33 a requirement which it does not enjoin. In fact, after the Constitution came into force, the power to legislate in respect of any item must be referable to an entry in the relevant list. Entry 2 in list I: Naval, Military and Air Force; any other Armed Forces of the Union, would enable Parliament to enact the Army Act and armed with this power the Act was enacted in July 1950. It has to be enacted by the Parliament subject to the requirements of Part III of the Constitution read with Article 33 which itself forms part of Part III. Therefore, every provision of the Army Act enacted by the Parliament, if in conflict with the fundamental rights conferred by Part III, shall have to be read subject to Article 33 as being enacted with a view to either restricting or abrogating other fundamental rights to the extent of inconsistency or repugnancy between Part III of the constitution and the Army Act. This is no more res integra in view of the decision of the Constitution Bench of this Court in *Ram Sarup v. Union of India* (1964) 5 SCR 931 : AIR 1965 SC 247, in which repelling the contention that the restriction or abrogation of the fundamental rights in exercise of the power conferred by Article 33 is limited to one set out in Section 21of the Act, this Court observed as under:

"........The learned Attorney-General has urged that the entire Act has been enacted by Parliament and if any of the provisions of the Act is not consistent with the provisions of any of the Articles in Part III of the Constitution, it must be taken that to the extent of the inconsistency Parliament had modified the fundamental rights under those articles in their application to the person subject to, that Act. Any such provision in the Act is as much law as the entire Act. We agree that each and every provision of the Act is a law made by Parliament and that if any such provision tends to effect the fundamental rights under Part III of the Constitution, that provision does not, on that account, become void, as it must be taken that Parliament has thereby in the exercise of its power under Article 33 of the Constitution made the requisite modification to affect the respective fundamental rights....."

Section 21 merely confers an additional power to modify rights conferred by Article 19 (a) and (c) by Rules and such Rules may set out the limits of restriction. But the specific provision does not derogate from the generality of power conferred by Article 33. Therefore, it is not possible to accept the submission that the law prescribing procedure for trial of offences by court martial must satisfy the requirement of Article 21 because to the extent the procedure is prescribed by law and if it stands in derogation of Article 21, to that extent Article 21 in its application to the Armed Forces is modified by enactment of the procedure in the Army Act itself.

16. Incidentally a reference was made to *Dalbir Singh v. State of Punjab* 1962 Supp 3 SCR 25 : AIR 1962 SC 1106, but it hardly illuminates the contours of controversy. The contention raised was that section 3 of the PEPSU Police (Incitement to disaffection) Act, 1953, was violative of Article 19 (1)(a) and was not saved by Article 19 (2). Repelling this contention a Constitution Bench of this Court held that the Police service is an arm of the State charged with the duty of ensuring and maintaining public order and since any breach of discipline on the part of its members might result in a threat to public order, Section 3 must be held, to be valid as having been enacted in the interest of public order within the meaning of Article 19 (2). Attempt was made to urge that as the Act in question was made by the President under Article 356 of the Constitution it would be an Act of Parliament in exercise of the power conferred by Article 33 and as the police force would be one such force as contemplated by Article 33 charged with the maintenance of public a order, the provisions of the Act would be beyond the challenge of Part III of the Constitution. This contention was negatived on the ground that Article 33 was not applicable because parliament had delegated the powers of State legislature to the President and, therefore, any law enacted by the President in exercise of this power would not have the force of Parliamentary legislation contemplated by Article 33. But this is hardly of any assistance. In *Lt Col M L Kohli*

v. Union of India AIR 1975 SC 612 : (1975) 4 SCC 814 the petitioner challenged certain provisions of the Army Act and it was contended that Article 33 does not cover ex-servicemen who are not serving members of the defence forces. In fact, at the hearing of the petition the contention was withdrawn and, therefore, it is not necessary to examine this decision any further.

17. Mr Tarkunde, however, contended that the observations of the Constitution Bench in *Ram Sarup's case* in respect of the provisions of the Act having been enacted by the Parliament in exercise of powers conferred by Article 33 and that each and every provision of the Act is a law made by Parliament and if any such provision tends to affect the fundamental rights under Part III of the Constitution, that provision does not, on that account become void as it must be taken that Parliament has in exercise of its power under Article 33 of the Constitution made the requisite modification to affect the respective fundamental rights, are obiter. Proceeding along this line it was submitted that the contention before the Constitution Bench was that Article 22 of the Constitution conferred a fundamental right on a person accused of an offence to be defended by a lawyer of his own choice, the denial of this right to the accused would be violative of Article 22 and the trial would be vitiated. It is true that this contention was repelled on the facts found, namely, that the petitioner made no request for being represented at the court martial by a counsel of his own choice. Rule 96 of the Army Rules provides that subject to the Rules, counsel shall be allowed to appear on behalf of the prosecutor and accused at general and district courts-martial if the Chief of the Army Staff or the convening officer declares that it is expedient to allow the appearance of counsel thereat and such declaration may be made as regards any particular general or district court-martial held in a particular place etc. The question of validity of this Rule was kept open. Frankly, there is some force in the contention of Mr. Tarkunde that once having found that the accused in that case made no request for being defended by a lawyer of his choice he could not be heard to complain of contravention or violation of the right under Article 22 and, therefore, the question whether the whole of the Act was enacted in exercise of the power conferred by Article 33 did not specifically arise. However, a contention was specifically canvassed before the Constitution Bench by the learned Attorney-General that court may proceed on the basis that the request as claimed on behalf of the accused in that case was made and turned down and yet the accused could not in that case complain of contravention of Article 22 of the Constitution and this contention was in terms answered. If in this context the observation can be said to be

obiter, it is nonetheless entitled to respect at our hands.

18. It was, however, contended that the question as to the validity of the Rules enacted in exercise of the power conferred by Section 191 having been kept open, this Court must examine the contention afresh. It was urged that what Article 33 protects is an Act made by Parliament and not subordinate legislation such as the Rules and the Regulations. Section 191 confers power on the Central Government to make Rules for the purposes of carrying into effect the provisions of the Act. Section 192 confers power on the Central Government to make regulations for all or any of the purposes of the Act other than those specified in section. 191. Section 193 provides that all Rules and Regulations made under the Act shall be published in the official gazette and on such publication shall have effect as if enacted in the Act. What character the Rules and the Regulations acquire when a deeming fiction is enacted that if enacted in accordance with the procedure prescribed they shall have effect as if enacted in the Act meaning thereby that they are to be treated as part and parcel of the enactment itself? In the *Chief Inspector of Mines v. Lala Karam Chand Thapar* (1962) 1 SCR 9, 23 : AIR 1961 SC 838 a Constitution Bench of this Court examined the position of Rules or Regulations made under an Act having the effect as if enacted in the Act. After examining various foreign decisions, the Court held as under:

> "The true position appears to be that the Rules and Regulations do not loose their character as Rules and Regulations, even though they are to be of the same effect as if contained in the Act. They continue to be Rules subordinate to the Act, and though for certain purposes, including the purpose of construction, they are to be treated as if contained in the Act, their true nature as subordinate Rule is not lost."

The same question came up before a Constitution Bench *in Kali Pada Chowdhury v Union* of *India* (1963) 2 SCR 904 and the majority has almost accepted the same view.

19. The effect of the expression 'as if enacted in this Act' has occasionally presented difficulty arising from the context in which the expression is used. If the expression were to mean that the Rules or Regulations enacted or framed in exercise of the power to enact subordinate legislation having the same force as the provisions of the statute which enables the subordinate legislation to be enacted, a question is bound to arise whether, if the provisions of the statute are not open to question the subordinate legislation would also be immune from the challenge to its validity. In

Institute of Patent Agents v. Lockwood 1894 AC 347 Lord Harschell was of the opinion that the expression 'as if enacted in this Act' would render the subordinate legislation as completely exempt from judicial review as the statute itself. However, in *R v. Minister of Health, Ex-parte Yaffe* 1931 AC 494, there was some disinclination to accept Lord Herschell's opinion at least to its fullest extent. While distinguishing Lockwood's case a note was taken of the fact that the Rules framed in exercise of the power conferred by section 101(3) of the Patents, Designs and Trade Marks Acts of 1883 and 1888 would be subject to control of Parliament and, therefore, Parliament was in control of the Rules for 40 days after they were passed and could have annulled them on a motion to that effect, and that would permit an inference that they had same strength and validity as the provisions of the statute itself. Distinguishing this position in *Yaffe's* case it was noticed that there was no parliamentary manner of dealing with the confirmation of the scheme by the Ministry of Health and, therefore, it cannot have the same efficacy and validity as the provisions of the statute. Subsequently, in *Miller v. Bootham (William) & Sons Ltd* (1944) KB 337: (1944) All ER 333, the conflict between the view of Lord Harschall in Lockwood's case and the view of Lord Dunedin in *Yaffe's* case was noticed but it was held to have no impact in that case because power was reserved with the Secretary of State in the later factories Act of 1937 to bring the earlier regulation in conformity with the intendment of the Act. It would, however, appear that this ancient formula often resorted to, to clothe subordinate legislation with the force of the provisions of the statute would require further consideration. . It is, however, not necessary to conclude this point because the primary contention was about the non-compliance with Rules rather than with their validity.

20. Rule 40 provides for composition of court-martial. It reads as under:

> "40. Composition of court-martial: (1) A general court martial shall be composed, as far as seems to the convening officer practicable, of officers of different corps or departments, and in no case exclusively of officers of the corps or department to which the accused belongs.
>
> (2) The members of a court-martial for the trial of an officer shall be of a rank not lower than that of the officer unless, in the opinion of the convening officer, officers of such rank are not (having due regard to the exigencies of the public service) available. Such opinion shall be recorded in the convening order.
>
> (3) In no case shall an officer below the rank of captain be a member

of a court-martial for the trial of a filed officer."

The power to convene the General Court Martial is conferred of the Central Government, the Chief of Army Staff or by any officer empowered in this behalf by warrant of the Chief of Army Staff. The officer empowered to convene a general court-martial is designated in the Rules as 'convening officer'. In the composition of court-martial there is both a positive and negative requirement to be fulfilled. The positions requirement is that it shall be composed of officers of different corps or departments and the negative inhibition is that in any case it shall not be composed exclusively of officers of the corps or departments to which the accused belongs. Both these requirements are subject to the overriding consideration that it may be so done as far as it seems to the convening officer practicable to do so. In other words, one or the other requirement may be given a go by if it is otherwise found not to be practicable. Keeping aside the functional requirement of practicability of complying with Rule 40, the convening officer in ordinary circumstance should arrange the composition of the general court martial as to include officers of different corps or departments and must avoid so composing the court-martial as to be exclusively of officers of the corps or department to which the accused belongs. There is a further requirement in sub-section (2) which will be presently examined. What constitutes Corps for the purposes of Rule 40 is the bone of contention between the parties. The expression 'department' did not present any difficulty. The definition of the expression 'department' is an inclusive definition. The expression would include any division or branch of a department. Learned Additional Solicitor-General stated that there is only one department in the Army and that is the department of Judge-Advocate. There is no other department. It is not necessary to dilate on this point because it was not contended on behalf of the petitioners that the personnel of the court-martial belonged to the same department.

21. The expression 'corps' has been defined to mean any separate body of persons subject to the Act which is prescribed as corps for the purposes of all or any of the provisions of the Act. And 'prescribed' means prescribed by Rules made under the Act. Rule 187 bears the marginal note: 'Corps prescribed under section 3 (vi). Each of the separate bodies of persons subject to the Act set out in sub-Rule (1) (a) to (y) is to be a corps for the purposes of Chapter III and section 43 (a) of the Act and Chapters II and III of the Act. Sub- Rule (3) provides that for the purposes of every other provision---i.e., other than Chapter III and section 43 (a) of the Act and Chapters II and III of the Rules --- each of the body of persons set out in

sub-clauses (a) to (f) shall be deemed to be a corps. They are: (a) every battalion; (b) every company which does not form part of battalion; (c) every regiment of cavalry, armoured corps or artillery; (d) every squadron or battery which does not form part of a regiment of cavalry, armoured corps or artillery; (e) every school of instruction, training centre, or regimental centre; and (f) every other separate t unit composed wholly or partly of persons subject to the Act (chart showing vertical hierarchy in the Army has not been included).

22. The President of India is the Supreme Commander of the Armed Forces [See Article 53(2)]. Under him is the Chief of Army Staff. The Indian Army is divided into five commands being Northern, Central, Western, Eastern and Southern Commands. Each area command has under its static formation areas, sub-area, etc. and fighting formation army corps: for example, the Western Command is said to have three army corps. Corps in this sense means army formation. Speaking generally, each army corp is composed of three or four divisions with an officer of the rank of Major General at its head; each division is divided into three or four Brigades, each Brigade being commanded by a brigadier; each Brigade is composed of three or four battalions so designated in the case of Infantry and Regiment in the case of Cavalry or its modern equivalent; each battalion or regiment being commanded by an officer of the rank of Lt Col, each battalion is divided in three or four companies in case of Infantry and three or four Batteries or Squadron in the case of cavalry, each such unit being led by an officer of the rank of a Major.

23. To start with, the expression 'army corps' should not be confused with the expression 'corps'. Both connote a distinct and different unit in the army. Section 7 and Rule 189 operate in a different situation. They merely specify who is the commanding officer of a person attached to corps, department or detachment. Corps forms a tiny small part of what is called Army Corps. The expression 'Army Corps' used in sections 8 and 125 with its content and juxtaposition leaves no room for doubt that the expression 'Army Corps' and 'corps' have different connotation. Once this is borne in mind, the meaning of the expression 'corps' in Rule 40, does not present any difficulty.

24. Reverting to sub-Rule (3) of Rule 187 which prescribes corps for the purposes of section 3 (*vi*), every battalion is a corps for the purposes of the Act and Rules. Now there may be a company but not forming part of a battalion and may be independent of any battalion and, therefore, sub clause (b) of sub-Rule (3) of Rule 187 treats such unattached Company

not forming part of a battalion as a corps by itself. That is equally true of regiment of cavalry, armoured corps or artillery. Undoubtedly, every school of instruction, training centre or regimental centre cannot form part of a battalion and must of necessity be a separate Corps. If we recall the composition as roughly sketched, every company is part of some battalion because each battalion is sub-divided into companies. And that is possibly the army unit which is being designated as Corps. Bearing in mind the designation of battalion in infantry and regiment in cavalry, the unit designated as battalion or regiment will be a corps for the purpose of the Act and the Rules. This conclusion is reinforced by reference to Rule 187(1) in which there are separate bodies of persons each by its very designation, duties and responsibilities and functional requirement would not be part of regular army battalion and, therefore, each has to be designated as a corps for the purposes of the Act and the Rules. If each battalion in the infantry or regiment in cavalry would be a corps for the purposes of Rule 40, the selection of personnel for composing a general court martial would not present difficulty. If on the other hand as contended for the petitioners that the expression 'corps' is an inter-changeable substitute for the expression 'army corps', the difficulty of setting up a general court-martial in strict compliance with Rule 40 would be insurmountable. This can be demonstrably established if the composition of the army as hereinabove set out is recalled for the limited purpose of pointing out that command is composed of army corps and each army corps is led by the officer of the rank of Lt General. Expression 'command' may be clarified in the sense that this country is divided into various commands such as Western Command, Northern Command, etc. Now, if various army corps form part of the command and if for setting up a general court- martial in strict compliance with Rule 40 is to be insisted upon, persons from different army corps have to be selected because as far as practicable officers of different army corps-substituting the expression for corps-for the time being will have to be selected. But the negative inhibition of Rule 40 will present an insurmountable difficulty in that any such general court martial shall not be composed exclusively of officers of the same corps. Translated into functional adaptability officers under the same army corps attached to various divisions, brigades under the various divisions, battalions under the brigades and companies under the battalions will be disqualified from serving on the general court martial because they all belong to the same 'army corps'. That could not be the object underlying Rule 40. Instead of vertical movement, if a downward movement in the army command is taken into account to ascertain the meaning of the expression 'corps',

Rule 40 will become workable and would be easy to comply with. What is positively desired is that for the composition of a general court-martial, one must strive to secure services of officers of different corps or departments and what must be eschewed is its being composed exclusively of officers of corps or departments to which the delinquent officer belongs. If we give a restricted meaning to the expression 'corps' the Rule becomes workable If wider meaning is given so as to substitute 'army corps' for 'corps' it would be wholly unworkable because officers will have to be summoned from another command altogether. Thus, if we take 'army corps' to mean the same thing as 'corps' and if the accused belongs to a certain army corps all officers belonging to various divisions under the same army corps, to all brigades under all the divisions of the same army corps, to all battalions under all brigades of the same army corps and to all companies under all battalions of the same army corps will be disqualified because they do not belong to the different corps and are likely to be stigmatized as officers exclusively belonging to the same corps. A vertical movement starting from the bottom which is indicated by reference to battalion and regiment in sub-Rule (3) of Rule 187 clearly indicates that the lowest formation in the battalion or the regiment is corps over and above those specifically designated as corps under Rule 187(1). Therefore, it clearly transpires that the expression 'corps' in Rule 40 must be given the same meaning as set out in sub-Rule (3) of Rule 187 and it would mean that every battalion in the infantry and every regiment in the cavalry would by itself be a corps.

25. This interpretation accords with the intendment underlying Rule 40. Rule 40 takes note of a possible official bias or personal bias on account of close association. If officers belonging to the same corps have to try brother officer, either there might be possible indulgence towards the brother officer or familiarity in working together may have bred such contempt that bias is inevitable. To decry and such possibility and to put personnel of general court-martial beyond reproach, to make it unbiased and objective, composition of court-martial was to be so devised by statutory Rules as to make it an ideal body having all the trappings of a court. Two fundamental principles in this behalf are that the judge must be unbiased and objective free from personal likes and dislikes or prejudice consequent upon association of close familiarity. People drawn from 'different corps' and avoiding officers of the same corps composing the general court-martial would ensure an objective, unbiased body. If this is the underlying intendment, it is achieved by giving the expression 'corps' a restricted meaning and not a wide meaning to make it synonymous with 'Army Corps' at the top, so that it may almost become impossible to

search only officers belonging to different army corps and avoid meaning the court-martial exclusively by officers belonging to same corps because a large body of officers would spill over the line. If on the other hand as is clearly indicated by sub-Rule (3) of Rule 187 a battalion or a regiment is treated as a corps then it is easy to provide composition of court-martial in strict compliance with Rule 40. Under a brigade there are number of battalions. Each battalion would be a corps. One can easily draw officers from different battalions as they would be belonging to different corps and one can avoid what is negatively inhibited, viz., a general court-martial being composed exclusively of officers of the corps to which the accused belongs. If the accused belongs to one battalion, even under the same brigade there are number of battalions, and each battalion being a corps, officers from battalions other than the battalion to which the accused belongs can be conveniently summoned because each battalion is under the same brigadier. In this manner officers belonging to different corps can be summoned and one can easily avoid a general court martial composed exclusively of officers of the corps to which the accused belongs. It would be unwise to reject this construction on the ground that it does not take note of and try to avoid command influence. Command influence is too vague a concept to call in aid for construction of a Rule. Viewed from either angle the expression 'corps' in Rule 40 is not used in the same sense in which the expression 'army corps' is used but it is used in the sense in which it is defined and elaborated in Rule 187.

26. It was contended that the interpretation of Rule 40 must be informed by the underlying intendment that officers composing the court-martial must be independent of command influence or influence of superior officers like the convening officer. This is unquestionably correct, save and except saying what meaning one must assign to a loose expression like 'command influence'. If by command one at the highest level such as commander-in-charge of area is the one likely to permeate his influence down to the lowest it would be impossible to set up a court-martial of officers belonging to entirely a different command. The expressions like the 'command influence' and the 'influence of superior officers' have to be understood in the context of the vertical hierarchy in the composition of army. Once it transpires that the expression 'corps' in Rule 40 has the same meaning as has been set out in Rule 187 and, therefore, a battalion would be a corps and an unattached company can be a corps by itself, it becomes easy and practicable to set up a court martial in which officers outside the corps would be available and such officers outside the same corps to which an accused belongs could certainly be said to be free

from command influence. But to urge that even if the officers of another battalion but forming part of the same brigade are selected the Brigadier being the top officer under whom various battalions must be operating, the command influence will permeate down, the same difficulty would arise as hereinbefore explicitly set out in setting up a court-martial. The intendment underlying Rule 40 is fully subserved by the interpretation, which the language employed indicates, put on the expression 'corps' in Rule 40.

27. Undoubtedly Rule 40 by its very language is not mandatory. Rule on its own force insists on compliance with its requirements as far as may be practicable. Even with this leeway, a strict compliance with the requirements of Rule 40 must be insisted upon and the departure on the ground of practicability will, if challenged, have to be proved-within the broad parameters of functional adjustability of the Army requirements. If the interpretation canvassed on behalf of the petitioners is accepted every time the soul of Rule 40 will be sacrificed at the altar of practicability while the interpretation which we put on the expression 'corps' in Rule 40 would help in avoiding shelter under the practicability clause and that in a very large number of cases strict compliance with Rule 40 can be insisted upon. If a court martial is set up not in consonance with Rule 40 and the defence of practicability is advanced the same can be examined with precision. Therefore, the expression 'corps' in Rule 40 is not synonymous with the expression 'army corps' and it must receive a restricted construction with narrow connotation as explained in Rule 187 (3).

28. There are two further requirements to be complied with while setting up a general court martial. Section 113 provides that a general court martial shall consist of not less than five officers, each of whom has held a commission for not less than three whole years and of whom not less than four are of a rank not below that of captain. Sub-Rule (2) of Rule 40 adds one more condition that the members of court-martial for trial of an officer shall be of a rank not lower than that of the officer unless in the opinion of the convening officer, officers of such rank are not (having due regard to the exigencies of public service) available. Such opinion has to be recorded in the convening order. Sub-Rule (3) of Rule 40 merely incorporates the mandate of Section 113.

29. Having formulated the necessary test for examining the validity of the composition of general court martial it is necessary to turn to the facts of each case in this behalf. Lt Col Prithi Pal Singh Bedi (Writ Petition No. 4903 of 1981) was holding the rank of Lieutenant Colonel and belonged

to the 226 Regiment of 43 Artillery Brigade of 9th Infantry Division of the Indian Army at the relevant time. The general court-martial set up to try him was composed of five officers. They are: Brigadier Kalkat, an officer in rank higher than the petitioner, Lt Col Khullar, Lt Col Yadav, Lt Col Nathu Singh and Lt Col Kohli, all of coordinate, same or of equal rank, and even though they all belong to 9th Infantry Division, they are drawn from different brigades and regiments and that becomes distinctly clear from the attachment of each set out in the order convening the general court-martial. To be precise, Lt Col Khullar was Officer Commanding 168 Field Regiment, Lt Col Yadav Bhopal Singh, SM was Officer Commanding 10 Dogra; Lt Col Nathu Singh, Punjab was Officer Commanding 5th Rajputana Rifles. It would appear at a glance that even though all the five officers belong to the 9th Division, none of them belongs to the same corps to which the petitioner belonged and none was lower in rank than the rank held by the petitioner. Therefore, the requirement of Rule 40 is strictly complied with and there is no contravention in letter and spirit thereof.

30. In the case of Capt Dharam Pal Kukrety (Writ Petition No. 1513 of 1979), the general court martial is composed of seven officers. Petitioner Kukrety was holding the rank of a Captain. Of the seven officers composing the court martial the senior-most is a Brigadier the next in rank is holding the rank of Lt Col and the remaining five are of the rank of Major. Their designations and attachments show that none of them is even equal in rank with the petitioner; each is holding a rank higher than the petitioner. Petitioner at the relevant time belonged to 25 Infantry Division which is a division of the 16th Corps of the Indian Army. And all the members composing the court-martial belonged to the 25th Infantry Division which itself is a division of the 15th Corps of the Indian Army. But the expression 'corps' qualifying '16th' is army corps and not corps as understood in Rule 40. None of the officers composing the general court-martial in the case belongs to the corps to which the petitioner belonged. Therefore, there is no violation of Rule 40.

31. The petitioner Capt Chander Kumar Chopra (Writ Petition No. 5930 of 1980) has alleged in his petition that he belongs to the 33 corps and that each such corps is divided into divisions. This will clearly show that by saying that he belongs to 33 corps he means to suggest that he belongs to 33 Army Corps. At the relevant time the petitioner was holding the rank of a Captain and was attached to 877 AT BN ASC C/o 99 APO. There is not one word in the petition that any of the officers composing the general court-martial set up to try him, belongs to his corps in the sense in which

the word has been interpreted by us. Nor has he alleged that any one lower in rank than a Captain has been nominated as a member of the general court-martial set up to try him. Therefore, even in this case there is nothing to show that Rule 40 has been violated.

32. It would be advantageous at this stage to call attention to the provision contained in section 130 of the Act and Rules 41 to 44 of the Rules. When either a general, district or summary court martial is assembled and the offender who is to be tried is brought before it, it is obligatory to read out the names of the presiding officer and the members composing the court martial to the accused and he is asked whether he objects to his being tried by any of the officers sitting on the court. Sub-section (2) of section 130 requires that if the accused objects to any such officer, his objection and the reply there to of the officer objected to shall be heard recorded and the remaining officers of the court shall in the absence of the challenged officer decide the objection. The provision contained in section 130 is elaborated in Rules 41 to 44. Rule 41 requires that as soon as the court assembles the order convening the court shall be laid before it together with a charge sheet and summary of evidence as also the ranks, names and corps of the officers appointed to serve on the court. A duty is cast on the court to first ascertain whether it has been convened according to the provisions of the Act and the Rules. In order to find out whether Rule 40 has been complied with or not, the corps to which each officer composing the court martial is attached is to be set out and which will reveal at a glance whether he is qualified to sit on the court. At this stage the accused does not enter into the picture. The duty is cast on the court itself to ascertain whether its constitution is in accordance with the Act and the Rules. Rule 42 cast a duty on the court to satisfy itself that the person who is to be tried is amenable to the provisions of the Army Act and that each charge framed against him discloses an offence under the Act and is framed is accordance with the Rules. Then comes Rule 43. After the court has satisfied itself that Rules 41 and 42 have been complied with the accused is to be brought before the Court. Rule 44 provides that on the accused being brought before the court, the order convening the court and the names of the presiding officer and the members of the court shall then be read over to the accused and he shall be asked as required by section 130 whether he has any objection to being tried by any officer serving in the Court. Whenever an objection is taken it has to be recorded, In order to ensure that any one objected to does not participate in disposing of the objection, clause (a) of the proviso to Rule 44 directs that the accused shall state the names of all officers constituting the court in respect of

whom he has any objection before any objection is disposed of. This is a mandatory requirement because the officer objected to cannot participate in the decision disposing of the objection. It is true that if the court is not constituted in accordance with the Act and the Rules, Rule 44 would hardly assist because as in this case if the contention is that Rule 40 was violated in constituting the court-martial and that each officer was disqualified from being a member of the court-martial, there is none left to dispose of the contention. In such a situation, Rule 44 may not be helpful because once such an objection is taken no one shall be competent to decide the objection. The provision conferring a right on the accused to object to a member of the court-martial sitting as a member and participating in the trial ensures that a charge of bias can be made and investigated against individual members composing the court-martial. This is preeminently a rational provision which goes a long way to ensure a fair trial. That stage is still to come and therefore we refrain from pronouncing on any allegation of bias against individual member of the court martial.

33. Similarly a very faint attempt made by Mr Sanghi inviting us to examine the merits of the charge against Lt Colonel Bedi should not lure us into doing so. That is our function at any rate at this stage and we steer clear the same.

34. Having examined the general contention as to the legality and validity of general court martial set up in each of these cases, we may now turn to certain specific contentions raised in each petition.

In re WP 4903 of 1981:

35. Mr Sanghi, learned counsel for the petitioner urged that pre condition to the trial by a general court martial having not been satisfied, the order convening the general court martial to try the petitioner is vitiated. Reliance was placed on Rules 22, 23, 24 and 25. They may be extracted:

> 22. **Hearing of Charge**: (1) Every charge against a person subject to the Act other than an officer, shall be heard in the presence of the accused. The accused shall have full liberty to cross examine any witness against him, and to call any witnesses and make any statement in his defence.
>
> (2) The commanding officer shall dismiss a charge brought before him if in his opinion, the evidence does not show that an offence under the Act has been committed, and may do so if, in his discretion, he is satisfied that the charge ought not to be proceeded with.

(3) At the conclusion of the hearing of a charge, if the commanding officer is of opinion that the charge ought to be proceeded with, he shall without unnecessary delay.

(a) dispose of the case summarily under section 80 in accordance with the manner and form in Appendix III; or

(b) refer the case to the proper superior military authority; or

(c) adjourn the case for the purpose of having the evidence reduced to writing; or

(d) if the accused is below the rank of warrant officer, order his trial by a summary court- martial.

Provided that the commanding officer shall not order trial by a summary court-martial without a reference to the officer empowered to convene a district court-martial or on active service a summary general court-martial for the trial of the alleged offender unless either-

(a) the offence is one which he can try by a summary court martial without any reference to that officer; or

(b) he considers that there is grave reason for immediate action and such reference cannot be made without detriment to discipline.

23. **Procedure for taking down the summary of evidence**- (1) Where the case is adjourned for the purpose of having the evidence reduced to writing, at the adjourned hearing the evidence of the witnesses who were present and gave the evidence before the commanding officer, whether against or for the accused, and of any other person whose evidence appears to be relevant, shall be taken down in writing in the presence and hearing of the accused before the commanding officer or such officer as he directs.

(2) The accused may put in cross-examination such questions as he thinks fit to any witness, and the questions together with the answers thereto shall be added to the evidence recorded.

(3) The evidence of each witness after it has been recorded as provided in the Rule when taken down, shall be read over to him, and shall be signed by him, or if he cannot write his name, shall be attested by his mark and witnessed as a token of the correctness of the evidence recorded. After all the evidence against the accused has

been recorded; the accused will be asked: "Do you wish to make any statement? You are not obliged to say anything unless you wish to do so, but whatever you say will be taken down in writing and may be given in evidence." Any statement thereupon made by the accused shall be taken down and read over to him, but he will not be cross-examined upon it. The accused may then call his witnesses, including, if he so desires, any witnesses as to character.

(4) The evidence of the witnesses and the statement (if any) of the accused shall be recorded in the English language. If the witness or accused as the case may be, does not understand the English language, the evidence or statement, as recorded shall be interpreted to him in a language which he understands.

(5) If a person cannot be compelled to attend as a witness, or if owing to the exigencies of service or any other grounds (including the expense and loss of time involved), the attendance of any witness cannot in the opinion of the officer taking the summary (to be certified by him in writing), be readily procured, a written statement of his evidence purporting to be signed by him may be read to the accused and included in the summary of evidence.

(6) Any witness who is not subject to military law may be summoned to attend by order under the hand of the commanding officer of the accused. The summons shall be in the form provided in Appendix III.

24. **Remand of accused**: (I) The evidence and statement (if any) taken down in writing in pursuance of Rule 23 (hereinafter referred to as the 'summary of evidence'), shall be considered by the commanding officer, who thereupon shall either-

    (a) remand the accused for trial by a court-martial; or

    (b) refer the case to the proper superior military authority; or

    (c) if he thinks it desirable, re-hear the case and either dismiss the charge or dispose of it summarily.

(2) If the accused is remanded for trial by a court- martial, the commanding officer shall without unnecessary delay either assemble a summary court-martial (after referring to the officer empowered to convene a district court-martial or on active service as summary general court-martial when such reference is necessary) or apply to the proper military authority to convene a court-martial, as the case

may require.

25. **Procedure on charge against officer**: (1) Where an officer is charged with an offence under the Act, the investigation shall, if he requires it, be held and the evidence, if he so requires, be taken in his presence, in writing, in the same manner as nearly as circumstances admit, as is required by Rule 22 and Rule 23 in the case of other persons subject to the Act.

(2) When an officer is remanded for the summary disposal of a charge against him or is ordered to be tried by a court-martial without any such recording of evidence in his presence, an abstract, of evidence to be adduced shall be delivered to him free of charge as provided in sub-Rule (7) of Rule 33."

36. The submission is that before a general court martial is convened as provided in Rule 37 it is obligatory for the commanding officer to hear the charge made against the accused in his presence giving an opportunity to the accused to cross-examine any witness against him and to call any witness and make any statement in his defence and that if the commanding officer is so satisfied he can dismiss the charge as provided in sub-Rule (2) of Rule 22. If at the conclusion of the hearing under Rule 22 the commanding officer is of the opinion that the charge ought to be proceeded with, he has four options open to him, one such being to adjourn the case for the purpose of having the evidence reduced to writing, called summary of evidence. Rule 23 prescribes the procedure for taking down the summary of evidence which, inter alia, provides recording of the evidence of each witness, opportunity to the accused to cross-examine each such witness, etc. Rule 24 provides that the summary of evidence so recorded shall be considered by the commanding officer who at that stage has again three courses open to him, to wrt, (a) remand the accused for trial by a court-martial, (b) refer the case to the proper superior military authority; and (c) if he thinks it desirable, re-hear the case and either dismiss the charge or dispose it of summarily. It was urged that in case of the petitioner Lt Col Bedi, the commanding officer did not hear the charge in his presence that no direction to prepare a summary of evidence in which he could participate was given and that without complying with the mandatory requirements of Rules 22 and 23 a direction has been given to convene the court-martial to try the petitioner. Rules 22 to 24 are mandatory in respect of every person subject to the Act other than an officer. Therefore, the requirements of Rules 22 to 24 are not mandatory in case of an officer and this becomes manifestly clear from sub-Rule (1) of Rule 25 which

provides that where an officer is charged with an offence under the Act, the investigation shall, *if he requires it*, be held, and the evidence, *if he so requires*, be taken in his presence in writing in the same manner as nearly as circumstances admit, as is required by Rule 22 and Rule 23 in the case of other persons subject to the Act. The opening words of Rule 22 clearly demonstrate the mandatory applicability of the provisions in Rule 22 and 23 Rule in case of persons subject to the Act other than officers. Any lurking doubt in that behalf is removed by the language of Rule 25 which provides that if an officer is charged with an offence under the Act, the investigation, if he required, shall be held and the evidence, if he requires shall be held and the evidence, if requires it, shall be taken in his presence. The petitioner is an officer. Therefore, the procedure prescribed in Rules 22 and 23 will not apply *proprio vigore* to him. If he wants Rules 22 and 23 Rule to be complied with, it is for him to make a request in that behalf. He has to make a two-fold request: (1) that the investigation shall be done in his presence; and (2) the summary of evidence shall also be drawn in his presence. Petitioner in this case has averred in his petition that the commanding officer did not hear the charge as required by Rule 22 and, therefore, he could not participate in the hearing of the charge nor could be cross-examine the witnesses and make his submissions. He further stated that no charge-sheet was given to him. He has averred that the order dated 10 November 1980, for taking down summary of evidence is void and illegal as it is violative of Rule 23 of the Rules. Mr Sanghi contended that failure to comply with Rules 22, 23 and 24 has denied to the petitioner an opportunity first to convince the commanding officer to dismiss the charge under sub-Rule (2) of Rule 22 and even if he could not have persuaded the commanding officer to dismiss the charge after the summary of evidence was recorded, he could have persuaded the commanding officer under Rule 24 either to refer the case to superior military authority or re-hear it and dismiss the charge and this denial of opportunity vitiates the subsequent trial by general court martial. Nowhere in the petition the epetitioner has specifically stated that he did make a request that the investigation shall be done in his presence and that the summary of evidence should be recorded in his presence. There is utter sphinx like silence on this point. In para 39 of the counter-affidavit on behalf of the respondents it is specifically stated that Rule 25 requires that if an officer wants Rules 22 and 23 to be complied with, he has to make a request in that behalf and that the petitioner never made such a request at the appropriate time and, therefore, cannot now make a grievance that Rules 22 and 23 have not been complied with. There is no rejoinder to the affidavit. Therefore, it is crystal clear that in the absence of a request from the petitioner as required by Rule 2S, failure to comply with Rules 22, 23 and 24 would not vitiate the trial by the general court-martial. *Rex v. Thomson* (1946) 4 Dom LR 579 was relied upon to buttress the submission that there has to be hearing of the charge by the officer Commanding in the presence of the offender and the offender should be afforded full opportunity to be heard before a court martial is convened and this is a mandatory requirement and the courts must draw a distinction between what is merely irregular and what is of such a character as to be of substance. It was urged that compliance with this procedure which affords full opportunity of participation cannot be treated as merely directory but must be held to be mandatory to ensure a just and fair trial and its violation must be held to vitiate the order convening the court martial and the order would be without jurisdiction. It may be pointed out that the offender in the case before the court in that case was a non-commissioned officer governed by the Army Act, 1881. He was thus a person other than an officer subject to the Army Act and the mandate of Rules 22 and 23 in his case would have applied in all its rigour but as has been pointed out the petitioner in the present case is an officer and unless he requires it, Rules 22 and 23 are not required to be complied with and, therefore, the decision does not advance his any further. Therefore, there is no merit in this contention.

37. Incidentally it was urged that to the extend Rule 25 erodes mandatory compliance with principles of natural justice as adumbrated in Rules 22, 23 and 24 it would be violative of fundamental rights guaranteed under Article 21 of the Constitution and would be *ultra vires* the Constitution. Referring to *Lee v. Showmen's Guild of Great Britain* (1952) 2 QB 329, it was urged that public policy would invalidate any stipulation excluding the application of the Rules of natural justice to a tribunal whose decision was likely to result in deprivation of personal liberty. Continuing along this line it was urged that to the extent the application of minimum principles of natural justice enacted in Rules 22, 23 and 24 depends for its applicability upon the demand by the officer it would be contrary to public policy which mandates that compliance with Rules of natural justice should not be made dependent upon a requisition by the person against whom the inquiry is held but it must be deemed to be obligatory and an integral part of any procedure prescribed for a Tribunal whose decision is likely to result in deprivation of personal liberty. It has already been pointed out that Parliament has the power to restrict or abrogate any of the rights conferred by Part III of the Constitution in their application to the members of the Armed Forces so as to ensure the proper discharge of duties and maintenance of discipline

amongst them. The Act is one such law and, therefore, any of the provisions of the Act cannot be struck down on the only ground that they restrict or abrogate or tend to restrict or abrogate any of the rights conferred by Part III of the Constitution and this would indisputably include Article 21. But even apart from this, it is not possible to subscribe to the view that even where the prescribed procedure inheres compliance with principles of natural justice but makes the same dependent upon the requisition by the person against whom the inquiry is held, it would be violative of Article 21 which provides that no person shall be deprived of his life or personal liberty except according to the procedure established by law. If the procedure established by law prescribes compliance with principles of natural justice but makes it dependent upon a requisition by the person against whom an inquiry according to such procedure is to be held, it is difficult to accept the submission that such procedure would be violative of Article 21 And as far as the Rules are concerned, they have made clear distinction between an officer governed by the Act and any other person subject to the Act. Expression 'officer' has been defined to mean a person commissioned, gazetted or in pay as an officer in the regular Army and includes various other categories set out therein. By the very definition an officer would be a person belonging to the upper bracket in the Armed Forces and any person other than an officer subject to the provisions of the Act would necessarily imply persons belonging to the lower categories in the army service. Now, in respect of such persons belonging to the lower category it is mandatory that Rules 22, 23 and 24 have to be followed and there is no escape from it except on the pain of invalidation of the inquiry. But when it comes to an officer, a person belonging to the upper bracket in the armed forces the necessary presumption being that he is a highly educated, knowledgeable, intelligent person, compliance with Rules 22, 23 and 24 is not obligatory but would have to be complied with if the officer so requires it. This is quite rational and understandable. One cannot be heard to say that he would not insist upon an inquiry in which he can participate which is his right, and then turn round and contend that failure to hold the inquiry in accordance with the principles of natural justice as enacted in Rules 22, 23 and 24 though he did not insist upon it, would not merely invalidate the inquiry but the Rule which requires compliance at the request of the officer is in itself on that account ultra vires. It was, however, urged that in view of the decisions of this Court in *Mohinder Singh Gill v. The Chief Election Commissioner, New Delhi* (1978) 2 SCR 272 : (1978) 1 SCC 405 and *Maneka Gandhi v. Union of India* (1978) 1 SCC 248, it is an incontrovertible proposition of law that even while finding a balance between need for expedition and need to give full opportunity to the person against whom the inquiry is held, "a body charged with a duty to act judicially must comply with the minimum requirements of natural justice and that if observance of natural justice in the area of administrative decision making so as to avoid devaluation of the principle by administrators already alarmingly insensitive to the rationale of audi alterm partem" that one can ever look upon with equanimity where this principle gives way before a tribunal charged with a duty to act judicially. As has been pithily observed by an author, such an overemphasis overlooking the other procedural safeguards prescribed, "indeed wears an engaging air of simplicity and reason but having examined the entire procedure one can say confidently that this simplicity is merely skin deep." Rules 22, 23 and 24 prescribe participation at a stage prior to the trial by the court martial. Undoubtedly, fairness in action and natural justice have been developing very much in recent years and if the power of the executive increases the courts have developed the doctrine in an evolving way so a striking out expedition is perilous [*Schmidt v. Secretary of State for Home Affairs*, 91969) 2 Ch D 149]. By rejecting the contention a striking expedition of this wholesome principle is not undertaken. It must, however, be pointed out that in a trial which is likely to result in deprivation of liberty the body which has ultimately the power to make an order which would result in deprivation of liberty, must hear the offender offering full participation and that principle cannot be diluted. However, procedure prescribed in Rules 22, 23 and 24 is at a stage anterior to trial by the court martial. It is the decision of the court martial which would result in deprivation of liberty and not the order directing that the charge be heard or that summary of evidence be recorded or that a court martial be convened. Even in normal trial under the Cr PC it has never been suggested that it is unfair to launch a criminal prosecution without first hearing the accused (see *Lord Salmond in Cozens v. North Doven Hospital Management Committee* [1962] 2 QB 330, 343]. Therefore, there is no substance in the contention that Rules 22, 23 and 24 in view of the provision contained in Rule 25 are ultra vires Article 21 of the Constitution.

38. Mr. Banerjee, learned Additional Solicitor-General in this context urged that even if it is felt that there is some violation of the provisions contained in Rules 22, 23 and 24 in case of an officer as the officer will have an opportunity to exhaustively participate in the trial by the court martial the irregularity emanating from non-compliance with Rules 22, 23 and 24 would not vitiate the order convening the court-martial. Reliance was placed on *Major G Barasay v. The State of Bombay* (1962)

2 SCR 195 : AIR 1961 SC 1762, in which the question arose whether an investigation by an officer of the Delhi Special Police Establishment who undertook investigation of the case and failed to comply with two preconditions incorporated in the proviso to section 5-A of the Prevention of Corruption Act, 1950, the investigation was vitiated and the trial upon such investigation would be bad. The High Court held that the two conditions had not been complied with by the investigating officer but after considering the entire evidence observed that the alleged irregularity would not justify the conclusion that the non observance of the conditions prescribed in the proviso to section 5-A of the Prevention of Corruption Act had resulted in failure of justice. This Court agreed with this conclusion. Drawing sustenance from this conclusion it was urged that irregularity in the course of investigation, if any, would not vitiate the trial but in such a situation the court must examine evidence more carefully. As we are of the opinion that the failure to comply with the requirements of Rules 22, 23 and 24 depended upon a requisition by the petitioner, his inaction or omission in that behalf would have no impact on the order convening the court-martial.

39. Reference was also made to *Flying Officer S Sundarajan v. Union of India* AIR 1970 Del 29 : 1970 Cr LJ 213, where a Full Bench of the Delhi High Court held that any error or irregularity in complying with the procedure prescribed by Rule 15 of the Indian Air Force Rules which is in *pari materia* with Rule 22 of the Army Rules would not vitiate the trial and ultimate conviction of the accused because of any error or irregularity at a stage before the accused is charged for the purpose of having the evidence reduced to writing and it will not vitiate the subsequent trial as the guilt of the accused has to be established not on the basis of what the commanding officer might have done or might not have done at the initial stage. It was further held that any irregularity in the procedure at that initial stage might have a bearing on the veracity of witnesses examined at the trial or on the bonafides of the commanding officer or on the defence that may be set up by the accused at the trial but the irregularity can by no means be regarded as affecting the jurisdiction of the court to proceed with the trial. Jurisprudentially speaking the view expressed is that Rule 15 is directory and its contravention has no impact on the subsequent trial. Frankly, we have our reservations about the view taken by the Full Bench of the Delhi High Court but as we have held that Rules 22, 23 and 24 have not been violated on account of the failure of the petitioner to insist upon their compliance which it was obligatory upon him to do, we refrain from expressing any opinion on this point.

40. Mr Sanghi next contended that it is obligatory upon the authorities concerned to appoint a court of inquiry whenever an inquiry affects the character or military reputation of a person subject to the Act and in such an inquiry full opportunity must be afforded to such person of being present throughout the inquiry and of making any statement or giving any evidence he may wish to make or give and of cross-examining any witness whose evidence in his opinion affects the character or military reputation and producing any witness in defence of his character or military reputation. There are some provisions in the Act which (*sic*) order setting up of a Court of Inquiry in the circumstances and for the purpose set out in the provisions. Section 89 permits collective fines to be imposed in the circumstances therein mentioned but the same can be done after obtaining the report of court of inquiry. In other words, where it is considered necessary and permissible under the Act to impose a collective fine it can be done after obtaining the report of a court of inquiry which will presage an appointment of such a court of inquiry. Similarly, section 106 comprehends the appointment of a court of inquiry when any person subject to the Act has been absent from his duty without due authority for a period of 30 days, and such court is required to inquire in respect of the absence of the person and the deficiency if any in the property of the Government entrusted to his care, or in any arms, ammunition, equipment, instruments, clothing or necessaries, and if satisfied of the fact of such absence without due authority or other sufficient cause, the court shall declare such absence and the period thereof, and the said deficiency, if any the commanding officer of the corps or department to which the person belongs shall enter in the court-martial book of the corps or department a record of the declaration. A reference to these two sections would show that where action can be taken after obtaining report of the court of inquiry it has been so specified. Now, when an offence is committed and a trial by a general court martial is to be held, there is no provision which requires that a court of inquiry should be set up before the trial is directed. Mr Sanghi, however, urged that on a correct interpretation of Rule 180, it would appear that whenever the character of a person subject to the Act is involved in any inquiry, a court of inquiry must be set up. Rule 180 does not bear out the submission. It sets up a stage in the procedure prescribed for the courts of inquiry, Rule 180 cannot be construed to mean that whenever or wherever in any inquiry in respect of any person subject to the Act his character or military reputation is likely to be affected setting up of a Court of inquiry is a sine qua non. Rule 180 merely makes it obligatory that whenever a court of inquiry is set up and in the course of

inquiry by the court of inquiry character or military reputation of a person is likely to be effected then such a person must be given a full opportunity to participate in the proceedings of court of inquiry. Court of inquiry by its very nature is likely to examine certain issue generally concerning a situation or persons. Where collective fine is desired to be imposed, a court of inquiry may generally examine the shortfall to ascertain how many persons are responsible. In the course of such an inquiry there may be a distinct possibility of character or military reputation of a person subject to the Act likely to be affected. His participation cannot be avoided on the specious plea that no specific inquiry was directed against the person whose character or military reputation is involved. To ensure that such a person whose character or military reputation is likely to be affected by the proceedings of the court of inquiry should be afforded full opportunity so that nothing is done at his back and without opportunity of participation, Rule 180 merely makes an enabling provision to ensure such participation. But it cannot be used to say that whenever in any other inquiry or an inquiry before a commanding officer under Rule 22 or a convening officer under Rule 37 of the trial by a court martial, character or military reputation of the officer concerned is likely to be affected a prior inquiry by the court of inquiry is sine qua non. Therefore, the contention being without merits must be negatived.

41. It was next contended that the petitioner was not supplied the relevant documents asked for by him and that, therefore, he is not being afforded a full and adequate opportunity to defend himself. Rule 33 ensures preparation for defence by the accused person. He has a right to call witnesses in his defence. The limited grievance is that by his letter dated 11 November 1980, he requested that documents concerning the case against him may be supplied to him. He also gave the name of Sub Gopal Chand as an essential witness. By his letter dated 14 November 1980, the petitioner requested to supply him the copies of the documents therein listed. As the trial by the court martial has not been commenced, we are sure that the authorities concerned will supply necessary documents to the petitioner in order to avoid even a remote reflection that he was not given adequate opportunity to defend himself.

42. In passing it is necessary to observe that the procedure prescribed for trial of sessions cases in Chapter XVIII of the Code of Criminal Procedure when compared with the procedure prescribed for trial by a general court martial there is very little deviation or departure and is more or less the procedure appears to be fair, just and reasonable. Dr O P Sharma, Judge-

Advocate-General, Indian Army, in his *Military Law in India*, p. 156, after comparing the two procedures observes that the procedure of trial by court martial is almost analogous to the procedure of trial in the ordinary criminal courts. He points out two demerits, viz., a distinct possibility of a successive trial by a criminal court and a court-martial exposing the accused to the hazards of double jeopardy, and the absence of a provision for bail. The horrendous delay of trial in ordinary criminal courts has its counterpart in delay in trial by court-martial also. Save and except this deficiency and one or two of minor character both the procedures are almost identical and this aspect has to some extent influenced our decision.

Writ Petitions 1513 of 1979 and 5930 of 1980:

43. Save and except the contention as to the validity of the com-position of the court martial no other specific contention was raised in these two petitions.

44. Reluctance of the apex court more concerned with civil law to interfere with the internal affairs of the Army is likely to create a distorted picture in the minds of the military personnel that persons subject to Army Act are not citizens of India. It is one of the cardinal features of our Constitution that a person by enlisting in or entering armed forces does not cease to be a citizen so as to wholly deprive him of his rights under the Constitution. More so when this Court held in *Sunil Batra v. Delhi Administration* (1979) 1 SCR 392, 495 : (1978) 4 SCC 494, that even prisoners deprived of personal liberty are not wholly denuded of their fundamental rights. In the larger interest of national security and military discipline Parliament in its wisdom may restrict or abrogate such rights in their application to the Armed Forces but this process should not be carried so far as to create a class of citizens not entitled to the benefits of the liberal spirit of the Constitution. Persons subject to Army Act are citizens of this ancient land having a feeling of belonging to the civilized community governed by the liberty-oriented constitution. Personal liberty makes for the worth of human being and is a cherished and prized right. Deprivation thereof must be preceded by an enquiry ensuring fair, just and reasonable procedure and trial by a judge of unquestioned integrity and wholly unbiased. A marked difference in the procedure for trial of an offence by the criminal court and the court martial is apt to generate dissatisfaction arising out of this differential treatment. Even though it is pointed out that the procedure of trial by court martial is almost analogous to the procedure of trial in the ordinary criminal courts, we must recall what Justice William O'Douglas observed: "[T]hat civil trial is held in an atmosphere conducive to the

protection of individual rights while a military trial is marked by the age-old manifest destiny of retributive justice. Very expression 'court martial' generally strikes terror in the heart of the person to be tried by it. And somehow or the other the trial is looked upon with disfavour." [Tough Test for Military Justice, *Times Magazine*, pp. 42 and 43]. In *Reid v. Covert* 1 L. Ed 2d 1148 : 354 US 1 (1957), Justice Black observed at p. 1174 as under:

> "Courts-martial are typically ad hoc bodies appointed by a military officer from among his subordinates. They have always been subject to varying degrees of 'command influence'. In essence, these tribunals are simply executive tribunals whose personnel are in the executive chain of command. Frequently, the members of the court-martial must look to the appointing officer for promotions, advantageous assignments and efficiency ratings-in short, for their future progress in the service. Conceding to military personnel that high degree of honesty and sense justice which nearly all of them undoubtedly have, the members of a court-martial, in the nature of things, do not and cannot have the independence of jurors drawn from the general public or of civilian judges."

Absence of even one appeal with power to review evidence, legal formulation, conclusion and adequacy or otherwise of punishment is a glaring lacuna in a country where a counterpart civilian convict can prefer appeal after appeal to hierarchy of courts. Submission that full review of finding and/or sentence in confirmation proceeding under Section 153 is provided for is poor solace. A hierarchy of courts with appellate powers each having its own power of judicial review has of course been found to be counterproductive but the converse is equally distressing in that there is not even a single judicial review. With the expanding horizons of fair play in action even in administrative decision, the Universal Declaration of Human Rights and retributive justice being relegated to the uncivilized days, a time has come when a step is required to be taken for at least one review and it must truly be a judicial review as and by way of appeal to a body composed of non-military personnel or civil personnel. Army is always on alert for repelling external aggression and suppressing internal disorder so that the peace loving citizens enjoy a social order based on Rule of law; the same cannot be denied to the protectors of this order. And it must be realized that an appeal from Ceaser to Ceaser's wife --- confirmation proceeding under Section 153 --- has been condemned as injudicious and merely a lip sympathy to form. The core question is whether at least there should be one appeal to a body composed of non-military personnel and who would enjoy the right of judicial review both on law and facts as also determine the adequacy of punishment being commensurate with the gravity of the offence charged. Judicial approach by people well-versed in objective analysis of evidence trained by experience to look at facts and law objectively, fair play and justice cannot always be sacrificed at the altar of military discipline. Unjust decision would be subversive of discipline. There must be a judicious admixture of both. And nothing revolutionary is being suggested. Our Army Act was more or less modelled on the UK Act. Three decades of its working with winds of change blowing over the world necessitate a second look so as to bring it in conformity with liberty oriented constitution and Rule of law which is the uniting and integrating force in our political society. Even UK has taken a step of far reaching importance for rehabilitating the confidence of the Royal Forces in respect of judicial review of decisions of court-martial. The UK had enacted a Court Martial (Appeals) Act of 1951 and it has been extensively amended in Court Martial (Appeals) Act, 1968. Merely providing an appeal by itself may not be very re- assuring but the personnel of the appellate court must inspire confidence. The court martial appellate court consists of the ex-officio and ordinary judges of the Court of Appeal, such of the judges of the Queen's Bench Division as the Lord Chief Justice may nominate after consultation with the Master of the Rolls, such of the Lords, Commissioners of Justiciary in Scotland as the Lord Chief Justice generally may nominate, such judges of the Supreme Court of the Northern Ireland as the Lord Chief Justice of Northern Ireland may nominate and such of the persons of legal experience as the Lord Chancellor may appoint. The court martial appellate court has power to determine any question necessary to be determined in order to do justice in the case before the court and may authorize a new trial where the conviction is quashed in the light of fresh evidence. The court also has power inter alia, to order production of documents or exhibits connected with the proceedings, order the attendance of witnesses, receive evidence, obtain reports and the like from the members of the court martial or the person who acted a Judge-Advocate, order a reference of any question to a Special Commissioner for Inquiry and appoint a person with special expert knowledge to act as an assessor. Frankly the appellate court has power of full judicial review unhampered by any procedural clap-trap.

45. Turning towards the USA, a reference to Uniform Code of Military Justice Act, 1950, would be instructive. A provision has been made for setting up of a court of military appeals. The Act contained many procedural reforms and due process safeguards not then guaranteed in

civil courts. To cite one example, the right to legally qualified counsel was made mandatory in general court-martial cases 13 years before the decision of the Supreme Court in *Gideon v. Wainwright* 572 US 535 (1963). Between 1950 and 1968 when the Administration of Justice Act, 1968, was introduced, many advances were made in the administration of justice by civil courts but they were not reflected in military court proceedings. To correct these deficiencies the Congress enacted Military Justice Act, 1968, the salient features of which are: (1) a right to legally qualified counsel guaranteed to an accused before any special court martial; (2) a military judge can in certain circumstances conduct the trial alone and the accused in such a situation is given the option after learning the identity of the military judge of requesting for the trial by the judge alone. A ban has been imposed on command interference with military justice, etc. Ours is still an antiquated system. The wind of change blowing over the country has not permeated the close and sacrosanct precincts of the Army. If in civil courts the universally accepted dictum is that justice must not only be done but it must seem to be done, the same holds good with all the greater vigour in case of court martial where the judge and the accused done the same dress, have the same mental discipline, have a strong hierarchical subjugation and a feeling of bias in such circumstances is irremovable. We, therefore, hope and believe that the changes all over the English speaking democracies will awaken our Parliament to the changed value system. In this behalf, we would like to draw pointed attention of the Government to the glaring anomaly that courts martial do not even write a brief reasoned order in support of their conclusion, even in cases in which they impose the death sentence. This must be remedied in order to ensure that a disciplined and dedicated Indian Army may not nurse a grievance that the substance of justice and fair play is denied to it.

With these observations we dismiss all the three petitions and vacate all interim orders. There shall be no order as to costs.

6

R. Viswan v. Union of India 1983 SCR (3) 60 : 1983 SCC (3) 401 : 1983 SCALE (1)497, decided on 6 May 1983 [Five Judge Bench].

JUDGMENT:

Original Jurisdiction: WP (Crl) Nos. 815, 843, 632/80, 844, 5116/81, 1301-04, 1383, 3460, 4510, 4511, 4512, 4551/80 & 3861, 3848, 8317/81 and 59 of 1982 (Under article 32 of the Constitution of India) and Special Leave Petition (Crl) Nos. 2061-65 of 1980. From the Judgment and Order dated 19 May 1980 of the Delhi High Court in Criminal Writ Petition Nos. 24-27/80 & 30/80.

BHAGWATI, J.

These writ petitions raise a short but interesting question of law relating to the interpretation of Article 33 of the Constitution. The question is whether section 21 of the Army Act 1950 read with Chapter IV of the Army Rules 1954 is within the scope and ambit of Article 33 and if it is, whether Central Government Notifications Nos. SRO 329 and 330 dated 23rd September 1960 making inter alia section 21 of the Army Act 1950 and Chapter IV of the Army Rules 1954 applicable to the General Reserve Engineering Force are ultra vires that Article since the General

Reserve Engineering Force is neither an Armed Force nor a Force charged with the maintenance of public order. It is a question of some importance since it affects the fundamental rights of a large number of persons belonging to the General Reserve Engineering Force and in order to arrive at a correct decision of this question, it is necessary first of all to consider the true nature and character of the General Reserve Engineering Force. In or about 1960 it was felt that economic development of the North and North Eastern Border areas were greatly handicapped by meagre and inadequate communications and defence of these areas also required a net work of roads for effective movement and deployment of Armed Forces. This was rendered all the more necessary because the relations of India with its neighbours were in a state of potential conflict and part of the Indian territory was under foreign occupation and there were also hostile forces inviting some sections of the people to carry on a campaign for secession. The Government of India therefore, with a view to ensuring coordination and expeditious execution of projects designed to improve existing roads and construct new roads in the border areas is order to improve the defence preparedness of the country, created several posts in the Directorate General of Works. Army Headquarters for work connected with the development of border roads as per letter dated 9 April 1960 addressed by the Under Secretary to the Government of India, Ministry of Defence to the Chief of the Army Staff. On 18 April 1960, within a few days thereafter, the Government of India sanctioned the post of Directorate General Border Roads in the rank of Major-General in the Directorate General of Works, Army Head Quarters; vide letter dated 18 April 1960 addressed by the Under Secretary to the Government of India, Ministry of Defence to the Chief of the Army Staff. The Director General Border Roads was placed in charge of this new organization which started originally as part of the Directorate General of Works, Army Head Quarters. But subsequently, for reasons of high policy, it was decided that this Organisation should not continue as part of the Directorate General of Works, Army Head Quarters but should be under the Board Roads Development Board set up by the Government of India as a separate self contained Authority under the Chairmanship of the Prime Minister with the Defence Minister as Deputy Chairman, the Financial Adviser (Defence) as Financial Adviser and a few other members nominated by the Prime Minister. The budget of the Border Roads Development Board formed part of the budget of the Ministry of Shipping and Transport but the financial control was vested in the Ministry of Finance (Defence). The Government of India by a letter dated 16th June 1960 addressed by the Secretary of the Border Roads Development Board to the Director General, Border Roads conveyed the sanction of the President to "raising and maintenance of a General Reserve Engineering Force for the construction of roads in the border areas and such other tasks as may be entrusted to it by the Border Roads Development Board." It was directed that the General Reserve Engineering Force will be "under the overall command of the Director General Border Roads under whom will be Regional Chief Engineers/Independent Deputy Chief Engineers who will exercise command Over the units of the Force placed under their control." The General Reserve Engineering Force (hereinafter referred to as GREF) was thus raised under the authority of the Government of India and it was placed under the overall command of the Director General, Border Roads.

Ever since then the Director General, Border Roads, has always been an army officer of the rank of Major General and he functions under the directions of the Border Roads Development Board, The General Reserve Engineering Force (GREF) is organised on army pattern in units and sub units with distinctive badges of rank and a rank structure equivalent to that in the army. The officers and other personnel of GREF arc required to be in uniform right from class IV to Class I personnel. Though GREF is undoubtedly a departmental construction agency, it is maintained by the Government of India to meet the operational requirements of the army whose operational planning is based on the availability of the units of GREF for operational purposes. In fact GREF pro- vided support to the Army during Indo-China conflict of 1962 and Indo-Pakistan conflicts of 1965 and 1971 and also assisted the Army in the maintenance of public order during the disturbances in Mijoram in 1966 and in Assam in 1980-81. The personnel of GREF are primarily drawn from two sources and they consist of (1) officers and men belonging to the Army and (2) officers and men recruited, through the Union Public Service Commission in case of officers and departmentally in case of other ranks. A ten per cent quota is reserved for recruitment of ex-servicemen. The posting of Army officers and men in GREF is done, not on any ad hoc basis, but in accordance with a well thought out manning policy laid down by the Government of India for the purpose of maintaining at all times and at all levels the special character of GREF as a force designed to meet the operational requirement of the Army. The manning policy was laid down by the Government of India in respect of officers. ...... The GREF Centre is organised on lines similar to an Army Regimental Centre and also functions in the same manner. It is located at a place adjoining an Engineer Regimental Centre, initially at Roorkee and now at Pune, so that it can, if necessary, draw upon the resources of the Engineer Regimental Centre. The new recruits are imparted training in the following three military disciplines: (a) Discipline, which includes drill, marching and saluting. (b) Combat training, including physical training i.e. standing exercises, beam exercises, rope work, route marches etc., harbour deployment drills, camp protection etc. (c) Combat Engineering Training, including field engineering, handling of service explosives, camouflage, combat equipment, bridging, field fortifications, wire obstacles etc.

GREF personnel are not trained in the use of arms, since the role to be performed by GREF is such that its personnel are not required to use arms and they need arms only for static protection and for use during emergency. Therefore in GREF issue of arms is restricted only to Army personnel and ex-servicemen apart from certain units like the Provost Units (GREF Police) which having regard to the nature of their duties, have necessarily to be armed.

The tasks which are to be carried out by GREF comprise not only maintenance of strategic roads but also support for the operational plans of the Army in place of Army Engineer Regiments. We shall presently elaborate these tasks in order to highlight the true character of GREF, but before we do so, we may point out that the role and organisation of GREF units have been reviewed from time to time in consultation with the Army Headquarters and as a result of a major review carried out after the Indo-Pakistan Conflict of 1971, the Army Headquarters defined the role and organisation of GREF units in a secret document dated 24 January 1973. It is clear from this document that, according to the Army Headquarters, a minimum of 17 Border Roads Task Forces and 34 Pioneer Companies are permanently required for providing engineer support to the Army and over the years, this minimum requirement has been fulfilled and 17 Border Roads Task Forces and 34 Pioneer Companies have been made permanent. These 17 Border Roads Task Forces and 34 Pioneer Companies have to be maintained as essential units of GREF for meeting the operational requirement of the Army, even if sufficient work load is not available in Border Areas at any given point of time. There are, in fact, at present 21 Border Roads Task Forces and 34 Pioneer Companies, that is, four Border Roads Task Forces more than the minimum required by the Army Authorities.

The requirement of these four additional Border Roads Task Forces is reviewed from time to time depending on the workload. What should be the composition of the Border Roads Task Forces is laid down in the document dated 24 January 1973 and this document also sets out the tasks to be carried out by the Border Roads Task Forces which may be briefly summarised as follows: (a) Maintenance of line of communication in rear areas of the theatre of operations including roads constructed by the Border Roads and roads maintained by CPWD, State PWD and MES. (b) Improvement and maintenance of operational roads and tracks constructed by combat engineers; (c) Construction and maintenance of AICs and helipads; (d) Improvement and repairs to airfields; (e) Construction of accommodation and all allied facilities for maintenance areas required for sustaining operations; (f) Construction of defence works and obstacles; and (g) Water supply in difficult terrain and deserts. These tasks are required to be carried out by the Border Roads Task Forces during operations with a view to providing engineering support to the army in its operational plans. The Border Roads Task Forces have to perform these tasks not only within the country up to the border but also beyond the border up to the extent of advance into enemy's territory. Even during peace time the Border Roads Task Forces have to be suitably positioned in the likely area of operations so that they can, in the event of hostilities, be quickly deployed on their operational tasks. The Border Roads Tasks Forces along with the Pioneer Companies attached to them are also included in the Order of Battle of the Army so that the support of these units to the Army is guaranteed and can be requisitioned at any time. These units of GREF are further sub-allotted to the lower army formations such as Command, Corps and Division and they appear on the Order of Battle of these formations. Their primary function is to carry out works projected by the General Staff, Army Headquarters to meet the operational requirements and these works, include, inter alia, construction and maintenance of roads operational tracks, airfields, ditch-cum-bund (water obstacles on the border) and field fortifications like bunkers fire trenches and Pill Boxes.

If after meeting the requirements of the General Staff, Army Headquarters, there is spare capacity available with these units of GREF, they undertake construction work on behalf of other ministries or departments, though even there, preference is given to strategic and other roads in sensitive border areas. The funds allocated for the Border Roads Organisation are non-plan funds meant exclusively to meet the requirements of the General Staff, Army Headquarters and they cannot be used for carrying out the works of other ministries or departments. When works are undertaken by GREF units on behalf of other ministries or departments, they are treated as works on agency basis and, where applicable, agency charges are collected by the Border Roads Organisation from the ministries or departments whose work is carried out by them. GREF units undertake, as far as possible, only those tasks which are similar in nature to the tasks for which they are primarily designed to meet Army requirements. It is apparent from the further affidavit of Lt Col S S Cheema that the major portion of the work carried out by GREF units consists of tasks entrusted by the General Staff, Army Headquarters and the tasks carried out on agency basis on behalf of other ministries or departments are comparatively of much lesser value. In fact, until 1966 no work on agency basis was undertaken by GREF units and during the period 1967 to 1970 less than 2 percent of the total work was executed by GREF units for other ministries or departments. Even during the years 1970-71 to 1980-81, the percentage of work carried out by GREF units on behalf of other ministries of departments did not on an average exceed 15 per cent of the total work. The figures for the year 1980-81 also reveal the same pattern.

During 1981-82 the work executed by GREF units for General Staff, Army Headquarters consisted of construction and maintenance of 12865 kms of roads out of the funds of the Border Roads Organisation and 310 kms of ditch-cum-bunds out of funds provided as the Defence Ministry while the agency work entrusted by the Ministry of Shipping and Transport did not cover more than 519 km of strategic roads, 216 kms of sensitive broader area roads and 376 kms of National Highways in border areas and the agency work entrusted by other ministries was limited only to 702 kms of roads. It will thus be seen that the major part of the work executed by GREF units consists of tasks entrusted by the General Staff, Army Headquarters and only a small percentage of work is being done on behalf of other ministries or departments when spare capacity is available.

So far as the personnel of GREF are concerned, they are partly drawn from the Army and partly by direct recruitment. Army personnel are posted in GREF according to a deliberate and carefully planned manning policy evolved with a view to ensuring the special character of GREF as a force intended to support the Army in its operational requirements. The posting of Army personnel in GREF units is in fact regarded as normal regimental posting and does not entitle the Army personnel so posted to any deputation or other allowance and it is equated with similar posting in the Army for the purpose of promotion, career planning, etc. The tenure of Army personnel posted in GREF units is treated as normal Regimental Duty and such Army personnel continue to be subject to the provisions of the Army Act 1950 and the Army Rules 1954 whilst in GREF. But quite apart from the Army personnel who form an important segment of GREF, even the directly recruited personnel who do not come from the Army are subjected to strict Army discipline having regard to the special character of GREF and the highly important role it is called upon to play in support of the Army in its operational requirements. Since the capacity and efficiency of GREF units in the event of outbreak of hostilities depends on their all time capacity and efficiency they are subjected to rigorous discipline even during peace time, because it is elementary that they cannot be expected suddenly to rise to the occasion and provide necessary support to the Army during military operations unless they are properly disciplined and in fit condition at all times so as to be prepared for any eventuality. The Government of India has in exercise of the power conferred upon it by sub-sections (1) and (4) of Section 4 of Army Act 1950 issued a Notification bearing SRO 329 dated 23 September 1960 applying to GREF all the provisions of that Act with the exception of those shown in Schedule A, subject to the modifications set forth in Schedule B and directing that the officers mentioned in the first column of Schedule C shall exercise or perform, in respect of members of the said Force under their command, the jurisdiction, powers and duties incident to the operation of that Act specified in the second column of Schedule C. This Notification makes various provisions of Army Act 1950 applicable to GREF and amongst them is Section 21 which provides:

21. **Power to modify certain fundamental rights in their application to persons subject to this Act**.- Subject to the provisions of any law for the time being in force relating to the regular Army or to any branch thereof, the Central Government may, by notification, make rules restricting to such extent and in such manner as may be necessary the right of any person subject to this Act:-

(a) to be a member of, or to be associated in any way with, any trade union or labour union or any class of trade of labour unions, or and society, institution or association or any class of institution or associations;

(b) to attend or address any meeting or to take part in any demonstration organised by any body of persons for any political or other purposes;

(c) to communicate with the press or to publish or cause to be published any book, letter or other documents.

The other sections which are made applicable deal with special privileges, offences, punishments, penal deductions, arrest and proceedings before trial, Court-Martial and other incidental matters. These sections which are made applicable are primarily intended to impose strict discipline on the members of GREF the same kind of discipline which is required to be observed by the regular Army personnel. The Government of India has also in exercise of the powers of conferred by Section 21, sub-section (4) of Section 102 and section 191 of the Army Act 1950 issued another Notification bearing SRO 330 on the same day, namely, 23 September 1960, directing that the Army Rules 1954 as amended from time to time shall, with the exception of Rules 7 to 18, 168, 172 to 176, 190 and 191, be deemed to be Rules made under the Army Act 1950 as applied to GREF. Rules 19, 20 and 21 of the Army Rules 1954 are material for the purpose of the present writ petitions and they provide inter alia as follows:

19. **Unauthorised organisations**- No person subject to the Act shall, without the express sanction of the Central Government:-

(i) take official cognizance of, or assist or take any active part in, any society, institution or organisation not recognised as part of the Armed Forces of the Union; unless it be of a recreational or religious nature in which case prior sanction of the superior officer shall be obtained;

(ii) be a member of, or be associated in any way with, any trade union or labour union, or any class of trade or labour unions.

20. **Political and non-military activities**- (1) No person subject to the Act shall attend, address, or take part in any meeting or demonstration held for a party or any political purposes, or belong to join or subscribe in the aid of, any political association or movement.

(2) No person subject to the Act shall issue an address to electors or in any other manner publicly announce himself of allow himself to be publicly announced as a candidate or as a prospective candidate for election to Parliament, the legislature of a State, or a local authority, or any other public body or act as a member of a candidate's election committee or in any way actively promote or prosecute a candidate's interests.

21. **Communications to the Press, Lectures, etc**- No person subject to the Act shall-

(i) publish in any from whatever or communicate directly or indirectly to the Press any matter in relation to a political question or on a service subject or containing any service information, or publish or cause to be published any book or letter or article or other document on such question or matter or containing such information without the prior sanction of the Central Government, or any officer specified by the Central Government in this behalf; or

(ii) deliver a lecture or wireless address, on a matter relating to a political question or on a service subject or containing any information or views on any service subject without the prior sanction of the Central Government or any officer specified by the Central Government in this behalf.

These rules obviously owe their genesis to Section 21 and they impose restrictions on the fundamental rights of members of GREF. Since the Army Act 1950 and Army Rules 1954 are made applicable by virtue of SRO Nos 329 and 330 dated 23 September, 1960, GREF personnel when recruited, are required to accept certain terms and conditions of appointment which include inter alia the following:

"5 (iv): You will be governed by the provisions of Central Civil

Service (Classification, Control and Appeal) Rules, 1965, as amended from time to time. Notwithstanding the above, you will be further subject to certain provisions of the Army Act, 1950, and Rules made there-under, as laid down in SROs 329 and 330 of 1960, for purposes of discipline. It will be open to the appropriate disciplinary authority under the Army Act 1950 to proceed under its provisions wherever it considers it expedient or necessary to do so.

5 (v): You will be required to serve anywhere in India or outside India and when so called upon by the Government or the appointing authority or your superior officer, you shall proceed on field service.

5 (vi): You shall, if required, be liable to serve in any Defence Service or post connected with the defence of India.

5 (xi): On your appointment, you will be required to wear the prescribed uniform while on duty, abide by such rules and instructions issued by your superior authority regarding discipline, turnout, undergo such training and take such departmental test as the Government may prescribe."

The result is that the directly recruited GREF personnel are governed by the provisions of Central Civil Service (Classification, Control and Appeal) Rules 1965 as amended from time to time but for purposes of discipline, they are subject to certain provisions of the Army Act 1950 and the Army Rules 1954 as laid down in SROs 329 and 330 dated 23 September 1960. The material facts in all the writ petitions which are being disposed of by this Judgment are similar and hence it is not necessary to set out separately the facts of each writ petition. It will suffice to set out the facts of writ petition No 815 of 1980 which was tried as the main writ petition and whatever we say in regard to the facts of this writ petition must apply equally in regard to the other writ petitions. The petitioners in writ petition No. 815 of 1980 are 24 in number and at all material times they were members of GREF. Out of them, petitioner Nos. 1 and 24 were deserters from service and warrants were issued for their arrest under the provisions of the Army Act 1950 but the Police Authorities were not able to apprehend them. So far as petitioners Nos. 2 to 23 are concerned, they were charged before the Court Martial for offences under section 63 of the Army Act 1950 in that they alongwith some other GREF personnel assembled in front of HQ Chief Engineer (Project) Vartak shouting slogans and demanding release of HQ CE (P) Vartak personnel placed under arrest, removed their belts and threw them on the ground in the vicinity of OC's

Office, participated in a black flag demonstration and failed to fall in line though ordered to do so by Brig Gosain, Chief Engineer Project, Vartak and also associated themselves with an illegal association called "All India Border Roads Employees Association". These 22 petitioners were tried by the Court Martial in accordance with the procedure prescribed by the Army Act 1950 and the Army Rules 1954 as applicable to the members of GREF and on being convicted, they were dismissed from service.

The petitioners thereupon preferred writ petition No. 815 of 1980 challenging the validity of SROs. 329 and 330 dated 23rd September 1960 since these Notifications had the effect of applying the provisions of the Army Act 1950 and the Army Rules 1954 to the members of GREF and restricting their fundamental rights. The petitioners contended that GREF was not a Force raised and maintained under the authority of the Central Government and SROs 329 and 330 dated 23 September 1960 were *ultra vires* the powers of the Central Government under sub-sections (1) and (4) of Section 4 of the Army Act 1950. The petitioners also urged that in any event the application of Section 21 of the Army Act 1950 read with Rules 19 to 21 of the Army Rules 1954 to the members of GREF was unconstitutional since it restricted the fundamental rights of the members of GREF in a manner not permitted by the Constitution and such restriction of the fundamental rights was not protected by Article 33, because the members of GREF was not "members of the Armed Forces or the Forces charged with the maintenance of public order" within the meaning of that Article. There was also one other contention advanced on behalf of the petitioners which, if well founded would render it unnecessary to examine whether GREF was a Force raised and maintained under the authority of the Central Government and the members of GREF were members of the Armed Forces or the Forces charged with the maintenance of public order and that contention was that Section 21 of the Army Act 1950 was in any event not justified by the terms of Article 33, since under that Article it was Parliament alone which was entrusted with the power to determine to what extent any of the fundamental rights shall, in application to the members of the Armed Forces or the Forces charged with the maintenance of public order, be restricted or abrogated so as to ensure the proper discharge of their duties and the maintenance of discipline amongst them and Parliament could not leave it to the Central Government to determine the extent of such restriction or abrogation as was sought to be done under Section 21. Section 21 was therefore, according to the petitioners, unconstitutional and void and along with Section 21 must fall Rules 19 to 21 of the Army Rules 1954.

The petitioners contended that in the circumstances they were entitled to exercise their fundamental rights under Clauses (a), (b) and (c) of Art. 19 (1) without any of the restriction imposed by Rules 19 to 21 of the Army Rules 1954 and if that be so, they could not be charged under section 63 of the Army Act 1950 on the facts alleged against them and their convictions by the Court-Martial were illegal and void and consequently they continued in service of GREF. The self same contentions were repeated on behalf of the petitioners in the other writ petitions. The respondents disputed the validity of these contentions and submitted that GREF was a Force raised and maintained under the authority of the Central Government and having regard to the special character of GREF and the role which it was required to play in support of the Army operations, the members of GREF could legitimately be regarded as members of the Armed Forces within the meaning of Article 33 and the Central Government was therefore entitled to issue SROs. 329 and 330 dated 23rd September 1960 making the provisions of the Army Act 1950 and the Army Rules 1954 and particularly Section 21 and Rules 19 to 21 applicable to the members of GREF. The respondents defended the validity of Section 21 and contended that it was a proper exercise of power by Parliament under Article 33 determining the extent to which the Fundamental Rights may, in their application to the members of the Armed Forces including GREF, be restricted or abrogated and it was not outside the power conferred on Parliament by that article and, read with Rules 19 to 21, it validly restricted the Fundamental Rights of the members of GREF. The respondents submitted that in the circumstances the petitioners were rightly charged under Section 63 of the Army Act 1950 and their convictions by the Court Martial and subsequent dismissals were valid. The respondents thus sought to sustain the validity of the action taken by the authorities against the petitioners.

Now the first question that arises for consideration on these rival contentions is as to the constitutional validity of Section 21. That section empowers the Central Government by notification to make rules restricting "to such extent and in such manner as may be necessary" three categories of rights of any person subject to the Army Act 1950, namely, (a) the right to be a member of or to be associated in any way with, any trade union or labour union, or any class of trade or labour unions, or any society, institution or association or any class of institution or associations; (b) the right to attend or address any meeting or to take part in any demonstration organised by any body of persons for any political or other purposes; and (c) the rights to communicate with the press or to publish or cause to be published any book, letter or other document. These rights which are permitted to be restricted are part of the Fundamental Rights under clauses (a), (b) and (c) of article 19(1) and under the constitutional scheme; they cannot be restricted by executive action unsupported by law. If any restrictions are to be imposed, that can be done only by law and such law must satisfy the requirements of clause (2), (3) or (4) of Article 19 according as the right restricted falls within clause (a), (b) or (c) of Article 19(1). The restrictions imposed must be reasonable and in case of right under clause (a) of article 19(1), they must be "in the interest of the sovereignty and integrity of India, the security of the state, friendly relations with foreign states, public order, decency or morality, or in relation to contempt of court, defamation or incitement to an offence" as provided in clause (2) of Article 19, in case of right under clause (b) of Article 19(1), they must be "in the interest of the sovereignty and integrity of India or public order" as provided in clause (3) of article 19 and in case of right under clause (c) of article 19(1), they must be "in the interest of the sovereignty and integrity of India or public order or morality" as provided in clause (4) of article 19. Then only they would be valid; otherwise they would be unconstitutional and the law imposing them would be void. Now here we find that Section 21 does not itself impose any restrictions on the three categories of rights there specified. If Section 21 had itself imposed any such restrictions, it would have become necessary to examine whether such restrictions are justified under clause (2), (3) or (4) of article 19, as may be applicable. But Section 21 leaves it to the Central Government to impose restrictions on these three categories of rights without laying down any guidelines or indicating any limitations which would ensure that the restrictions imposed by the Central Government are in conformity with clause (2), (3) or (4) of Article 19, whichever be applicable. It confers power on the Central Government in very wide terms by providing that the Central Government may impose restrictions on these three categories of rights "to such extent and in such manner as may be necessary".

The Central Government is constituted the sole judge of what restrictions are considered necessary and the Central Government may, in terms of the power conferred upon it, impose restrictions it considers necessary, even though they may not be permissible under clauses (2), (3) and (4) of Article 19. The power conferred on the Central Government to impose restrictions on these three categories of rights which are part of the Fundamental Rights under clauses (a), (b) and (c) of Article 19(1) is thus a broad uncanalised and unrestricted power permitting violation of the constitutional limitations. But, even so, section 21 cannot be condemned as invalid on this ground, as it is saved by article 33 which permits the enactment of such a provision. Article 33 carves out an exception in so far as the applicability of Fundamental Rights to members of the Armed Forces and the Forces charged with the maintenance of public order is concerned. It is elementary that a highly disciplined and efficient armed force is absolutely essential for the defence of the country.

Defence preparedness is in fact the only sure guarantee against aggression. Every effort has therefore to be made to build up a strong and powerful army capable of guarding the frontiers of the country and protecting it from aggression. Now obviously no army can continuously maintain its state of preparedness to meet any eventuality and successfully withstand aggression and protect the sovereignty and integrity of the country unless it is at all times possessed of high morale and strict discipline. Morale and discipline are indeed the very soul of an army and no other consideration, howsoever important, can outweigh the need to strengthen the morale of the armed forces and to maintain discipline amongst them. Any relaxation in the matter of morale and discipline may prove disastrous and ultimately lead to chaos and ruination affecting the well being and imperilling the human rights of the entire people of the country. The constitution makers therefore placed the need for discipline above the fundamental rights so far as the members of the Armed Forces and the Forces charged with the maintenance of public order are concerned and provided in Article 33 that Parliament may by law determine the extent to which any of the Fundamental Rights in their application to members of the Armed Forces and the Forces charged with the maintenance of public order, may be restricted or abrogated so as to ensure the proper discharge of their duties and the maintenance of discipline among them. Article 33 on a plain grammatical construction of its language does not require that Parliament itself must by law restrict or abrogate any of the Fundamental Rights in order to attract the applicability of that Article.

What it says is only this and no more, namely, that Parliament may by law determine the permissible extent to which any of the Fundamental Rights may be restricted or abrogated in their application to the members of the Armed Forces and the Forces charged with the maintenance of public order. Parliament itself can, of course, by enacting a law restrict or abrogate any of the Fundamental Rights in their application to the members of the Armed Forces and the Forces charged with the maintenance of public order as, in fact, it has done by enacting the Army Act, 1950, the provisions of which, according to the decisions of a Constitution Bench of this Court in *Ram Swarup v. Union of India* are protected by article 33 even if found to affect one or more of the Fundamental Rights. But having regard to varying requirement of army discipline and the need for flexibility in this sensitive area, it would be inexpedient to insist that Parliament itself should determine what particular restrictions should be imposed and on which Fundamental Rights in the interest of proper discharge of duties by the members of the Armed Forces and the Forces charged with the maintenance of public order maintenance of discipline among them. The extent of restrictions necessary to be imposed on any of the Fundamental Rights in their application to the members of the Armed Forces and the Forces charged with the maintenance of public order for the purpose of ensuring proper discharge of their duties and maintenance of discipline among them, would necessarily depend upon the prevailing situation at a given point of time and it would be inadvisable to encase it in a rigid statutory formula. The Constitution makers were obviously anxious that no more restrictions should be placed on the Fundamental Rights of the members of the Armed Forces and the Forces charged with the maintenance of public order than are absolutely necessary for ensuring proper discharge of their duties and the maintenance of discipline among them, and therefore they decided to introduce a certain amount of flexibility in the imposition of such restrictions and by article 33, empowered Parliament to determine the permissible extent to which any of the Fundamental Rights in their application to the members of the Armed Forces and the Forces charged with the maintenance of public order may be restricted or abrogated, so that within such permissible extent determined by Parliament, any appropriate authority authorised by Parliament may restrict or abrogate any such Fundamental Rights. Parliament was therefore within its power under article 33 to enact Section 21 laying down to what extent the Central Government may restrict the Fundamental Rights under clauses (a), (b) and (c) of Article 19(1), of any person subject to the Army Act, 1950, every such person being clearly a member of the Armed Forces.

The extent to which restrictions may be imposed on the Fundamental Rights under clauses (a), (b) and (c) of Article 19(1) is clearly indicated in clauses (a), (b) and (c) of section 21 and the Central Government is authorised to impose restrictions on these Fundamental Rights only to the extent of the rights set out in clauses (a), (b) and (c) of section 21 and no more. The permissible extent of the restrictions which may be imposed on the Fundamental Rights under clauses (a), (b) and (c) of Article 19 (1) having been laid down in clauses (a), (b) and (c) of section 21, the Central Government is empowered to impose restrictions within such permissible limit, "to such extent and in such manner as may be necessary." The guideline for determining as to which restrictions should be considered necessary by the Central Government within the permissible extent determined by Parliament is provided in Article 33 itself, namely, that the restrictions should be such as are necessary for ensuring the proper discharge of their duties by the members of the Armed Forces and the maintenance of discipline among them. The Central Government has to keep this guideline before it in exercising the power of imposing restrictions under Section 21 though, it may be pointed out that once the Central Government has imposed restrictions in exercise of this power, the court will not ordinarily interfere with the decision of the Central Government that such restrictions are necessary because that is a matter left by Parliament exclusively to the Central Government which is best in a position to know what the situation demands. Section 21 must, in the circumstances, be held to be constitutionally valid as being within the power conferred under Article 33.

That takes us to the next question whether the Central Government was entitled to issue SROs. 329 and 330 applying certain provisions of the Army Act 1950 and the Army Rules 1954 to the members of GREF. We will first consider the question of validity of SRO 329 because if that notification has been validly issued and the provisions of section 21, subsection (4) of section 102 and section 191 of the Army Act 1950 made applicable to the members of REF, SRO 330 applying certain provisions of the Army Rules, 1954 to the members of GREF in exercise of the powers conferred under section 21, sub-section (4) of section 102 and section 191 of the Army Act 1950 would be fortiori be valid. Now SRO 329 is issued by the Central Government under sub-sections (1) and (4) of section 4 of the Army Act 1950 which provide inter alia as under:

> "Section 4(1). The Central Government my, by notification, apply with or without modifications, all or any of the provisions of this Act to any force raised and maintained in India under the authority of that Government, and suspend the operation of any other enactment for the time being applicable to the said force.
>
> (2) ......
>
> (3) ......
>
> (4) While any of the provisions of this Act apply to the said force, the Central Government, by notification, direct by what authority any jurisdiction, powers or duties incident to the operation of these provision shall be exercised or performed in respect of the said force.

The Central Government is empowered under sub-section (1) of section 4 to apply any of the provisions of the Army Act, 1950 to any force raised or maintained in India under the authority of that Government and when any such provisions of the Army Act, 1950 are applied to that force under sub-section (1), the Central Government can by notification issued under sub-section (4), direct by what authority, the jurisdiction, powers and duties incident to the operation of those provisions shall be exercised or performed in respect of that force. SRO 329 applying certain provisions of the Army Act, 1950 to the members of GREF and directing by what authority, the jurisdiction, powers and duties incident to the operation of those provisions shall be exercised or performed in respect of GREF, would therefore be within the power of the Central Government under sub-section (1) and (4) of section 4, if GREF could be said to be a force raised and maintained in India under the authority of the Central Government. The question is: what is the true meaning and scope of the expression "any force raised and maintained in India under the authority of the Central Government." The word "force" is not defined anywhere in the Army Act, 1950. There is a definition of the expression "the forces" in section 3 (xi) but it does not help, because the expression we have to construe is "force" which is different from "the forces". There is however an indication to be found in sub-section (2) of section 4 which throws some light on the sense in which the word "force" is used in sub-section (1) of section 4. Section 4, sub-section (2) clearly contemplates that the "force" referred to in sub-section (1) of section 4 must be a force organised on similar lines as the army with rank structure. So far as GREF is concerned, there can be no doubt that it is a force organised on army pattern with units and sub units and rank structure. Moreover, as is clear from the letter dated 16th June, 1960 addressed by the Secretary, Border Roads Development Board to the Director General Border Roads, GREF is a force raised and maintained under the authority of the Central Government. The Central Government therefore had power under sub-sections (1) and (4) of section 4 to issue SRO 329 applying some of the provisions of the Army Act, 1950 to GREF and directing by what authority the jurisdiction powers and duties incident to the operation of these provisions shall be exercised or performed in respect of GREF. But the question is, and that is the more important question to which we have to address ourselves, whether, even if GREF was a force raised and maintained under the authority of the Central Government, the Central Government could, in exercise of the powers conferred under sub-section (1) of section 4, validly-apply section 21 to the members of GREF. Section 21 empowers the Central Government to make rules restricting "to such extent and in such manner as may be necessary" the rights set out in clauses (a), (b) and (c) of that section and in exercise of this power, the Central Government has made rules 19 to 21 to which reference has already been made by us. Now as already pointed out above, section 21 is protected against invalidation by Article 33, since it lays down in clauses (a), (b) and (c) the possible extent to which the fundamental rights of any person subject to the Army Act, 1950 may be restricted and every person subject to the Army Act 1950 would clearly and indubitably be a member of the Armed Forces within the meaning of Article 33. But if section 21 were to be applied to persons who are not members of the Armed Forces of the forces charged with the maintenance of public order, Article 33 would not afford any protection to section 21 in so far as it applies to such persons and the application of section 21 to such persons would be unconstitutional. We must therefore proceed to consider whether the members of GREF could be said to be members of the Armed Forces within the meaning of Article 33. If they cannot be said to be members of the Armed Forces, the application of section 21 to them would not have the protection of Article 33 and would be clearly void.

The history, composition, administration, organisation and role of GREF which we have described above while narrating the facts clearly show that GREF is an integral part of the Armed Forces. It is undoubtedly a departmental construction agency as contended on behalf of the petitioners but it is distinct from other construction agencies such as Central Public Works Department etc., in that it is a force intended primarily to support the army in its operational requirement. It is significant to note that the Border Roads organisation, which is in over all control of GREF was originally created as part of Army Headquarters and it was only later, for reasons of high policy, that it was separated from Army Headquarters and placed under the Border Roads Development Board. Though the budget of the Border Roads organisation forms part of the budget of Ministry of Shipping and Transport, the financial control is vested in the Ministry of Finance (Defence). The entire infrastructure of GREF is modelled on the pattern of the Army and it is organised into units and sub-units with command and control system similar to that in the Army. The personnel of GREF right from class IV to class I have to be in uniform with distinctive badges of rank and they have a rank structure equivalent to that of the Army. GREF is primarily intended to carry out defence and other works projected by the General Staff, Army Headquarters and it is only where spare capacity is available that GREF undertakes works of other ministries or departments on agency basis and there also, preference is given to strategic and other roads in sensitive areas. The funds which are provided to the Border Roads organisation are meant exclusively for carrying out the works entrusted by the General Staff, Army Headquarters and so far as the works carried out for other ministries or departments on agency basis are concerned, the funds of the Border Roads organisation are not permitted to be used for carrying out those works and they are paid for by the respective ministries or departments and where applicable, agency charges for executing the works are also collected. The statistics given in the earlier part of the judgment show that the major portion of the work executed by GREF units consists of tasks entrusted by the General Staff, Army Headquarters and only a small percentage of the work is being done on behalf of other ministries or departments. GREF units carry out essentially those tasks which are otherwise carried out by Army Engineering Regiments and they provide engineering support to the Army both during peace time as also during hostilities. It was found necessary as a result of a major review carried out by Army Headquarters after 1971 that a minimum of 17 Border Road Task Forces and 34 Pioneer Companies would be permanently required for providing engineering support to the Army and accordingly 17 Border Road Task Forces and 34 Pioneer Companies have been made permanent and their composition has been reorganised in accordance with the recommendations of the Army Headquarters. These 17 Border Road Task Forces and 34 Pioneer Companies are being maintained as essential units of GREF for meeting the operational requirements of the Army, even if sufficient work is not available for them at any given point of time. The operational planning of the Army is in fact based on availability of these 17 Border Road Task Forces and 34 Pioneer Companies and during operations, they have to carry out tasks which would otherwise have been done by equal number of Army Engineering Regiments. It may be pointed out that these 17 Border Road Task Forces and 34 Pioneer Companies have replaced corresponding number of Army Engineering Regiments and Pioneer Companies in the Army. The tasks required to be carried out by the Border Road Task Forces have already been described in some details in the opening part of the Judgment while narrating the facts and we need not repeat the same over again. Suffice it to state that these tasks are required to be carried out by the Border Road Task Forces during operations with a view to providing engineering support to the Army in its operational plans. The Border Road Task Forces have to perform these tasks and provide engineering support to the Army not only up to the border but even beyond up to the exent of advance into enemy territories. Even in peace time, the Border Road Task Forces have to undertake works projected by General

Staff, Army Headquarters to meet their operational requirements and these work include construction and maintenance of roads, operational tracks, ditch-cum-bund (water obstacles on the broder), field fortifications like bunkers, fire trenches and pill boxes, helipads and airfields. It is also significant to note that the Border Road Task 1 Forces and Pioneer Companies attached to them are included in the order of Battle of the Army which implies that support of these units to the Army is guaranteed and can be requisitioned at any time The Border Road Tack Forces are also sub-allotted to lower army formations and they appear on the order of Battle of these formations. GREF units consisting of these Border Road Task Forces and Pioneer Companies are placed under the direct control of the Army during emergencies when the entire control of this Force is entrusted to the Chief of the Army Staff.

Even during peace time, the Chief of the Army Staff exercises control over the discipline of the members of GREF units through the applicability of the provisions of the Army Act 1950. The Director General, Border Roads who is in over-all control of GREF units is always an army officer of the rank of Major General and his confidential reports are written by the Chief of the Army Staff. The signal communication of GREF is also integrated with the Army communication set up not only during operations but also in normal peace time. It is also a factor of vital significance which emphasises the special character of GREF as a force intended to provide support to the Army in its operational plans and requirements that Army personnel are posted in GREF units according to a carefully planned manning policy so that GREF units can in times of war or hostilities be able to provide effective support to the Army. The tenure of office of the Army personnel in GREF units is regarded as normal regimental duty and is equated with similar appointments in the Army for the purpose of promotion, career planning etc. Even the directly recruited personnel of GREF are given training at the GREF Centre before they are posted and the training given is in three military disciplines which we have described in detail in the opening part of the Judgment. The training includes not only drill, marching and saluting but also combat training including physical training such as standing Exercises, beam exercises, rope work, route marches etc. and combat engineering training including field engineering, handling of service explosives, camouflage, combat equipment, bridging, field fortifications, wire obstacles etc. Moreover, the directly recruited personnel are taken up only after they voluntarily accept the terms and conditions of employment which include inter alia conditions 5 (iv), 5 (v), 5 (vi) and 5 (xi) which have been reproduced in full while narrating the facts. These conditions make it clear the directly recruited personnel may be required to serve anywhere in India and outside India and when directed, they would have to proceed on field service and if required, they would also be liable to serve in any Defence Service or post connected with the defence of India. It is also stipulated in these conditions that on their appointment, the directly recruited personnel would have to wear the prescribed uniform while on duty and that they would be subject to the provisions of the Army Act 1950 and the Army Rules 1954 as laid down in SROs 329 and 330 for purposes of discipline. **It is abundantly clear from these facts and circumstances that GREF is an integral part of the Armed Forces and the members of GREF can legitimately be said to be members of the Armed Forces within the meaning of Article 33.**

The petitioners however tried to combat this conclusion by pointing out that the services constituted under Border Roads Engineering Service Group A, Rules 1977 and the Border Roads Engineering Service Group B, Rules, 1977 both of which were made by the President in exercise of the powers conferred under article 309 and brought into force with effect from 20th September 1977, were expressly designated as Central Civil Services and that in reply to Unstarred Question No 1100, the Minister for Defence stated on 18 June 1980 that "GREF as at present organized is a civilian construction force" and similarly in reply to Unstarred Question No. 6002, the Minister of Defence observed on 1 April 1981 that "the civilian employees serving with the Border Roads organisation and GREF are not under administrative control of Ministry of Defence but are under the administrative control of the Border Roads Development Board" and so also Minister of Defence stated on 25th February 1983 in answer to Unstarred Question No. 938 that "the members of the General Reserve Engineer Force of the Border Roads organisation are civilian employees of the Central Government."

The petitioners contended on the basis of these statements that GREF was not an Armed Force but was a civilian construction agency and the members of GREF could not possibly be regarded as members of the Armed Forces so as to fall within the scope and ambit of Article 33. This contention though it may appear at first blush attractive, is in our opinion not well founded and must be rejected. It is undoubtedly true that as stated by the Minister of Defence, GREF is a civilian construction force and the members of GREF are civilian employees under the administrative control of the Border Roads Development Board and that the engineer officers amongst hem constitute what may be designed as "Central Civil

Services, within GREF, but that does not mean that they cannot be at the same time form an integral part of the Armed Forces. The fact that they are described as civilian employees and they have their own special rules of recruitment and are governed by the Central Civil Service (Classification, Control and Appeal) Rules, 1965 is not determinative of the question whether they are members of the Armed Forces. It may be noted that even the members of the Civil General Transport Companies constituted under Government of India, War Department, notification No. 1584 dated 29 June 1946 as also the members of the Independent Transport Platoons have been treated as members of the Armed Forces for the purpose of application of the provisions of the Army Act 1950 by SRO 122 dated 22 July 1960 and SRO 282 dated 17 August 1960. So also when personal of Military Engineer Service have to function in operational areas under the army, they too are brought under the provisions of the Army Act 1950 for the purpose of discipline. The question whether the members of GREF can be said to be members of the Armed Forces for the purpose of attracting the applicability of Article 33 must depend essentially on the character of GREF, its organisational set up, its functions, the role it is called upon to play in relation to the Armed Forces and the depth and intimacy of its connection and the extent of its integration with the Armed Forces and if judged by this criterion, they are found to be members of the Armed Forces, the mere fact that they are non-combatant civilians governed by the Central Civil Services (Classification Control and Appeal) Rules 1965, cannot make any difference. This view which we are taking on principle finds ample support from the decision of this Court in *Ous Kutilingal Achudan Nair v. Union of India* where the question was whether certain employees in the Defence Establishment such as cooks, chowkidars, laskers, barbers, carpenters, mechanics, boot-makers, tailors etc. who were noncombatant civilians governed by the Civil Service Regulations for purpose of discipline, leave, pay etc. and were eligible to serve up to the age of 60 years unlike the members of the Armed Forces, could be validly called "members of the Armed Forces" covered by Article 33, because it Was only if they were members of the Armed Forces within the meaning of that article that the restrictions imposed upon their right to form association could be sustained. This Court speaking through Sarkaria, J. held that the employees in question were members of the Armed Forces and gave the following reasons in support of its view:

> "The members of the Unions represented by the appellants fall within this category. It is their duty to follow or accompany the Armed personnel on active service, or in camp or on the march. Although

270

they are non-combatants and are in some matters governed by the Civil Service Regulations, yet they are integral to the Armed Forces. They answer the description of the "members of the Armed Forces" within the contemplation of Article 33."

Here also it is indisputable on the facts and circumstances mentioned above that the functions and duties of GREF are integrally connected with the operational plans and requirements of the Armed Forces and the members of GREF are, to use the words of Sarkaria, J. "integral to the Armed Forces". There can be no doubt that without the efficient and disciplined operational role of GREF the military operations in border areas during peace as also in times of war will be seriously hampered and a highly disciplined and efficient GREF is absolutely essential for supporting the operational plans and meeting the operational requirements of the Armed Forces. It must therefore be held that the members of GREF answer the description of "members of the Armed Forces" within the meaning of Article 33 and consequently the application of section 21 of the Army Act 1950 to the members of GREF must be held to be protected by that Article and the Fundamental Rights of the members of GREF must be held to be validly restricted by section 21 read with Rules 19 to 21 of the Army Rules 1954. If that be so, the petitioners were liable to be charged under section 63 of the Army Act 1950 for the alleged violations of Rules 19 to 21 and their convictions by Court Martial as also subsequent dismissals must be held to be valid. Before we part with this point, we may point out that an anguished complaint was made before us on behalf of the petitioners that there is considerable disparity between the Army personnel posted in GREF units and the other officers and men of GREF in so far as the terms and conditions of service, such as, salary, allowances and rations are concerned. It is not necessary for us to consider whether this complaint is justified; it is possible that it may not be wholly unjustified but we may point out that in any event it has no real bearing. It all on the question whether the members of GREF can be said to be members of Armed Forces. Since, the members of GREF are drawn from two different sources, it is possible that the terms and conditions of service of the personnel coming from the two sources may be different. The Army personnel posted in GREF units naturally carry their own terms and conditions of service while the other officers and men in GREF are governed by their own distinctive terms and conditions. It is difficult to appreciate how differences in terms and conditions of service between GREF personnel coming from two different streams can possibly have any impact on the character of GREF as a force integral to the Armed Forces. It is immaterial for the purpose of determining whether the members of GREF are members of the Armed Forces as to what are the terms and conditions of service of the members of GREF and whether they are identical with those of Armed personnel appointed on the same or equivalent posts in GREF units. But, we may observe that in case it is found that the terms and conditions of service of officers and men in GREF directly recruited or taken on deputation are in any way less favourable than those of Army personnel appointed to the same or equivalent posts in GREF, the Central Government might well consider the advisability of taking steps for ensuring that the disparity, if any, between the terms and conditions of service, such as, salary, allowances, rations etc. Of Army personnel posted in GREF units and other officers and men in GREF is removed.

It may be pointed out that a faint attempt was made on behalf of the petitioners to contend that their convictions by Court Martial were illegal since their trial was not in accordance with law. This contention was strongly resisted on behalf of the respondents and it was positively averred in the affidavit of Lt Col Shergill that disciplinary action was initiated and punishment awarded by the competent disciplinary authority after the offences were proved in accordance with law and all possible help and opportunity was extended to the petitioners and others who were tried to defend themselves with the help of defending officers of their choice or of civil lawyers. Lt Col Shergill stated in the clearest terms in his affidavit in reply that "out of 357 personnel kept under military custody, 287 have been released on the basis of their unconditional apology and those who failed to do so, have been tried by GCM/SCM summarily and awarded punishment, on the basis of the gravity of the offence proved against them. During the trial, all possible help was provided under the rules and they were allowed to meet/employ lawyers of their choice to defend the case. In all the cases, defending officers as per their choices have also been detailed from departmental side. The trials were held strictly in accordance with the procedure laid down in the rules, and there is no denial of natural justice." Having regard to this positive statement made on oath by Lt Col Shergill, it is not possible for us to hold that the convictions of the petitioners by the Court Martial were not in accordance with law. In any event, the allegations of the petitioners in this behalf raised disputed questions of fact which it is not possible for us to try in a writ petition.

We cannot in the circumstances be called upon to quash and set aside the convictions of the petitioners by the Court Martial or their subsequent dismissals from service on the ground that they were not in accordance with law.

There was also one other contention advanced on behalf of the petitioners and it raised a question of violation of Article 14 of the Constitution. The contention was that the members of GREF were governed both by the Central Civil Services (Classification, Control and Appeal) Rules 1965 and the provisions of the Army Act 1950 and the Army Rules 1954 in matters of discipline and therefore whenever a member of GREF was charged with misconduct amounting to an offence under the Army Act 1950, it was left to the unguided and unfettered discretion of the authorities whether to proceed against the employee under the Central Civil Services (Classification, Control and Appeal) Rules 1965 or under the Army Act 1950 and the Army Rules 1954 and SROs 329 and 330 applying the provisions of the Army Act, 1950 and the Army Rules 1954 to members of GREF for purposes of discipline were therefore discriminatory and violative of Article 14. We do not think there is any substance in this contention. In the first place, the nature of the proceedings which may be taken under the Central Civil Services (Classification, Control and Appeal) Rules 1965 against an erring employee is different from the nature of the proceedings which may be taken against him under the provisions of the Army Act 1950 read with the Army Rules 1954, the former being disciplinary in character while the latter being clearly penal.

It is significant to note that Section 20 of the Army Act 1950 which deals with dismissal, removal or reduction of any person subject to that Act and clauses (d), (e), (f), (g) and (k) of Section 71 which provide for punishment of cashiering, dismissal, reduction in rank forfeiture of seniority and forfeiture of pay and allowances, have not been made applicable to the members of GREF by SRO 329 with the result that, so far as disciplinary proceeding are concerned, there is no overlapping between the provisions of the Central Civil Services (Classification, Control and Appeal) Rules 1965 and the provisions of the Army Act 1950 and the Army Rules 1954 as applied to the members of GREF. Secondly, it is not possible to say that the discretion vested in the authorities whether to take action against an erring member of GREF under Central Civil Services (Classification Control and Appeal) Rules 1965 or under the Army Act 1950 and the Army Rules 1954 is unguided or uncanalised.

It has been denied in the affidavit of Lt. Col. Shergill that unguided discretion any power is vested in the disciplinary authority to proceed against an employee of GREF either under the Central Civil Services (Classification, Control and Appeal) Rules 1965 or the Army Act 1950 and the Army Rules 1954 or to switch over from one proceeding to the other at the any stage. Lt Col Shergill has stated positively in his affidavit that clear and detailed administrative guidelines have been laid down for the purpose of guiding the disciplinary authority in exercising its discretion whether to take action against an employee of GREF under the Central Civil Services (Classification, Control and appeal) Rules 1965 of the Army Act 1950 and the Army Rules 1954 and these guidelines have been set out in full in Annexure R-5 to his affidavit. Thirdly, the decision in *Northern India Caterers Ltd. v. Punjab* on which the contention of the petitioners is based has been over-ruled by this Court in *Maganlal Chhaganla v. Municipal Corporation, Greater Bombay* where it has been held that "the contention that the mere availability of two procedures will vitiate one of them, that is, the special procedure is not supported by reason or authority." And lastly, it may be noted that in any event the provisions of the Army Act 1950 and the Army Rules 1954 as applied to the members of GREF are protected by Article 33 against invalidation on the ground of violation of Article 14.

The present contention urged on behalf of the petitioners must also therefore be rejected. We may make it clear it is only in regard to the members of GREF that we have taken the view that they are members of the Armed Forces within the meaning of Article 33. So far as casual labour employed by GREF is concerned, we do not wish to express any opinion on this question whether they too are members of the Armed Forces or not, since that is not a question which arises for consideration before us. The writ petitions are accordingly dismissed with no order as to costs. The special leave petitions will also stand rejected.

Petitions dismissed.

7

Delhi Police Non-Gezetted Karmchari Sangh v. Union of India AIR 1987 SC 379 : 1987 SCC (1) 115 : 1986 SCALE (2)872, date of Judgement 20 November 1986 [Two Judge Bench].

JUDGMENT:

1. This appeal by certificate is directed against the Judgment of a Division Bench of the Delhi High Court, in CW No 731 of 1971. The prayer in the Writ Petition is for the issuance of an appropriate writ, order or direction declaring (a) the Police Forces (Restriction of Rights) Act No 33 of 1966 (for short the Act) as *ultra vires* the Constitution, (b) the Police Forces (Restriction of Rights) Rules 1966 and Police Forces (Restriction of Rights) Amendment Rules, 1970 (for short the Rules) *ultra vires* of Act 33 of 1966 and the Constitution of India, (c) that the Circular dated 1 April 1971 as invalid, illegal, *ultra vires*, null and void and (d) for a declaration that the Delhi Police Non-Gazetted Karmchari Sangh, petitioner No. 1 in the Writ Petition, is a legally and validly constituted service organization.

2. The first appellant is the Non-Gazetted Karmachari Sangh (for short the 'Sangh') and the appellant Nos. 2 to 7, its members. The High Court dismissed the petition holding that the challenge was not sustainable and that neither the Act nor the Rules violated any provisions of the Constitution. The High Court dealt at length with the preliminary objections that a challenge based on the violation of any fundamental right was not permissible in view of the emergency declared by the President of India, in December, 1977. This need not detain us now in this Judgment.

3. The appellants' case is that the Act referred above violates Article 19(1) (c) of the Constitution of India and that the restrictions imposed by it, being arbitrary, violates Article 14 of the Constitution. The Non-Gazetted members of the Delhi Police Force wanted to form an organization of their own and for that purpose constituted the Karmachari Union in 1966 and applied for its registration under the Trade Union Act, 1926. Initially the registration asked for was declined. Then Act 33 of 1966 was enacted. It came into force on 2 December 1966. An application for recognition was again made on 9 December 1966. Recognition was granted by the Central Government on 12 December 1966. The Non-Gazetted members of the Delhi Police Force were permitted to become members of the Sangh. On 12 December 1966, the Central Government made rules under the Act which were amended in December 1970. The Circular in question was

issued under these rules. The Circular attempts to derecognize the Sangh. This occasioned the filing of the writ petition.

4. Before considering the rival contentions urged before us, it would be useful to refer to the salient features of the Police Forces (Restriction of Rights) Act, 1966 to appreciate its ambit and the restrictions imposed by its provisions. The Act was enacted to delineate the restrictions imposed of the rights conferred by Part III of the Constitution, in their application to the members of the forces charged with the maintenance of public order so as to ensure the proper discharge of their duties' and the maintenance of discipline among them. The Parliament obviously has this power under Article 33 of the Constitution of India. The provisions of the Act seek to place certain restrictions on members of the police force in exercise of their fundamental rights guaranteed by Article 19(1)(c) to form Association or Unions. Section 3 of the Act reads as follows:

"3(1). No member of a police force shall without the express sanction of the Central Government or of the prescribed authority—

(a) be a member of, or be associated in any way with, any trade union, labour union, political association or with any class of trade unions, labour unions or political associations; or

(b) be a member of, or be associated in any way with, any other society, institution, association or organisation that is not recognised as part of the force of which he is a member or is not of a purely social, recretional or religious nature; or

(c) communicate with the press or publish or cause to be published any book, letter or other document except where such communication or publication is in the bona fide discharge of his duties or is of a purely literary, artistic or scientific character or is of a prescribed nature.

Explanation: If any question arises as to whether any society, institution, association or organization is of a purely social, recreational or religious nature under clause (b) of this subsection, the decision of the Central Government thereon shall be final.

(2) No member of a police force shall participate in or address, any meeting or take part in any demonstration organized by any body of persons for any political purposes or for such other purposes as may be prescribed."

Section 4 of the Act provides for penalties if Section 3 is contravened by any person. Section 5 gives power to the Central Government by notification in the official gazette, to amend the schedule by including therein any other enactment relating to a force charged with the maintenance of public order or omit there from any enactment already specified therein. Section 6 gives the rule making power to the Central Government.

5. The only contention that now survives is whether the impugned statute, rules and orders are violative of the fights of the appellants guaranteed under Article 19(1)(c) of the Constitution of India. This appeal could be disposed of by a short Order. Appellants No. 2 to 7 are no longer in service. They have been dismissed. As such they do not have the necessary *locus standi* to sustain this petition. But the appellants' counsel submitted that the first petitioner—the Sangh, was still interested in pursuing this appeal and that persuaded us to hear the appeal on merits.

6. It is true that recognition was given to the Sangh originally. Subsequently by order dated 1 April 1971, the Sangh was derecognized. This was pursuant to the amended rules. Rule 3 provided:

> "No member of the police forces shall participate in, or address, any meeting or take part in any demonstration organised by any body of persons (a) for the purpose of protesting against any of the provisions of the Act or these rules or any other rules made under the Act; or (b) for the purpose of protesting against any disciplinary action taken proposed to be taken against him or against any other member of a police force; or (c) for any purpose connected with any matter pertaining to his remuneration or other conditions of service or his condition of work or living condition, or the remuneration, other conditions, of any other member or members of a police force.
>
> Provided that nothing contained in clause (c) shall preclude a member of a police force from participating in a meeting convened by an association of which he is a member and which has been accorded sanction under sub-section (1) of section 3 of the Act, where such meeting is in pursuance of or for the furtherance of, the objects of such association."

The above rules were amended by a notification dated 19 December 1970 the material change for our purpose being an amendment in the proviso to clause (c) of rule 3. The original proviso to clause (c) was substituted by another proviso which reads as follows:

> "Provided that nothing contained in clause (c) shall preclude a

member of a police force from participating in a meeting—

(i) which is convened by an association of police-officers of the same rank of which he is a member and which has been granted recognition under clause (b) of sub-section (1) of section 3 of the Act;

(ii) which has been specifically provided for in the articles of association or/and has been, by general or special order, permitted by the Inspector General of Police having regard to the object of such meeting and other relevant factors; and

(iv) which has been convened to consider the agenda circulated to all concerned according to the relevant provisions of the articles of association, after giving intimation in advance to the ' Inspector General of Police or an officer nominated by him." (Emphasis supplied).

Rule 5 was added to the Rules by virtue of which minutes had to be recorded of the meetings of a recognized association. The Inspector General of Police could send observers by virtue of rule 6 to such meetings. Outsiders were prohibited from attending the meetings of the association without permission of the Inspector General of Police by Rule 7. Rules 8, 9 & 11 may also be usefully read:

"8. Recognition: Members of police force belonging to the same rank desiring to form an association may make an application for the grant of recognition under clause (b) of subsection (1) of section 3 and such application shall be in writing under the hand of a representation of such association addressed to the Inspector General of Police who shall be the authority to grant, refuse or revoke such recognition;

Provided that before refusing or revoking recognition, the Association shall be given a reasonable opportunity of making representation against the proposed action.

9. Suspension of recognition: The Inspector General of Police may in the interests of the general public or for the maintenance of discipline in the police-force and with the prior approval of the Central Government, the State Government or as the ease may be the Administrator of the Union Territory suspend the recognition granted under rule 8 for a period not exceeding three months which may be extended for a further period of three months by the Central Government, State Government or as the case may be the Administrator of the Union Territory so however that the total period

for which such recognition may be suspended shall, not, in any case, exceed six months.

11. Special provision regarding recognition already granted: Recognition granted prior to the commencement of the Police Forces (Restriction of Rights) Amendment Rules, 1970, to any association the articles of association of which are not in conformity with these rules shall, unless the said articles of association are brought in conformity with the provisions of these rules within a period of thirty days, stand revoked on the expiry of the said period."

7. It is the change effected by the new Proviso to Rule 3(c) which has come in for attack at the hands of the appellants. Previously all non-gazetted officers of the Delhi Police Department could be members of the Sangh. Now, the amended proviso to rule 3(c) mandates that only members of the Police Force having the same rank could constitute themselves into one Association. The effect of this amended rule is that the Sangh will have to be composed of various splinter associations consisting of members holding different ranks. This according to the appellants violates not only Article 19(1)(c) which protects freedom of association, but also the provisions of the Act.

The immediate provocation for filing the writ petition was the Circular by which the recognition granted to the Sangh was revoked. The operative part of the Circular reads as follows:

"Rule 11 of the Police Force (Restriction of Rights) Amendment Rules, 1970 published vide extraordinary Gazette of India notification No. GSR-2049 dated 19 December 70 lays down that recognition granted prior to the commencement of these rules, to any association the articles of which are not in conformity with these rules shall unless the articles are brought in conformity with the provisions of these rules within a period of 30 days, stand revoked on the expiry of the said period.

2. Whereas the Constitution of the Delhi Police Non-Gazetted Karmchari Sangh which was granted recognition vide Government of India, Ministry of Home Affairs letter No.8/70/66-P.I., dated 12 December 66 and which contains a number of provisions not in conformity with the above rules, the recognition already granted to the Delhi Police Non-Gazetted Karmachari Sangh, stands revoked.

3. This may be brought to the notice of all ranks.

4. A copy of this circular may be published in the Delhi Police Gazette."

The appellants' counsel submits that recognition of the association carries with it the right to continue the association as such. It is a right flowing from the fact of recognition. To de-recognize the association in effect offends against the freedom of association. It is urged that once the Government had granted recognition to the Sangh and approved its constitution neither the Parliament nor any delegated authority can take away that recognition or dictate to the association who could be its members. The right available to the members of the association at the commencement should continue as such without any hindrance.

8. Before considering the questions of law raised by the appellants' counsel with reference to the decided cases, it would be useful to bear in mind the fact that this association consists of members of Police Force who by virtue of this fact alone stands on a different footing from other associations. The Constitution of India has taken care to lay down limitations on such, associations from exercising rights under Article 19(1)(c). Article 33 read with Article 19(4) of the Constitution offers an effective reply to the contention raised by the appellants. Article 33 reads as follows:

"Parliament may, by law, determine to what extent any of the rights conferred by this Part shall, in their application to the members of the Armed Forces or the Forces charged with the maintenance of public order, be restricted or abrogated so as to ensure the proper discharge of their duties and the maintenance of discipline among them."

Article 19(4) reads as follows:

"Nothing in sub clause (c) of the said clause shall affect the operation of any existing law in so far as it imposes, or prevent the State from making any law imposing, in the interests of the sovereignty and integrity of India or public order or morality, reasonable restrictions on the exercise of the right conferred by the said sub-clause."

That the Sangh and its members come within the ambit of Article 33 cannot be disputed. The provisions of the Act and rules taking away or abridging the freedom of association have been made strictly in conformity with Article 33. The right under Article 19(1)(c) is not absolute. Article 19(4) specifically empowers the State to make any law to fetter, abridge or abrogate any of the rights under Article 19(1)(c) in the interest of public order and other considerations. Thus the attack against the Act and rules can be successfully met with reference to these two Articles as members of the Police Force, like the appellants herein, are at a less advantageous position, curtailment of whose fights under Article 19(1)(c) comes squarely within Article 33 in the interest of discipline and public order. This conclusion of ours is sufficient to dispose of this appeal. However, we will deal with the submissions made before us for the completeness of the Judgment.

9. The scope of Article 19(1)(c) came up for consideration before this Court in *Damyanti Naranga v. Union of India* [1971] 3 SCR 840. The question related to the Hindi Sahitya Sammelan, a Society registered under the Societies Registration Act, 1860. The Parliament enacted the Hindi Sahitya Sammelan Act under which outsiders were permitted to become members of the Sammelan without the volition of the original members. This was challenged and this Court held that any law altering the composition of the Association compulsorily will be a breach of the right to form the association because it violated the composite right of forming an association and the right to continue it as the original members desired it.

10. Here we have an entirely different situation since we are dealing with a group distinct in its nature and composition from others. Here we are dealing with a force that is invested with powers to maintain public order. Article 33 enables Parliament to restrict or abrogate the fundamental rights in their relation to the Armed Forces including Police Force. In *Ous Kutilingal Achudan Nair v. Union India* [1976] 2 SCR 769 this Court had to consider two questions; whether the employees of the defence establishment such as cooks, barbers and like civil employees were "members of the Armed Forces" and if so whether they could be validly deprived of their right to form unions in violation of Article 19(1)(c). This Court held that they fell within the category of members of the Armed Forces and that the Central Government was competent by notification to make rules restricting or curtailing their right to form associations, Article 19(1)(c) notwithstanding.

11. In *Raghubar Dayal Jai Prakash v. Union of India* [1962] 3 SCR 547, this Court had to deal with this question in relation to the functions of an incorporated body the objects of which were, *interalia*, to regulate forward transactions in the sale and purchase of various commodities, Freedom of association is a fundamental right. It was contended that if a law regulated the recognition of an association under certain conditions subject to which alone recognition could be accorded or continued, such

conditions were bad. This Court had to consider whether the freedom of association implied or involved a guaranteed right to recognition also. The contention was that if the object of an association was lawful, no restriction could be placed upon it except in the interest of public order and that freedom to form an association carried with it the right to determine its internal arrangements also. Repelling this contention this Court held that restrictions cannot be imposed by statute for the purpose of regulating control of such associations. While the right to freedom of association is fundamental, recognition of such association is not a fundamental right and the Parliament can by law regulate the working of such associations by imposing conditions and restrictions on such functions.

12. It cannot be disputed that the fundamental rights guaranteed by Article 19(1)(c) can be claimed by Government servants. A Government servant may not lose its right by joining Government service. Article 33 which confers power on the Parliament to abridge or abrogate such rights in their application to the Armed Forces and other similar forces shows that such rights are available to all citizens, including Government servants. But it is, however, necessary to remember that Article 19 confers fundamental rights which are not absolute but are subject to reasonable restrictions. What has happened in this case is only to impose reasonable restrictions in the interest of discipline and public order.

13. The validity of the impugned rule has to be judged keeping in mind the character of the employees we are dealing with. It is true that the rules impose a restriction on the right to form association. It virtually compels a Government servant to withdraw his membership of the association as soon as recognition accorded to the said association is withdrawn or if, after the association is formed, no recognition is accorded to it within six months. In other words, the right to form an association is conditioned by the existence of the recognition of the said association by the Government. If the association affairs recognition and continues to enjoy it, Government servants can become members of the said association; if the said association does not secure recognition from the Government or recognition granted to it is withdrawn, Government servants must cease to be members of the said association. That is the plain effect of the impugned rule. These rules are protected by Articles 33 and 19(4) of the Constitution. Besides, it is settled law that the right guaranteed by Article 19(1)(c) to form associations does not involve a guaranteed right to recognition also.

14. The main grievance of the appellants is that the first appellant-Sangh when recognised, comprised of Police Officers of various ranks,

the common factor being that all its members were non-gazetted police officers. This composition was changed by the impugned rules. Not only is the composition changed; the entire Sangh stood derecognised for failure to alter its constitution complying with the new rules. This attack cannot be sustained. Section 3 of the Act permits the rule making authority to define any group of Police Force that can form an Association. It also gives power to prescribe the nature of activity that each' such association of members can indulge in. It, therefore, follows that if rules can be framed defining this aspect, a rule can also be framed enabling the authorities to revoked or cancel recognition once accorded, if the activities offended the rules.

15. The further grievance of the appellant is that non-gazetted officers who once formed one block have been further divided with reference to ranks and that this again is an inroad into their right under Article 19(1)(c). This submission has been already met. Besides, this classification based on ranking has its own rationale behind it. We are dealing with a Force in which discipline is the most important pre-requisite. Non-gazetted officers consist of men of all ranks; the lowest cadre and officers who are superior to them. If all the non-gazetted officers are grouped together irrespective of rank, it is bound to affect discipline. It was perhaps, realizing the need to preserve discipline that the changes in the rule were effected. We are not satisfied that there has been violation of any law in doing so. On a careful consideration of the questions involved in this appeal, we hold that the High Court was right in its decision.

We accordingly dismiss the appeal.

8

Intelligence Bureau Employees' Association v. Union of India (1997) 11 SCC 348, decided on 24 April 1996 [Two Judge Bench].

These writ petitions filed under Article 32 of the Constitution relate to functioning of the Intelligence Bureau Employees' Association (hereinafter referred to as "the petitioner Association"), a society registered under the Societies Registration Act, 1860. The petitioner Association is claimed to be an association of the employees working in the Intelligence Bureau (for short "IB") of the Government of India. It was registered as a society on 23 June 1979. On 3 May 1980 the Joint Director of IB issued a circular memorandum wherein it was stated that the Government has now made it clear that in a security organization like the IB there is no scope for an employees' association and, in this context it was mentioned that attempts were being made to vitiate the generally satisfactory personnel relationship which has existed within the organization and that communications addressed to senior officers, not excluding the Head of the organization, were often couched in intemperate language verging on abuse and that this displayed highly indisciplined conduct not befitting members of an organization like the IB. In the said circular it was, however, stated that the grievances of the employees would be the basic concern of all members of the organization though the primary responsibility for this would vest in the administration and a special responsibility would also be cast on the staff councils which would have to function in a representative manner and form an essential adjunct of the Grievances Redressal machinery of the organization. By this writ petition the petitioners are seeking to challenge the validity of the said circular memorandum on the ground that it is violative of the fundamental rights of the petitioners guaranteed under Articles 14 and 19 of the Constitution.

2. During the pendency of the writ petition, Article 33 of the constitution has been amended by the Constitution (Fiftieth Amendment) Act, 1984 which received the assent of the President of India on 11 September 1984. As a result of the said amendment Article 33 has been substituted by the following provision:

"33. Power of Parliament to modify the rights conferred by this Part in their application etc.—Parliament may, by law, determine to what extent any of the rights conferred by this Part shall, in their application to,—

    (a)   the members of the Armed Forces; or

(b)   the members of the Forces charged with the maintenance of public order; or

(c)   persons employed in any bureau or other organisation established by the State for purposes of intelligence or counter-intelligence; or

(d)   (d)   persons employed in, or in connection with, the telecommunication systems set up for the purposes of any Force, bureau or other organization established by the State for purposes of any Force, bureau or organization referred in clauses (a) to (c),

be restricted or abrogated so as to ensure the proper discharge of their duties and the maintenance of discipline among them."

3. Under the un-amended Article 33 the rights conferred by Part III could be restricted or abrogated by a law made by Parliament in respect of members of the Armed Forces and members of Forces charged with maintenance of public order. As a result of the fiftieth amendment the scope of the provision has been enlarged and persons employed in any bureau or other organization established by the State for the purpose of intelligence or counter-intelligence, which could include the IB, and persons employed in or in connection with the telecommunication system set up for the purpose of any force, bureau or organization referred to in the preceding clauses have been brought within the ambit of Article 33. The said amendment in the Constitution was followed by the Intelligence Organizations (Restriction of Rights) Act, 1985, Act No. 58 of 1985, which received the assent of the President of India on 6 September 1985. Section 3 of the said Act makes the following provisions:

"3. (1) No member of an Intelligence Organization shall,—

(a)   be a member of, or be associated in any way with, any trade union, labour union, political association or with any class of trade unions, labour unions or political associations; or

(b)   be a member of, or be associated in any way with, or raise funds for, or hold office in, or function in any other manner for, any other society, institution, association or organization that is not recognised by the Central Government as part of the Intelligence Organization of which he is a member or is not of a purely social, recreational or religious nature; or

(c)   communicate with the press or publish or cause to be published any book, letter, pamphlet, poster or other document except with the prior permission of the head of the Intelligence Organization; or

(d)   except for purposes of official duty, contact or communication with any person or any matter relating to functioning, structure, personnel or organizational affairs of the Intelligence Organization of which he is a member;

(e)   use the name of the Intelligence Organization of which he is a member for purposes not authorized by the head of the Intelligence Organization or in any other manner except for purposes relating to the official work and functioning of the Organization itself.

Explanation.—If any question arises as to whether any society, institution, association or organization is of a purely social, recreational or religious nature under clause (b) of this sub-section, the decision of the Central Government thereon shall be final.

(2) No member of an Intelligence Organization, shall participate in, or address, any meeting or take part in any demonstration organized by any body of persons for any political purposes or for such other purposes as may be prescribed."

4. We have heard Shri Rawal who is appearing as a counsel for the petitioner Association and is appearing in his personal capacity as Petitioner 2. Shri Rawal has sought to challenge the validity of the fiftieth amendment in the Constitution but he has not been able to show how the said amendment which enlarges the scope of Article 33 so as to include persons engaged in activities connected with the activities of the Armed Forces and Forces charged with the maintenance of public order referred to in the un-amended Article 33 is destructive of the basic structure of the Constitution so as to transgress the limitations placed on the amending power under article 368 of the constitution. The only contention that was urged by Shri Raval was that the fiftieth amendment is discriminatory in nature inasmuch as it takes away the rights that were enjoyed by the members of the petitioner Association without giving them anything in return. Merely because as a result of the impugned amendment the members of the petitioner Association can be deprived of their rights under Part III of the Constitution does not mean that the amendment is destructive of the basic structure of the Constitution. We are, therefore, unable to accept

the contention urged by Shri Raval assailing the validity of Article 33 as amended by the fiftieth amendment.

5. Shri Rawal has not been able to show any infirmity in Act No. 58 of 1985 which has been enacted under the provisions of Article 33 as amended once the said amendment in Article 33 is found to be valid. A perusal of the provisions of Section 3 of the said Act shows that there is no complete prohibition in respect of employees of an Intelligence Organization becoming a member of an association. The prohibition is only in respect of associations specified in clause (a) of sub-section (1) of section 3, i.e, trade unions, labour unions, political associations or with any class of trade unions, labour unions or political associations. Under clause (b) of sub-section (1) it is permissible to form associations which are purely social, recreational or religious in nature. It is also permissible to form any other association or organisation provided it is so recognised by the Central Government. It is thus open to the petitioner Association, if it so chooses, to move the Central Government for recognition and if it fulfils the requirements laid down by the Central Government for such recognition, the said request shall be given due consideration by the Central Government.

6. It would thus appear that after the amendment of Article 33 by the fiftieth amendment and enactment of Act No. 58 of 1985 the circular memorandum has lost its significance and no purpose would be served by going into the validity of the same. The writ petitions have, therefore, become infructuous and are accordingly dismissed as having become infructuous.

No orders as to costs.

9

Union of India v. L D Balam Singh (2002) 9 SCC 73: [2002] 3 SCR 385: 2002 (2) LC 790(SC), decided on 24 April 2002 [Two Judge Bench].

JUDGMENT:

1. While it is true that Army personnel ought to be subjected to strictest form of discipline and Article 33 of the Constitution has conferred powers on to the Parliament to abridge the rights conferred under Part III of the Constitution in respect of the members of the Armed Forces, but does that mean and imply that the Army Personnel would be denuded of the Constitutional privileges as guaranteed under the Constitution? Can it be said that the Army Personnel form a class of citizens not entitled to the Constitution's benefits and are outside the purview of the Constitution? To answer above in the affirmative would be a violent departure to the basic tenets of the Constitution. An Army Personnel is as much a citizen as any other individual citizen of this country. Incidentally, the provision as contained in Article 33 does not by itself abrogate any rights and its applicability is dependent on Parliamentary legislation. The language used by the framers is unambiguous and categorical and it is in this perspective Article 33 may be noticed at this juncture. The said article reads as below:-

2. A plain reading [of Article 33] thus would reveal that the extent of restrictions necessary to be imposed on any of the fundamental rights in their application to the armed forces and the forces charged with the maintenance of public order for the purpose of ensuring proper discharge of their duties and maintenance of discipline among them would necessarily depend upon the prevailing situation at a given point of time and it would be inadvisable to encase it in a rigid statutory formula. The Constitutions makers were obviously anxious that no more restrictions should be placed than are absolutely necessary for ensuring proper discharge of duties and the maintenance of discipline amongst the Armed Force Personnel and therefore Article 33 empowered the Parliament to restrict or abridge within permissible extent, the rights conferred under Part III of the Constitution in so far as the Armed Force Personnel are concerned. In this context reference may be made to the decision of the Supreme Court in the case of *R Viswan v. Union of India* AIR 1983 SC 658) : (1983) 3 SCC 401 also a judgment of the Calcutta High Court in the case of *Lt Col Amal Sankar Bhaduri v. Union of India* (1987 CLT 1) of which one of us (U C Banerjee, J.) was a party.

3. This Court in the case of *Prithi Pal Singh v. Union of India* AIR 1982 SC 1413 observed:

> "It is one of the cardinal features of our Constitution that a person by enlisting in or entering armed forces does not cease to be a citizen so as to wholly deprive him of his rights under the Constitution. More so when this Court held in *Sunil Batra v. Delhi Administration* (1979) 1 SCR 392 at p. 495 : AIR 1978 SC 1675 at p. 1727 that even prisoners deprived of personal liberty are not wholly denuded of their fundamental rights. In the larger interest of national security and military discipline Parliament in its wisdom may restrict or abridge such rights in their application to the Armed Forces but this process should not be carried so far as to create a class of citizen not entitled to the benefits of liberal spirit of the Constitution. Persons subject to Army Act are citizens of this ancient land having feeling of belonging to the civilized community governed by the liberty oriented Constitution."

4. While answer to the first question posed above is in the affirmative, the contextual facts bear out and pose a further issue as regards availability of substantive and procedural safeguards under a specific legislation the High Court answered it in the affirmative since such procedural safeguards are said to be mandatory in nature.

5. Adverting to the factual matrix presently under consideration, it appears that on a petition filed under Articles 226/227 of the Constitution of India, the respondent herein prayed for quashing of the charge-sheet, sentence of the General Court Martial, order of confirmation of General Officer Commanding and also to quash the trial of the General Court Martial. The facts of the matter however briefly are as below:

The petitioner was serving the Indian Army having joined the same on 28 October 1976. He was posted to 18 Cavalry C/o 56 APO during the year 1990-91 at Patiala Cantt. He was residing with his family in a Government married accommodation being House No. 255/30 K S Colony, Patiala Cantt. On 28 December 1991 a search of his residence was conducted by Army Officers/Officials and allegedly opium weighing 4.900 Kgs was recovered from his family quarter. The petitioner was thereafter placed under arrest in military custody and was put in the quarter guard of his unit aforesaid and FIR No. 378 was lodged at Police Station Sadar Patiala on 28 December 1991. A sample of the opium recovered was forwarded to the Chemical Examiner for analysis and the remaining quantity of the opium, a contraband was kept with the Police.

6. The summary of evidence was ordered by the Commanding Officer of 64 Cavalry and on the basis of directions from the Brigade Commander, the petitioner was put to trial by the General Court Martial. The petitioner was tried under Section 69 of the Army Act for an offence punishable under Section 18 of the Narcotic Drugs and Psychotropic Substances Act, 1985 (hereinafter referred to as NDPS Act). After the trial was over, the petitioner was convicted and sentenced by the General Court Martial.

7. Before adverting, however, to the rival contentions as advanced before this Court, it would be worthwhile to refer to the relevant provisions of the Army Act and the Rules framed thereunder. Chapter VI of the Army Act, 1950 stands ascribed to the offences and Section 69 therein deals with the civil offences, which reads as below :-

> "69. **Civil offences Subject to the provisions of Section 70**: Any person subject to this Act who at any place in or beyond India, commits any civil offence, shall be deemed to be guilty of an offence against this Act and, if charged therewith under this section, shall be liable to be tried by a court- martial and, on conviction, be punishable as follows, that is to say:-
>
> (a) if the offence is one which would be punishable under any law in force in India with death or with transportation, he shall be liable to suffer any punishment, other than whipping, assigned for the offence, by the aforesaid law and such less punishment as is in this Act mentioned; and
>
> (b) in any other case, he shall be liable to suffer any punishment, other than whipping, assigned for the offence by the law in force in India, or imprisonment for a term which may extend to seven years, or such less punishment as is in this Act mentioned."

8. It is on this score that Section 109 in Chapter X ought also to be noticed at this juncture. The Section reads as below:

> 109. **Power to convene a general court-martial**: A general court-martial may be convened by the Central Government or the Chief of the Army Staff or by any officer empowered in this behalf by warrant of the Chief of the Army Staff.

9. Having outlined the factual score as above and upon noting of the two

several provisions of the Army Act, it would be worthwhile to note Section 18 of the Narcotic Drugs and Psychotropic Substances Act, 1985 (NDPS Act). Needless to record that the petitioner was tried under Section 69 of the Army Act for an offence punishable under Section 18 of the NDPS Act the trial did take place before a General Court Martial and conviction and sentence was also passed therein. It is this sentence and conviction which stands challenged in the writ petition moved before the High Court, as noticed above. The NDPS Act admittedly contains certain safeguards and the law reports are replete with case laws pertaining to these safeguards. Dilution of the safeguards as prescribed in the statute has strongly been criticised and negated and the same were ascribed to be strictly mandatory in nature. The issue thus: whether by reason of the respondent being a member of the Armed Forces would stand denuded of such a safeguard in the event the General Court Martial takes note of an offence under a specific statute. Article 33 of the Constitution though conferred a power but has not been taken recourse to put a bar or restraint as regards the non-availability of the statutory safeguards in terms therewith. Before proceeding further, however, it would be convenient to note certain provisions of the NDPS Act, namely, Sections 18, 42, 50, which read as under:

"18. Punishment for contravention in relation to opium poppy and opium

Whoever, in contravention of any provision of this Act or any rule or order made or condition of licence granted there under, cultivates the opium poppy or produces, manufactures, possesses, sells, purchases, transports, imports inter-State, exports inter-State or uses opium shall be punishable

(a) where the contravention involves small quantity, with rigorous imprisonment for a term which may extend to six months, or with fine which may extend to ten thousand rupees, or with both;

(b) where the contravention involves commercial quantity, with rigorous imprisonment for a term which shall not be less than ten years but which may extend to twenty years and shall also be liable to fine which shall not be less than one lakh rupees which may extend to two lakh rupees:

Provided that the court may, for reasons to be recorded in the judgment, impose a fine exceeding two lakh rupees.

(c) in any other case, with rigorous imprisonment which may extend to ten years and with fine which may extend to one lakh rupees.

42. **Power of entry, search, seizure and arrest without warrant or authorisation**:

(1) Any such officer (being an officer superior in rank to a peon, sepoy or constable) of the department of central excise, narcotics, customs, revenue, intelligence or any other department of the Central Government including para-military forced or armed forces as is empowered in this behalf by general or special order by the Central Government, or any such officer (being an officer superior in rank to a peon, sepoy or constable) of the revenue, drugs control, excise, police or any other department of a State Government as is empowered in this behalf by general or special order of the State Government, if he has reason to believe from personal knowledge or information given by any person and taken down in writing, that any narcotic drug, or psychotropic substance, or controlled substance in respect of which an offence punishable under this Act has been committed or any document or other article which may furnish evidence of the commission of such offence or any illegally acquired property or any document or other article which may furnish evidence of holding any illegally acquired property which is liable for seizure or freezing or forfeiture under Chapter VA of this Act is kept or concealed in any building, conveyance or enclosed place, may between sunrise and sunset :-

(a) enter into and search any such building, conveyance or place;

(b) in case of resistance, break open any door and remove any obstacle to such entry;

(c) seize such drug or substance and all materials used in the manufacture thereof and any other article and any animal or conveyance which he has reason to believe to be liable to confiscation under this Act and any document or other article which he has reason to believe may furnish evidence of the commission of any offence punishable under this Act or furnish evidence of holding any illegally acquired property which is liable for seizure or freezing of forfeiture under Chapter VA of this Act; and

(d) detain and search and, if he thinks proper arrest any person whom he has reason to believe to have committed any offence punishable under this Act:

Provided that if such officer has reason to believe that a search warrant or authorisation cannot be obtained without affording opportunity for the concealment of evidence or facility for the escape of an offender, he may enter and search such building, conveyance or enclosed place at any time between sunset and sunrise after recording the grounds of his belief.

(2) Where an officer takes down any information in writing under Sub-Section (1) or records grounds for his belief under the proviso thereto, he shall within seventy-two hours send a copy thereof to his immediate official superior.

50. Conditions under which search of persons shall be conducted:-

(1) When any officer duly authorised under Section 42 is about to search any person under the provisions of Section 41, Section 42 or Section 43, he shall, if such person so requires, take such person without unnecessary delay to the nearest Gazetted Officer of any of the departments mentioned in Section 42 or to the nearest Magistrate.

(2) If such requisition is made, the officer may detain the person until he can bring him before the Gazetted Officer or the Magistrate referred to in sub-section (1).

(3) The Gazetted Officer or the Magistrate before whom any such person is brought shall, if he sees no reasonable ground for search, forthwith discharge the person but otherwise shall direct that search be made.

(4) No female shall be searched by anyone excepting a female.

(5) When an officer duly authorised under section 42 has reason to believe that it is not possible to take the person to be searched to the nearest Gazetted Officer or Magistrate without the possibility of the person to be searched parting with possession of any narcotic drug or psychotropic substance, or controlled substance or article or document, he may, instead of taking such person to the nearest Gazetted Officer or Magistrate, proceed to search the person as provided under section 100 of the Code of Criminal Procedure, 1973

(2of 1974).

(6) After a search is conducted under sub- section (5), the officer shall record the reasons for such belief which necessitated such search and within seventy-two hours send a copy thereof to his immediate official superior."

10. As regards the mandatory effect of the provisions as contained in Section 50 above, the Constitution Bench of this Court in *State of Punjab v. Baldev Singh* (1999) 6 SCC 172 has the following to state :

"24. There is, thus, unanimity of judicial pronouncements to the effect that it is an obligation of the empowered officer and his duty before conducting the search of the person of a suspect, on the basis of prior information, to inform the suspect that he has the right to require his search being conducted in the presence of a Gazetted officer or a Magistrate and that the failure to so inform the suspect of his right, would render the search illegal because the suspect would not be able to avail of the protection which is inbuilt in Section 50. Similarly, if the person concerned requires, on being so informed by the empowered officer or otherwise, that his search be conducted in the presence of a Gazetted officer or a Magistrate, the empowered officer is obliged to do so and failure on his part to do so would also render the search illegal and the conviction and sentence of the accused bad.

25. To be searched before a Gazetted officer or a Magistrate, if the suspect so requires, is an extremely valuable right which the legislature has given to the person concerned having regard to the grave consequences that may entail the possession of illicit articles under the NDPS Act. It appears to have been incorporated in the Act keeping in view the severity of the punishment. The rationale behind the provision is even otherwise manifest. The search before a Gazetted officer or a Magistrate would impart much more authenticity and creditworthiness to the search and seizure proceedings. It would also verily strengthen the prosecution case. There is, thus, no justification for the empowered officer, who goes to search the person, on prior information, to effect the search, of not informing the person concerned of the existence of his right to have his search conducted before a Gazetted officer or a Magistrate, so as to enable him to avail of that right. It is, however, not necessary to give the information to the person to be searched about his right in writing. It is sufficient if

such information is communicated to the person concerned orally and as far as possible in the presence of some independent and respectable persons witnessing the arrest and search. The prosecution must, however, at the trial, establish that the empowered officer had conveyed the information to the person concerned of his right of being searched in the presence of a Magistrate or a Gazetted officer, at the time of the intended search. Courts have to be satisfied at the trial of the case about due compliance with the requirements provided in Section 50. No presumption under Section 54 of the Act can be raised against an accused, unless the prosecution establishes it to the satisfaction of the court, that the requirements of Section 50 were duly complied with."

11. On the factual matrix Mrs Indu Malhotra appearing for the respondent rather emphatically contended that it is an admitted situation that there is non-compliance of Sections 41 and 42 of the NDPS Act since no search warrants were issued and officers conducting the search were admittedly not duly authorised under the Act and by reason therefor the resultant effect of state of the situation as above, rendered the entire proceeding stand vitiated. The decision in Baldev Singh (supra) mainly dealt with the provisions of Section 50, which would be dealt with shortly hereafter but presently having a perusal of the relevant statutory provisions (in particular Sections 41 and 42) the submission as above cannot but be termed as it has been inevitable and inescapable. A recent decision of this Court in *Roy V.D. v. State of Kerala* 2001 SCC (Cri) 42 however, lends credence to conclusion as above since this Court as a matter of fact dealt with the true purport of Sections 41 and 42 of the NDPS Act. The felicity expression as contained therein, however, prompts us to note the same in extenso as below:-

"15. It is thus seen that for exercising powers enumerated under sub-section (1) of Section 42 at any time whether by day or by night a warrant of arrest or search issued by a Metropolitan Magistrate or a Magistrate of the First Class or any Magistrate of the Second Class who has been specifically empowered by the State Government in that behalf or an authorisation under sub-section (2) of Section 41 by an empowered officer is necessary. Without such a warrant or an authorisation, an empowered officer can exercise those powers only between sunrise and sunset. However, the proviso permits such an empowered or authorised officer to exercise the said powers at any time between sunset and sunrise if he has reason to believe that such a search warrant or authorisation cannot be obtained without affording opportunity for the concealment of evidence of facility for the escape of an offender and he records the grounds of his belief.

16. Now, it is plain that no officer other than an empowered officer can resort to Section 41(2) or exercise powers under Section 42(1) of the NDPS Act or make a complaint under clause (d) of sub-section (1) of Section 36-A of the NDPS Act. It follows that any collection of materials, detention or arrest of a person or search of a building or conveyance or seizure effected by an officer not being an empowered officer or an authorised officer under Section 41(2) of the NDPS Act, lacks sanction of law and is inherently illegal and as such the same cannot form the basis of a proceeding in respect of offences under Chapter IV of the NDPS Act and use of such a material by the prosecution vitiates the trial.

17. To the same effect is the view expressed by this Court in *State of Punjab v. Balbir Singh* (1994 (3) SCC 299 : 1994 SCC (Cri) 634). In para 13 Jayachandra Reddy, J. speaking for the Court observed thus: (SCC p. 313): "13. Therefore, if an arrest or search contemplated under Sections 41 and 42 is made under a warrant issued by any other Magistrate or is made by any officer not empowered or authorised, it would per se be illegal and would affect the prosecution case and consequently vitiate the trial."

19. The learned Additional Solicitor General, however, relying upon conclusion No.(3) in para 57 of *State of Punjab v. Baldev Singh* (1999 6 SCC 172 : 1999 SCC (Cri) 1080) contends that a search and seizure in violation of Sections 41 and 42 of the NDPS Act does not vitiate the trial but would render the recovery of illicit article suspect and would only vitiate the conviction and sentence of the accused if the conviction has been recorded solely on the basis of such an illicit article, so the High Court was right in not quashing the proceedings. We are afraid, we cannot accede to the contention of the learned Additional Solicitor General."

12. The appellant herein, however, rather emphatically voiced two specific counts in support of the appeal. On the first, it has been contended that by reason of the fact of the petitioner being a 'person' belonging to the Armed Forces, question of usual formalities as regards the procedural aspect under NDPS Act would not arise, as such infraction of Section 42 of the NDPS Act cannot be said to be of any consequence : On the second

count it has been the definite contention that since Section 50 specifically records "about to search any person" and since the contraband item has been in fact recovered from the private residence of the respondent herein, Section 50 cannot be said to be of any application. It is on this score the charge-sheet, though not included in the paper book, but upon leave of the Court, was produced and placed reliance upon in support of the appeal. We also deem it fit and convenient to note the charge-sheet herein below:-

CHARGE SHEET

The accused No 1059403N LD (Subs) Balam Singh of 18 Cavalry, attached to 64 Cavalry is charged with:-

Army Act Section 69

COMMITTING A CIVIL OFFENCE, THAT IS TO SAY, POSSESSING OPIUM IN CONTRAVENTION OF SECTION 18 OF THE NARCOTIC DRUGS AND PSYCHOTROPIC SUBSTANCES ACT, 1985

in that he,

at Patiala on 28 Dec 91 was found in illegal possession of 4 kgs and 900 grams of   opium.

Place: Patiala Sd/ x x x x   (SD Singh) Colonel

Date: 12 Mar 92   Commanding Officer

                                                              The 64 Cavalry

To be tried by General Court Martial.

                                                  Sd/ x x x x

Station: Patiala   (Kamaljit Singh)

C/o 56 APO   Major General

Dated: 14 Mar 92   General Officer Commanding,

                                                      1 Armoured Division

13. We shall have the occasion to deal with the specific grievance as

submitted in support of the respondent's contention later on in this judgment, but for the present suffice it to record that the same stated to be relating to possession of opium in contravention of Section 18 of the NDPS Act since he was found in illegal possession of 4 Kgs and 900 grams of opium at Patiala on 28 December 1991. The charge-sheet, however, is stated to be, as noticed above, issued under Section 69 of the Army Act by one Shri S D Singh, Colonel/Commanding Officer 64th Cavalry and it is this charge-sheet which has been directed by the General Officer Commanding, Major General Kamaljit Singh to be tried by the General Court Martial.

14. In the writ petition filed before the High Court after the conclusion of the Court Martial proceedings and recording of the finding of guilt of the charge the petitioner/respondent herein specifically raised a plea of the charge being vague. Before, however, we deal with the same let us get back to the two specific counts noticed hereinbefore, namely, procedural aspect and non-applicability of Section 50. Dealing with the second count first, as regards non-applicability of Section 50 by reason of the factum of the same being made applicable to the person and not the place, we cannot but record our concurrence therewith. Section 50 sub- section (1) by reason of the language used therein, does not and cannot have any manner of application in the facts presently under consideration.

15. Turning attention on to the procedural aspect, be it noticed that Section 18 is an offence which cannot but be ascribed to be civil in nature in terms of the provisions of Army Act if Section 18 is to be taken recourse to then and in that event the provisions of the statute come into play in its entirety rather than piecemeal. The charge leveled against the respondent is not one of misdeeds or wrongful conduct in terms of the provisions of the Army Act but under the NDPS Act. In the event, we clarify, a particular statute is taken recourse to, question of trial under another statute without taking recourse to the statutory safeguards would be void and the entire trial would stand vitiated unless, of course, there are existing specific provisions therefor in the particular statute. Needless to record that there were two other civilian accused who were tried by the Court at Patiala but were acquitted of the offence for non-compliance of the mandatory requirements of the NDPS Act. Once the petitioner was put on trial for an offence under the NDPS Act, the General Court Martial and the Army authorities cannot reasonably be heard to state that though the petitioner would be tried for an offence under Section 18 of the NDPS Act, yet the procedural safeguards as contained in the statutory provision would not be

applicable to him being a member of the Armed Forces. The Act applies in its entirety irrespective of the jurisdiction of the General Court Martial or other Courts and since the Army authorities did not take into consideration the procedural safeguards as is embodied under the Statute, the question of offering any credence to the submissions of Union of India in support of the appeal does not and cannot arise. There is no material on record to show that the authorities who conducted the search and seizure at the house of the respondent herein has in fact done so in due compliance with Section 42 of the statute which admittedly stand fatal for the prosecution as noticed above as a matter of fact, two of the civilians stand acquitted therefor.

16. Lastly, it has been contended by the respondent that the charge-sheet is not only vague, but devoid of all material particulars and does not even fulfil the requirements of the Army Rules and the entire proceedings in any event stand vitiated. We are, however, not expressing any opinion thereon, neither the same is required for the purposes of disposal of this matter. Suffice it to record, however, that the same has some substance.

17. Having considered the matter in the perspective as above, we do not find any infraction of any law in the judgment of the High Court; neither the judgment can be faulted in any other way. This appeal, therefore, fails and is thus dismissed.

10

Union of India v. Ex Flt Lt GS Bajwa (2003) 9 SCC 630 : (2003) 3 SCR 1092 decided on 2 May 2003, Two Judge Bench.

1. The Union of India has preferred this appeal by special leave against the judgment and order of the High Court of Delhi dated 3 August 1995 in Civil Writ Petition No. 245 of 1986 whereby the High Court allowed the writ petition filed by the respondent herein and while setting aside the order of dismissal passed by the Court Martial after trial, directed his reinstatement in the same post which he held when he was dismissed, but made his continuation in the same post subject to medical fitness. It also directed payment of 50 per cent of the back wages to the respondent from the date of dismissal till the date of the judgment.

2. The case of the respondent in the writ petition was that he was commissioned in the Indian Air Force on 27 June, 1970 and was appointed to the substantive rank of Flight Lieutenant on 27 June 1976. In the year 1976 he was posted at Udhampur. In the course of his duties he found certain irregularities in the matter of transportation of explosives, which were being transported piecemeal at higher rates. He, therefore, brought this to the notice of the authorities and pointed out that Air Marshal Dilbagh Singh had passed orders, which were beyond his jurisdiction and financial powers resulting in loss to the Union of India. He claimed that on account of his alertness and fearlessness in pointing out these irregularities, the Union of India saved a considerable amount. However, by this act of his he incurred the wrath of Air Marshal Dilbagh Singh who instructed his subordinate officers to "fix" him. He was illegally and improperly admitted in the Psychiatric Ward between 15 June 1979 and 10 July 1979 and thereafter between 22 August 1979 and 19 October 1979.

3. The case of the respondent was that on June 18, 1982 Wing Commander S L Gupta directed him to undergo an examination by the Medical Board on June 21, 1982 with a view to his re-categorization of last medical category. This order was patently illegal and, therefore, the respondent did not obey the order. On account of his disobedience of the order passed by the Wing Commander, a General Court Martial was ordered to try him on the charge of disobeying the lawful command given by his superior officer and also for improper conduct prejudicial to the good order and Air Force discipline. Accordingly the respondent was charged of offences punishable under sections 41(2) and 65 of the Air Force Act, 1950 (hereinafter referred to as 'the Act'). According to the respondent the

proceedings before the General Court Martial were conducted illegally and improperly and in breach of law inasmuch as the respondent was denied legal assistance in the Court Martial proceedings even though he was charged of a serious offence which, on proof, entailed a sentence of imprisonment for a term which could extend to 14 years under section 41(2) and 7 years under Section 65 of the Act. Moreover he was denied copies of the day to day proceedings which were essential for his defence. He was also denied a fair opportunity to examine witnesses in defence. The General Court Martial proceeded to try the respondent and ultimately found him guilty by its verdict pronounced on 21 June 1983. The General Court Martial imposed the sentence of dismissal from service. The appeal preferred by the respondent to the Central Government was dismissed on 14 January 1985 which compelled him to file the writ petition challenging the Court Martial proceedings and praying for a declaration that the order passed by the General Court Martial was null and void. He also prayed for all consequential benefits including compensation for illegal detention in Psychiatric Ward and for his illegal arrest on 21 June 1983.

4. The Union of India controverted the allegations made in the Writ Petition and at the threshold took the objection that the question regarding his illegal confinement in Psychiatric Ward and his illegal arrest were barred by the principle of constructive *res judicata* as he had moved several writ petitions and special leave petitions earlier raising those contentions but had failed in each one of them. It was submitted that the GCM conducted the proceedings in accordance with law and there was no breach of a statutory provision or breach of principle of natural justice. The order of Wing Commander S L Gupta was a lawful order and its disobedience by the respondent attracted the provisions of section 41 of the Act which made it an offence punishable with a term of imprisonment which may extend to 14 years.

5. The High Court rejected the contention of the respondent that the order passed by Wing Commander was an illegal order and that its disobedience did not amount to a disobedience of a lawful order for purposes of section 41 of the Air Force Act. Relying upon the judgment of the Supreme Court in *Ranjit Thakur v. Union of India* (1987) 4 SCC 611 it was held that the said order of Wing Commander Gupta was not an illegal order and that order had been issued bona fide and in public interest.

6. The High Court also rejected the contention of the respondent that the orders directing him to appear before the Medical Board, as well as the trial before the General Court Martial, were mala fide acts committed at

the instance of Air Marshal Dilbagh Singh. It noticed that it was sometime in the year 1976 that the respondent claimed to have exposed some mal practice which cast a reflection on Air Marshal Dilbagh Singh. The General Court Martial proceedings were initiated in the year 1983. The submission, that the action was malafide, was therefore, farfetched. Moreover Air Marshal Dilbagh Singh against whom mala fide was alleged was not even a party in the writ petition. The General Court Martial proceedings were initiated in the year 1983. The submission, that the action was malafide, was therefore, farfetched. Moreover Air Marshal Dilbagh Singh against whom mala fide was alleged was not even a party in the writ petition. The submission was, therefore, rejected.

7. The High Court then proceeded to consider the submission urged before it that an illegality had been committed in as much as the petitioner was deprived of his fundamental right by not being permitted to be represented by a counsel of his choice at the State expense in the Court Martial proceedings. The High Court observed in this regard that it is a fundamental right of an Indian citizen to have assistance of a legal expert when he is to face a trial for an offence punishable with imprisonment, as his personal liberty is at stake. If such an accused was not in a position to engage an advocate at his own cost, then it becomes the fundamental duty of the State to provide him legal assistance at the cost of the State. Reliance was placed on the judgment of this Court in *Suk Das v. Union Territory of Arunachal Pradesh* AIR 1986 SC 991 to support the view that the accused has a fundamental right under Article 21 of the Constitution of India to obtain free legal service at the cost of the State, if he is unable to engage the services of a lawyer on account of poverty or indigence. The High Court noticed that in the instant case as soon as the respondent was intimated about the constitution of General Court Martial to try him, he made an application to the President of India on 2 May 1983 bringing to his notice his inability to engage an advocate at his own cost and requested that he may be provided funds for engaging an advocate to defend him in the said General Court Martial. A copy of this application was also given to the GCM. Moreover, since the respondent apprehended that the other subordinate officers may not be in a position to give him proper and necessary assistance in defending him on account of their fear of Air Marshal Dilbagh Singh, his request to have an advocate for defending him, in view of his apprehension, could not be said to be unreasonable or improper.

8. The Union of India on the other hand contended that neither in the Air

Force Rules nor in the Air Force Act is there has any provision to appoint a legal practitioner at State expense to defend the accused before a Court Martial and, therefore, such a request could not be granted. The Rules only provide that an accused may be represented by any officer subject to Air Force laws who shall be called the 'defending officer' or assisted by any person whose services he may be able to procure who shall be called the 'friend of the accused'. The submission urged on behalf of the Union of India was rejected by the High Court on the reasoning that even if there was no such provision in the Act or the Rules, the principles laid down by the Supreme Court in the case of *Suk Das* (supra) were applicable and, therefore, the respondent had a fundamental right under Article 21 of the Constitution of India to be represented by a legal practitioner. Article 21 commanded that no person shall be deprived of his personal liberty except in accordance with the procedure established by law and, therefore, it followed that when a person was to be prosecuted, he must be afforded sufficient opportunity to defend himself and, consequently, he must be given legal aid. Failure to provide such legal aid vitiated the trial and in these circumstances the trial was not proper and legal.

9. The learned Judge further observed that Rule 102 of the Air Force Rules which provided for an accused being represented by a 'defending officer' or a 'friend of the accused' hardly satisfied the test of giving proper opportunity to the accused to defend himself. The prosecution was conducted by a prosecutor before the General Court Martial and the Judge Advocate is appointed to assist the Court. The Judge Advocate is an officer belonging to the department of the Chief Legal Adviser or an officer approved by the Chief Legal Adviser. The role of the Judge Advocate is to explain to the Court the legal provisions in order to assist the Court to come to the right conclusion. Thereafter the High Court observed:

> "In the instant case there was a prosecutor for the prosecution and the Judge Advocate was also appointed. The Judge Advocate always represents the Chief Legal Advisor in a Court Martial as per the provisions of Section 111 of the Air Force Act. Thus, the prosecution had the aid of a prosecutor as well as a Judge Advocate whereas in the instant case though the petitioner was insisting to have appointment of a Civil Advocate, the same was not appointed. No doubt initially a Defending Officer was helping the petitioner but he had also withdrawn in the midst of the trial. But merely because the petitioner was given the assistance of the Defending Officer, it could not be said that the petitioner and the prosecution were in equal position.

In view of the presence of the prosecutor and the assistance of Judge Advocate, the non-appointment of a Civil Advocate for the petitioner has put the petitioner in an unequal position."

10. The High Court, therefore, held that the denial of petitioner's request for being represented by an advocate resulted in miscarriage of justice, particularly in a case where the prosecution itself alleged that the accused was suffering psychologically to some extent. Refusal of any legal aid from a legal expert or a person having expertise in law to such an accused amounted to miscarriage of justice. The High Court was of the view that the respondent was handicapped in conducting his defence which was obvious from the fact that when he was required to cross-examine the witnesses he requested the Court Martial to grant him time so that he could consult his advocate in this regard. For the same reason the respondent could not explain to the Court Martial the relevancy of the witnesses whom he wished to summon. He apprehended that he may disclose his defence if he attempted to explain the relevancy of the concerned witnesses and that would cause serious prejudice to him in the trial.

11. It was pointed out by the Union of India before the High Court that in his application to the President of India, the respondent has asked for appointment of the two advocates named therein. An accused cannot insist on having an advocate of his choice to defend him at State expense. The High Court observed that even if an Advocate of his choice could not be given, the State was bound to provide him legal assistance and this could be done if a panel of advocates was prepared by the State and the respondent was called upon to make his selection. The High Court, therefore, concluded that the non-appointment of an advocate to defend the accused resulted in miscarriage of justice and, therefore, the trial of the petitioner stood vitiated.

12. Another grievance of the respondent was that he had given two lists of witnesses, the first consisting of 24 names and the second of 7 names. But when he requested the General Court Martial to summon those witnesses the Judge Advocate advised the General Court Martial that the respondent should be asked to explain the relevancy of those witnesses and accordingly the respondent was called upon to disclose the relevancy of each witness and on what point he wished to examine him. The High Court held that technically as well as legally the direction of the Court Martial was proper and correct, but the Court Martial ought not to have acted too technically since the respondent was not in a position to state the relevancy of the witnesses without disclosing his defence and, therefore, apprehended that

he while attempting to disclose the relevancy of witnesses may disclose his defence to his prejudice.

13. The High Court noticed that the respondent, when called upon to explain the relevancy of the witnesses, stated that he would write letters to the witnesses who were out of Delhi. They were officers of the Indian Air Force, some of them retired and some of them in service. Only after getting their replies, he could state their relevancy to the Court and also whether he wanted to examine any of them. He sought an adjournment on 3 June 1983 and prayed that the matter be adjourned till 17 June 1983. However, he was granted an adjournment only for 4 days. The High Court observed that it failed to understand how the General Court Martial expected that the respondent would be in a position to contact witnesses residing at Bombay, Bangalore etc. and get their replies in 4 days. Thus by adjourning the hearing on 3 June 1983 to 7 June 1983 the General Court Martial denied reasonable opportunity to the respondent to examine his defence witnesses.

14. The High Court then considered the complaint of the respondent that he was not supplied copies of the proceedings taking place every day despite his repeated requests. The non supply of copies of evidence and proceedings amounted to denial of reasonable opportunity to the accused to defend himself and was also against the principles of natural justice. The High Court accepting the submission held that the denial of copies of the evidence and proceedings recorded every day, to the petitioner also resulted in denying reasonable opportunity to him to defend.

15. Lastly the High Court considered the grievance of the respondent that the prosecutor, the Judge Advocate and the members of the General Court Martial met behind close doors and changed the recorded proceedings and evidence after careful editing. Portions favourable to the respondent were removed and the depositions were changed to suit the prosecution and the original statements destroyed. The High Court examined portions of the typed record of proceedings produced by the petitioner and found that on the same date some portion of the statement of the Judge Advocate as well as the witnesses were typed on different typewriters. The High Court also noticed that the evidence of witnesses was recorded by the Court in long hand and it was not dictated directly to the typists and the statements were subsequently typed by the typists. Even the signatures of the witnesses were not taken nor did the signatures of the Court appear on those documents. The High Court, thereafter, concluded:

Therefore, in these circumstances, the procedure followed by the Court in conducting the trial in question is also not proper as the original statements of the witnesses recorded by the Court in its own hand in the open court are not preserved and when the petitioner is alleging that there was tempering with the evidence recorded, it has become very difficult for us to come to a conclusion that the allegations made by the petitioner are baseless or false in the absence of the original record.

16. In view of these findings the High Court held that the trial of the petitioner was vitiated and consequently the punishment awarded to him was set aside.

17. Shri Raju Ramachandran, learned Additional Solicitor General appearing on behalf of the appellant-Union of India assailed the judgment of the High Court and submitted that the finding recorded by the High Court that the failure of the appellant to provide a counsel to the respondent at State expense resulted in breach of the fundamental right of the respondent guaranteed under Article 21 of the Constitution of India, was recorded by the High Court in ignorance of the provisions of Article 33 of the Constitution of India which expressly empowers the Parliament to modify the rights conferred by Part III of the Constitution in their application to the members of the armed forces. The High Court was, therefore, in error in not considering the provisions of the Act, as a law made by Parliament under Article 33 of the Constitution of India modifying and restricting the right conferred by Article 21 of the Constitution of India. In a Court Martial trial the appellant was not required to provide a counsel at State expense to the respondent, whose rights were governed by the provisions of the Air Force Act and the Rules. They provided that the appellant may be represented by an officer called "the defending officer" or assisted by any person whose services he may be able to procure who shall be called "the friend of the accused." The respondent was in fact permitted to engage a counsel at his own expense but he failed to do so. Even the friend of the accused, had to withdraw at the request of the respondent. The respondent cannot be, therefore, heard to say that prejudice was caused to him on account of non-compliance of any of the provisions of the Act or the Rules. He further submitted that in recording a finding that the respondent and the prosecution were not equally placed in the proceedings before the Court Martial, the High Court completely misunderstood the duties of the Judge Advocate and the role played by him in proceeding before the Court Martial. He also assailed the other findings recorded by the High Court.

18. Learned counsel appearing on behalf of the respondent submitted that the findings recorded by the High Court are unassailable and he urged further grounds, which were not urged before the High Court, to support the conclusion reached by the High Court.

19. It is indeed surprising that while considering the submissions urged on behalf of the respondent alleging the breach of his fundamental right under Article 21 of the Constitution of India, the High Court neither noticed the provisions of Article 33 of the Constitution of India nor does it appear to have been brought to its notice. **Article 33 of the Constitution of India expressly empowers the Parliament to determine by law the extent to which any of the rights conferred by Part III of the Constitution, in their application, inter alia, to the members of the armed forces, shall be restricted or abrogated to ensure the proper discharge of their duties and the maintenance of discipline among them. The Parliament can, therefore, in exercise of powers conferred by Article 33 of the Constitution of India restrict or abrogate the fundamental rights guaranteed under Part III of the Constitution in their application to the members of the armed forces. It, therefore, follows that if any provision of the Act or the Rules restricts or abrogates any right guaranteed under Part III of the Constitution of India, it cannot be challenged on the ground that it is violative of the fundamental right as guaranteed under Part III. It is no doubt true that the restriction or abrogation is dependent on Parliamentary legislation and only a law passed by virtue of Article 33 can override Articles 21 and 22 of the Constitution of India.** The law on the subject is fairly well settled and we may only refer to some of the authorities on the subject. In *Ram Sarup v. Union of India* AIR 1965 SC 247 a Constitution Bench of this Court upholding the submission urged by the Learned Attorney General observed:

"The learned Attorney General has urged that the entire Act has been enacted by Parliament and if any of the provisions of the Act is not consistent with the provisions of any of the articles in Part III of the Constitution, it must be taken that to the extent of the inconsistency Parliament had modified the fundamental rights under those articles in their application to the person subject to that Act. Any such provision in the Act is as much law as the entire Act. We agree that each and every provision of the Act is a law made by Parliament and that if any such provision tends to affect the fundamental right under Part III of the Constitution, that provision does not, on that account, become void, as it must be taken that Parliament has thereby, in the exercise of its power under Article 33 of the Constitution, made the requisite modification to affect the respective fundamental right. We are however of opinion that the provisions of section 125 of the Act are not discriminatory and do not infringe the provisions of Article 14 of the Constitution. It is not disputed that the persons to whom the provisions of section 125 apply do form a distinct class. They apply to all those persons who are subject to Act and such persons are specified in section 2 of the Act."

20. In *Lt Col Prithi Pal Singh Bedi v. Union of India* (1982) 3 SCC 140 this Court observed:

"Article 33 confers power on the Parliament to determine to what extent any of the rights conferred by Part III shall, in their application to the members of the Armed Forces, be restricted or abrogated so as to ensure the proper discharge of duties and maintenance of discipline amongst them. Article 33 does not obligate that Parliament must specifically adumbrate each fundamental right enshrined in Part III and to specify in the law enacted in exercise of the power conferred by Article 33 the degree of restriction or total abrogation of each right. That would be reading into Article 33 a requirement which it does not enjoin. In fact, after the Constitution came into force, the power to legislate in respect of any item must be referable to an entry in the relevant list. Entry 2 in List I: Naval, Military and Air Forces; any other Armed Forces of the Union, would enable Parliament to enact the Army Act and armed with this power the Act was enacted in July 1950. It has to be enacted by the Parliament subject to the requirements of Part III of the Constitution read with Article 33 which itself forms part of Part III. **Therefore, every provision of the Army Act enacted by the Parliament, if in conflict with the fundamental rights conferred by Part III, shall have to be read subject to Article 33 as being enacted with a view to either restricting or abrogating other fundamental rights to the extent of inconsistency or repugnancy between Part III of the Constitution and the Army Act.**"

21. This Court referred to the observations in *Ram Sarup* (supra) and held that the question was no longer *res integra* in view of the decision of the Constitution Bench. The Court, therefore, rejected the submission that the law which prescribed procedure for trial of offences by Court Martial must satisfy the requirement of Article 21 because to the extent the procedure

is prescribed by law and if it stands in derogation of Article 21, to that extent Article 21 in its application to the armed forced is modified by enactment of the procedure in the Army Act itself. The Court noticed that there operate two conflicting public interests; the maintaining of discipline in the Armed Forces to safeguard national security, to ensure enjoyment by the people of India of their fundamental rights, and the right of members of Armed Forces themselves to fundamental rights.

22. In *Delhi Police Non-Gazetted Karmachari Sangh v. Union of India* (1987) 1 SCC 115 the challenge to the Act and the Rules impugned therein was on the ground of infringement of fundamental right guaranteed under Article 19(1)(c) read with Article 19(4) of the Constitution of India. It was argued in that case that recognition of the Association carries with it the right to continue the Association as such. It is a right flowing from the fact of recognition. To derecognise the Association in effect offends against the freedom of association. This Court held:

"13. That the Sangh and its members come within the ambit of Article 33 cannot be disputed. The provisions of the Act and Rules taking away or abridging the freedom of association have been made strictly in conformity with Article 33. The right under Article 19(1)(c) is not absolute. Article 19(4) specifically empowers the State to make any law to fetter, abridge or abrogate any of the rights under Article 19(1)(c) in the interest of public order and other considerations. Thus the attack against the Act and Rules can be successfully met with reference to these two articles as members of the police force, like the appellants herein, are at a less advantageous position, curtailment of whose rights under Article 19(1)(c) comes squarely within Article 33 in the interest of discipline and public order."

23. Having regard to the authorities it must be held that the provisions of the Act cannot be challenged on the ground that they infringe the fundamental right guaranteed to the respondent under Article 21 of the Constitution of India. Since the Air Force Act is a law duly enacted by Parliament in exercise of its plenary legislative jurisdiction read with 33 of the Constitution of India, the same cannot be held to be invalid merely because it has the effect of restricting or abrogating the right guaranteed under Article 21 of the Constitution of India or for that reason under any of the provisions of Chapter III of the Constitution.

24. It was not disputed before the High Court, nor was it disputed before us, that the Act and the Rules framed thereunder do not oblige the State/

Union of India to engage at the cost of the State a counsel for the officer who faces his trial before the Court Martial. The High Court relying on the judgment of this Court in *Suk Das v. Union Territory of Arunachal Pradesh* (supra) held that **the respondent had a fundamental right under Article 21 of the Constitution of India to obtain free legal service at the cost of the State if he was unable to engage the services of a lawyer on account of poverty or indigence. It clearly erred in applying the principles laid down in that case. That was not a case dealing with a member of the armed forces governed by a law enacted by Parliament, which restricted or abrogated the right with a view to ensure the proper discharge of duties and the maintenance of discipline among members of the armed forces, and which the Parliament was authorized to enact by virtue of Article 33 of the Constitution.**

25. We also fail to understand how the respondent can claim that he was unable to engage the services of a counsel on account of poverty or indigence. The respondent was an officer of the Indian Air Force and was holding the rank of Flight Lieutenant. He had served the Indian Air Force for many years. The mere fact that he wrote to the President of India stating that he was not in a position to engage an Advocate at his own cost, was not sufficient to hold that he was unable to do so on account of poverty or indigence. In any event, there being no provision under the Act or the Rules to provide a defence counsel at a State expense, the respondent could not claim such a right *de hors* the Act and the Rules on the ground of Article 21 of the Constitution of India which stood restricted by the Act.

26. We may notice at this stage that it is not as if the respondent was not permitted to engage a counsel at his own expense. The Court Martial permitted him to engage a counsel at his own expense. After seeking several adjournments on this ground, the respondent ultimately informed the Court Martial that he was not in a position to engage counsel at his own expense. In view of these facts the respondent cannot place any reliance on the judgment of this Court in *Major General Inder Jit Kumar v. Union of India* (1997) 9 SCC 1. In that case, as was submitted by the respondent, time was given to the appellant to engage a defence counsel. In the instant case, as we have observed earlier, the respondent was also given such an opportunity but he did not engage a defence counsel of his choice at his own expense. Moreover in *Major General Inder Jit Kumar* (supra) the Court was not called upon to consider the claim of the appellant therein to be represented by a counsel of his choice at State expense. In fact the respondent has no such right under the Act. The respondent does not even

have a right to claim an advance from the State for engaging a counsel at his own expense. In *Union of India v. Major A Hussain* (1998) 1 SCC 537 a grievance was made before this Court by the respondent therein that since further advance of Rs 15,000/- was not given to him to engage another defence counsel he could not effectively defend his case. Repelling the argument this Court observed:

> "The High Court, however, failed to take notice of the fact that the respondent was not entitled to any advance for the purpose of engaging the defence counsel and earlier as a special case an advance of Rs10,000 had been sanctioned. No Rule or Army Instruction has been shown under which the respondent was entitled to an advance."

27. It is futile ....

28. So far as the facts of this case are concerned it is clear from the record that the respondent was informed that he was not entitled to a civil defence counsel of his choice at State expense but he was given the option of engaging a civil counsel of his choice under own arrangement and at his own expense. He was also informed that he could give the name of any service officer whom he wished to have as his defending officer and whose services will be made available to him free of cost. Upon a written request of the respondent the services of Sqn Leader V K Sawhney, an officer with legal qualifications having substantial experience as a defending officer in trial by Court Martial was made available to him as "the friend of the accused" by the convening authority. The respondent was also advised that he could accept the services of the said officer as his defending officer, if he so desired. Inspite of the options given to the respondent and inspite of several adjournments, the respondent did not engage a counsel at his own expense. When the defence case commenced, the respondent dispensed with the services of the "friend of the accused", whose services he had asked for in writing.

29. We are, therefore, satisfied in the facts and circumstances of the case that the provisions of the Act and the Rules were scrupulously followed in the conduct of the Court Martial proceedings and the respondent chose to defend himself without seeking the help of the defending officer or the friend of the accused. It, therefore, does not lie in his mouth to complain that he was prejudiced in his defence on account of the State not providing him defence counsel at State expense. The finding recorded by the High Court is, therefore, wholly unsustainable.

30. The High Court then considered the provisions of Rule 102 of the

Rules and held that merely providing for the accused being represented by the defending officer or friend of the accused hardly satisfied the test of giving proper opportunity to the accused to defend himself. According to the High Court the prosecution was assisted by a prosecutor and the Judge Advocate whereas the respondent was insisting for engagement of an advocate at State expense, which was not granted. No doubt a defending officer had been given to the petitioner but he had also withdrawn in the midst of the trial. It cannot, therefore, be said that the petitioner and the prosecutor were in equal position.

31. The High Court erroneously referred to the respondent being assisted by a defending officer when in fact he was being assisted by a "friend of the accused", who was nominated at his own request. As noticed earlier, it was the respondent who dispensed with the assistance of the friend of the accused and, therefore, he cannot make a grievance of it. But the approach of the High Court belies a complete misconception of the functions and duties of the Judge Advocate and the role played by him in a Court Martial proceeding. The High Court proceeded on the assumption that the Judge Advocate, who represents the Chief Legal Adviser in Court Martial proceedings, is there to assist the prosecution and he alongwith the prosecutor constitute a team against which is pitted the hapless accused in the trial. In doing so the High Court completely misdirected itself and laboured under a complete mis-apprehension of the duties and the role of the Judge Advocate.

32. Under Rule 110 of the Air Force Rules, 1969 an officer, who is disqualified for sitting as a Court Martial, shall be disqualified for acting as Judge Advocate at that Court Martial. This rule ensures that the Judge Advocate also enjoys the same impartiality as the President and Members of the Court Martial. The powers and duties of the Judge Advocate have been laid down in Rule 111 which provides that the prosecutor or the accused, is at all times, entitled to his opinion on any question of law relative to the charge or trial, whether he is or out of court, subject, when he is in court to the permission of the court. He is responsible for informing the court of any informality or irregularity in the proceedings. Whether consulted or not, he shall inform the convening officer and the court of any informality in the proceedings or defect in the charge, or in the constitution of the court, and shall give his advice on any matter before the court. At the conclusion of the case he shall, unless both he and the court consider it unnecessary, sum up the evidence and give his opinion upon the legal bearing of the case before the court proceeds to deliberate upon its finding. The Judge Advocate has,

equally with the Presiding Officer, the duty of taking care that the accused does not suffer any disadvantage in consequence of his position as such or of his ignorance or incapacity to examine or cross-examine witnesses or otherwise, and may, for that purpose, with the permission of the court, call witnesses and put questions to witnesses, which appear to him necessary or desirable to elicit the truth. In fulfilling his duties, the Judge Advocate must be careful to maintain an entirely impartial position. Rule 111, therefore, which lays down the powers and duties of the Judge Advocate leaves no room for doubt that though a participant in the proceeding, he is not partisan. He holds a brief neither for the prosecutor nor for the defence. He must guide the Court Martial when questions of law arise and render his honest opinion regardless of the consideration whether it helps the prosecution or the defence. He is neither a friend of the prosecutor nor an adversary of the defence. He has to maintain an entirely impartial position charged with the duty of taking care that the accused does not suffer any disadvantage in consequence of his position as such. The Judge Advocate performs a solemn obligation to advise honestly and to guide dispassionately the Court Martial with the objective to ensure a fair trial and justice according to law. The duties with which he is charged and the impartiality expected by him must assure the person being tried that he shall not suffer any disadvantage on account of his position as such and that whenever necessary intervention by Judge Advocate shall ensure even handed justice. We, therefore, do not agree with the conclusion reached by the High Court that the procedural safeguards under the Act do not provide a level playing field and that the dice is heavily loaded against the accused in a trial before the Court Martial. We cannot lose sight of the fact that even the Judge Advocate is administered an oath/affirmation before he enters upon his office. He is bound by his oath to carry out the duties of his office in accordance with the Act and the Rules without partiality, favour or affection and not on any account, at any time, whatsoever, disclose or discover the vote or opinion on any matter of any particular member of the Court Martial, unless required to give evidence thereof by a court of justice or a Court Martial in due course of law. The impartiality of the Judge Advocate, is thus, ensured and it can never be contended that in the scheme of the Act and the Rules the role of the Judge Advocate is only to assist the prosecutor to secure the conviction of the accused.

33. The next finding of the High Court is with regard to the approach adopted by the Court Martial in regard to the relevancy of witnesses, which the respondent was called upon to disclose. The High Court itself found that there was nothing wrong in the Court calling upon the respondent to

disclose the relevancy of each witness and the point on which the respondent wished to examine him. The High Court, however, went on to observe that the Court ought not to have acted too technically since the respondent was not in a position to state the relevancy of the witnesses without jeopardizing his defence. The reason given by the High Court does not impress us. If the direction of the Court Martial was in accordance with law, there could be no justification to hold that obedience of law itself resulted in prejudice to the respondent. In our view, in the facts and circumstances of the case, the Court Martial was fully justified in calling upon the respondent to satisfy the Court that it was necessary to examine those witnesses in the trial. We say so because a large number of witnesses were sought to be examined. Many of them were Air Force officers, which included some former Chief of the Air Staff as also the Chief of the Air Staff. One fails to understand what possibly could be the relevancy of these witnesses when the charge against the respondent was that he had disobeyed the order of his superior officer by not complying with the direction to submit himself to a medical examination by the Board. To us it appears that the request was not even bona fide and was a mere delaying tactics. This apprehension appears to be justified in view of the fact that the respondent asked for adjournment of the case by 14 days. The purpose for which adjournment was sought was that he would be writing to the witnesses concerned and only after getting their response he would decide whether to examine them before the Court Martial as his witnesses. This depicts the peculiar approach of the respondent. He prayed for an adjournment not on the ground that there was some difficulty in producing these witnesses on a particular day, but on the ground that he had not communicated with them and only after communicating with them and getting their response, he would be in a position to tell the Court whether he would examine them and if so, which of them, as his witnesses. On such a ground, the Court Martial would have been justified in rejecting the prayer but the Court Martial granted him 4 days time and accordingly adjourned the proceedings at his request. The High Court has found fault with the Court Martial in not giving to the respondent sufficient time to get replies from the witnesses. It has gone to the extent of holding that the Court Martial denied reasonable opportunity to the respondent to examine his defence witnesses. We are of the view that this finding is wholly unsustainable.

34. In the first instance Rule 89 of the Air Force Rules provides that when a court is once assembled and the accused had been arraigned, the court shall, subject to the provisions of Rule 88, continue the trial from day to day unless it appears to the court that an adjournment is necessary for

the ends of justice, or that such continuance is impracticable. The normal rule, therefore, is that the trial must continue from day to day and this is with a view to expeditious disposal of the matter before the Court Martial. Unfortunately the practice of seeking unnecessary adjournments has become rampant with the resultant delay in disposal of matters before adjudicatory authorities and the courts. This practice has been deprecated by this Court. In *Union of India v. Major A Hussain* (Supra), this Court observed (SCC p. 649, para 23):

> "Proceedings of a court-martial are not to be compared with the proceedings in a criminal court under the Code of Criminal Procedure where adjournments have become a matter of routine though that is also against the provisions of law."

35. We, therefore, hold that no illegality was committed either in calling upon the respondent to explain the relevancy of the witnesses or in refusing a long adjournment, on the request of the respondent.

36. In the facts and circumstances of the case the grievance of the respondent that he was denied reasonable opportunity to examine his defence witnesses is baseless.

37. The next grievance of the respondent which found favour with the High Court is that he was not supplied copies of the proceedings every day, though he had repeatedly asked for the same. The appellant pointed out that neither under the Air Force Act, 1950 nor the Air Force Rules, 1969 is there any provision for supply of copies of the evidence and the proceedings every day. But there is a provision which permits the charged officer to inspect the record of proceedings. Therefore, the request for supply of copies every day was not tenable. The High Court held that merely because there are no provisions in the Act and the Rules to supply copies, the Court cannot deny the copies of evidence and the record of proceedings to the accused and such denial amounts to denial of reasonable opportunity to defend himself, as it was in violation of the principles of natural justice.

38. Rule 125 of the Air Force Rules, 1969 provides as follows:

> "125. **Right of person tried to copies of proceedings**. - Every person tried by a court martial shall be entitled on demand, at any time after the confirmation of the finding and sentence and before the proceedings are destroyed, to obtain free of cost from the officer or person having the custody of the proceedings, a copy thereof,

including the proceedings upon revision, if any."

39. Rule 100 is as follows:

> "100. **Custody and inspection of proceedings**. The proceedings shall be deemed to be in the custody of the judge advocate (if any), or, if there is none, of the presiding officer, but may, with proper precaution for their safety, be inspected by the members of the court, the prosecutor and accused, respectively, at all reasonable times before the court is closed, to consider the finding."

40. It will thus be seen that there is a specific provision in the Rules which provides for copies of the proceedings to the person tried by the Court Martial free of cost at any time after the confirmation of the finding and sentence and before the proceedings are destroyed. Clearly, therefore, the respondent was not entitled to a copy of the proceedings day to day as claimed by him. However, Rule 100 in terms provides that the proceedings may be inspected by the accused at all reasonable times before the court is closed to consider the finding. Nothing, therefore, prevented the respondent from inspecting the proceedings and preparing his defence. Rule 100 itself incorporates the principle of natural justice by giving to the respondent an opportunity to go through the proceedings and for this purpose to inspect the same at all reasonable times. This meets the requirement of principles of natural justice and the respondent cannot complain on the ground that he was not given a copy of the proceedings day to day. The High Court was, therefore, clearly wrong in coming to the conclusion that the principles of natural justice were violated by non supply of copies of proceedings day to day.

41. The next allegation of the respondent which was considered by the High Court was to the effect that the Judge Advocate, the Prosecutor and the Court Martial were meeting in closed chamber and then the original depositions were being changed to favour the prosecution and after removing portions favourable to the respondent, the statements of witnesses were being re-typed and original statements were destroyed. The High Court observed that the Court was recording the proceedings in long hand and thereafter it was being typed. Some pages of such typed record showed that some portions of the submissions of the Judge Advocate as well as the witnesses were typed on different typewriters. From this the High Court jumped to the conclusion that the procedure followed by the Court in conducting the trial was not proper as the original statements of the witnesses recorded by the Court in its own hand in the open Court were not preserved and

the respondent's allegation that records were tampered with could not be said to be baseless or false. The respondent relied upon an affidavit filed before the High Court by one Shri H S Siddhu who attended the Court Martial proceeding and stated that once he visited the room next to the Court Martial Room and he found typists typing Court Martial records. He found that the proceedings made by the Judge Advocate in manuscript were being typed by one of the typists. The said manuscript had several amendments made in red ink and even a whole para had been redrafted. Thereafter the respondent had requested the Court Martial to obtain his signatures on each and every page of the manuscript proceedings on each day and to give him a copy of the proceedings at the end of the day but that request was refused. The respondent has not filed any affidavit of his own but has chosen to file an affidavit of a former officer, which also does not clearly establish that the records were being tampered with. Obviously when the Judge Advocate records proceedings in long hand, the same has to be given a final shape before it becomes a part of the record. That cannot be said to be tampering with the record. Moreover the mere fact that copies of the proceedings were typed on two different typewriters does not necessarily lead to the conclusion that the evidence was changed or the record was tampered. Very often, with a view to quick disposal of work, the material to be typed may be distributed to more than one typist. We, therefore, find no force in the submission that the members of the Court Martial, the Judge Advocate and the Prosecutor tampered the record of proceedings with a view to prejudice the case of the respondent. No specific instance was pointed out to us to substantiate this charge.

42. We shall now take up for consideration the submissions urged before us, which were not urged before the High Court.

43. It was submitted that the power to convene a Court Martial cannot be delegated. In the instant case it was contended by the learned counsel for the respondent that the order convening the Court Martial was signed by Air Cdr D S Sabhikhi on behalf of the Air Marshal. The heading of the document which is Annexure-R is as follows:

"Orders by Air Marshal D A Lafotaine, AVSM, VM, Air Officer in-charge Personnel, Air Headquarters, IAF."

44. A ground was taken before the High Court that the convening of the General Court Martial was signed by an officer, in whose name no delegation or such authority had ever been made. In reply thereto the appellant had submitted that the convening order was signed by the said

officer on behalf of the Air Officer in-charge Personnel (AOP), who had after due application of mind, issued the order for convening the above Court Martial. It was not disputed before us that the AOP was empowered to convene a Court Martial. The only question which, therefore, requires consideration is whether the order convening the General Court Martial was passed by the AOP and it was only formally communicated under signatures of Air Cdr concerned or whether the Air Cdr, named therein, who was not empowered, himself passed the convening order. With a view to avoid any controversy on this factual position, we directed the appellant to produce before us the original file. We have perused the file and we find that the order for convening the General Court Martial was approved by Air Marshal D A Lafotaine, AOP. There is, therefore, no force in the submission that the convening order was unauthorized and, therefore, illegal.

45. The next submission urged before us, which does not appear to have been urged before the High Court, was that the order given by Wing Commander S L Gupta on 18 June 1982 was itself illegal and, therefore, the respondent was not bound to obey that order. It was argued before us that there was an undertaking by the appellant before this Court with regard to the stay of medical board proceedings, which was due on 1 May 1980. No such recorded undertaking has been brought to our notice and it is sought to be argued on the basis of the counter-affidavit filed in the instant proceedings before the High Court that even the appellant understood that an oral undertaking had been given to the Court not to hold a medical board till 1 May 1980. It is not possible for us to accept the ipse dixit of the respondent that there was an oral undertaking given to this Court. All undertakings given to this Court are recorded and even when an oral understanding is reached, one would find some reference to it in the proceedings of the Court. In the absence of any such material on record the contention of the respondent that the appellant was bound by the oral undertaking not to proceed with the medical board must be rejected. In any event even if it is accepted, that an oral undertaking was given, it was only to the effect that no medical board will be held till 1May 1980. There is no undertaking given thereafter. The order of Wing Commander Gupta was issued on 18 June 1982, more than two years later.

46. It was urged before us for the first time that the prayer made by the respondent on 7th June, 1983 for examining himself as a defence witness was refused. The respondent contends that the said prayer was recorded in the proceedings. However, no proceeding was brought to our notice

wherein it was recorded that the respondent shall not be allowed to examine as a defence witness. On the contrary, it appears from the extract of proceedings of the Court Martial, referred to by the appellant in its counter affidavit, that at page 180 of the proceedings the following was recorded:

> "The court also decides to inform the accused that since he has not brought out any fresh points in his submission and rejoinder, the court decides to proceed further in the interest of justice.
>
> The court is opened and the above decision is announced to the accused in open court. On being asked the accused confirms that he has no witnesses to examine in his defence. The court informs the accused that since he has no witnesses to examine, the defence case may be treated as closed. The accused confirms that he does not wish to examine any witness in his defence and that the defence case is closed."

47. In these circumstances the submission that the respondent was not permitted to examine himself as a defence witness must be rejected.

48. In the result this appeal is allowed, the impugned judgment and order of the High Court of Delhi dated 3 August 1995 is set aside and the Writ Petition being CWP No 245 of 1986 dismissed. There shall be no order as to costs.

11

Mohammed Zubair Corporal v. Union of India (2017) 2 SCC 115, decided on 15 December 2016, Three judge Bench.

1. The Appellant was enrolled as an airman in the Indian Air Force (IAF) on 19 December 2001. On 10 January 2005, the Appellant submitted an application seeking permission to keep a beard on religious grounds, since he is a Muslim. The Air Officer Commanding rejected the application on 1 February 2005 and the Appellant was informed on 9 February 2005 of the rejection, which was on the ground of the Air Headquarters' Policy dated 24 February 2003. On 22 March 2005 the Appellant submitted another application to the Air Officer Commanding seeking reconsideration of the earlier decision.

He was granted an interview with him on 10 June 2005, when he was informed of the necessity to maintain uniformity amongst Air Force personnel because of which his request had been rejected. The Air Officer Commanding, however, addressed a communication dated 23 June 2005 to the Headquarters Maintenance Command (HQMC) seeking a clarification on the legal issues raised by the Appellant. In the meantime on 20 June 2005 the Appellant proceeded on annual leave.When he returned on 1 August 2005, he was found to sport a beard. On 1 August 2005 he was informed by Wing Commander that contrary to Air Force Regulations, he was found to have a beard while in service uniform. The Appellant was instructed to shave off his beard and to report at 0700 hrs on 2 August 2005, failing which it was stated that "severe disciplinary action" would be initiated against him.

The Appellant declined to shave off his beard. Since in the meantime a clarification had been sought from HQMC, he was permitted to grow a beard on a provisional basis until his earlier application was finalized. By a communication dated 26 August 2005 HQMC Nagpur, informed 3 BRD, AF that under the current policy of the Air Force (Air HQ/C 23406/24/PS) dated 24 February 2003 and 9 July 2003 an Airman was not permitted to have a beard on religious grounds. On receipt of this letter, the Appellant was directed to shave off his beard and informed that the provisional permission granted to him on 3 August 2005 was withdrawn.

2. On 17 September 2005 the Appellant filed a writ petition before the Punjab & Haryana High Court in which by an interim order dated 20 September 2005 a Single Judge stayed the operation of the Air Force

Order dated 5 September 2005. The Air force authorities moved the High Court for vacating the interim stay but the application was dismissed on 9 February 2006. A Special Leave Petition was filed before this Court which was disposed of on 28 September 2007 with a request to the High Court to dispose of the petition expeditiously. By an order of the High Court dated 14 July 2008 the writ petition was dismissed. A Letters Patent Appeal was dismissed by the High Court on 31 July 2008. In the meantime, a notice to show cause was issued to the Appellant calling upon him to explain as to why he should not be discharged from service. In reply to the notice, the Appellant asserted his right to retain a beard. The Appellant was eventually discharged from service under Rule 15(2)(g)(ii) of the Air Force Rules 1969 in June 2016.

3. In the writ proceedings before the High Court, which were instituted on 17 September 2005 the Appellant sought the following reliefs:

"a writ of Certiorari or any other appropriate writ, order or direction for quashing of Annexure P-5 vide which the petitioner, a Muslim has been directed to shave his beard by 20 September 2005, the same (Annexure P-5) being illegal, without any sanction of law and in contravention of paragraph 425(b) of the Regulations of the Indian Air Force and policy letters dated 08 May1980 and 10 August 1982 (Annexures P-1 and P-2);

With a further prayer that the operation of the impugned order (Annexure P-5) may kindly be stayed till the disposal of this writ petition since Air Force Regulations and policies explicitly confer upon Muslims a right to sport beard and provide for no discretion to the respondents to take away this right under any circumstance."

The challenge was to the direction issued to the Appellant to shave off his beard on 20 September 2005 on the ground that it was contrary to para 425(b) of the Regulations governing the Indian Air Force and to the policy letters of 8 May 1980 and 10 August 1982.Even prior to the institution of the writ petition, the Appellant had been discharged from service. Strictly speaking a mere challenge to the direction by which he was called upon to shave off his beard would not subserve the cause of the Appellant once he stood discharged from service. Be that as it may, the Division Bench of the High Court by its judgment and order dated 31 July 2008 came to the conclusion that the purpose of para 425(b) is to ensure that the identity of a person is not altered during the course of service so as to render recognition possible.The Division Bench affirmed the judgment of the learned Single

Judge to the effect that maintaining a beard was not an integral part of the religion professed by the Appellant. In the view of the High Court, the matter pertained to the Armed Forces where a certain degree of discipline had to be maintained and the rules and regulations broadly accommodate "the basic interest of various religions in a secular manner".

4. The policy governing the growth of hair, including facial hair, in the Air Force has been enunciated in paragraph 425 of the Air Force Regulations, 1964, and provides as follows:

425. Growth of Hair etc. by Air Force Personnel.

Except as in sub para (b), the hair of the head will be kept neatly cut and trimmed. The hair of airman under detention/sentence will be cut no shorter than is customary/ throughout the service except on medical advice and except where on an application made by the airman he has been permitted to keep long hair. Face will be clean shaven. Whiskers and moustaches, if worn will be moderate length.

Personnel whose religion prohibits the cutting of the hair or shaving of the face of its members will be permitted to grow hair or retain beard. However, such hair and/ or beards will be kept clean, properly dressed and will not be removed except on medical grounds or on application duly approved.

Clause (a) of para 425 mandates firstly, that Air Force personnel must keep their hair neatly cut and trimmed. Secondly, facial hair has to be shaved and every airman must have a clean shaven face. Thirdly, whiskers and moustaches though permitted have to be of a moderate length. The rest of the clause deals with Airmen under detention or sentence with which the present case is not concerned. Clause (b) of para 425, however, stipulates that an airman will be permitted to grow hair or to retain a beard where the religion professed by him prohibits the cutting of hair or shaving of facial hair. In that case, the hair and/or beard must be kept clean and properly dressed and cannot be removed except on medical grounds or on an application which is duly approved. The touchstone for being allowed to grow one's hair or to retain a beard is where there is a religious command which prohibits either the hair being cut or a beard being shaved.

5. The Air Force is a combat force, raised and maintained to secure the nation against hostile forces. The primary aim of maintaining an Air Force is to defend the nation from air operations of nations hostile to India and to advance air operations, should the security needs of the country

322

so require. The Indian Air Force has over eleven thousand officers and one lakh and twenty thousand personnel below officers' rank. For the effective and thorough functioning of a large combat force, the members of the Force must bond together by a sense of Espirit-de-corps, without distinctions of caste, creed, colour or religion.There can be no gainsaying the fact that maintaining the unity of the Force is an important facet of instilling a sense of commitment, and dedication amongst the members of the Force. Every member of the Air Force while on duty is required to wear the uniform and not display any sign or object which distinguishes one from another. Uniformity of personal appearance is quintessential to a cohesive, disciplined and coordinated functioning of an Armed Force. Every Armed Force raised in a civilised nation has its own 'Dress and Deportment' Policy.

6. India is a secular nation in which every religion must be treated with equality. In the context of the Armed Forces, which comprise of men and women following a multitude of faiths the needs of secular India are accommodated by recognising right of worship and by respecting religious beliefs. Yet in a constitutional sense it cannot be overlooked that the overarching necessity of a Force which has been raised to protect the nation is to maintain discipline. That is why the Constitution in the provisions of Article 33 stipulates that Parliament may by law determine to what extent the fundamental rights conferred by Part III shall stand restricted or abrogated in relation inter alia to the members of the Armed Forces so as to ensure the proper discharge of their duties and the maintenance of discipline among them.

Article 33 provides as follows:

> 33. Power of Parliament to modify the rights conferred by this Part in their application to Forces, etc.-- Parliament may, by law, determine to what extent any of the rights conferred by this Part shall, in their application to-

> (a)   the members of the Armed Forces; or

> (b)   the members of the Forces charged with the maintenance of public order; or

> (c)   persons employed in any bureau or other organisation established by the State for purposes of intelligence or counter intelligence; or

> (d)   persons employed in, or in connection with, the

telecommunication systems set up for the purposes of any Force, bureau or organisation referred to in clauses (a) to (c), be restricted or abrogated so as to ensure the proper discharge of their duties and the maintenance of discipline among them."

7. In the Indian Air Force, the norms governing the growth of hair and retention of facial hair is governed by paragraph 425. Policy documents have also been issued from time to time. On 28 April 1980, the Air Head Quarters issued a letter responding to queries made in respect of Armed Force personnel professing Islam. The letter opined that personnel professing Islam are covered by the exception under paragraph 425(b) of the Regulations and that the beard should be "of such length when covered by a fist no hair shall be visible outside." Subsequently, on 10 August 1982 it was stipulated by a policy letter that no permission was required by Muslim Air Force personnel to keep a beard so long as the airman sported a beard at the time of joining service.However, if an airman who is a Muslim desired to sport a beard after joining service, he would be permitted to submit a formal application informing his commanding officer of this fact and to sport a beard from that date. The airman would not be allowed to remove the beard except on medical grounds or on an application approved by the Commanding Officer. On 6 October 1999 a comprehensive policy was formulated in supersession of the Headquarters' letter dated 10 August 1982.The policy document laid down that service personnel professing Islam were not required to obtain formal permission if they already sported a beard at the time of joining service. However, if a person desired to grow a beard after joining service, he was required to submit a formal application to the Commanding Officer who would ascertain the reason and ensure that the beard was maintained in a neat, trim and tidy manner. The beard would not be allowed to be shaved off without specific permission. The provisions in relation to the length of the beard for Muslim airmen contained in the earlier policy were reiterated.

8. In February 2003 the policy was re-examined so as to implement a common code of conduct applicable to air force personnel. On 24 February 2003 a revised policy was issued with the concurrence of the Union government in the Ministry of Defence in supersession of the earlier policy dated 6 October 1999. Para 2(a) of the policy governs personnel who profess Sikhism.Para 2(a) provides thus:

Sikh personnel who wear turban and keep beard at the time of commission/enrolment would continue to do so. These personnel must maintain the beard neatly dressed/tied and rolled and not kept flowing. They are to wear the turban while in uniform/civil dress whether inside or outside the camp except during PT/Games and activities related to operations where wearing of turban is not feasible. At all such occasions, Sikh personnel are to wear turban/patka or handkerchief over the knot of hair as appropriate. Sikh personnel keeping short hair and beard are to wear turban as applicable to those maintaining long hair.

Paragraph 2(b) of the policy states thus:

(b) Only those Muslim personnel, who had kept beard along with moustache at the time of commissioning /enrolment prior to 01 Jan 2002, would be allowed to keep beard and moustache. Such personnel are to maintain it in a manner that it is neat, trimmed and tidy and not more than the length which could be covered by one fist. Muslims who have grown beard after joining service should shave off the beard. Under no circumstances, a Muslim person who had beard at the time of joining service before 01 Jan 2002 shall be allowed to maintain beard without moustache.Moustache would be a part of the beard".

Para 2(c) allows non-sikh personnel to sport a beard for a short period towards fulfilment of specified religious rights and ceremonies for a period not exceeding thirty days. Para 2(c) stipulates that while in uniform, the personal appearance of an individual should not give any religious bias. Hence Tilak/Vibhuti on the forehead, a thread on the wrist or arm of the airman and a trinket in the ear (etc.) are not to be worn.

9. On 9 June 2003 a letter was issued by the Air Headquarters containing a clarification in the following terms :

4. In an effort to allay the fears or misconception of the Non-Sikh personnel, it is clarified that all those personnel whose religion/ religious practices demand sporting of beard and moustaches; they could continue to wear the beard as long as such a permission has been granted to them prior to issuance of this letter or they had beard and moustaches, as part of their religious practices, at the time of joining the Air Force. In pursuance of this directive, Commanders are to ensure that necessary endorsements are made in the personal documents of such individuals and photographs depicting such changes in the facial appearances are affixed to them. The Identity Cards also need to be changed accordingly.

The above letter states that personnel whose religion requires sporting a beard and moustache would be allowed to grow a beard provided (i) permission was granted prior to the issuance of the letter; and(ii) a beard and moustache was grown at the time of joining the Air Force.

In pursuance of this directive, commanders have been required to make endorsements in the personal documents depicting in the photographs affixed such changes in the facial appearance. Identity cards have to be changed accordingly. The policy document now specifically provides that if permission had been granted to non-Sikh personnel prior to 9 June 2003, they could continue to sport a beard or if they had as a part of religious practice done so at the time of joining the Air Force.

10. During the course of the hearing, we had inquired of Shri Salman Khurshid, learned senior counsel appearing on behalf of the Appellants whether there is a specific mandate in Islam which "prohibits the cutting of hair or shaving of facial hair". Learned senior counsel, in response to the query of the Court, indicated that on this aspect, there are varying interpretations, one of which is that it is desirable to maintain a beard. No material has been produced before this Court to indicate that the Appellant professes a religious belief that would bring him within the ambit of para 425(b) of the Regulations which applies to "personnel whose religion prohibits the cutting off the hair or shaving off the face of its members".The policy letters which have been issued by the Air Headquarters from time to time do not override the provisions of para 425(b) which have a statutory character. The policy circulars are only clarificatory or supplementary in nature. The policy letter of 8 May 1980 did initially permit an airman professing Islam to sport a beard of a prescribed length. This was revisited by the Air Headquarters on 10 August 1982 and a distinction was made between the cases of Muslim personnel who had already sported a beard at the time of joining service (in whose case no permission was required) and cases where personnel desire to sport a beard after joining service (in which case a formal application informing the Commanding Officer was required to be submitted).

On 6 October 1999 the Air Headquarters while reiterating this distinction made it clear that if an airman seeks to grow a beard after joining service he would require the approval of the Commanding Officer who would ascertain the reasons for his decision, advice the individual to maintain the beard in a neat, trim and tidy manner and that once permitted he would not be allowed to shave off his beard. Evidently, these provisions have been introduced having due regard to the security concerns inherent in maintaining identity in the Armed Forces. Maintenance of identity is a crucial element in the safety and security of the Forces, particularly in the context of the threat of infiltration. The policy was again revisited on 24 February 2003.

This time a limited protection was granted for those who had a beard prior to 1 January 2002 at the time of enrolment but the policy also stated that no person would after joining service be allowed to maintain a beard. This position was clarified on 9 June 2003 by stating that personnel whose religion demands sporting a beard, would be allowed to do so provided they were granted permission prior to the date of the letter or had grown a beard at the time of joining Air Force. So long as the provisions of para 425 (which have a statutory effect) are not breached, a mere policy can be revisited and modulated in the interest of the Force. The policy documents are only clarificatory in nature. Policies can be duly modified to subserve the best interest of the Force, which is inextricably intertwined with the need to protect the nation against grave threats of destabilization and disorder. The discipline of this Force is paramount.

11. We see no reason to take a view of the matter at variance with the judgment under appeal. The Appellant has been unable to establish that his case falls within the ambit of para 425(b) of the Regulations. In the circumstances, the Commanding Officer was acting within his jurisdiction in the interest of maintaining discipline of the Air Force. The Appellant having been enrolled as a member of the Air Force was necessarily required to abide by the discipline of the Force. Regulations and policies in regard to personal appearance are not intended to discriminate against religious beliefs nor do they have the effect of doing so. Their object and purpose is to ensure uniformity, cohesiveness, discipline and order which are indispensable to the Air Force, as indeed to every armed force of the Union.

12. For these reasons, we see no merit in the Civil Appeal No. 8644 of 2009.

The Civil Appeal shall stand dismissed. However, with no orders as to costs.

13. In the view of the above, Civil Appeal No. 8643 of 2009 is dismissed accordingly.

    CJI. [T S THAKUR]

    J. [Dr D Y CHANDRACHUD]

    J. [L. NAGESWARA RAO]

New Delhi

December 15, 2016

Indian airmen can't keep a beard as it is against their respective service rules, the same has been confirmed by the Supreme Court of India.

In this case, two Muslim petitioners had argued in the Supreme Court that keeping a beard was a facet of their fundamental right to freedom of religion, and they sought equality with Sikhs. The petitioners challenged the IAF authorities' confidential order dated 24 February 2003, which prohibited Muslim personnel from growing beard.

Indian Air Force in June 2016 dismissed a Muslim soldier who was insisting on sporting a beard on religious grounds. The military termed him as an "undesirable soldier" and subsequently, his sacking was upheld by an Armed Forces Tribunal in Kochi bench. Tribunal ruled that under Article 25 keeping a beard is not a fundamental right or a facet of Islam.

The Supreme Court on 15 December 2016 held that all personnel working in Indian Air Force are not allowed to keep a beard merely by citing religious grounds. Under Article 25 of the Constitution, religion is the fundamental right of all citizens, but it is subject to several other conditions as prescribed by the constitution itself and several other legislations as enacted from time to time. Further, the protection under the Constitution is only to the prima facie tenets of a particular religion and not every other incidental thing. The court justified these policies of the government by saying that "such uniformity of policies are secular by its very nature and not merely framed to govern the conduct of the Air Force personnel of any particular religion.

The apex court refused to consider growing beard as a part of the Islam, just like it is as per the religious practices of Sikhism. The Court said,

"In a constitutional sense article 33 stipulates that up to what extent the fundamental rights of the citizens could be restricted or abrogated by a law made by the parliament. It is necessary to note that article 33 empowers the parliament to modify fundamental right in the case of application to the armed forces." The court also noted the fact that for an effective functioning of a large combat force, the team members must bond together by a true sense of espirit-de-corps, without any differentiation of caste, creed, religion or color.

12

Lt Col Amal Sankar Bhaduri v. Union of India, (1987) Cal LT 1 (HC), 91 CWN 631, decided on 24 December 1985, Kolkata High Court.

Judgment:

1. An interesting question as regards the jurisdiction of the Writ Court in matters of court martial in general, falls for determination in this Writ Petition.

2. While it is true that Army personnel ought to be subjected to strictest form of discipline and Article 33 of the Constitution has conferred powers on to the Parliament to abridge the rights conferred under Part III of the Constitution in respect of the members of the Armed Forces, but does that mean and imply that the Army personnel would be denuded of the Constitutional privileges as guaranteed under the Constitution. Can it be said that the Army personnel form a class of citizens not entitled to the Constitution's benefits and are outside the purview of the Constitution. To answer above in the affirmative in my view, would be a violent departure to the wishes of the framers of our Constitution. Army personnel are as much citizen as any other individual citizen of this country. At this juncture it would be worthwhile to refer to Article 33 of the Constitution. Article 33 has been engrafted in the Constitution to enable the Parliament by law to restrict the rights as contained in Part III of the Constitution. The extent of restrictions necessary to be imposed on any of the fundamental rights in their application to the armed forces and the forces charged with the maintenance of public order for the purpose of ensuring proper discharge of their duties and maintenance of discipline among them would necessarily depend upon the prevailing situation at a given point of time and it would be inadvisable to encase it in a rigid statutory formula. The Constitution makers were obviously anxious that no more restrictions should be placed than are absolutely necessary for ensuring proper discharge of duties and the maintenance of discipline amongst the Armed Force Personnel and therefore Article 33 empowered the Parliament to restrict or abridge within permissible extent, the rights conferred under Part III of the Constitution in so far as the Armed Force Personnel are concerned [In this context reference may be made to the decision of the Supreme Court in the case of *R. Viswan v. Union of India* (1983)].

3. The Supreme Court in the case of *Prithi Pal Singh v. Union of India* reported in 1983CriLJ647 observed:

"It is one of the cardinal features of our Constitution that a person by enlisting in or entering Armed Forces does not cease to be a citizen so as to wholly deprive him of his rights under the Constitution. More so when this Court held in *Sunil Batra v. Delhi Administration* 1978CriLJ1741 that even prisoners deprived of personnel liberty are not wholly denuded of their fundamental rights. In the larger interest of national security and military discipline Parliament in its wisdom may restrict or abridge such rights in their application to the Armed Forces but this process should not be carried so far as to create a class of citizen not entitled to the benefits of liberal spirit of the Constitution. Persons subject to Army Act are citizens of this ancient land having feeling of belonging to the civilized community governed by the liberty oriented -- Constitution."

4. At this stage it is convenient to deal with the other aspect of the matter as regards the maintainability of the petition under Article 226 of the Constitution as contended by the respondent, viz.; that the ban imposed by Article 227(4) also applies to Article 226.

5. At the outset it is to be noted that unlike Article 227, there is no express limitation in Article 226 itself excluding the power of Superintendence over Military Tribunal from the scope of that Article. It is now well settled that the Law Courts would not be justified in incorporating an expression or a word in a particular provision of the statute as it would be presumed that such omission has been effected by the Law makers knowingly. To add to or to supplement the words of a statute would be contrary to all recognized principles of construction. Our Constitution makers have deliberately thought it fit not to impose the same restriction in Article 226 as it is in Article 227(4). The framers of the Constitution obviously, therefore, did not intend that there should be a similar embargo in respect of Military Tribunals under Article 226 of the Constitution. Whereas in Article 227 the power of interference is restrictive in nature the powers conferred under Article 226 is of very wide amplitude. The power of interference extends even to the extent of quashing an impugned order on the ground of error of law. The respondents contended that as the Court has the power of Superintendence both under Article 226 as also under Article 227, both the Articles should be read together in a harmonious manner and as such the restriction in Article 227(4) should also be read as existing in Article 226 of the Constitution. In my view however the same cannot be accepted. Jurisdiction of the High Court under Article 226 is of very wide amplitude. On a plain reading of Article 226 and Article 227 of

the Constitution, in my view, it cannot be said that the two Articles are in pari material. The extent of Courts Jurisdiction under the two Articles is not the same and no logical reason exists for engrafting in Article 226, the limitation imposed by Article 227(4) of the Constitution. The language of Article 227(4) clearly manifests that the same was not intended to have a broader application. The user of 'This Article' in Article 227(4) clearly depicts the intention of the Constitution makers. Whenever the makers of our Constitution thought it fit to restrict the powers of the Law Courts, the same has been expressed in explicit language. Article 392(B) or Article 363 may be, considered in this context. It, therefore, appears that there is no overlapping of jurisdiction neither the scope of Articles 226 and 227 are the same.

6. The next contention is in regard to the Constitution of Court Martial. Before dealing with the rival contentions in that regard it would be worthwhile at this juncture to refer to the relevant provisions of the Army Act and the Rules.

7. Section 109 of the Army Act provides that a General Court Martial may be convened by the Central Government or the Chief of Army Staff or by any Officer empowered in this behalf by warrant of the Chief of Army Staff.

8. Section 113 provides that a General Court Martial shall consist of not less than five Officers each of whom has held a commission for not less than three whole years and of whom not less than four are of a rank not below that a Captain.

9. As regards the composition of General Court Martial, Rule 40 of the Army Rules 1954 also lends assistance to Section 113 of the Army Act. Rule 40 provides as follows:--

(i) A General Court Martial shall be composed as far as seems to the convening Officer practicable, of officers of different corps or departments and in no case exclusive of Officers of the corps or department to which the accused belongs;

(ii) The members of a Court Martial for the trial of an officer shall be of a rank not lower than that of the officer unless, in the opinion of the convening officer, officers of such rank are not (having due regard to the exigencies of the public service) available. Such opinion shall be recorded in a convening order.

(iii) In no case shall an Officer below the rank of captain be a member of a Court Martial for the trial of a field officer.

Mr. Ghosh appearing for the writ petitioners contended that the Court Martial has been illegally constituted in violation of Rules 40(2) of the Army Rules of 1954 and as such the Court Martial has no jurisdiction to try the petitioner. Admittedly, the petitioner is a Lt Col in the Army but the respondents Nos. 9, 10 and 11 hold substantive rank of Major though at present in the acting rank of Lt Col. Relying on these state of facts, Mr Ghosh strongly contended that three out of its five members of the Court Martial are of a lower substantive rank than that of a petitioner and the constitution of the Court Martial is thus in contravention of Rules 40(2) of the Army Rules and hence illegal.

10. In support of his contentions Mr Ghosh also placed reliance on Rule 2(d)(ii) of the Army Rules. Rule 2(d)(ii) defines 'rank' to mean 'substantive rank'.

11. Mr RN Das, however, tried to repel the submissions of Mr. Ghosh on two counts. Firstly that the petitioner did not object to be tried by the members constituting the Court Martial when it first assembled on 15 March 1985 and secondly the definition in Rule 2(d) (ii) of the Army Rules will not apply to Rules 40(2) of the Army Rules. Mr. Das contended that the rank is not defined in the Army Act. Therefore, Section 113 of the Army Act rank includes both acting and substantive ranks and the definition of 'rank' in Rule 2(d) (ii) if read with Rules 40(2) of the Army Rules would lead to a conflict as regards the meaning of rank in Section 113 of the Army Act. Mr Das contended that Rules 40(2) is practically identical with Section 113 of the Army Act and the Law Courts ought not to put an interpretation which may lead to a conflict between the provisions of the Army Act and the Rules framed thereunder.

12. At this juncture, however, it would be useful to refer to the relevant set of facts vis-a-vis the contention of the parties in that regard.

13. In December 1984 the petitioner was asked to name his defending officer, whereupon the petitioner named two officers in order to preference, the second being Major Chawda. But by reason of non-availability of the two officers named, and on being further asked to suggest his defending officer, the petitioner named further four officers. The petitioner, however, having had no confirmation as regards his defending officer, engaged a civilian lawyer from Gauhati. The civilian lawyer was not, however, available prior to 16 April 1985, intimation whereof was sent to the authorities. On 13 March 1985, that is, two days prior to the assembly

of the Court Martial, Major Chawda was assigned to the petitioner as his defending officer. The petitioner, however, expressed his unwillingness to be defended by Major Chawda and the latter in fact reported the same to the authorities. On 15 March 1985 the petitioner submitted a Memorandum to the Court stating that he did not wish to be defended by Major Chawda. Nevertheless, Major Chawda, however, appeared as Defending Officer. In the writ petition, the petitioner has stated that he wanted Major Chawda to object to the Constitution of the Court, but he did not do so, saying that 'he did not wish to annoy the Court'. However, the petitioner insisted that the Court be adjourned till 16 April 1985 so that civilian counsel of his choice could be available for defending him. This request was granted by the Court.

14. On this state of facts it is to be considered as to whether the conduct of the petitioner can be said to be barred by the doctrine of estoppel, waiver or acquiescence.

15. In Spencer Bower and Turner, *The Law Relating to Estoppel by Representation*, it has been stated: Not even the plainest and most express contract or consent of a party to litigation can confer jurisdiction on any person not already vested with it by the law of the land, or add to the jurisdiction lawfully exercised by any judicial tribunal; it is equally plain that the same results cannot be achieved by conduct or acquiescence by the parties. Any such attempt to create or enlarge jurisdiction is in fact the appointment of a Judicial Officer by a subject, and as such constitutes a manifest usurpation of the Royal Prerogative. On the other hand where nothing more is involved than a mere irregularity of procedure or (e.g.) non-compliance with statutory conditions precedent to the validity of a step in the litigation, of such a character that, if one of the parties be allowed to waive the defect, or to be estopped by conduct from setting it up, now new jurisdiction is thereby impliedly created and no existing jurisdiction impliedly extended beyond its existing boundaries, the estoppel will be maintained, and the affirmative answer of illegality will fail.

16. Accordingly, in all cases of the first class, that is, where it is sought by estoppel to enlarge the jurisdiction of any tribunal of limited jurisdiction, or to confer jurisdiction on any tribunal or person to whom it is not given by law, it has been held that it is impossible by contract to achieve these ends contrary to the provisions of a statute; and similarly no estoppel can be invoked to produce a similar result. In the second class, in which the representation is set up merely as a remedy for an irregularity in procedure it has been held that this end may be achieved by estoppel or waiver.

17. In some branches of the law the terms of the relevant statute preclude the parties from contracting out of the jurisdiction of the prescribed tribunal; and, in such cases, just as no agreement between the parties can oust the jurisdiction of the tribunal, neither can it be ousted by the invocation of an estoppel.

18. In the case of *RW McClaughry v. Peter C. Deming* Law Ed. US 183 1049, Peckham J. observed that consent can confer no jurisdiction on a Court Martial but composed entirely of Officers of the regular army of the United States in direct violation of the 77th Article of war which declares that such Officers shall not be competent to sit on Court Martial to try the Officers or soldiers of other forces. Similar view has also been expressed in the case of *Simpson v. Crowle* 1921(3) KB 243 in which it has been held that as the claim was solely for an injunction and not for an injunction as ancillary to a cause of action within Section 56 of the County Courts Act, 1888, the County Court Judge had no jurisdiction and that the mere fact that the parties proceeded with the trial without the point as to the jurisdiction having been raised did not confer jurisdiction upon the County Court Judge.

19. In the case of *Ram Lal Roshonlal & Co. v. B C Paul & Sons (P) Ltd* AIR1960Cal547 this Court held that defect in or lack of or basis incompetence in jurisdiction can never be waived.

20. In the case of *KR Shenoy v. Chief Officers, Town Municipal Council, Udipi* [1975]1SCR680 the Supreme Court observed that an excess of statutory power cannot be validated by acquiescence in or by the operation of an estoppel.

21. The issue was further examined by the Supreme Court in the case of *Superintendent of Taxes, Dhubri v. OnkarmalNathmal Trust*, AIR1975SC2065 in which the Supreme Court observed :

> "Furthermore, the waiver, even where both sides have agreed to waive the operation of a statutory provision, cannot extend to a case in which the effect may be either to oust the jurisdiction conferred by statute or to confer a jurisdiction which, according to the statute, is not there."

In that view of the matter, I am unable to accept the contention of Mr. Das that simply because of the fact that the petitioner did not object to be tried by the members constituting the Court Martial when it first assembled on 15 March 1985 it would be deemed to be a complete waiver of the right as regards the challenge on the ground of jurisdiction. To hold it otherwise would be a complete departure from the well established principles of law. Consent in any event, cannot confer jurisdiction if there is none, I, however, find some jurisdictions in Mr Ghosh's submission on the factual aspect that there was in fact no consent or waiver as regards the constitution of the Court Martial.

22. Further it is also to be noted that there ought to be an express pleading in regard to the point of estoppel, waiver or acquiescence which is, however, lacking in the case under consideration.

23. The respondents next contended that Rules 40(2) of the Army Rules is practically identical with Section 113 and the definition of 'rank' in Rule 2(d)(ii) ought not to be read in Rules 40(2) of the Army Rules. It was further contended that if the definition of 'rank' is read in Rules 40(2) it would lead to conflict which the Law Courts ought always try to avoid. Law Courts ought to interpret the statute to make it viable and operative and ought not to put an interpretation which may lead to its invalidity or the provisions being rendered nugatory.

24. The Army Act read as a whole, does not lend any support to the respondent's contention neither the expression nor the concept of 'acting rank' occurs anywhere in the statute. There is thus no warrant for saying that the word 'rank' used in the Act includes an 'acting rank'. It does follow, therefore, far less, logically, that such a wide meaning must be given to the word 'rank' in Section 113. The expression 'acting rank' occurs only in Special Army Instructions relating to pay, pension, promotion, leave, etc., (but not regarding composition of a Court Martial). These Instructions have no statutory force and are subordinate to the Act, and cannot, therefore, be used for interpreting the Act.

25. A perusal of Section 113 of the Act shows that the word 'rank' occurs in the Section only in the last part, i. e., as regards the requirement that at least four of the five officers must be of a rank not below that of a Captain.

26. It is apparent from Section 113 that this section is only dealing with the minimum requirements for the composition of a Court Martial. One of those requirements is that at least four members of the Court Martial must be above the rank of Captain, i.e., they must be Majors or above. This is the context in which the word 'rank' occurs. In this context reliance was placed on the decision of the Madras High Court in the case of in Re: Kandassery AIR 1919 Mad24. In that decision the statute required that sanction for prosecution must be given by a District Magistrate and the Court held that

a person who was an acting District Magistrate and discharging the same function as the District Magistrate was competent to grant the sanction. In my view, however, the decision noted above has no manner of application and it is clearly distinguishable on facts. In Section 113 of the Army Act there is no reference to any functionary by any official title.

27. In the course of argument, some emphasis was placed on the fact that the definition contained in Rule 2(d) (ii) of the Army Rules was brought in by amendment in 1979. This does not mean that before 1979 the meaning of 'rank' in the Army Rule was different that before 1979 'rank' included 'acting rank'. It is well known that definitions are not infrequently brought in by subsequent amendment to declare what was always the true meaning of particular expression, so as to avoid possible confusion or difficulties which may have arisen because of the absence of a definition earlier. It cannot be presumed that the Rule making authority would introduce a definition of a 'word' in the Rules which would run counter to the meaning of that 'word' in the Act. On the contrary, it is to be presumed that it is in conformity with the meaning of that 'word' in the Act. Simply because there is no definition of 'rank' in the Army Act, it is not a correct method of interpretation to say that word should be given as wide a meaning as possible and that it, therefore, includes 'acting rank'.

28. The word 'rank' in Section 113 of the Act, in my view means what the word normally conveys--i.e., substantive rank, and not 'acting rank', which is a special extended meaning and not a normal meaning. There is nothing in the Act to indicate that this special or extended meaning is intended to be included in Section 113. In the case of *Commissioner of Wealth Tax, Andhra Pradesh v. Officer-in-Charge (Court of Wards)* [1976]10ITR133(SC), the Supreme Court observed:--

> "We think that it is not correct to give as wide a meaning as possible to terms used in a statute simply because the statute does not define an expression. The correct rule is that we have to endeavour to find out the exact sense in which the words have been used in a particular context. We are entitled to look at the statute as a whole and give an interpretation in consonance with the purposes of the statute and what logically follows from the terms used. We are to avoid absurd results."

29. It was further contended by the respondent authority that Section 17 of the General Clauses Act ought to be allowed a full play in the matter of interpreting Section 113 of the Army Act as well as the Rules 40(2)

particularly as the Central Government (the Rule-making Authority) must have been aware that the Army Rules of 1954 are, by virtue of Section 193, to have effect 'as if enacted in the Act', i.e., on a par with the provisions of the Act. In my view Section 17 of the General Clauses Act, however, does not in any way advance the matter further. It is to be noted that both Section 113 and Rules 40(2) of the Rules for General Court Martial, however, have separate and different objects and purposes and the two provisions operate in different fields.

30. Section 113 prescribes firstly the minimum number required for a valid Court Martial and secondly prescribes the minimum experience that each should, possess, i.e., each must have held a commission for a period not less than 3 years, and thirdly the minimum qualifications that the members should possess, i.e., that at least four should hold a rank not below that of Captain. Rules 40(2), however, deal with a different aspect. It lays down that the members of the Court Martial must not be of lower in rank than that of the officer who is being tried by them. This is an additional requirement. Section 113 stops after laying down the minimum rank of officers constituting a Court Martial and it does not deal with any other aspect of the constitution of a Court Martial, e.g., the further question of the ranks of the members of the Court Martial vis-a-vis that of the officer being tried by them. This aspect is left to the Army Rules. Section 191(2)(e), of the Army Act expressly confers power to frame rules providing for the convening and constitution of Court Martial. If the Legislature was of the view that Section 113 (which deals with the composition of Court Martial) was exhaustive, there would not have been any point in expressly conferring power to make rules for the constitution of Court Martial. Rules 40(2) has been framed in pursuance of Section 191(2)(e) of the Act.

31. Thus in my view, Rules 40(2) does not conflict in any way with Section 113 of the Act. It only imposes an additional requirement, viz., that the members of the Court Martial should not be of lower in rank than that of the officer being tried. There is no difficulty at all in reading Rules 40(2) harmoniously with Section 113 neither there is any repugnancy. This is also the understanding of the army authorities, as will appear from the Manual of Military Law, Vol I, at para 17 on page 25.

32. There is no conflict between Rules 40(2) and Section 113 and such an interpretation is fully consistent with the principle running throughout Military Law that a man should be tried by his peers. A substantive Lt Col can be tried by members of a Court Martial who are of the substantive rank of Lt Col or of a higher rank. He cannot be tried by a Major. This very

same principle is embodied in para 518 of the Defence Service Regulations dealing with composition of a Court of Inquiry, viz., 'when the character of military reputation of an Officer is likely to be a material issue, then Presiding Officer of the Court of Inquiry whenever possible will be senior in rank and other members at least equivalent in rank to that Officer.'

33. In this context the observations of the Supreme Court in the case of *Commissioner of Sales Tax, Gujarat v. Union Mining Agency* [1981]1SCR870 is very opposite.

34. ....

35. The Supreme Court further observed that there is no dispute with the proposition that the meaning of a word or expression defined may have to be departed from on account of the subject or context in which the word had been used and that will be giving effect to the opening sentence in definition section, namely, 'unless the context otherwise requires'. In view of this qualification, the Court has not only to look at the words but also to look at the context, the collocation and the object of such words relating to such matter and interpret the meaning intended to be conveyed by the use of the words in a particular Section. But where there is no obscurity in the language of the Section, there is no scope for the application of the rule ex visceribus actus. This Rule is never allowed to alter the meaning of what is of itself clear and explicit. The authorities relied upon by the High Court are, therefore, not applicable.

36. The next contention urged on behalf of the petitioner is in regard to the non-compliance of the conditions precedent to the exercise of power convening a Court Martial. Before dealing with this aspect of the matter it is worth considering the relevant statutory provisions in particular Rule 37 of the Army Rules of 1954 framed under the Act of 1950. Rule 37 reads as follows:-

> "37. **Convening of General and District Court-Martial.**(1) An Officer before convening a Central or District Court-Martial shall first satisfy himself that the charges to be tried by the Court are for offences within the meaning of the Act, and that the evidence justifies a trial on those charges, and if not so satisfied, shall order the release of the accused, or refer the case to superior Authority.
>
> (2) He shall also satisfy himself that the case is a proper one to be tried by the kind of Court-Martial which he proposes to convene.
>
> (3) The Officer convening a Court-Martial shall appoint or detail the

officers to form the Court and may also appoint or detail, such waiting Officers as he thinks expedient. He may also, where he considers the services of an interpreter to be necessary, appoint or detail an interpreter to the Court.

(4) The officer convening a Court-Martial shall furnish to the senior member of the Court with the original charge sheet on which the accused to be tried and, where no judge-advocate has been appointed, also with a copy of the summary or abstract of evidence and the order for the assembly of the Court-Martial. He shall also send to all the other members, copies of the charge-sheet and to the judge-advocate when one has been appointed, a copy of the charge-sheet and a copy of the summary or abstract of evidence."

Rule 37(1) and (2) of the Rules, in my view, makes it obligatory on the part of the convening Officer to the effect that the officer must himself look into the evidence and there is an element of personal satisfaction, There ought also to be a consideration of the evidence and upon such consideration the convening Officer must be satisfied that such evidence justifies the trial of the Officer on the proposed charges that is to say that there ought to be a proper and independent formation of opinion based on records.

37. Incidentally, though a definite case has been made out by the petitioner that there was no proper application of mind by the convening officer and as such the requirement of Rule 37(2) was not complied with. The respondents, however, have chosen not to deal with the, said allegations in the counter affidavit. The convening officer though made a party in the writ petition has not come out with any affidavit which is, in my view, cannot be overlooked by the Court. Statute enjoins certain functionaries to perform certain duties and that particular functionary when made a party ought to have come out with a case in regard to the compliance of statutory requirement. A third person by virtue of a simple authority to sign and affirm, in my view, is not a proper person to comply with strict rigours of law. In any event, in the counter affidavit filed by the respondent authorities it has been stated as follows:

"I say that the General Officer (Commanding), Bengal Area, the convening Authority had fully satisfied himself in terms of Army Rule 37(1) in respect of charge and evidence. He had gone through the legal opinion of the Assistant Judge Advocate General 4 Corps on the evidence and charges and had satisfied himself in all respects before convening the General Court-Martial."

38. In the present case the respondent No. 2 was the convening officer whether the respondent No. 2 himself looked into the evidence and was satisfied with the findings justifying a trial of the petitioner on the proposed charges ought to be a matter within the personal knowledge of the convening officer being the respondent No. 2 in the present proceedings. The affidavit as it appears, have been affirmed by an officer who is not even a party to the proceeding and therefore, no credence to the statement can or ought to be placed thereon and the criticism of Mr Ghosh, in my view, is amply justified in the facts of the case.

39. In any event, the statement in the counter affidavit goes to show that the respondent No. 2 had gone through the legal opinion of the Assistant Judge Advocate General on the evidence and charges and had satisfied himself from that opinion and the evidence and charges before convening the General Court-Martial. This by itself shows that the respondent No. 2 arrived at his satisfaction upon consideration of the opinion of the Assistant Judge Advocate General which, in my view, is not permissible since Rule 37(1) requires that the convening Officer must apply his mind and look into the evidence himself. On a plain reading of the Rule what is required is the independent application of mind and not on the basis of someone else's opinion.

40. Mr. Das, however, appearing for the respondent authority referred to the Defence Services Regulations. Para 459 reads as follows:--

> **"Reference to the Judge Advocate General's Department before trial**--In all cases for trial by a General Court Martial, and all cases under the Army Act, of indecency, fraud, theft except ordinary theft, civil offences except simple assaults, the charge-sheet and summary of evidence, and all the exhibits will be referred to by the convening officer to the Deputy/Assistant JAG of the Command before trial is ordered. The convening officer who also referfor advice any other cases of doubt or difficulty. In all cases the doubts or difficulties and the matters of which advice is required will be specifically stated in the applications."

41. On a plain reading of para 459 of the Defence Services Regulations it is clear and apparent that though the Regulation contemplates reference to Judge Advocate General before trial commences but the Regulation does not provide that the convening officer to act on the opinion or advice of the Judge Advocate General. Reference to the Judge Advocate General for advice of the Convening Officer can only be effected in case of doubt

or difficulty but not otherwise. In this context reference to para 459 of the Defence Services Regulations and in particular para 452 (d) ought to be noted. Under para 452 (d) it has been clearly laid down that the commander under whose authority the convening order has been issued must personally satisfy himself as required in Rule 37 and a certificate to that effect must also in every such case be attached to the convening order. It appears further from the records that an endorsement has been made at the foot of the opinion of the Assistant Judge Advocate General by another officer to the effect that the petitioner should be tried by a Court-Martial. Immediately below there is another endorsement by the respondent No. 2, dated 14 January 1984 to read: "I agree, Convene GCM". In my view agreeing with an opinion formed by someone else that the petitioner should be tried by a Court-Martial is not sufficient compliance with Rule 37(1) of the Army Rules.

42. Assuming, however, that the Convening Officer has formed an opinion and that formation of opinion is a precondition of the convening of a General Court-Martial, but the Writ Courts, in my view, would be within its jurisdiction on the given set of facts to enquire whether the formation of opinion has been justified or not. It ought not to be best sight of that the matter before this Court is not one which concerns the findings of fact arrived at by a disciplinary authority or a case where the Labour Court has come to certain findings of fact which are being challenged in a writ proceeding. The Supreme Court in the case of *State of Uttar Pradesh v. Sardar DK Yadav* AIR 1968 SC 1186, observed that it is well established that where the jurisdiction of an administrative authority depends upon a preliminary finding of fact the High Court is entitled in a proceeding for a writ to be determined upon its own independent judgment whether or not that finding is correct.

43. Further in the case of *Rohtas Industries v. S D Agarwal* [1969]3SCR108, the Supreme Court observed that whenever a provision of law confers certain power on an authority on its forming certain opinion on the basis of certain facts the Courts cannot and ought not to be precluded from examining whether the relevant facts on the basis of which the opinion is said to have been formed were in fact existed.

44. The same issue was further examined by the Supreme Court in the case of *M.A. Rashid v. State of Kerala* [1975]2SCR93. The Supreme Court observed:

> "Where powers are conferred on public authorities to exercise the

same when 'they are satisfied' or when 'it appears to them', or when 'in their opinion' a certain state of affairs exists; or when powers enable public authorities to take 'such action as they think fit' in relation to a subject matter, the Courts will not readily defer to the conclusiveness of an executive authority's opinion as to the existence of a matter of law or fact upon which the validity of the exercise of the power is predicated."

45. The Supreme Court further observed:

"Administrative decisions in exercise of powers even if conferred in subjective terms are to be made in good faith on relevant consideration. The Courts inquire whether a reasonable man could have come to the decision in question without misdirecting himself on the law or the facts in a material respect. The standard of reasonableness to which the administrative body is required to conform any range from the Courts' own opinion of what is reasonable body might have decided. The Courts will find out whether conditions precedent to the formation of the opinion has a factual basis."

46. The decision of the Supreme Court in the case of *Mrs. Labbkuwar Bhagawan Shaha v. Janardan Mahadev Kala* AIR 1963 SC 535, in my view, is strictly not relevant in the present context. It was strongly urged that there exists some evidence which requires investigation. But in my view, the evidence must be such so as to at least prima facie establish though not conclusively that the petitioner had committed the offence charged. If it falls short of this or if the evidence is untrustworthy then same would not be sufficient evidence in the eve of law. In fine, the Convening Officer ought to be satisfied that the evidence which is already on record justifies a trial of the petitioner on the proposed charge.

47. On the state of law as discussed above, it is, therefore, to be seen as to whether there was any factual basis for such formation of opinion against the petitioner. For convenience take such an analysis ought to be effected in relation to the charges leveled against the petitioner.

48. The 1st charge reads as follows:

"The accused No MH-0166A Lt Col (Substantive) Amal Shankar Bhaduri of Military Hospital, Panagarh attached to base hospital Barrackpore an officer holding of permanent commission in the regular army is charged with :-

Without sufficient cause overstaying leave granted to him,

in that he, at Panagarh having been granted leave of absence from 09 May 1983 to 11 May 1983, with permission to prefix 06 May 1983 being Sunday, to proceed to his home, failed without sufficient cause, to rejoin duty a Military Hospital at Panagarh on 12 May 1983."

49. As against the aforesaid charge the Parade Register being exhibit 'P' before the authority shows that the petitioner was present on 12 May 1983 and was on the ration strength of the Unit. The attendance register being exhibit 'Q' also categorically suggests that the petitioner was present on 12 May 1983. The oral evidence of DW Acharya as also DW Maj Mahlewat go to show that the petitioner was present on 12 May 1983. It is, however, on record as against this evidence that the petitioner was not seen by Maj Pandarinath and Nayak Subedar Dogra at the Unit on 12 May 1983. It is to be noted in this context that Maj Praharaj has countersigned the parade state register on 12 May 1983 certifying the correctness of the entries. Maj Praharaj however was not called as a witness. PW 19 Gorai has stated that he saw the petitioner at Delhi on the morning of 12 May 1983 and PW 10 Inder Singh and PW 2 Dogra stated that they received the petitioner at Panagarh Station on 13 May 1983. PW 1 has stated that this was about 6 or 6-30 AM at Panagarh on 13 May 1983. The petitioner produced a certificate issued by the Railway Authorities being exhibit 'T' stating therein that the Kalka Mail passed through Panagarh at 8-44 AM on 13 May 1983. Another significant fact to be noted is that Kalka Mail stops at Durgapur and not at Panaragh. Therefore, the petitioner could not have possibly availed of Kalka Mail on 12 May reaching Panagarh on 13 May between 6 and 6-30 AM in the morning. The parade state register being exhibit 'P' further shows that Gorai himself was present at Panagarh on 12 May 1983. In that view of the matter, question of Gorai seeing of the petitioner at Delhi on 12 May 1983 is beyond any strength of imagination.

50. The petitioner has stated in his written statement that he had gone to Delhi on 7 May 1983 as the whereabouts of his son were not known and he returned to Panagarh on 11 May 1983. Thereafter, on the morning of 12 May 1983 he left Panagarh for Durgapur at about 7-30 AM for his friend's house and from whose house he could avail of the STD telephone facility as he was still trying to find out the whereabouts of his son, who was still missing. The petitioner further stated that he came back to Panagarh at about 1-40 PM and afterwards met Maj Mahlewat and his son. Later in the day as per the written statement of the petitioner he again went to Durgapur but as he could not come back that night, so he took the first

train to Panagarh on the morning of 13 May 1983 when he was received at the Station.

51. The documentary evidence, in my view, does not militate against the statement of the petitioner. On the contrary it corroborates the petitioner's version.

52. Having regard to the contemporary documentary evidence evidencing that' the petitioner was present on 12 May 1983 and having regard to the testimony of two PWs as also certain correspondence signed by the petitioner on 12 May 1983 as appears from. Exhibit 'H' in my view, no prima facie case said to have been established against the petitioner in respect of the charge. Such formation of opinion in the matter initiating a general Court Martial does not stand to reason and can be said to be utterly perverse, entitling the Writ Court to quash the same. This is apart from the factum that the charge is of very trivial nature and the state of evidence does not justify the formation of opinion or the satisfaction of the convening officer in regard to the initiation of Court Martial proceedings against the petitioner.

53. The second charge reads as follows:

"An act prejudicial to good order and military discipline,

in that, he at Panagarh, while officer commanding military hospital, Panagarh improperly and without authority permitted No. 13920Ck L/Nk M C Gorai a sahayak, to be absent from duty from 12 May to 31 May 1983."

54. Section 63 of the Army Act provides that any person who is guilty of any act or omission which, though not specified in this Act is prejudicial to good order and military discipline usually on conviction by Court Martial be liable to suffer imprisonment for a term which may extend to seven years or such less punishment as is in this Act mentioned. Admittedly, the second charge has been levelled under Section 63 of the Army Act.

55. The charge itself manifests that another officer absented himself from duty without leave for which responsibility is said to have been foisted on the petitioner though the concerned officer was not proceeded with. In my view, at best the offence would be of aiding and abetting rather than an offence under Section 63 being an act prejudicial to good order and military discipline. Absence from duty without leave amounts to an offence under Section 39(b) of the Army Act with which L/NkGorai could have been charged but not the petitioner under Section 63 of the Army Act.

Aiding and abetting itself is an offence under Section 66 of the Army Act. As such the charge in any event, is wholly misconceived and in the view I have taken no trial could take place under Section 63 of the Army Act.

56. Apart from what is noted above, the principle question that arises for consideration in this regard is whether there existed any obligation or a duty under the Act or the Rules upon the petitioner to ensure presence of the petitioner's subordinate staff or an officer for duty. Unfortunately both the Act and the Rules are silent on that score. In my view, the answer is and ought to be in the negative. As noted above, there is no obligation on the part of the petitioner to ensure presence of his subordinate officers and as such breach of good order and military discipline cannot be attributed to the petitioner. In this context, Note 3(a) of Section 63 of the Army Act is of some significance and as such the same is set out hereunder:

> "3.(a) 'An omission' to be punishable under this Section must amount to neglect which is wilful or culpable. If wilful, i.e., deliberate it is clearly blameworthy. If it is not wilful, it may or may not be blameworthy, and the Court must consider the whole circumstances of the case, and in particular the responsibility of the accused. A high degree of care can rightly be demanded of a person who is in charge of a motor vehicle or public money or property, or who is handling fire-arms or explosives, where a slight degree of negligence may involve loss or danger to life; in such circumstances a small degree of negligence may be blameworthy. On the other hand, neglect which results from more forgetfulness, error of judgment or inadvertence, in relation to a matter which does not rightly demand a very high degree of care, would not be judged blameworthy so as to justify conviction and punishment. The essential thing for the Court to consider is whether in the whole circumstances of the case as they existed, at the time of the offence the degree of neglect proved is such as, having regard to their military knowledge of the amount of care which ought to have been exercised, renders the neglect substantially blameworthy and deserving of punishment."

Further the language of Section 63 is 'prejudicial to good order and military discipline'. The word 'ought' used in this Section shows that both conditions must be satisfied. I am, however, unable to accept the contention of Mr Das that the action of the petitioner as regards the absence of L/NkGorai amounts to an act prejudicial to good order or prejudicial to military discipline. Furthermore, the daily attendance register as well as the parade state register show the presence of L/NkGorai from 12 May 83 to 31 May

83. Contemporary documents maintained by the military administration cannot be ignored. It is the interesting feature of this matter is that the MajPraharaj, the administrative officer has signed the parade state register but was not called to testify the circumstances under which the name of L/NkGorai finds place in the register maintained by the authority. Another redeeming feature as regards this charge is the lack of evidence as regards the acts or omissions or involvement of the petitioner in the matter. None of the witnesses have mentioned in their respective depositions any act or omission on the part of the petitioner in regard to the factum of permission to L/NkGorai to be absent from duty without leave.

57. On the materials on record, therefore, I am of the view that the charge under Section 63 of the Act in no way can be substantiated as against the petitioner.

58. The third charge with which the petitioner was charged reads as follows:

"Such an offence as is mentioned is Clause (f) of Section 52 of the Army Act with intent to defraud,

in that he at Panagarh on 25 June 1983 with intent to defraud caused a railway concession voucher (IAFT--1720A) bearing No L/30, 754311 dated 28 June issued in the name of brother of No. 139 2012 L/Nk M. C. Gorai of military hospital, Panagarh for journey from Panagarh to New Delhi and back vide (IAFT--1720A) bearing No. L/30, 764312 dated 28 June78 to be used by Shri Ashok, his personal servant."

59. The charge has been framed under Section 52(f) of the Army Act. In order to appreciate the submissions made in this regard, it is necessary to refer to Section 52 of the Army Act. Section 52 reads as follows:

"52. **Offences in respect of property**.--Any person subject to this Act who commits any of the following offences, that is to say (a) commits theft of any property belonging to the government, or to any military, naval or air force mess, band or institution, or to any person subject to military, naval or air force law; or

(b) dishonestly misappropriate or converts to his own use any such property ; or

(c) commits criminal breach of trust in respect of any such property ; or

(d) dishonestly receives or retains any such property in respect of which any of the offences under Clauses (a), (b) and (c) has been committed, knowing or having reason to believe the commission of such offence ; or

(e) wilfully destroys or injures any property of the Government entrusted to him ; or

(f) does any other thing with intent to defraud, or to cause wrongful gain to one person or wrongful loss to another person;

shall, on conviction by Court Martial, be liable to suffer imprisonment for a term which may extend to ten years or such less punishment as is in this Act mentioned."

60. Section 52 of the Army Act deals with offences in respect of property. Section 52(a) to (e) show that each of the sub-sections is dealing with a specific act in regard to the property belonging to the Government or to the Armed Forces. In my view, Section 52(f) ought to be construed *ejusdem generis*. This view finds support from the decision of the Bombay High Court in the case of *Maj SG Barsay v. The State* AIR 1958 Bom 354. The Bombay High Court observed :

"In our opinion this contention is not well founded. Accused No. 1 is charged in this case is having entered into a criminal conspiracy with five others. Two of whom are public servants and three are not public servants. It is no doubt true that the offences falling under Section 5(i)(c) and (d) of the Prevention of Corruption Act might fall under Section 52(b) of the Army Act. Section 52 of the Army Act deals with offences in respect of government property or property belonging to any military, naval or air force mess, band or institution or to any person subject to military, naval or air force law. Several clauses in that section deal with different kinds of offences which are liable to be committed in respect of such property. In our opinion the language of Section 52 Clause (f) must be construed *ejusdem generis* and would not include the offence of criminal conspiracy, much less criminal conspiracy entered into by persons not governed by the provisions of the Act."

61. The petitioner has been charged as having caused Ashok to wrongfully use a particular railway concession voucher, in my view, considering the true purport of the language used in Section 52 the same would not come under Section 52(f) of Army Act. I am in respectful agreement with the view expressed by the Bombay High Court and am of the view that even if

the petitioner had entered into an agreement with Ashok who wrongfully used the concession voucher, but such an agreement does not fall within the ambit of Sub-section (f) or amounts to an offence under Section 52(f) and as such the convening Officer could not have possibly been satisfied or formed an opinion on a charge under Section 52(f). The Writ Court as such for the reasons abovenoted would be within its jurisdiction to declare such satisfaction as perverse.

62. Further, on a perusal of the evidence on record as regards the charge concerned, it appears that there is not enough evidence that the ticket on which Ashok travelled was obtained in exchange of the concession voucher issued in the name of Gorai's brother, neither there is my evidence about the involvement of the petitioner in regard to the user of a concession voucher by Ashok. Ashok was examined and there is no evidence to the effect that the petitioner gave him any concession voucher or tickets neither Ashok has said that the petitioner instructed him to use the concession voucher. There is thus absolutely no evidence at all that the petitioner caused Ashok to use that particular voucher. Strenuous submissions have been made by Mr. Das as regards a chit found on the desk of the petitioner. Admittedly, the concession vouchers are issued by the administrative officer and the chit however does not bear the signature of the petitioner. If the chit had been given by way of instruction, it would have in the normal course of events been signed by the petitioner. The other significant feature would be that if the chit was supposed to be instruction it would have found its place in the administrative office rather than at the desk of the commanding officer, a fortnight after the concession had been issued. From the records it appears that one Maj Tewari was the Administrative Officer at the material time issued the voucher. Maj. Tewari would have been the best person to depose as to the circumstances under which the concession voucher was issued. So also one Baldeb Singh being the writer of the voucher. None of these two persons have been called to depose. The absence of which in my view, cannot be ignored. Another aspect of the matter, viz., the evidence of Tindal being PW 20, the officiating Head Clerk, in the office of the Administrative Officer, keeps absolute silence as regards the chit affair. He does not say that any instructions were given by the petitioner for issue of the concession voucher or that he was asked to issue the voucher by the petitioner. The only evidence which is on record on which emphasis to was laid by Mr. Das is the evidence of Maj. Pandari Nath. The gist of his evidence as appears from record is that the chit being exhibit 'A' was the instruction on the basis of which the concession voucher was issued in the name of Gorai's brother. In my view, by reason of the preponderance

of evidence to the contrary and on consideration of the document itself the same can never be termed to be a basic document culminating in the issuance of a concession voucher. The petitioner in this regard, says that Gorai telephoned him from his house requesting that he should be issued a concession voucher for himself and his brother. The petitioner scribbled the requirement of Gorai but did not pass any instruction to his sub-ordinate staff for any such issue neither he has signed the chit for the purpose of giving effect to the said requirement. It was kept on his desk and no further step was taken in that regard.

63. Further on a proper construction of Section 52(f), it is clear and manifest that there must be an intent to defraud in regard to which, in my view, there is no evidence from which inference could reasonably be made that the petitioner by his acts intended to defraud.

64. That being the position, the charges, in my view, are perverse in nature capable of being quashed by the Court in exercise of its writ jurisdiction.

65. Last contention of Mr. Das appearing for the authority is that the Court cannot and ought not to go into the question of perversity since there is no specific prayer for quashing of a charge-sheet being Annexure 'H' to the writ petition. Admittedly, the petitioner prayed for the issuance of a high prerogative writ of mandamus commanding the respondent to act in accordance with law and to recall, rescind and withdraw the impugned convening order No. 00/084/262/A3 dated 9 March 1985 convening the General Court Martial to proceed against the petitioner being Annexure 'I' to the petition and to desist from proceeding further with the said Court Martial against the petitioner or any further acting upon the impugned order dated 9 March 1985. A writ of certiorari was also prayed for quashing or setting aside the order dated 9 March 1985 as also a writ of prohibition restraining the respondent from proceeding with a General Court Martial by reason of the convening order dated 9 March 1985. The order dated 9 March 1985 directs the petitioner to be tried by a Court Martial and the trial is in respect of the charges mentioned in Annexure 'H'. While it is true that there ought to be a prayer for quashing the charge sheet but absence of which would not justify to refuse the writ when the exigencies of the particular case demand it so. This view finds support from the decision of the Supreme Court in the case of *Chiranjit Lal v. Union of India*[1950]1SCR869. In that decision the Supreme Court observed:-

"Article 32 of the Constitution of India gives such very wide discretion in the matter of framing our writs to suit the exigencies of particular cases and the application of the petitioner cannot be thrown out simply on the ground that the proper writ or trial has not been prayed for."

66. In my view, technical rules of pleading ought not to stand in the way in the matter of grant of appropriate relief when the facts warrant such a decision and the Court ought not to exercise jurisdiction simply on the ground that there is no proper prayer for the same. The reliefs ought to be militated as per the situation and circumstances so as to afford complete reliefs to the person seeking the aid of Law Courts. If on the existing material there is no ground for the formation of an opinion in the matter of initiation of a General Court Martial then in my view, there can hardly be any point in continuing with the General Court Martial and going through the formality of a trial and such a course would merely result in unnecessary harassment without serving the cause of justice.

67. In that view of the matter, this writ petition succeeds. The charge sheet being Annexure 'H' to the petition as well as the order convening the General Court Martial being Order dated 9 March 1985 are quashed and set aside. There shall, however, be no order as to costs.

68. [Stay of] Operation of the Order as prayed for is granted for a period of three weeks after the X-mas vacation.

13

The Union of India v. Mohammed Ansari, WP (C) 4074 of 2012 decided on 02 August 2013 [Two Judge Bench].

Judgment & Order:

1. Whether members of General Reserve Engineer Force, commonly known as GREF, which is involved in construction, making and maintenance of roads in the border areas, can be regarded as members of Armed Forces? Can the members of GREF be regarded as persons subject to the Army Act, 1950? Whether a member of the GREF can seek a relief, which a person is, otherwise, entitled to receive from the Central Administrative Tribunal constituted under the Administrative Tribunals Act, 1985? Do the members of GREF fall, for all intents and purposes, within the ambit of Armed Forces Tribunal Act, 2007? Can a person, as a member of GREF, invoke extra-ordinary jurisdiction of the High Court under Article 226 and/or Article 227 of the Constitution of India on a subject, which is, otherwise, covered by Armed Forces Tribunal Act, 2007? These are some of the prominent questions, which the present writ petition has raised.

2. The material facts, leading to the present writ petition, made under Article 226 of the Constitution of India, may be set out as under:

(i) The respondent herein made an application, in the Central Administrative Tribunal, Guwahati Bench, his case being, in brief, thus:

(a) The respondent herein was appointed, in Boarder Roads Engineering Services (in short, BRES), as an Assistant Executive Engineer (Electrical & Mechanical) in the year 1985 by order, dated 03 June1985, by the Government of India, Ministry of Shipping and Transport. The respondent herein was promoted, on 30 May1997, to the post of Executive Engineer (Electrical & Mechanical) by the letter, dated 12 July 2005, issued by Boarder Roads Development Board (in short, BRDB).

(b) The respondent herein has already put in 26 years 8 months of service as an officer of the Organised Group A Services and, as a Superintending Engineer, he has already put in more than 6 years 7 months of service and that having so put in uninterrupted service for such a long period of time, he has become entitled to get the benefit of non-functional upgradation, meant for officers of Organised Group

A Services in Pay Band 4 and Pay Band 3, but he has been arbitrarily denied his due financial upgradation solely on the ground that he has not done the stipulated command posting of two years in terms of Para (c) of the BRDB's Note, dated 10 January 2011. In this regard, the authorities concerned are oblivious of the fact that in the hierarchical structure of the GREF, there is just one command appointment for 14 aspirants and if the stipulated period of two years of command post is required to be ensured for each of the 14 aspirants, such as, the respondent herein, who are, otherwise, eligible for such command appointment, then, an applicant, to become eligible for financial up-gradation, would take a period of 30 years; whereas a person, such as, the respondent herein, would have, otherwise, been entitled to receive financial up-gradation if the requirement of command appointment had not been insisted upon. The respondent herein accordingly sought for appropriate reliefs. The application, so made by the respondent, gave rise to Original Application (in short, OA) No.102/2012.

3. Resisting, at the very threshold, the OA, so filed by the respondent herein as applicant, the present petitioners, as respondents in the OA, contended that the Central Administrative Tribunal had no jurisdiction to deal with grievances of the applicant-respondent herein inasmuch as all members of the GREF, for reasons of discipline, fall under the Ministry of Defence by virtue of notifications, issued in this regard by the Central Government by taking recourse to Section 4 of the Army Act, 1950, and the Army Rules, 1954, for the purpose of discipline of the members of the GREF, and they become, thus, members of the Armed Forces and, as a member of the Armed Forces, a member of the GREF cannot invoke the learned Central Administrative Tribunal's jurisdiction inasmuch as the learned Tribunal's jurisdiction stands barred by the provisions of Section 2(a) of the Administrative Tribunals Act, 1985.

4. Notwithstanding the preliminary objection, so raised, the learned Tribunal passed an order, on 18 June 2012, holding that it had the jurisdiction to entertain an OA filed by the members of the GREF.

5. Aggrieved by the decision, so reached, on the question of maintainability of the OA, the respondents, in the OA, have filed, as petitioners, this writ petition seeking to invoke this Court's jurisdiction under Article 226 and get the order, dated 18 June 2012, passed by the learned Tribunal, set aside and quashed.

6. We have heard Mr. Mr. R. Sharma, learned Assistant Solicitor General of India, for the petitioners, and Mr. S. Bhattacharjee, learned counsel, appearing for the respondent. We have also heard Mr. U.K. Nair, learned counsel, who has appeared as *amicus curiae*.

7. While considering the present writ petition, it needs to be noted that there is no dispute before us that in terms of the provisions of Section 2(a) of the Administrative Tribunals Act, 1985, Central Administrative Tribunal is not empowered to deal with matters relating to any member of the Naval, Military or Air Forces or of any other Armed Forces of the Union. Logically extended, this makes it clear that if the members of the GREF are members of the Armed Forces, then, the Central Administrative Tribunal would have, in the light of the provisions of the Administrative Tribunals Act, 1985, no jurisdiction to deal with their cases.

8. The question, therefore, would be whether a member of the GREF can be regarded as a member of Armed Forces, for, such a member, if regarded, in law, as a member of the Armed Forces, then, would the provisions, embodied in the Administrative Tribunals Act, 1985, not be available to such a member?

9. The first question, therefore, which falls for consideration, is: whether a member of the GREF is a member of Armed Forces? This question is no longer *res integra* inasmuch as a Constitution Bench of the Supreme Court, in *R. Viswan v. Union of India* (AIR 1983 SC 658), had the occasion to deal with the question of applicability of the Army Act, 1950, to the members of the GREF.

10. In *R. Viswan*'s case (supra), wherein the application of some of the provisions of the Army Act, 1950, and the Rules, framed there under, to the member of the GREF, by issuance of notifications by the Government of India, was the main subject of challenge, it was contended by *R. Viswan*, a member of the GREF, that in the light of the provisions of Article 33 of the Constitution of India, the GREF is neither an Armed Force nor a Force charged with the maintenance of public order and, hence, the notifications, issued for applying certain provisions of the Army Act, 1950, and Chapter IV of the Army Rules, 1954, to the GREF, were *ultra vires*.

11. Having analysed the provisions of the Constitution, the provisions of the Army Act and the conditions of service of a member of the GREF, the Court, in *R. Viswan*'s case (supra), concluded, at para 14, that the member of the GREF are members of the Armed Forces within the meaning of Article 33 of the Constitution of India. The relevant observations, made, in this regard, in *R. Viswan*'s case (supra), read thus:

*"We may make it clear that **it is only in regard to the members of GREF that we have taken the view that they are members of the Armed Forces within the meaning of Article 33.** So far as casual labour employed by GREF is concerned, we do not wish to express any opinion on this question whether they too are members of the Armed Forces or not, since that it is not a question which arises for consideration before us. The writ petitions are accordingly dismissed with no order as to costs. The special leave petitions will also stand rejected."* (Emphasis is added)

12. From what have been observed and held above, in *R. Viswan* (supra), there can be no escape from the conclusion that the members of the GREF are also the members of Armed Forces within the meaning of Article 33. In this regard, the Supreme Court, in *R. Viswan* (supra), also held that GREF is an integral part of the Armed Forces and the members of GREF can legally be said to be members of the Armed Forces within the meaning of Article 33. The relevant observations, appearing in *R. Viswan* (supra), read as under:

*"10. It is undoubtedly true that as stated by the Minister of Defence, **GREF is a civilian construction force and the members of GREF are civilian employees under the administrative control of the Border Roads Development Board and that the engineer officers amongst them constitute what may be designed as "Central Civil Services, within GREF, but that does not mean that they cannot be at the same time form an integral part of theArmed Forces.** The fact that they are described as civilian employees and they have their own special rules of recruitment and are governed by the Central Civil Service (Classification, Control and Appeal) Rules, 1965 is not determinative of the question whether they are members of the Armed Forces. The question whether the members of GREF can be said to be members of the Armed Forces for the purpose of attracting the applicability of Article 33 must depend essentially on the character of GREF, its organisational set up, its functions, the role it is called upon to play in relation to the Armed Forces and the depth and intimacy of its connection and the extent of its integration with the Armed Forces **and if judged by this criterion, they are found to be members of the Armed Forces, the mere fact that they are non-combatant civilians governed by the Central Civil Services (Classification Control and Appeal) Rules 1965, cannot make any difference** (AIR 1983 SC 658 to 673, 674). Applying the aforesaid criteria in determining the status*

*of members of GREF, the Court held: "**It is abundantly clear from those facts and circumstances that GREF is an integral part of the Armed Forces and the members of GREF can legitimately be said to be members of the Armed Forces within the meaning of Article 33.**" (Emphasis is added)*

13. From the above observations, made in *R. Viswan* (supra), it becomes clear that GREF is a civilian construction force and the members of the GREF are civil employees under the administrative control of the Border Roads Development Board. At the same time, however, GREF is an integral part of the Armed Forces and the members of GREF can legally be said to be members of the Armed Forces within the meaning of Article 33 and, hence, the provisions ofthe Army Act, 1950, are, for the purpose of discipline, extended, though to a limited extent, to the members of the GREF. The fact that the members of the GREF are described as civil employees and they have their own special rules of recruitment and are governed by the Central Civil Service (Classification, Control and Appeal) Rules, 1965, is not determinative of the question whether they are members of the Armed Forces or not. The answer to the question, whether the members of the GREF can, for the purpose of attracting applicability of Article 33, be said to be members of the Armed Forces, must depend essentially on the character of the GREF, its organizational set up, its functions and the role it is called upon to play in relation to the Armed Forces and the depth and intimacy of its connection and the extent of its integration with the Armed Forces. The mere fact that the members of GREF are non-combatant civilians and they are governed by the Central Civil Services (Classification Control and Appeal) Rules 1965, cannot make any difference.

14. What emerges from the above discussion is that notwithstanding the fact that the provisions of the Central Civil Services (Classification, Control and Appeals) Rules, 1965, are applicable to a member of GREF, a member of GREF is nonetheless a member of the Armed Forces by virtue of the notifications, which have been issued by the Central Government by taking recourse to its powers under Section 4 of the Army Act, 1950, and since a member of the GREF is a member of the Armed Forces within the meaning of Article 33 of the Constitution of India, Section 2(a) of the Administrative Tribunals Act, 1985, would make the provisions, embodied in the Administrative Tribunals Act, 1985, inapplicable to the members of the GREF inasmuch as Section 2(a) of the Administrative Tribunals Act, 1985, clearly lays down that the provisions of this Act shall not apply to, amongst others, any member of the Naval, Military or Air Force or of any other Armed Forces of the Union. A member of the GREF, therefore, cannot invoke the provisions of Section 14 and/or Section 19 of the Administrative Tribunals Act, 1985.

15. The above inference gets strengthened from the order, dated 09 January 1998, passed, in Special Leave Petition (Civil) No.8096/1995 (*Union of India v. Smt. Vidyawati*).

16. In *Vidyawati's* case (supra), husband of the petitioner, *Vidyawati*, was appointed, on temporary basis, in GREF and was, subsequently, awarded *quasi permanent* status and, later on, promoted to the post of Cook. *Vidyawati's* husband, Murarilal, suffered from heart ailment in the month of December, 1980, and remained under treatment for heart ailments until he was discharged on being declared physically unfit for service. Less than nine months after his discharge from GREF, *Vidyawati's* husband, Murarilal, died. *Vidyawati*, then, applied to the authorities concerned seeking to obtain retiral benefits arising out of the death of her husband. As the same were not madeavailable to her, she applied to the Central Administrative Tribunal, Allahabad Bench. This application gave rise to Original Application No.1195/1993. The present petitioners, as respondents in the OA No.1195/1993, resisted the maintainability of the proceeding on the ground that the GREF is an integral part of the Armed Forces in terms of the Government of India's letter, dated 14 August 1985, and SRO No.329, dated 23 September 1969, and, hence, the Central Administrative Tribunal had no jurisdiction. Having taken into account the fact that service of *Vidyawati's* husband was governed by the Central Civil Services (Temporary Service) Rules, 1965, the learned Tribunal concluded, in its order, dated 27 July 1994, that it had the jurisdiction in the matter and, accordingly, directed the Union of India to work out the *gratuity* payable to the husband of the applicant, *Vidyawati*. Aggrieved by the order, so made, the Union of India filed a Special Leave Petition, which gave rise to Special Leave Petition (Civil) No.8096/1995.

17. The Supreme Court passed an order, on 09 January1988, in *Vidyawati's* case (supra), taking the view that members of GREF cannot, in the light of the decision, in *R. Viswan* (supra), move Central Administrative Tribunal and, hence, the impugned decision of the learned Tribunal that it had jurisdiction to deal with the matter was not sustainable. The Supreme Court accordingly set aside the order, dated 27 July 1994, passed by the learned Tribunal with liberty, however, givento the applicant, *Vidyawati*, to move the High Court for appropriate reliefs, if she is so desired.

18. We may pause, at this stage, to point out that at the time, when the order, dated 09 January 1988, was made, the decision, in *L. Chandra Kumar v. Union of India,* reported in (1997) 3 SCC 261, had not been rendered and while ousting the jurisdiction of the High Court, under Articles 226 and 227 of the Constitution of India, the Administrative Tribunal's Act, 1985, preserved and saved the Supreme Court's powers under Article 136 and, hence, a person, aggrieved by an order of a Central Administrative Tribunal, could have challenged the same by invoking Article 136.

19. Coupled with the above, we may also point out that though the order, dated 09 January 1988, was passed, in *Vidyawati's* case (supra), by the Supreme Court in a Special Leave Petition, it needs to be borne in mind that the Supreme Court's observations, while making the order, dated 09 January 1988, would amount to declaration of law under Article 141 of the Constitution of India and shall be binding on all courts and tribunals within the territory of India. A reference, in this regard, may be made to the case of *Kunhayammed v. State of Kerala,* reported in (2000) 6 SCC 359, more particularly, para 27 and para 44 (v), wherein the Supreme Court has clearly laid down that if provision for appeal is made against an order passed by a court and an appeal is preferred, then, the decision of the lower court/forum getsmerged into the decision of the appellate court and it is the decision of the appellate court, which subsists, remains operative and is apt for enforcement in the eye of law, but the position of the Special Leave Applications, made under Article 36, is, somewhat, different in the sense that the jurisdiction, conferred by Article 136 of the Constitution, is divisible into two stages inasmuch as the first stage is up to the disposal of the prayer for special leave to file an appeal and the second stage commences if and when the leave to appeal is granted and the special leave petition is converted into an appeal. In no uncertain words, laid down the Supreme Court, in *Kunhayammed's* case (supra), that the doctrine of merger is not a doctrine of universal or unlimited application; rather, it depends on the nature of jurisdiction exercised by the superior forum and the content or subject-matter of challenge laid shall be determinative of the applicability of the doctrine of merger and that the superior jurisdiction should be capable of reversing, modifying or affirming the order put in issue before it. It is further observed, in *Kunhayammed's* case (supra), that under Article 136 of the Constitution, the Supreme Court may reverse, modify or affirm the judgement/decree/order appealed against only when it exercises appellate jurisdiction (i.e., after the leave to appeal is granted) and not while it exercises the discretionary jurisdiction on the question as to whether the petition for special leave to appeal shall be granted or not and, thus, the doctrine or merger, in such cases, comes into play if the special leave to appeal is granted and not when the question as to whether the leave would be granted or not is considered and decided. It has been pointed out, in *Kunhayammed*'s case (supra), by the Supreme Court that an order, refusing special leave to appeal, may be a non-speaking order or a speaking one and, in either case, it does not attract the doctrine of merger inasmuch as an order, refusing special leave to appeal, does not stand substituted in place of the order under challenge and that what such an order implies is that the Supreme Court was not inclined to exercise its discretion so as to allow the appeal being filed.

20. It is extremely pertinent to note that in *Kunhayammed*'s case (supra), the Supreme Court has concluded that if an order refusing leave to appeal is a speaking order, i.e., when reasons are assigned for refusing the grant of leave, then, the order has two implications. Firstly, the statement of law, contained in such an order, is a declaration of law by the Supreme Court within the meaning of Article 141 of the Constitution. Secondly, other than the declaration of law, whatever is stated in the order, are the findings recorded by the Supreme Court, which would bind the parties thereto and also the Court, tribunal or authority in any proceedings subsequent thereto by way of judicial discipline, the Supreme Court being the Apex Court of the country. (See also State of *Arunachal Pradesh v. Nefa Udyog* 2004(2) GLT 724. (Emphasis is added)

21. In the light of the decision, reached by the Supreme Court, in *Vidyawati*'s case (supra), one can have no escape from the conclusion, and we do conclude, that as far as Central Administrative Tribunal is concerned, a member of the GREF is not covered, in the light of the decision in *R. Viswan* (supra) read with the decision in *Vidyawati*'s case (supra), by the provisions of the Administrative Tribunals Act, 1985, and, hence, a member of the GREF would be disentitled from invoking the jurisdiction of the Central Administrative Tribunal.

22. The incidental question, which has arisen, in the present writ petition, is: whether a member of the GREF is covered by the provisions embodied in the Armed Forces Tribunal Act, 2007?

23. The answer to the question, posed above, brings us to Section 2 of the Armed Forces Tribunal Act, 2007, which reads as under:

"**Applicability of the Act** : *(1) The provisions of this Act shall apply to all persons subject to the army Act, 1950, (46 of 1950) the Navy*

Act, 1957 (62 of 1957) and the Air Force Act, 1950 (45 of 1950) (2)
This Act shall also apply to retired personnel subject to the Army
Act, 1950 (46 of 1950) or the Navy Act, 1957 (62 of 1957) or the Air
Force Act, 1950 (45 of 1950) including their dependants, heirs and
successors, in so far as it relates to their service matters."

24. From a bare reading of the provisions of Section 2 of the Armed Forces Tribunal's Act, 2007, what becomes transparent is that Armed Forces Tribunal Act, 2007, applies, *inter alia,* to a person, who is subject to the Army Act, 1950.

25. In the case of GREF, the provisions of the Army Act, 1950, have been applied, though to a limited extent, by virtue of notifications, which have been issued, in this regard, by the Central Government taking recourse to the powers under Section 4. For the purpose of clarity, Section 4 of the Army Act, 1950, being relevant, is reproduced below:

"4.   **Application of Act to certain forces under Central Government**:-

(1) The Central Government may, by notification, apply, with or without modifications, all or any of the provisions of this Act to any force raised and maintained in India under the authority of that Government, and suspend the operation of any other enactment for the time being applicable to the said force.

(2) The provisions of this Act so applied shall have effect in respect of persons belonging to the said force as they have effect in respect of persons subject to this Act holding in the regular Army the same or equivalent rank as the aforesaid persons hold for the time being in the said force.

(3) The provisions of this Act so applied shall also have effect in respect of persons who are employed by or are in the service of or are followers of or accompany any portion of the said force as they have effect in respect of persons subject to this Act under clause (i) of sub- section (1) of section (2).

(4) While any of the provisions of this Act apply to the said force, the Central Government may, by notification, direct by what authority any jurisdiction, powers or duties incident to the operation of these provisions shall be exercised or performed in respect of the said force."

26. A minute reading of the provisions of Section 4 of the Army Act, 1950, clearly reveals that when the provisions of the Army Act, 1950, are made applicable to a person or group of persons, then, such a person or group of persons would be treated as a person or persons subject to the Army Act, 1950. Viewed from this angle, when the Central Government has extended, by notifications, the provisions of the Army Act, 1950, to the members of the GREF, the members of the GREF would, ordinarily, be required to be treated as persons subject to the Army Act, 1950.

27. What is, however, inescapable to note is that the Army Act has not been applied, as a whole, to the members of the GREF. Far from this, limited numbers of provisions have been made applicable to the members of the GREF for the purpose of maintaining discipline. When the Army Act, 1950, has not been made applicable, as a whole, to a member of GREF, the effect is that a member of GREF would, ordinarily, be a person subject to the Army Act, 1950, particularly, when one notices that the Central Government is empowered, under Section 4(1) of the Army Act, 1950, to apply all or any of the provisions of the Army Act, 1950, to any force raised and maintained in India under the authority of the Central Government.

28. Thus, even though limited provisions of the Army Act, 1950, have been made applicable to the members of the GREF, Section 4 of the Army Act, 1950, when read as a whole, makes it abundantly clear that though limited provisions of the Army Act, 1950, have been made applicable to the members of the GREF, the members of the GREF would nevertheless be regarded as persons subject to the Army Act, 1950, to the extent that the provisions of the Army Act, 1950, in a given situation, cover their act and in respect of the provisions of the Army Act, 1950, which have been made available to the members of the GREF, a member of the GREF has to take recourse to the Armed Forces Tribunal Act, 2007. For instance, Armed Forces Tribunal has, by virtue of Section 15 of the Armed Forces Tribunal Act, 2007, appellate jurisdiction against any order, decision, finding or sentence, which may be passed by a Court Martial.

29. Situated thus, it becomes abundantly clear that not only a member of the Armed Forces, but even a member of the GREF, who is tried by a Court Martial, has the right to prefer appeal by taking recourse to Section 15 of the Armed Forces Tribunal Act, 2007. However, all the provisions of the Army Act, 1950, having not been made applicable to the members of the GREF, neither all punishments, as embodied under Section 71 of the Army Act, 1950, can be imposed on a member of the GREF, nor can he, in all eventualities, invoke Section 15 of the Armed Forces Tribunal Act, 2007. In this regard, it is noteworthy that by virtue of SRO 329, dated 03.09.1960, issued by the Government of India, in exercise of its power conferred by sub-Section (1) of Section 4 of the Army Act, 1950, the provisions of the Army Act and the Rules, framed there under, have been applied to the members of the GREF. While so applying the provisions of the Army Act, 1950, to the members of the GREF, the application of the provisions of the Army Act and the Rules, framed there under, has been kept minimal for the purpose of maintaining discipline. Thus, while the provisions of Section 21 of the Army Act, 1950, has been made applicable to the members of the GREF, the provisions of Section 71 of the Army Act, 1950, have not been made applicable in *toto* inasmuch as the provisions, embodied in clauses (d), (e), (f), (g) and (k) of Section 71, which prescribes the penalties of cashiering, dismissal from the service, reduction in rank, forfeiture of seniority of rank and forfeiture of all arrears of pay and allowances, respectively, have not been made applicable. As a corollary thereto, the provisions of the Central Civil Services (Control, Classification and Appeals) Rules, 1965, would be applicable to those matters, which have been left exempted by the Government of India's Notification aforementioned. Obviously, therefore, the GREF personnel, if aggrieved by the imposition of any of the penalties prescribed by clauses (a), (b), (c), (h), (i), (j) and (l) of Section 71 of the Army Act, 1950, would have the right to prefer appeal under Section 50 of the Armed Forces Tribunal Act, 2007. For remaining service related matters, a member of the GREF would be covered by the provisions of the Central Civil Services (Control, Classification and Appeals) Rules, 1965, of course, all the provisions of the Constitution of India.

30. The above inference, that a member of the GREF can be dealt with by taking recourse to the Central Civil Services (Control, Classification and Appeals) Rules, 1965, when he is tried by a court-martial and has not been imposed punishment(s), which SRO 329, dated 23.09.1960, exempts, gets strengthened from the decision, in *Union of India v. Sunil Kumar Sarkar* (2001) 3 SCC 414, wherein a General Court-Martial was initiated against a GREF personal and, on conclusion of his trial, he, having been found guilty of some of the charges framed against him, was sentenced to undergo rigorous imprisonment for one year, which was, later on, reduced to six months. Because of the exemption of clause (e) of Section 71 of the Army Act, 1950, which, otherwise, provides for dismissal from service, the respondent, *Sunil Kumar Sarkar*, could not be dismissed despite being sentenced to undergo rigorous imprisonment for six months. However, as the conviction of the respondent, Sunil Kumar Sarkar, could not have automatically resulted into his dismissal from service, a proceeding under Rule 19 of the Central Civil Services (Control, Classification and Appeals) Rules, 1965, was initiated and this proceeding came to be challenged by the respondent. The Supreme Court, in Sunil Kumar Sarkar (supra) took the view that conviction and punishment of imprisonment by General *Court Martial*, under the Army Act, 1950, and punishment of dismissal by disciplinary authority, under the Central Civil Services (Control, Classification and Appeals) Rules, 1965, would not amount to double jeopardy, because, a disciplinary procedure, as contemplated by Article 311(2)(a) of the Constitution, is a summary procedure provided to take disciplinary action against a government servant, who is already convicted in a criminal proceeding, and Rule 19 of the Central Civil Services (Control, Classification and Appeals) Rules, 1965, is in conformity with the above provisions of the Constitution. The Supreme Court further held, in *Sunil Kumar Sarkar* (supra), that the two proceedings aforementioned operate in two different fields though the crime or the misconduct might arise out of the same act. The Court Martial proceedings deal with the penal aspect of the misconduct, but the proceedings under the Central Civil Services (Control, Classification and Appeals) Rules, 1965, deal with the disciplinary aspect of the misconduct. The two proceedings do not overlap. The relevant observations, made by the Supreme Court, in *Sunil Kumar Sarkar* (supra), read as under:

> "**8.** *The Division Bench also found fault with the order of dismissal passed by the disciplinary authority on the ground that the same was solely based on the conviction suffered by the respondent in the court-martial proceedings. The Court in this regard held that the disciplinary authority had a predetermined mind when he passed the order of dismissal. Here again, in our opinion, the Division Bench did not take into consideration Rule 19 of the Central Rules which contemplates that if any penalty is imposed on a government servant on his conviction in a criminal charge, the disciplinary authority can make such order as it deems fit (dismissal from service is one such order contemplated under Rule 19) on initiating disciplinary proceedings and after giving the delinquent officer an opportunity of making a representation on the penalty proposed to be imposed. As a matter of fact, this type of disciplinary procedure is contemplated in the Constitution itself as could be seen in Article 311(2) (a). Rule 19 of the Central Rules is in conformity with the above provisions of the Constitution. This, as we see, is a summary procedure provided*

to take disciplinary action against a government servant who is already convicted in a criminal proceeding. The very foundation of imposing punishment under Rule 19 is that there should be a prior conviction on a criminal charge. Therefore, the question of having a predetermined mind does not arise in such cases. All that a disciplinary authority is expected to do under Rule 19 is to be satisfied that the officer concerned has been convicted of a criminal charge and has been given a show-cause notice and reply to such show-cause notice, if any, should be properly considered before making any order under this Rule. Of course, it will have to bear in mind the gravity of the conviction suffered by the government servant in the criminal proceedings before passing any order under Rule 19 to maintain the proportionality of punishment. In the instant case, the disciplinary authority has followed the procedure laid down in Rule 19, hence, we cannot agree with the Division Bench that the said disciplinary authority had any predetermined mind when it passed the order of dismissal.

*11. Before concluding we must point out that during the course of arguments, a doubt was raised as to the maintainability of the concurrent proceedings initiated against the respondent by the authorities. **The respondent in this case has been punished for the same misconduct both under the Army Act as also under the Central Rules. Hence, a question arises whether this would tantamount to "double jeopardy" and is in violation of Article 20 of the Constitution of India. Having considered the arguments addressed in this behalf, we are of the opinion that so far as the concurrent proceedings initiated by the Organisation against the respondent both under the Army Act and the Central Rules are concerned, they are unexceptionable. These two proceedings operate in two different fields though the crime or the misconduct might arise out of the same act. The court-martial proceedings deal with the penal aspect of the misconduct while the proceedings under the Central Rules deal with the disciplinary aspect of the misconduct. The two proceedings do not overlap. As a matter of fact, Notification No SRO-329 dated 23-9-1960 issued under the Central Rules and under sub-sections (1) and (4) of Section 4 of the Army Act makes this position clear. By this notification, the punishments that could be meted out under the Central Rules have been taken out of the purview of the court-martial proceedings under the Army Act. We further find support for this view of ours in the judgment of this***

Court in R. Viswan v. Union of India. " (Emphasis added).

31. Consequently, in the past, a member of the GREF, when tried by a Court Martial, could have, ordinarily, invoked, against the order, decision or finding, the High Court's jurisdiction under Article 226; but such recourse cannot, in the light of *R. Viswan*'s case (supra), be had, now, in respect of matters, which are covered by the Armed Forces Tribunal Act, 2007. However, as persons, subject to the Army Act, they would not fall under the Armed Forces Tribunal Act, 2007, in respect of those matters, which are covered by the Central Civil Services (Control, Classification and Appeals) Rules, 1965, inasmuch as in respect of those matters, which are covered by Central Civil Services (Control, Classification and Appeals) Rules, 1965, a member of the GREF would not be able to take recourse to the Armed Forces Tribunal Act, 2007, because Armed Forces Tribunal Act, 2007, would not, in the light of the provisions of the Armed Forces Tribunal Act, 2007, have jurisdiction to deal with the matters, which are covered by the Central Civil Services (Control, Classification and Appeals) Rules, 1965, and, hence, in such cases, his remedy would lie, in an appropriate case, in taking recourse to Article 226 of the Constitution of India inasmuch as jurisdiction of the Armed Forces Tribunal Act, 2007, does not oust, and could not have ousted, in the light of the decision, in *L. Chandra Kumar* (supra), the High Court's jurisdiction, under Article 226, by virtue of Section 14 of the Armed Forces Tribunal Act, 2007.

32. What surfaces from the above discussion is that the present respondent, as a member of the GREF and a member of the Armed Forces, cannot, in the light of the decision, in *R. Viswan* (supra) read with the decision, in *Vidyawati*'s case (supra), and could not have taken recourse to the provisions of the Administrative Tribunals Act, 1985. Consequently, the learned Central Administrative Tribunal has/had no jurisdiction in the matter of the petitioner's (i.e., the present respondent's) grievance as regards refusal to grant him financial up-gradation and, at the same time, the respondent's grievance shows that even the Armed Forces Tribunal cannot redress, and could not have redressed, his grievance as regards refusal to grant him financial up-gradation. The remedy of the respondent, therefore, lies in making appropriate application in the High Court, under Article 226 of the Constitution of India, or in instituting appropriate suit for remedy of his grievances.

33. In the result and for the reasons discussed above, this writ petition succeeds and the impugned order, dated 18 June 2012, passed by the learned Tribunal is hereby set aside and quashed.

34. ....

35. With the above observations and directions, this writ petition shall stand disposed of.

36. No order as to costs.

Bibliography

Ackerman Bruce, The Emergency Constitution, *Yale Law Journal*, Vol. 113, 2004, pp. 1029–91.

Ahlberg K and Brunn N., 'Sweden: Transition through collective bargaining', in Blanpain, R., Blanke T. and Rose E., (Eds.).2005.*Collective Bargaining Wages in Comparative Perspective: Germany, France, the Netherlands, Sweden and the United Kingdom*, The Hague: Kluwer Law International, pp. 117-145.

Argent Pierre d', 'Military Law in Belgium', in Nolte George (ed.). 2003. *European Military Law Systems*, Berlin: De Gruyter Recht, pp. 183-232.

Arnold, Roberta, Military Criminal Procedure and Judicial Guarantees: The Example of Switzerland, *Journal of International Criminal Justice*, Vol. 3 (3), 2005, pp. 749-777.

Ashworth Andrew. 2005. *Sentencing and Criminal Justice*, Cambridge: Cambridge University Press.

Austin Granville. 2003. *Working A Democratic Constitution: A History of the Indian experience*, New Delhi: Oxford India Paperback.

Bakken Tim, A Woman Soldier's Right to Combat: Equal Protection in the Military, *Wm. & Mary J. Women & L.*, Vol. 20, 2014, pp. 271-294.

Bartle R. and HeineckenL. (eds.).2006. *Military Unionism in the Post-Cold War Era: A Future Reality?* London: Routledge Press.

Bastick Megan, *Integrating a Gender Perspective into Internal Oversight within Armed Forces*, Geneva: DCAF, OSCE, OSCE/ODIHR, 2014, pp. 64.

Basu Durga Das. 2009. *Shorter Constitution of India*, Vol I and II, Gurgaon: LexisNexis, Butterworths Wadhwa.

Besselink F.M., 'Military law in the Netherlands' in: G. Nolte (Ed.), 2003. European Military Law Systems, Berlin: De Gruyter Recht, pp. 548-644.

Blackette Jeff, 2009. *Rant on Court Martial and Service Law*, Oxford: Oxford University Press.

Blum Gabriella, The Crime and Punishment of States, *The Yale Journal of International Law*, Vol. 38, 2013, p. 57-122.

Born, H., Fluri P., and Johnsson A., (eds.).2003. Handbook on Parliamentary Oversight of the Security Sector: Principles, Mechanisms and Practices, Geneva: Geneva Centre for the Democratic Control of Armed Forces, Inter-Parliamentary Union.

Bradley, A.W., Ewing, K.D. and Knight, C.J.S. 2015.*Constitutional and Administrative Law*, UK: Pearson Education Limited.

Brickman Annika, Military Trade Unionism in Sweden, *Armed Forces and Society*, Vol. 2, No. 4, August 1976, pp. 529-537.

Buckingham Jake, Current trends surrounding the constitutional freedom of political communication, *Bond University Student Law Review*, Vol. 4, Issue 1/2, 2016, pp. 1-12.

Bulmer Elliot. 2017. *What is a Constitution? Principles and Concepts*, International Institute for Democracy and Electoral Assistance (International IDEA), Sweden.

Caforio G., 'Unionization of the Military: Representation of the Interests of Military Personnel' in: CaforioG., (ed.). 2006.*Handbook of the Sociology of the Military*, New York: Springer, pp. 311-323.

Caforio, G. (ed.). 2003. *Handbook of the Sociology of the Military*, New York: Kluwer Academic/ Plenum Publishers.

Callaghan, J., and F. Kernic (eds.). 2003.*Armed Forces and International Security: Global Trends and Issues*, Munster: Lit Verlag.

Callaghan J., 'Unions and the German Armed Forces: The Citizens in Uniform', in Bartle Richard and Lindy Heinecken (ed.). 2006.*Military Unionism in the Post-Cold War Era: A future reality?* London: Routledge, pp. 165-176.

Careiras, H. 2006.*Gender and the Military: Women in the Armed Forces of Western Democracies*, London: Routledge.

Carswell, Andrew J., Classifying the conflict: A soldier's dilemma, *International Review of the Red Cross*, Vol. 91, No. 873, March 2009, pp. 143-161.

Clode Charles M. 1869. *Military Forces of the Crown: Their Administration and Government*, London: John Murray.

Crawford J., The Criteria for Statehood in International Law, *British Yearbook of International Law*, Vol. 48, 1977, pp. 93-182.

Cusack, Colin, We've Talked the Talk, Time to Walk the Walk: Meeting International Human Rights Law Standards for US Military Investigations, *Military Law Review*, Volume 217, Fall 2013, pp. 48-90.

Defence Instructions (General), Political Activities of Defence Personnel, the Department of Defence, Canberra Act 2600, 4 October 2007.

Dixit K. C., Addressing Stress-Related Issues in Army, *IDSA Occasional Paper No 17*, Institute for Defence Studies and Analyses, New Delhi, 2011.

Dixit, K. C. 2012. *Building Army's Human Resource for Sub-Conventional Warfare*, New Delhi: Pentagon Press.

Fidell Eugene R. and Sullivan Dwight H., (ed.). 2002. *Evolving Military Justice*, Annapolis: Naval Institute Press.

Finner, Samuel E. 2002. *The Man on Horseback: The Role of the Military in Politics*, USA: Transaction Publishers.

Fleck, D. (ed.), 2008. *The Handbook of International Humanitarian Law*, Oxford: Oxford University Press.

Flynn Sean Patrick, The More? Uniform Code of Military Justice (and a practical way to make it better), *Notre Dame Law Review*, Vol. 92, No. 5, 2017, pp. 2179-2201.

Frowe Helen. 2011. *The Ethics of War and Peace: An Introduction*, London: Routledge.

GerkrathJorg, 'Military Law in France', in Nolte George (ed.), 2003, *European Military Law Systems*, Berlin: De Gruyter Recht, pp. 275-336.

Gibson Michael R., International Human Rights Law and the Administration of Justice through Military Tribunals: Preserving Utility while

Precluding Impunity, *Journal of International Law and International Relations,* Vol. 4(1), 2008, pp. 1-48.

Gross Oren and Fionnuala Ni Aolain. 2006. *Law in Time of Armed Conflict: Emergency Powers in Theory and Practice*, Cambridge: Cambridge University Press.

Hansen Victor, The Impact of Military Justice Reforms on the Law of Armed Conflict: How to Avoid Unintended Consequences, *Michigan State International Law Review*, Vol. 12 (2), 2013, p. 229-272.

Harrel, M., and Miller L., 1997. *New Opportunities for Military Women: Effects Upon Readiness, Cohesion and Morale*, California, Rand: Santa Monica.

Hartle Antony E. 2004. *Moral Issues in Military Decision Making*, USA: University of Kansas.

Haynes Jeff, 'The Principles of Good Governance', in Cleary Laura R. and Teri McConville (ed.). 2006. *Managing Democracy in Democracy*, Routledge, pp. 17-31.

Head Michael and Scott Mann. 2009. *Domestic Deployment of the Armed Forces: Military Powers, Law and Human Rights*, USA: Ashgate.

Heinecken L., Ban Military Unions, They're a Threat to National Security! So Where to from Here,*Strategic Review for Southern Africa*, Vol. 31, No. 2, 2009, pp. 1-18.

Heinecken L., Military Unionism and the Management of Employee Relations within the Armed Forces: A Comparative Perspective, *International Journal of Comparative Labour Law and Industrial Relations*, Vol. 4, No. 26, 2010, pp. 401-420.

Hummel N., Citizens in Uniform: A Legal Impulse Toward Unionization of European Armed Forces, pp. 1-36.

International Legal Protection of Human Rights in Armed Conflict, United Nations, Office of the High Commissioner of Human Rights, 2011,HR/PUB/11/01.

Jain M.P. 2018. *Indian Constitutional Law*, Gurgaon: LexisNexis.

Jha U.C., 2017. *Indian Military Domestic Deployment: Armed Forces Special Powers Act and Human Rights*, Vij Books India Pvt. Ltd.

Jha U.C., 2009. *The Military Justice System in India: An Analysis*, Gurgaon: LexisNexis, Butterworths, Wadhwa.

Kalhan Anil, Gerald P. Conroy, Mamta Kaushal, Sam Scott Miller and Jed S. Rakoff, Colonial Continuities: Human Rights, Terrorism, and Human Security, *Columbia Journal of Asian Law*, Vol. 20 (1), 2006, pp. 93-234.

Kartikeya Sameer Sharan, Social Media and India Army's New-Age Soldier, *CLAWS Journal*, Summer 2017, pp. 120-133.

King Anthony, Women in Combat, *The Three Sword Magazine*, Vol. 29, 2015, pp. 22-26.

Koltermann Jens O., Citizen in Uniform: Democratic Germany and the Changing *Bundeswehr, Parameters*, Summer 2012, p.108-126.

Kumar Nilendra, 2013. *Law Relating to the Armed Forces in India: An Exhaustive Treatise on Military Laws*, New Delhi: Universal Law Publishing Co. Pvt. Ltd.

Leigh I. D. and Born H. 2008.*Handbook on human rights and fundamental freedoms of armed forces personnel*, Warsaw: OSCE/ODIHR.

Lillich, Richard B., The Paris Minimum Standards of Human Rights Norms in a State of Emergency, *American Journal of International Law*, Vol. 79, 1985, pp. 1072-81.

Malan M., 'The Implications of Unionisation for the Combat effectiveness of the Armed Forces' in: *A compilation of Articles Relating to the Revision of South African Defence Legislation*, South Africa: Institute for Defence Policy, 1994.

Malik, V P, Human Rights in the Armed Forces, *Journal of Human Rights*, Vol. 4, 2005.

Mandeville L., Syndicalism and the French Military System, *Armed Forces and Society*, Vol. 2, No. 4, 1976, pp. 539-552.

Mangala A. C., 1992. *Commentary on Military Law in India*, Calcutta: Eastern Law House.

Mark Tushnet, Constitution-Making: An Introduction, *Tex. L. Rev.* Vol. 91, Issue 3, 2013, p. 1983.

Marston Daniel P. and Chander S. Sundaram (ed.). 2007. *A Military History of India and South Asia: from the East India Company to the Nuclear Era*, London: Praeger Security International.

Martin M. L., 'The French military and union rights: At the margin of full citizenship', in: Bartle R. andHeineckenL. (eds.).2006.*Military Unionism in the Post-Cold War Era: A Future Reality*, London: Routledge Press, pp. 177-197.

Menezes S. L. 1999. *Fidelity and Honour: The India Army*, New Delhi: Oxford India Paperback.

Michelle Grattan, Most Troops Home by Next Year's End, *The Age*, 17 April 2012, Melbourne edition, p. 4.

J. Mittelstadt J., The Army is a Service, Not a Job: Unionization, Employment, and the Meaning of Military Service in the Late-Twentieth Century United States, *International Labour and Working-Class History*, No. 80, 2011, pp. 29-52.

Mnisi, Eric Z., National Security and the Constitutional Right to Join Military Trade Unions: Is Constitutional Amendment an Imperative, *Scientia Militaria, South African Journal of Military Studies*, Vol. 45, No. 2, 2017, pp. 129-139.

Moskos, C., Williams J.A. and Segal D. (eds.). 2000. *The Post-modern Military: Armed Forces after the Cold War*, Oxford: Oxford University Press.

Moskos C., From Institution to Occupation. Trends in Military Organization, *Armed forces and Society*, Vol. 4, No. 4, 1977, pp. 41-50.

Nesterov, V.S. and Pruefert A.D. 2006.*Military Unionism: The Establishment of Professional Organizations/Trade Unions of Servicemen and their Present Position*, Moscow: Ves Mir.

Nolte George (ed.). 2003. *European Military Law Systems*, Berlin: De Gruyter Recht.

Osiel, M. 1999, *Obeying Orders: Atrocity, Military Discipline and the Laws of War*, New Brunswick, NJ: Transaction Publishers.

Nolte Georg and Heike Krieger, 'Military Law in Germany', in Nolte George (ed.), 2003, *European Military Law Systems*, Berlin: De Gruyter Recht, pp. 337-4261.

Pal Samaraditya. 2016.*India's Constitution: Origin and Evolution*, Vol. I and III, Gurgaon: LexisNexis.

Ram Samay. 2011. *Stress, Suicides and Fratricides in the Army: Crisis*

Within, New Delhi: Vij Publications India Pvt. Ltd.

Reuter Emily, Second Class Citizen Soldiers: A Proposal for Greater First Amendment protections for America's Military Personnel, *Wm. & Mary Bill Rts. J.*, Vo. 16, issue 1, 2007, pp. 315-344.

RoweP.,The Soldier as a Citizen in Uniform: A reappraisal, *New Zealand Armed Forces Law Review*, Vol. 7, 2007, pp. 1-17.

Rowe P. 2006. *The Impact of Human Right Laws on Armed Forces*. UK: Cambridge University Press.

Rowe, P. and Whelan, C. (eds). 1985. *Military Intervention in Democratic Societies*, London: Croom Helm.

RoznaiYanis. 2017. *Unconstitutional Constitutional Amendments: The Limits of Amending Powers*, Oxford: OUP.

Sassoli, M. and McChesney A., Conscripts' rights and military justice training manual, Chisinau: Centre for Recruits' and Servicemen's Rights Protection of the Republic of Moldova, 2002.

Sato Hiromi, Modes of International Criminal Justice and General Principles of Criminal Responsibility, *Journal of International Law*, Vol. 4, No. 3, 2012, pp. 765-807.

Schlueter, D.A. 2004.*Military Criminal Justice: Practice and Procedure*, Charlottesville, Virginia: LexisNexis.

Segal D. R., 'Worker democracy in military organization', in: Taylor W.J., Arango R.J. and Lockwood R.S. 1997.*Military Unions: US Trends and Issues*, Beverly Hills/London: SAGE Publications, pp. 28-53.

Sharma O.P., 1990. *Military Law in India*, Bombay: M.N. Tripathi Pvt Ltd.

Shelton, D. 2005.,*Remedies in International Human Rights Law*, Oxford: Oxford University Press.

Silk, James J., International Criminal Justice and the Protection of Human Rights: The Rule of Law or the Hubris of Law? *The Yale Journal of International Law*, Vol. 39, Spring 2014, pp. 94-114.

Simons, Beth A. 2009. *Mobilizing for Human Rights: International Law in Domestic Politics*, Cambridge: Cambridge University Press.

Soldiers and Human Rights: Lawyers to right of them, lawyers to left of them, *The Economist*, 9 August 2015.

Sorensen Henning, Danish military trade unions and their political role, in Bartle Richard and Lindy Heinecken (ed.). 2006.*Military Unionism in the Post-Cold War Era: A future reality?* London: Routledge, pp. 197-211.

Snider, T.W., Adler A.B. and Castro C.A. (eds.). 2005. *Military Life: The Psychology of Serving in Peace*, Westport, Connecticut: Praeger.

The Constitution of Sweden, Published by SverigesRiksdag, 2016, SE-100 12, Stockholm, Sweden.

Tomkins Adam, In Defence of the Political Constitution, *Oxford Journal of Legal Studies*, Vol. 22 (1), 2002, pp. 157-175.

Toney, Raymond J. and Shazia N. Anwar, International Human Rights Law and Military Personnel: A Look Behind the Barrack Walls, *American University International Law Review*, Vol. 14, No. 2, 1998, pp. 519-543.

Trechsel Stefan. 2005. *Human Rights in Criminal Proceedings*, Oxford: Oxford University Press.

Vidhu Rama G., 2011. *Court Martial Process: Empirically Studied*, New Delhi: VijBooks India Pvt Ltd.

Wade E.C.S. and Phillips George Godfrey, 1985, *Constitutional and Administrative Law*, Longman.

Walzer Michael, 'Two Kinds of Military responsibility', in Matthews Lloyed J. and Dale E. Brown (ed.). 1989. *The Parameters of Military Ethics*, New York: Pergamon-Brassey, International Defence Publishers Inc., pp. 67-72.

Wilkinson Steven I., 2015, *Army and Nation: The Military and Indian Democracy since Independence*, Ranikhet: Permanent Black.

Yossi Nehushtan and Megan Davidson, *Retrospective Rule Making and the Rule of Law: Between Fairness, Morality and Constitutionality*, *Ind. J. Const. & Admin. L.*, Vol. 2, 2018, pp. 27-43(2018).

Zapalla Salvatore. 2003. *Human Rights in International Criminal Proceedings*, Oxford: Oxford University Press.

Index